A STORY OF
AMERICA FIRST

A STORY OF AMERICA FIRST

The Men and
Women Who
Opposed U.S.
Intervention in
World War II

Ruth Sarles

Edited with an Introduction by
Bill Kauffman

Westport, Connecticut
London

Library of Congress Cataloging-in-Publication Data

Sarles, Ruth, 1906–1996.
    A story of America First : the men and women who opposed U.S. intervention in
World War II / Ruth Sarles ; edited with an introduction by Bill Kauffman.
       p. cm.
    Includes bibliographical references and index.
    ISBN 0–275–97512–6 (alk. paper)
       1. America First Committee.   2. World War, 1939–1945—United States.
3. Neutrality—United States—History—20th century.   I. Kauffman, Bill, 1959–
II. Title.
D753 .S34 2003
940.54'0973—dc21   2001058029

British Library Cataloguing in Publication Data is available.

Library of Congress Catalog Card Number: 2001058029
ISBN: 0–275–97512–6

First published in 2003

Praeger Publishers, 88 Post Road West, Westport, CT 06881
An imprint of Greenwood Publishing Group, Inc.
www.praeger.com

Printed in the United States of America

The paper used in this book complies with the
Permanent Paper Standard issued by the National
Information Standards Organization (Z39.48–1984).

10 9 8 7 6 5 4 3 2 1

Copyright Acknowledgments

The author and the publisher gratefully acknowledge permission for use of the
following material:

"Appendix B: An Interview with Robert Douglas Stuart, Jr.," is reprinted with
permission of the author.

Every reasonable effort has been made to trace the owners of copyright materials in
this book, but in some instances this has proven impossible. The author and publisher
will be glad to receive information leading to more complete acknowledgments in
subsequent printings of the book and in the meantime extend their apologies for any
omissions.

Contents

A photo essay follows Chapter 4

Preface

William H. Regnery II

My grandfather was born October 12, 1877 on a farm near Sheboygan, Wisconsin.

His father, Wilhelm, immigrated from Ensch, Germany, which still is a lovely little village hard on the Mosel River and smack dab in the middle of the wine region of the same name. There Wilhelm learned the trade of a Kuefer, one who makes wine barrels and looks after the making of wine. Today there are many in the area who share the same surname and even a few in the wine business.

My grandfather's mother, Johanna, was the daughter of immigrants who came from Frendenburg, Germany. One hundred and fifty years later the village remains probably much the same as when they left it, with its imposing church and castle ruins. It is located only a few miles south of Ensch, and on a recent visit I found no relatives left.

Wilhelm Regnery and Johanna Jung were married in Sheboygan, Wisconsin November 7, 1876, a union that did not enjoy the support of the bride's parents. The couple returned to Germany for their honeymoon, which probably marked the most carefree and financially comfortable time of the marriage. The birth of my grandfather followed within the usual interval and he was given the Christian names of William Henry. Within a year the family moved to St. Lucas, Iowa.

There is no record of the circumstances surrounding the trek west but it's a good guess that strained family relations were responsible. The selection of the destination remains a mystery, and, while there were no friends encouraging relocation, the concentration of German immigrants in the area provided a welcoming beacon. In any event, the young couple purchased forty acres of land that came with a two-room log cabin. There they set up housekeeping and in quick succession five children were born.

My grandfather's next ten years were spent on the Iowa prairie just after it was settled but before the closing of the frontier farther west. It was a hard

William H. and Frances Regnery, circa 1938

life that was made more difficult by his father's poor farming instincts and, of course, the trade he learned in Germany was of no value in this part of the New World.

I remember my grandfather reminiscing about his childhood. What sticks in my mind are the winter experiences: the five-mile walk through unplowed snow to a one-room schoolhouse, the Christmas treat of one whole orange, and the eager search for the early spring dandelions that represented the first fresh vegetables since the fall. The taste for this ersatz lettuce never left him, as one of his own sons would later recall.

St. Lucas is still a sturdy farm hamlet albeit with a diminishing retail base. The desire for retiring farmers to stay put is evidenced by several new homes. The area maintains its German heritage and the exchange of property stays within the neighborhood. The descendants of John Baptist Blong, who sold and then rebought my grandfather's farmstead, still live and farm in its environs. Julia Schmitt at ninety-five years old is the last of the family who can remember my grandfather from his visits to town; he would stay with her father, his boyhood friend, at their farmhouse. Julia took me to her childhood house and showed me the area just to the south upon which my grandfather's infinitely less comfortable cabin sat.

The following description of my grandfather's family life was taken from an account given to us by Julia and written by her mother Anna Blong Busche in

the mid-1920s. "He [Wilhelm] was a laborer and did mason work and plaster-
ing. They were poor. But he worked hard, my parents were good to him, gave
as much work as they could during harvest time. Work was scarce . . . at a time
when the mother of little William was sick in bed and Mr. Regnery had to go
to work, my mother send [sic] me over to take care of the kids. Mother was
good to them and always helped them whenever she could." A further indication of how difficult life must have been for the family is found in the cem-
etery behind the Catholic Church. There a gravestone marks the burial place
of baby Johann: "Geborn. 8 Dec., 1883 Gest. 15 Aug, 1884." As they shared
the same Christian name the child was undoubtedly named for his maternal
grandfather. However, the stonecutter misspelled the surname and it came out
as "Reyenry." Surely, if there was any extra money a corrected marker would
have been ordered.

My grandfather's youth and formal education effectively ended with the
family's arrival in Kansas City. He was eleven or twelve when they arrived and
quickly went to work to help out his family of seven and soon to be eight.
Anna Bushe continues her long distance account of the family. "His mother
wrote to my mother for some time, say five or six years. At one time she wrote
it is a little better money for Willy and Nick are working [in] a store. After
that his mother got sick and died."

In a marvelous account of his family and growing up in a pleasant Chicago
suburb of Hinsdale in the twenties and thirties, my uncle, Henry Regnery, had
this to say about his father's stay in Kansas City: " The twelve years or so my
father lived in Kansas City were not a happy time of his life. . . . He never
spoke of Kansas City with much affection; the happy memories of his childhood
and boyhood were always of the farm and St. Lucas."

In the same volume, my uncle goes into some detail about the extent to
which his brief formal education was hardly an end in itself but served to allow
him to continue at his own pace. "My father had an excellent mind and won-
derfully retentive memory, and used every opportunity to develop his faculties
and improve himself. He soon began buying books . . . some of these I remember—his well-worn set of Stevenson . . . a good edition of Shakespeare, which
he knew well, an Encyclopedia Britannica, and a Webster's dictionary. . . . He
used English correctly and well . . . had a beautiful handwriting and spoke good
German."

In the mid- to late 1890s, family lore has my father and a friend flipping a
coin as to the division of two promising job opportunities: the one with the
William Volker Company and the other with the *Kansas City Star.* My grandfather went into the distribution business while his friend ended up at the
newspaper, which he ultimately ran.

William Volker was a German immigrant whose business acumen was
equalled only by his charitable instinct. As his business prospered, he returned
his time and capital to civic enterprises. His name is still on display in Kansas
City. The foundation he established was distributing a seven-figure income

until, according to his wishes, it was dissolved in the late 1980s. He married late and died childless and became my grandfather's mentor if not surrogate father.

In 1902, Volker sent my grandfather to Chicago to look after his interests in a textile coating company. The firm's principal product was roller window shades. Within a few years Volker, through an early example of stock options, had conveyed 30 percent of the company to my grandfather, who was for all intents and purposes CEO. A like amount of equity was in the hands of Stanley Kempner, who was in charge of sales. In 1912, Kempner left the company in an argument over the division of profits and my grandfather acquired his stock with a loan from Mr. Volker. From then on my grandfather was in full charge of the corporation. The enterprise flourished and so did his family.

My grandfather married in 1903 to Frances Thrasher, whom he met at the Volker Company. He was twenty-six and she was one year older. Her family moved west from Virginia-Maryland after the Civil War, and she was born in Atchison, Kansas. Her father had served in the Union army from 1861 to 1864 and ended his enlistment a captain. Given the temper of the times and their border location it is not surprising that his brother died in Confederate grey.

The couple lived in an apartment in Chicago where their first child, William, was born in 1904. Two years later with a second child on the way and money in the bank, the family built a pleasant farm-style house in the suburbs and moved to Hinsdale. This was quite an accomplishment for a man not yet thirty who hailed from a log cabin. This modest house would welcome the next three children and by the arrival of the fourth in 1912 the house must have been ready to buckle under the weight and activity of the growing family. The following year my grandfather moved to a house better sized to his family, which was to expand one more time. The new home had begun life as a farm-house and with it came a square block of residual land which was put to good use by the four boys.

The teens and twenties were a period of rapid growth for the company. My grandfather became a man of influence in the commercial affairs of the city. While he must have made many business friends, the only one I remember hearing about was General Robert E. Wood of Sears and Roebuck. Wood ran the Quartermaster Corps in World War I and after mustering out of the army joined Sears. His recognition of the mobility that the automobile would provide the American public prompted Sears's suburban expansion, which allowed them to pull away decisively from their crosstown rival Montgomery Wards. My grandfather became associated with the Chicago Boys Club and was active in the organization along with Gen. Wood until the end of his life.

Upon the death of his wife my grandfather's father remarried and raised a second family. By the end of the expansion my grandfather had four full siblings and three half-siblings who lived to maturity. Uncle Frank joined him in the business but died of the flu during the great epidemic of 1918. The others, including his father, stayed in the Kansas area. To some extent he provided for all of them and a trust he established is still, in 2002, making payments to relatives and will do so for another generation.

The decade of the twenties was a high old time for American and my grandfather's business interests. But during the decade he made sure to return something to the community and his employees. In 1921, he incorporated the Marquette Charitable Foundation, which was one of the first philanthropic foundations chartered in Illinois. It made contributions, always anonymously, to charities, and among his favorites were the Boy Scouts of America and the Chicago Boys Club. During this period he established one of the first profit sharing plans at his company. It was entirely funded by corporate contributions and helped thousands of retired employees lead a comfortable life when social security was either not available or a pittance.

During the thirties, the economic dislocations suggested experimentation and new initiatives. My grandfather supported Roosevelt in 1932 and 1936. But his political sympathies did not extend to Mayor Cermak, who died from a bullet intended for Roosevelt. As a memorial, Twenty-second Street, which was the Volker Company's street address, was renamed Cermak Road. This did not sit well with my grandfather, who had a long running feud with Cermak and was not about to immortalize a political opponent on the letterhead of his company. His solution was to change the company's address from Cermak Road to Jefferson Street, which bordered one side. Roosevelt's promotion of more radical New Deal programs and interventionist policies abroad caused my grandfather to withdraw his support in the late thirties.

I don't know the details of my grandfather's decision to become one of the principal backers of the America First Committee, but I suspect it was not dissimilar to the motive of Bob Stuart, who founded the organization. When we decided to publish this account I contacted Bob who lives, as I do, in the Chicago area. He was interested in the project and suggested we meet for lunch. During our conversation, I asked what prompted his involvement. His response came easily and immediately. In delivering his reply he used the collective "we" to include his colleagues. He said, "We lived through the results and promises of the first war and didn't want to be dragged again into Europe's business." The American public was solidly opposed to entering the war in Europe, and the success of the America First Committee was a reflection of this position.

Directly after the Japanese attack at Pearl Harbor the organization was disbanded. Early in 1942, my grandfather through Bob Stuart communicated to Ruth Sarles and offered to hire her for $3,000 to write an account of the America First Committee ". . . for presenting, in due time, to those interested and to the public in general, the spirit which inspired so many of those connected with the America First Committee. . . ." Miss Sarles had been involved in the public relations office in Washington, had a good fix on the scope of organization, and, unlike her male colleagues, was not in uniform and could devote her time to writing the account.

Sarles's first chore was to determine the temper of the book. Would it be polemical or straightforward? She sought counsel from many sources but it was Charles Lindbergh who, in a letter to her dated March 31, 1942, offered the best advice. "If your history of the Committee is based primarily upon factual statements, letters, addresses, etc., it will constitute a permanent record of the pre-war period, and be referred to in the future by responsible historians and research workers. On the other hand, if you attempt to do too much explaining, you will immediately label your book with such partisanship that responsible writers will be hesitant to refer to it in the future." With the tenor of the book clear in her mind she was ready to begin.

Within months it had become clear the book's budget was going to be exceeded. In a letter to her dated May 21, 1942, my grandfather allayed her fear of prematurely exhausting her resources by writing, "As to the cost of the project, it is my opinion that this is very much of a secondary matter; I believe it more important that the work should be finished up in the best manner possible. So, as far as I am concerned, I am ready to continue on as in the past."

In fact the project stretched into the next year and a draft was circulated in early 1943. At this time the question of publication was brought up and in a letter from my grandfather of March 2, 1943, he stated, "My own opinion is that this is not the time to publish the book. . . ." In a somewhat cryptic letter to Ruth Sarles dated January 31, 1946, my grandfather suggests that she "pack up the items mentioned in the first and third paragraphs of your letter and ship them to me. . . . I will store them in our vault and, at the first opportunity, ask General Wood what disposition is to be made of them."

I presume he was referring to the finished manuscript which moldered for fifty years in a storeroom. Just before his death my uncle, Henry Regnery, retrieved the manuscript and donated it with his own papers to The Hoover Institution. While there were a number of copies made and distributed, I have a duplicate of my grandfather's original which served as the basis for an edited version which is represented by this book.

From his correspondence, it is clear that my grandfather and probably Gen. Wood intended to see Ruth Sarles's history published. While 1943 might not have represented the ideal year, my brothers and I decided that 2002 is a good time to make available to the public a work that, as my grandfather stated, "is not only of great importance as a historical record but also may serve, in due time, to give the American public and others a picture of the events occurring for about a year and a half before Pearl Harbor."

The war years were not kind to my grandfather. In 1941 he was sixty-four and apparently not in the best of health. In the summer of 1937 he had gone to Europe and wrote to my father that "there are many real nice walks around here with attractive scenery but most of these call for hill climbing which leaves me out of it." In the same letter he comments that "I have for the past two weeks done more outright loafing than ever in my lifetime and cannot say that I enjoyed it thoroughly—although there is a luxury connected with the lack of responsibility to others that is novel." His physical well-being was badly compromised by a severe beating he suffered at the hands of two muggers who were laying for him as he made his predictable way from the commuter train stop in Chicago to his office. Whether by coincidence or result, shortly thereafter he suffered his first heart attack and according to my uncle Henry's family history "recovered and continued to go into the office every day, but he was no longer the vigorous man he had been." In 1946, he wrote Ruth Sarles that "for reasons of health I no longer travel."

Regrettably, my memories of my grandfather date from about this time. I remember him only as a frail, rather small, man who spoke very little. I recollect him too lightly dressed for the snowy day and bent into the wind crossing a street. My family would often join Pop and Grandma for Sunday dinner, which was invariably standing rib roast, roasted or mashed potatoes, peas, salad, and buttery dinner rolls. I can remember my grandfather at the head of the table ably cutting slices to order.

My grandfather died in 1954 and I heard of his death on a Saturday after returning home from a movie matinee. As befitting a man of his stature, the large Catholic church which he heavily supported was full of mourners on a cold mid-January day when his funeral service was conducted.

My grandfather started with no resources, but given the use of $100,000 in corporate capital, increased the value of the enterprise which at his death had a net worth of $17 million and a market value of considerably more. He left life as he had entered it; he had conveyed his wealth to his family, charities, friends, and church. To his extended family he is regarded as a "founder" and his influence is still felt fifty years later. I was close to all my uncles, who were themselves successful men, and I never heard one of them by jest or carelessness diminish any action or opinion of their father. He was spoken of with not only great affection but outright admiration by all of his children. He earned the approbation of family and saw all his children successful in life. He lived a rewarding life and must have died a contented man.

Editor's Introduction

Bill Kauffman

No one will [ever] know what . . . odium has been heaped upon honorable men and women because they dared to lift their voices for peace and for our country.[1]

—John T. Flynn, June 1941

Sixty years after these United States entered a Second World War that would leave more than 400,000 American boys dead and 670,000 wounded; that would displace tens of millions of Americans in a domestic diaspora that did more than any other event in American history to feed the national malady of rootlessness; that concentrated unprecedented power in the national government, particularly its executive branch; and that led directly into a cold war with the Soviet Union that would consume trillions of taxpayers' dollars—the hundreds of thousands of American men and women who opposed U.S. intervention are still slandered as, at best, provincial ignoramuses, and at worst, morally scrofulous bigots.

The pacifist editor of *The Nation*, the "liberals' liberal" Oswald Garrison Villard, anticipated an eventual reassessment of the antiwar side, hoping for a day "when the history of these times is written by men marveling that a Hitler beyond seas could so have swept the greatest republic from its moorings."[2] That accounting has yet to come.

Even today, the very words "America First" are nearly verboten, as Virginia Governor Douglas Wilder discovered in 1991, when he adopted these as the slogan of his short-lived campaign for the Democratic presidential nomination. The condescending, faintly racist lectures that the black Wilder endured from the smug publicists of the bipartisan establishment were nothing compared with the bucketfuls of spit hurled at Patrick J. Buchanan, whose three consecutive insurgent campaigns refined, and defined, the America First position in the age of global capitalism.

The 800,000-strong America First Committee—born at Yale Law School, died at Pearl Harbor—was the largest antiwar organization in American history and constituted "the greatest 'common denominator' mass action the country has ever known,"[3] in the words of its chairman, General Robert E. Wood. Consisting of prairie Populists and patrician mugwumps, Midwestern Socialists and anti–New Deal Republicans, Sinclair Lewis, e.e. cummings, Gore Vidal, Charles Lindbergh, Gerald Ford, Lillian Gish, and John F. Kennedy, the America Firsters spanned the homegrown spectrum. They were united not by liberalism or conservatism nor even by antipathy to war—though in the peaceable AFC kingdom, the lion, say Hanford MacNider, the American Legion founder from Mason City, Iowa, might be found lying with the lamb, for instance the pacifist suffragette and best-selling ladies' novelist Kathleen Norris. What united America Firsters of left and right, coast and plains, was a sense that the very survival of their country was at stake.

The America Firsters were not misty-eyed nostalgics pining for lost and unrecoverable worlds, but they did understand that the America that would emerge from another European war would be irreversibly altered. MacNider, with an air of desperation, argued that "Europe and Asia have been in constant battle over the balance of power for thousands of years. They will be at it long after all of us here are gone. If we put ourselves back into it now, we shall lose this republic."[4] Typically, the biographer of the renegade New Dealer George N. Peek, an America First national committeeman, writes that "Peek had a deep, almost fanatical love for the kind of America which had provided opportunities for him and other young men in the early twentieth century."[5] To Peek and others, the debate of 1940–41 was over no mere question of war and peace but rather the very existence of the America that they had known and loved. (In our time, the novels of the Kentucky farmer Wendell Berry often use the Second World War as the fault line dividing the old America from the new.)

The pacifist Milton Mayer—one of those antiwar Jews whose not inconsiderable numbers have been lost in the fog of myth—characterized the "isolationists" as largely a mixture of "Anglophobic enemies of empire and imperialism in the best American spirit" and "tens of millions of genuinely neutralist Americans of purest patriotism who wanted no part of what Jefferson called 'the broils of Europe,' together with liberal internationalists . . . who all too clearly recalled the failure of the First World War to make the world safe for democracy and saw war, not Germany or Nazism but war itself, as the scourge of liberty." This "isolationist amalgam" was "much more representative of the country" than the narrow interventionist movement, which was concentrated among the monied classes of the eastern seaboard.[6]

The purpose of the America First Committee, according to one of its leading figures, former Undersecretary of State William R. Castle, was "to defeat hysteria; to make people think from an American point of view; to counteract as far as possible the pro-war propaganda of other organizations and individuals;

to work for sensible and complete preparation for defense; to do everything possible to maintain our American way of life."[7]

The policy implications thereof could be characterized as isolationist, in that the AFC sought to isolate the United States from the war fever riddling Europe and Asia; quasi-pacifistic, in that war itself was to be avoided unless a direct attack was made on the territorial United States; and libertarian, in that war and preparations therefore were believed to undermine traditional American liberties.

Yale Law School is an odd matrix in which a rebellious antiwar populism might gestate, but there you are. What became the America First Committee was born in the New Haven home of Robert Douglas Stuart, Jr., a law student and son of the first vice president (and later president) of Quaker Oats. Ruth Sarles tells the story in the narrative of Chapter 2, and Stuart recollects those days in an interview in Appendix B. For now, suffice to say that this band of lackbeards, many of them barely beyond their teenage years, grew up to be presidents of the United States (Gerald R. Ford) and Yale (Kingman Brewster), a Democratic vice presidential candidate (R. Sargent Shriver), a Supreme Court associate justice (Potter Stewart), and ambassadors to Great Britain (Brewster), Norway (Stuart), and Pakistan (Eugene Locke).

The AFC has been willfully misunderstood these many years; its most venomous critics—later revealed to be agents of British intelligence—called it a "Nazi transmission belt," whereas the court historians content themselves with dismissing it as a group of perhaps well-meaning but dangerously misguided Middle American rubes. In a classic smear job, John Roy Carlson (a.k.a. agent provocateur Avedis Derounian) wrote in his best-seller *Under Cover* (1943), "There were many in the America First Committee who were sincere and devout . . . but . . . the overwhelming majority were fascist party-liners."[8] But for a "right-wing" organization the America First Committee sure did include a lot of pacifists, radicals, and old liberals—and women in critical roles, Ruth Sarles among them. ("The peace problem is a woman's problem," said Congresswoman and America First speaker Jeannette Rankin, "because men have a natural fear of being classed as cowards if they oppose war."[9])

Though Ruth Sarles, as a paid employee, was outranked in America First by Chicago novelist Janet Ayer Fairbank, the AFC vice chairwoman who pulled rank as habitually as other women pull at their stockings, Sarles was the Capitol Hill face of America First and thus the most influential woman in the most influential antiwar organization in American history. And yet because America First, like most losing causes, has been traduced out of its rightful place in our history, and because this manuscript was never published, Ruth Sarles (later Ruth Sarles Benedict) has long passed into anonymity; like the farmwives whose mixture of faith, indomitability, and eccentricity once gave America its pith, she merits not even a footnote in feminist encyclopedias.

Ruth was a small-town Ohio gal in love with the big city, but as a prose stylist, Dawn Powell she wasn't. Her memos and letters have too little sass and gossip—though one imagines her as Jean Arthur, the career-girl cynic with a heart of gold, waking at 5:30 A.M., riffling through five daily newspapers before sunup, writing talking points and speeches for "cornball" Midwesterners, and driving Senator Champ Clark home when he'd had too much to drink. Yet she was also diligent, thorough, and horrified by the prospect of her countrymen being slaughtered in another European bloodbath.

Ruth Sarles was born January 28, 1906, in the Cincinnati suburb of Norwood, Ohio, from whose high school she was graduated in 1923. "She is the life of the class, always smiling, always in a good humor and liked by everyone,"[10] reported the Norwood yearbook. Her father was a chemical engineer, though her lineage consisted largely of Baptist ministers and missionaries. Ruth earned an A.B. degree in English at Denison University, graduating in 1928. She ranked fifty-third in her class of 143, scoring well in philosophy and political science but middling in math, sociology, and—piquantly for those ill-disposed toward this book—history. She later earned a masters degree in international law at American University.

Her Denison yearbook photos reveal a self-confident young woman. She was "a mighty good 'fellow' to talk with—that's Ruth," reported the yearbook biographer. "She is a member of all the university publications, being the principal woman staff member of the school weekly, a heavy contributor to the humor sheet, and an associate editor of the yearbook. A dancer in the junior revue, Ruth might plan on a histrionic future, if gentlemen keep on preferring blondes."[11]

Ruth preferred politics. After Denison, she worked as a librarian in the political science library at the University of Cincinnati before lighting out for Washington, where she had the great fortune to join one of the unheralded but noble men of interwar progressivism, Frederick J. Libby, at Libby's National Council for Prevention of War (about which there is more in Appendix A). For eight years she worked for the NCPW, editing *Peace Action* and the NCPW *Bulletin* and meeting many of the prominent Socialists and pacifists and isolationists of the 1930s. Ruth herself was not quite a Socialist, or a pacifist, or an isolationist, but rather something of an old-fashioned idealistic liberal by way of Ohio; think of Oswald Garrison Villard growing up in suburban Cincinnati.

In January 1941, Sidney Hertzberg mentioned to her that he was setting up a research bureau for America First. "I wasn't very enthusiastic"[12] at first, said Ruth, but within a few weeks she was circulating on Capitol Hill, supplying sympathetic legislators with facts and figures, and relaying Washington gossip to the Chicago headquarters. She worked primarily with the Senate; she regarded Senators Burton K. Wheeler (D-Mont.), Robert M. La Follette, Jr. (P-Wis.), Robert A. Taft (R-Ohio), and George Aiken (R-Vt.) as the most impressive of the lot.[13]

In 1943, Ruth married Bertram Benedict, an editor, later to be part owner, of Editorial Research Reports, a Washington-based service that supplied "background facts on national and international issues to newspaper editors and writers."[14] He had also written *The Larger Socialism,* a sympathetic critique of American socialism whose major argument was that it was insufficiently American, and that for every Debs of Terre Haute there were a polyglot dozen just off the boat and ready to tell Ohioans how to live.

After writing "A Story of America First," Ruth joined the Washington *Daily News;* her beats were the Capitol and then "food"—not its preparation but its scarcity in less fortunate countries. In 1947–48 she worked for her husband's Editorial Research Reports, and then in 1948 she joined the State Department, eventually serving as an intelligence research specialist with a particular interest in India and Ceylon (Sri Lanka). She retired in 1959.

So the America Firster, pacific dynamo from the National Council for Prevention of War, spent the last dozen years of her working life toiling for the departments of state under Truman and Eisenhower, composing "psychological intelligence reports" for the U.S. Information Agency, and monitoring the "propaganda of local Communist parties."[15] The war had indeed changed everything.

To Ruth's credit, she—unlike, say, the guileful careerist Chester Bowles—did not hide her America First affiliation when applying for various positions within the federal government. She was unapologetic and forthright. And besides, not even the most diligent ferreter of Old Right moles would bother with Ruth: in her State Department application form, she admitted membership in two political organizations: Americans for Democratic Action and United World Federalists.

In retirement, she and her husband had a boat, crab pot, and oyster bar on Tabb's Creek in Tidewater Virginia; they later moved to Oxford, on Maryland's Eastern Shore. Ruth kept busy with volunteer work on behalf of the black population in Easton, Maryland. She returned to Washington after Bertram's death in 1978 and ended her days in the Thomas House in Washington, D.C. (Upon Bertram's death at age eighty-six, the family requested that memorials be made to Amnesty International USA and the American Friends Service Committee.)

Ruth Sarles Benedict was "in her early seventies, but appeared younger," when she met Wayne S. Cole, the dean of historians of American isolationism.[16] Cole visited her several times and found her "sensible, and impressive." The five-foot, two-inch Sarles Benedict "was a bright, spunky, direct, no-nonsense little lady with real integrity and courage." And she was unrepentant, telling Cole that she felt "no sense of guilt" about her role in America First.[17] In his interview notes, Cole emphasizes, "She does *not* assume that she was wrong."[18] In this she was like most America Firsters; for every contrite Gerald Ford there were a dozen men like University of Chicago president Robert Hutchins, who defended his 1940–41 antiwar liberalism even to uncomprehending interviewers in the 1970s.

Political scientist J. Garry Clifford of the University of Connecticut visited Mrs. Benedict twice in the 1980s. Because "she was an old-fashioned liberal pacifist, I thought her perspective was insufficiently recognized as a motive, or dynamic, in the antiwar effort." She "felt less comfortable with [the] conservatives" of America First than she did with the liberals, "although she liked General Wood very much and was fascinated by Lindbergh," recalls Clifford. "I remember her telling me that she would not go into Senator Robert Reynolds' (D-N.C.) office alone because he was such a notorious womanizer. She mentioned that Bennett C. Clark drank so much that he was ineffective and that she drove him home from the office more than once." These are the stories that she left out of "A Story of America First." ("Another angle about her, partly revealed in our talks, is that she was a very attractive woman in 1941 . . . and she would use her attractiveness to 'woo' (so to speak) her sources of information," remarks Clifford.)[19]

Five years before her death, Sarles wrote a brief reminiscence about her years with the AFC for *Chronicles'* seminal "America First 1941/1991" issue. She concluded,

I am now 85 years old, and a firm believer in the examined life. I lost a few friends because of my America First ties. My Canadian mother, as pro-Royal as any Briton, offered me redemption through confession. Even as recently as the early 1980s a friend harshly took me to task for my past. Like most people in the peace movement I did not want to "isolate" America. I was an internationalist who welcomed the emergence of my country from that cocoon of aloof self-containment to full participation in the interdependent world community. Nevertheless, I cannot feel apologetic that I went against the mainstream before World War II, because I believed in the correctness of our stand. No one—but no one—knows what might have happened if the Japanese had not attacked Pearl Harbor and saved President Roosevelt the agonizing decision if and when his country should get fully into the war.[20]

She lived to the age of ninety, and though afflicted with Parkinson's disease she remained bright and lively, no valetudinarian she.

Ruth Sarles is lost to history. She fought the good fight, the American fight, then documented it in a 759-page manuscript that never found a publisher. She lived a full and rich life with the man she married. In best defiant American fashion, she was feistily impenitent. And why shouldn't she be? From the America First perspective, the "good war" destroyed the American republic by delivering us unto empire, unto perpetual war against a dizzying series of New Hitlers that continues to this day. It cut us loose from our constitutional moorings, and so far have we drifted that in the last decade President Bush the First has rained death upon Iraq and President Clinton has waged an air war against Serbia without, in either case, a formal declaration of war, and anyone who suggests that our presidents are violating Article 1, Section 8 of the U.S. Constitution (which vests Congress with the sole power to "declare war") is looked upon as, at best, a pettifogging oddball, and at worst, the getaway driver for Timothy McVeigh.

Who—what—was America First? Charles Lindbergh was its most compelling public face, and by far its best-known member; many students of the period are also well acquainted with John T. Flynn and General Robert E. Wood. And the other 799,997 or so members? A motley crew of knuckle-draggers and Jew-baiters and hate-mongers, according to the court historians. What was by far the largest antiwar organization in our history has been calumnied—partly out of ignorance, but partly out of sheer malice and hatred of the old America. Ruth Sarles's manuscript is a priceless corrective to this misperception, and in this introduction and Appendix A ("Who Were the America Firsters?") I hope to explain the America First Committee through profiles of various of its eminences who shone less brightly than Lindbergh but who, in the aggregate, define the committee and its integrally American quality.

(For a general history of the committee, Wayne S. Cole's *America First: The Battle Against Intervention 1940–1941* remains the standard. Justus D. Doenecke's documentary history *In Danger Undaunted: The Anti-Interventionist Movement of 1940–1941 as Revealed in the Papers of the America First Committee* is invaluable, as are the prodigious Doenecke's bibliographic efforts, most recently *Anti-Intervention: A Bibliographic Introduction to Isolationism and Pacifism from World War I to the Early Cold War* [1987].)

YALE AS KEY

Ruth Sarles in the text and Robert D. Stuart, Jr. in Appendix B discuss the New Haven cradle of America First at some length, but it bears repeating that the handful of Yale men who were present at the creation went on to spectacular careers as pillars of the postwar American Establishment: Potter Stewart of Jackson, Michigan, class of '37 and chairman of the *Yale Daily News*, sat next to Bob Stuart in law school class and went on to sit on the Supreme Court. Kingman Brewster, class of '41 and chairman of both the *Yale Daily News* and the Yale chapter of the AFC, later became president of the university. (The president during 1940–41, Charles Seymour, was an ardent interventionist.) Young Bob Stuart, Seymour's nemesis as the talented and indefatigable boy director of America First, served as U.S. ambassador to Norway from 1984 to 1989 and as chairman of the Council of American Ambassadors, an emeritus trustee of Princeton, and a member of the Atlantic Council of the United States. Whatever muck was thrown at these men in 1940–41 seems not to have stuck—at least as long as their reputations were in the hands of their contemporaries, who knew their characters and understood the essentially Old Republic nature of the America First Committee.

One of the odder footnotes in this saga is that founding member Gerald R. Ford, the Yale Law student who had been an All-American center at the University of Michigan, was one of the earliest resignations from the committee. He withdrew not because he'd had second thoughts about the wisdom of Roos-eveltian policy, but because he feared that his involvement might cost him his position as assistant football coach at Yale.[21] Like Arthur Vandenberg less than a decade later, the Michigan Republican never looked back: he was a committed interventionist throughout his congressional career, never finding a U.S. in-tervention or military appropriation he didn't like, and though he somewhat reluctantly oversaw the removal of U.S. troops from Vietnam, he was never again heard to call for military disengagement from any part of the world. Fittingly, he began his political ascent by defeating an isolationist Republican incumbent, Representative Bartel J. Jonkman.

In his autobiography, *A Time to Heal* (1979), Ford (or his ghost) avoids mention of the America First Committee but writes, "Before the war, I'd been an isolationist. Indeed, while at Yale, I had expressed the view that the U.S. ought to avoid 'entangling alliances' abroad. But now [1946] I had become an ardent internationalist. My wartime experiences had given me an entirely new perspective. The U.S., I was convinced, could no longer stick its head in the sand like an ostrich."[22] Now, there's a fair-minded depiction of his erstwhile comrades.

Ford's America First tie never became an issue in his national career. Nor did the check for $100 that young John F. Kennedy sent to the AFC—along with a note saying, "what you are all doing is vital"[23]—haunt Camelot as an isolationist specter. John F. Kennedy's older brother, Joseph Kennedy, Jr., or-ganized the Harvard Committee Against Military Intervention and helped or-ganize the campus branch of the America First Committee. One of Robert D. Stuart's best friends, Robert Sargent Shriver, Jr., also ran on a national ticket, as Democrat George McGovern's vice presidential candidate in 1972, after the mental-illness history of McGovern's first choice, Missouri Senator Thomas Eagleton, became unspinnable. Shriver's America First connection was not an issue in 1972—after all, it was cousin-german to McGovernite opposition to the Vietnam War—nor was there any mention of Shriver's involvement in America First and the allied College Men for Defense First in the 1961 hearings on his nomination to be director of the Peace Corps.

Shriver was a Democrat and Stuart was something of a mild New Dealer, but a third Yale man, advertising executive Chester Bowles, was the quintes-sential prep school liberal.

Bowles, of Choate and Yale, looked back on his avaricious school chums and wrote, "Following graduation in 1924 most of my classmates rushed off to highly paid jobs on Wall Street. As far as I know, I was the only one who even considered public service."[24] Selfless of him, no doubt, but the altruistic Bowles spurned "public service" and opted for advertising, where he honed the dis-sembling art that would prove so useful later in life as a diplomat. The adver-tising firm of Benton & Bowles prospered even during the depression, em-ploying 400 people and doing an annual business of $15 million in 1935.

The price of these riches was circumspection. As Bowles wrote Sidney Hertz-berg, publicity director of the AFC, "several of our clients feel very emphatic against the stand that I have taken. . . . Advertising is one helluva business—you can never call your soul your own."[25]

The stand to which he referred was Bowles' deep-set opposition to U.S. intervention in the European war. The papers of the America First Committee reveal Bowles to be a regular dynamo: dashing off memos, writing speeches, offering advice freely (which was emphatically *not* part of the Benton & Bowles m.o.).

Yet Chester Bowles would remember in his memoir, "When World War II broke out in 1939, I was sorely torn about whether or not we should become involved."[26] So sorely torn that he became a national committeeman of the AFC, and one of its most active. He somehow neglects to use the words "America First" in his autobiographical sketch, noting only that "[w]hile opposing United States participation in World War II unless we were attacked, I rejected the isolationist argument that we could cut ourselves off from the rest of man-kind"[27]—a mendacious misrepresentation of what Bowles's whilom comrades believed. But the savvy careerist knows when to throw old friends overboard. It takes chutzpah for an ardent New Dealer to publicly support Franklin D. Roosevelt for a third term at the 1940 convention while writing Senator Robert Taft in May 1940 that "our only hope" of peace "lies in the election of a person like yourself for the Presidency who really believes that at any cost America must remain on her own side of the ocean,"[28] but the Man from Madison Avenue was nothing if not supple. Unable to call even his soul his own, Bowles pursued the career in public service he had so reluctantly rejected in favor of riches in 1924. He served as governor of Connecticut, U.S. representative from Connecticut, U.S. ambassador to India and Nepal, and undersecretary of state in the Kennedy administration. He sedulously avoided any mention of his America First affiliation in any of his confirmation hearings. And as one scholar notes, "Although he was ordinarily meticulous in preserving his extensive correspondence, the letters he exchanged with other America First and non-interventionist figures in 1940 and 1941 are missing from his files."[29]

So thorough was Bowles's postwar transmogrification that Howard B. Schaf-fer, surveying Bowles's later career as a liberal interventionist, writes that ob-servers "find it both astonishing and ironic"[30] that his first political campaign sought to isolate the nation from the European War.

Yet Yale produced honorable men as well, among them the nation's leading scholar of international law, Edwin M. Borchard (1884–1951), a close adviser to the founders of the America First Committee—which Borchard, for reasons that seem more prudential than craven, refrained from joining.

Borchard's ascent in the academy was "almost meteoric,"[31] as Justus D. Do-enecke has written. Son of a Manhattan merchant, he was professor of law at Yale Law School from 1917 until 1950. At Yale, Borchard was "affable among friends, provocative and rigorous in the classroom, and tenacious in debate."[32]

A believer in the efficacy of international law and the salubrious effects of international trade, Borchard was also the leading advocate of *Neutrality for the United States*, as he and William Potter Lage titled their 1937 book.

Borchard and Lage took their epigraph from President Washington's Farewell Address, that warning against alliance and interference in European affairs that is read in the Senate every February on Washington's birthday by a junior senator who gets stuck with this senatorial equivalent of KP duty. The body will then spend the next 364 days of the year repudiating the bulk of Washington's advice. With the possible exception of the Ten Commandments, never has a document been so venerated and yet so violated.

Decrying "the cult of unneutrality,"[33] Borchard and Lage lay out the case for U.S. neutrality—in shorthand, peace and prosperity—and tally the cost of that "excessive partiality for one foreign nation" and the "insidious wiles of foreign influence"[34] against which Washington warned. As the gray eminence at the epicenter of America First—Yale Law School—Borchard might be assumed to have been the kindly dean of the AFC. Yet he never joined. As he wrote Robert E. Wood on September 24, 1941, two weeks after Charles Lindbergh's haymaking Des Moines speech,

> The importance of the work done by the America First Committee and the malicious smears of which it has been made a target would ordinarily lead me immediately to accept your invitation of September 22nd [to join the AFC's national committee].
>
> Nevertheless, there are considerations which I think are important, considerations which kept me from joining the Committee on the occasion of the original invitation of Douglas Stuart, a former student of mine. In spite of the fact that this administration knows that I am not sympathetic to what they are doing, they call upon me from time to time for advice. In addition, I represent interests before the Department which might be injured by my openly joining the Committee. Again, I am called upon by Senators and others from time to time and occasionally take public positions. This influence is I think better and more convincing if I refrain openly from joining a committee whose object is, so to speak, partisan—in the best possible way, I admit—and which sponsors speakers and policies which oblige it to be partisan.
>
> Perhaps I am wrong, but I think my influence with Senators and members of Congress is greater than it would be, however small it is, if I retain a certain detached position, without concealing the fact, however, which I have made clear, that I oppose the entrance of the United States into this war. I have gone so far as to sponsor meetings of the America First Committee around this section of the country, which shows where my loyalty lies. But under the circumstances I still think it better not to join the Committee as a member.[35]

This may seem a bit fastidious, and it carries intimations of careerism, but Borchard was neither trimmer nor coward. Some men are simply not joiners. (Borchard was on the national committee of the American Civil Liberties Union—one of many liberal isolationists, as we shall see.) After the war, he stuck to his guns, or should we say his ploughshares, condemning "the United Nations [as] an instrument for Great Power domination, the Nuremburg trials and the Potsdam Agreement [as] acts of vengeance, and the Truman Doctrine [as] a commitment to unlimited intervention."[36]

Borchard died a neutralist in a once-neutral country whose leaders now viewed the doctrine as synonymous with appeasement. His advice would echo that of the first president, and be ignored just as thoroughly. As he and William Potter Lage concluded, "The United States must recover its role as an impartial healer, and abandon that of unintelligent preacher."[37]

If Borchard was the leading scholar of diplomacy within the AFC orbit, the committee's most notable diplomatic supporter was William R. Castle, who had been President Hoover's undersecretary of state.

The Honolulu-born Castle organized the Washington, D.C., chapter of the America First Committee and hosted its first meeting at his house. Castle's father had served as Hawaii's minister to Washington; the son retained an affection for his homeland and wrote a history of the islands. Perhaps it was ancestral voices speaking, but Castle was also something of a Nipponophile. His chief responsibilities under Hoover had been Japanese relations and disarmament; by 1940, the two concerns intersected.

Castle cautioned against the rising anti-Japanese sentiment in Washington and predicted that the Rooseveltian embargo would lead to war. He wrote Herbert Hoover after Pearl Harbor, "You and I know that this continuous putting pins in rattlesnakes finally got this country bitten. We also know that if Japan had been allowed to go on without these trade restrictions and provocations, she would have collapsed from internal economic reasons alone within a couple of years."[38]

Castle's great-nephew, Alfred E. Castle, speculates that "Since Castle was most concerned and vocal about Roosevelt's policies in Asia, many of the most active interventionists ignored him." He was yellow-baited on occasion by the publicists of the War Party, but as the Japanese had yet to bomb Pearl Harbor, it was difficult to work up a good gust of hatred for the demonic little Nips.

Despite—or because of—his nativity in an island that would become an American colony, Castle had a Hooverian antipathy toward empire. The "only strictly American interest in the Far East was trade,"[39] as Alfred Castle summarized his great-uncle's view. Moreover, the United States "had no interests in Indo-China." Diabolical isolationist, that Castle.

GIVE PEACE A CHANCE?

The pacifist tincture of America First has been consistently, deliberately, and sometimes dishonestly obscured by some "peace historians." I shan't speculate as to motive, but certain of them view peace as a property of the ideological left, no matter that it was liberal Democratic presidents who entangled the United States in the First and Second World Wars, the Korean conflict, and the Vietnam War. The fact that the largest antiwar organization in American history came, in significant part, from the Right may be too unsettling to them.

The complexities of the antiwar Right may be glimpsed in the diaries of Charles Lindbergh. Though the flyer got on well with pacifists, as he generally did with men and women of goodwill, he recorded in his diary, "What luck it is to find myself opposing my country's entrance into a war I *don't* believe in, when I would so much rather be fighting for my country in a war I *do* believe in. Here I am stumping the country with pacifists and considering resigning as a colonel in the Army Air Corps [which he did three days later, on April 28, 1941, in response to President Roosevelt's disparagement of Lindbergh as a Copperhead], when there is no philosophy I disagree with more than that of the pacifist, and nothing I would rather be doing than flying in the Air Corps."[40]

Bob Stuart and General Robert E. Wood, national chairman of America First, were in nowise pacifists, and wanted to keep the AFC free of too much pacific taint. For instance, Stuart advised Fred Burdick, the committee's lobbyist in the House of Representatives, to change his "Peace Digest" letter to "something like 'America First News Digest,' because the Committee has always attempted to avoid any titles connoting pacifism."[41] General Wood, after reading Ruth Sarles's manuscript, asked her to preface "war" with "foreign" or "European"; he objected even to the term "antiwar." The general explained, "I think these corrections are very important. As you have it, it would give the impression that we were a group of pacifists. It is true there were pacifists who supported the movement, but the leadership of the movement was not in the least pacifist in tone."[42] Thus is history rewritten in the first draft.

Ruth Sarles wrote Page Hufty, AFC director of organization, on December 5, 1941, that although she "understood the aversion of AF leaders to too close association with persons tarred with the 'peace' brush," it did seem "a pity not to make use of their training and experience. You have a few of us now—and I doubt if we have hurt AF."[43]

In the years between the wars, no one painted with the peace brush so energetically as Frederick J. Libby (1874–1970), director of the National Council for Prevention of War, friend and employer of Ruth Sarles, and a close associate of many leaders of the America First Committee, which was, as he wrote Stuart on November 8, 1941, "a potential catalyst of incalculable political power. I suspect that this is a major reason why the Administration dislikes you so much."[44]

Libby's mother was a schoolteacher, and his father was a country doctor in Maine, padding along after his horse "faithful old 'Dick,'"[45] accepting payment in apples or potatoes from cash-poor farmers. (It is remarkable how many of these men and women were of New England stock, giving lie to America First sympathizer John P. Marquand's observation that "There has never been any isolationist sentiment to speak of . . . among those who are in the New England tradition."[46]) Libby was the sort of Old American who was simply not understood by the New Americans of the War Party.

Frederick Libby was a Quaker pacifist with a decided preference for conservative Republicans; as such, he made perfect sense in republican America but seems a truly outré eccentric when assessed in the darksome days of empire. "Libby had strong Republican leanings and made no secret of his admiration for such figures as Colonel Charles A. Lindbergh, Senator Robert A. Taft, and Wall Street lawyer John Foster Dulles,"[47] wrote Justus D. Doenecke.

To say that Libby admired Lindbergh is an understatement. "Lindbergh was the only man I ever knew whose spirit seemed literally transparent," marveled Libby in his autobiography. "He made me think of Jesus's characterization of Nathaniel as a man 'in whom is no guile.'"[48]

Though guile is a knee-jerk reflex in the successful lobbyist, Libby, too, was marked by its absence. He founded the National Council for Prevention of War in 1921 and was still at its helm until his retirement in November 1954 at the age of eighty, though by then the NCPW had been reduced to a shadow of its pre-empire influence. Peace was not a paying proposition in the years after 1941.

William H. Regnery was "one of the 'good angels'"[49] of the NCPW, wrote Libby, as he also was to the America First Committee. More than anyone other than Ruth Sarles, Regnery was responsible for "A Story of America First," for he subsidized and encouraged Sarles throughout her labor on this manuscript.

Regnery (1877–1954) was born on a farm near Sheboygan, Wisconsin. The family moved to a forty-acre farm in Fayette County, Iowa, when he was one, and when the boy was eleven or twelve they moved again, this time to Kansas City. In November 1902 young Regnery, whose formal education began and ended in a Catholic parochial school, was sent to Chicago by the William Volker Company to tend to the company's interests in the Western Shade Cloth Company, which made cloth for shades and, eventually, for bookbinding, tags, labels, and signs. A year later he was married, and by 1912 William H. Regnery was the major shareholder of the Western Shade Cloth Company (which would later be known as Joanna Western Mills Company).

"Although we had nearly a thousand employees in the Chicago plant, he knew most of them by name and they all knew him,"[50] wrote Regnery's son, the bookman Henry Regnery, in a family memoir. (This observation might be taken almost verbatim from Janet Ayer Fairbank's description of the Chicago factory owner in her novel *The Smiths*, which I discuss in Appendix A.)

Contrary to the stereotype of the reactionary businessman that must always be plastered on America First manufacturers lest things get too interesting, William H. Regnery was a Progressive. He was a director of Hull House and friend to Jane Addams. He was pro-Roosevelt in 1932 and 1936 and was "strongly in favor of the NRA [National Recovery Administration]."[51] He helped to subsidize the experimental Quaker settlement of Penn-Craft, in which unemployed coal miners and their families were instructed in the agrarian arts. (Regnery's son Henry spent the first three years of his marriage to his wife, Eleanor, at Penn-Craft.)

A pacifist, Regnery turned against Roosevelt over the war, which he feared would plunge his country into a long dark night of tyranny and intolerance.

(The story is told that shortly after Pearl Harbor, a young Japanese woman was hired to work in the Western Shade Cloth office. A delegation of women employees marched into Regnery's office to tell him "that unless we get rid of that Japanese girl they are all going to quit." Regnery replied, "They don't need to come in to tell me that. Tell them to go ahead and quit." None did; the Japanese woman became a long-term employee.)[52]

Anti-racism parables aren't supposed to find a place in accounts of the America First Committee; they confuse matters overmuch. For instance, Lawrence S. Wittner, one of the foremost scholars of American pacifism, wrote in his standard *Rebels Against War: The American Peace Movement, 1933–1983*, "Even more odious in the eyes of pacifists were isolationism's links to anti-Semitism and racism. Christian Front members poured into America First, despite the efforts of its leaders, while other neo-fascist groups seriously infiltrated isolationist ranks. Many of America First's leaders held strikingly racist views."[53] This is simply untrue. The only "strikingly racist" America First leader Wittner mentions is Charles Lindbergh, whose private comments about Jews were far milder than those of, say, Franklin and Eleanor Roosevelt.

Wittner is so determined to distance the chaste (and usually hopelessly ineffectual) "peace movement" of the Left from the popular opposition to American intervention in Europe in 1940–41 that he chastises Libby and the NCPW for objecting to FDR's military buildup. "[C]arried away by an almost fanatical opposition to the Administration, the N.C.P.W. veered into the isolationist camp. It distributed hundreds of thousands of copies of speeches by isolationist Senators Borah, La Follette, Nye, McCarran, and Walsh, as well as by the very symbol of nationalist isolationism, Charles Lindbergh."[54] In return, America First donated $1,000 to NCPW in 1941 for its work in opposing Lend-Lease. Though I respect Wittner's work, this is the language of the court historian, explaining principled pacifist opposition to a military buildup as the product of "fanaticism."

THE REAL ANTI-FASCISTS

General Robert E. Wood explained to a young scholar during the Second World War, "I assumed acting chairmanship of the Committee because I believed that our participation in the war was a graver threat—economically, socially and spiritually—to the welfare of our country than anything else, even the defeat of England. . . . As a patriot, I could take no other course than to work against what threatened to hurt my country."[55]

Notice General Wood's phraseology—"spiritually" was no mere afterthought. The committee was secular, of course, and contained probably more than its share of village atheists, but as 1941 rolled along to its morbid conclusion, an almost religious fervor suffused the America Firsters. Wood is echoed in an August 1942 note by former Democratic Representative Samuel B. Pettengill, who is worth quoting at length:

Until America First came along, in 25 years I have seen only one political movement in this country which was not wrapped around the dollar motive. That was the prohibition movement. I did not agree with that movement. I thought federal prohibition was a mistake. Nevertheless, I paid tribute to the idealism and disinterestedness of those who gave time and money, not for themselves, but to put over what they conceived to be a great reform. Then came America First. I spoke with Lindbergh in Chicago, and with Nye and Cudahy in the Convention Hall in Philadelphia, as well as numerous smaller meetings. These meetings contained some crackpots, Roosevelt baiters, possibly a few disloyalists. No movement is free from these elements. Theodore Roosevelt described them as the lunatic fringe. I think General Wood did a magnificent job in refusing to make compromises with any group suspected of having a greater loyalty to the Italian or German flag than the Stars and Stripes. But outside of these few there was a spiritual quality about these meetings of America First that I have not witnessed in twenty-five years. These countless thousands of men and women were giving their *time* and *money* and *prayers* for *no sordid motive*. It might be said that they were selfish. The mothers of young men were selfish for their sons. They hated to think of their young bodies eaten by rats in the trenches of some foreign land. But *this kind* of *selfishness* is the *soul of patriotism*.[56]

Pettengill, a South Bend, Indiana, lawyer who had been elected as a Democratic U.S. representative in 1930 and served until his defeat in 1938, turned against the New Deal over the issue of fascism. Not the German or Italian varieties, mind you, but the American. Anticipating John T. Flynn's classic analysis of fascism, *As We Go Marching* (1944), Pettengill charged in 1940 that "the second or third New Deal is fundamentally fascist." He asserted that "we are moving toward some form of National Socialism and away from our form of government."[57] He assumed leadership of the Committee for Constitutional Government, which had been formed in 1937 in response to FDR's court-packing proposal. Pettengill's detestation of FDR led him to switch parties, and in 1942 he served as chairman of the Republican National Finance Committee. (Across the bottom of a Pettengill memo Sarles had scrawled, "former congressman who BEAUED me around."[58] His part of the extant correspondence is circumspect enough. "You are a part of the America I hope this country will be,"[59] Pettengill wrote Sarles, in the sort of campaign boilerplate that might pass for sweet nothings on Capitol Hill.)

By June 1941, Ruth Sarles saw such Roosevelt administration initiatives as conscription and "price-fixing" as a move toward "fascism pure and simple."[60] This is just one of the many ironic twists that have contorted the popular image of the antiwar movement: slandered in retrospect as vaguely "fascist" because they opposed a U.S. war against fascist Germany, many America Firsters were motivated above all by a fear of fascism at home. (Fending off the "f"-word exasperated the libertarianish America Firsters as well as their supporters: Frederick J. Libby wrote Stuart in November 1941, "In view of the whispering campaign about the supposed 'fascism' of the America First Committee, I should very much like to have people see what a fine person you are."[61])

Ruth Sarles proposed that the AFC "do something on civil liberties,"[62] though just what was never clear. Certainly the AFC was distinguished by a sharp civil libertarian streak: for instance, national committeeman Amos R.E. Pinchot had been a founder of the National Civil Liberties Bureau, which was to become the American Civil Liberties Union. Robert Maynard Hutchins feared, "If the United States is to proceed through total war to total victory over totalitarian states, it will have to become totalitarian, too."[63] That did not happen; but the United States that emerged from the war was changed, perhaps forever, and not necessarily for the better.

The Jeffersonian side in our long national debate has been so soundly thrashed time and again that to contemporary ears, the America Firsters can sound alternately quaint and hysterical. Although Frederick J. Libby rejected the dichotomy of interventionists and isolationists and preferred the "American Party" and the "War Party," the interventionists have come down to us in historiography as the "American Party," whereas the isolationists have about them a vaguely disloyal odor. In our own day, "left" and "right" have ceased to be of much use in mapping the political landscape, and they are of surprisingly little help even when examining 1940. Seven decades of New Dealish fairy tales to the contrary, when Sarles's NCPW coworker Jeannette Rankin referred to President Roosevelt as "the Dictator"[64] she was not mouthing the platitudes of the "economic royalist" but hurling the epithet of the radical egalitarian Populist.

Historian Joan Hoff Wilson has demonstrated that Rankin's progressive isolationism-pacifism "had its roots in Jeffersonian agrarian values, in a nonconsumer oriented life style, in direct, decentralized government, in reform at home before reform of the world."[65]

This is a pretty fair summary of the worldview of many America Firsters of the "Left," Norman Thomas and the Socialists aside. They tended to be of rural rather than urban origin; they eschewed the collectivism of the socialists in favor of economic intervention in the La Follette vein: that is, in defense of small domestic producers and against export-oriented big business.

LINDBERGH, THE JEWS, AND THE INDELIBLE SMEAR

The state of affairs can only be described as topsy-turvy when America First, whose sympathies were made plain in its very name, was denounced as "traitorous"[66] by Communist Party USA leader William Z. Foster, an arrant Soviet tool whose funeral was held at the Lenin Mausoleum in Moscow's Red Square. But then, principled dissent has never been a good career move in American politics.

Once you're gone, you can't come back, as a ragged fellow once sang, and Foster's calumny is the standard-issue view of Middle America's antiwar movement. Leon M. Birkhead, the Unitarian minister and unregistered foreign agent who headed the British Security Coordination front group Friends of Democ-

racy, slandered America First as a "Nazi transmission belt," a slur that has had
a distressingly long life. (A Unitarian warhawk is just another odd bird in the
strange aviary of 1940–41.) In recent years, the noisome Ed Koch, former New
York City mayor turned pundit, kecked that the America First Committee
"supported Hitler and the Nazis in 1941," the sort of ignorant bombast that
weary Gothamites have come to expect from their ex-mayor. ("Ed Koch isn't
fit to carry the goggles of The Lone Eagle,"[67] wrote Pat Buchanan in January
1999, when Scott Berg's surprisingly favorable biography of Lindbergh occa-
sioned a renewed interest in the aviator, much to Koch's horror.)

Koch's roorback was a direct descendant of such World War II agitprop as
Under Cover by John Roy Carlson (the pen name of the interventionist Friends
of Democracy agent Avedis Derounian) and *Sabotage! The Secret War Against
America*, by Michael Sayers and Albert E. Kahn of the Reverend Birkhead's
Friends of Democracy.

Sabotage! is a lurid exposé in the tradition of *Reefer Madness* and *I Married
a Communist*. In breathless, if not deathless, prose, it seeks to link the small
and pathetic pro-Nazi German American Bund and various anti-Semitic cranks
to anyone who had the patriotic temerity to question U.S. intervention in the
European war. The evidence is scant: America First and her leaders formally
and consistently denounced Nazism, anti-Semitism, and any groups infected
by these un-American bugs, ranging from the obviously disloyal Bundists to
the rather more problematic social justice movement of Father Charles Coughlin. ("We don't want you people,"[68] General Wood told the Coughlinites point-
blank.) Nevertheless, Sayers and Kahn look under every cloaca. In the manner
of 1950s segregationists who trumpeted the Communist Party's endorsement
of Negroes sharing water fountains with whites, they note a single favorable
mention of America First in a Ku Klux Klan rag. The aviator Laura Ingalls,
later convicted for failing to register as a German agent, spoke at several smaller
America First rallies; she flew planes and felt kindly toward Nazis—need we
say more? Lindbergh in drag! (In fairness, Wayne S. Cole writes that Ingalls's
"part in the Committee's campaign is a serious blot on its record. But she
worked through America First less than half of its history. She addressed none
of the largest America First rallies. For every meeting addressed by this German
agent during the Committee's history, patriotic America First speakers addressed dozens."[69])

Sayers and Kahn conclude that America Firsters "became the dupes of the
enemies of the United States,"[70] a locution that would receive frequent use in
the Red hunts of the 1950s and the harassment of anti–Vietnam War protesters
in the late 1960s and early 1970s.

America First's leaders kept the organization as free as possible from infec-
tion by anti-Semites and those with kindred derangments. New York was the
only city that posed much of a problem in this regard; General Wood wrote
John T. Flynn in February 1941 that he had

heard that some of the members of our Queens Chapter are Christian Front or Silver Shirt members. We have kept our committee clean by refusing to take as members of our national committee anyone connected with other organizations or affiliated with those organizations in any way, particularly those that are as undesirable as I understand these two are. As far as I know, we have none of them in the Middle West and I do not know much about them. From what little I have heard of them they are not desirable fellow associates and we do not want them as members of our local committee.[71]

But of course, it always comes back to Lindbergh. The story of his Des Moines speech of September 11, 1941, is treated at length in Ruth Sarles's manuscript, and she does the great service of reprinting the speech in full. Read for yourself, and decide.

Lindbergh had anticipated the firestorm before the America First Committee was even a mote in Harold Ickes's eye. On October 7, 1939, he wrote in his diary that ex-President Hoover, William Castle, and others were trying to corral him into the GOP, "although I have no special interest in that party. . . . I have but little fear of being classed as a Republican for long. I have too little interest in either politics or popularity. One of the dearest of rights to me is being able to say what I think and act as I wish. I intend to do this, and I know it will cause trouble. As soon as it does, the politicians will disown me quickly enough—and I will be only too willing. . . . At least I shall hold my self-respect—and possibly that of a number of other people."[72]

Lindbergh was crucified, but those "other people" who continued to respect him were legion.

Among the many myths of America First demonology is the one in which anyone with the least shred of reputability divorced himself from the AFC after Lindbergh's Des Moines speech. ("The voice is the voice of Lindbergh," spewed the *San Francisco Chronicle*, "but the words are the words of Hitler."[73])

The committee did lose valuable allies over the Des Moines speech. Kathryn Lewis, daughter of the pugnaciously antiwar United Mine Workers leader John L. Lewis, resigned, though she told Stuart "that my own position on the war has not changed."[74] (Nor had her father's. He remained convinced that Roosevelt's intent was that "the United States first becomes a militaristic nation, and second, becomes an imperialistic nation, to carry out the dreams of conquest of some would-be dictator."[75])

John T. Flynn also castigated Lindbergh. And Socialist Party leader Norman Thomas wrote General Wood, "I know that Colonel Lindbergh is not anti-Semitic and that he meant good rather than evil by his address." But "what truth there was in it [his address] with regard to the Jews, should have been put before a private conference with Jews, not before a mass meeting and the radio public." He closed with his regret "that our friend the Colonel will not take the advice on public relations which he would expect an amateur in aviation to take from an expert."[76]

The sin, it seems, is a bad p.r. sense, not a hateful heart. Where were Benton and Bowles when America First needed them?

Greatly confusing the matter was the minor detail that Lindbergh was *right:* Jewish groups *were* solidly behind the push for war. And that gives the responses of AFC committee members a certain schizophrenic quality.

Sterling Morton of salt company fame wrote Stuart that he was deeply troubled by the colonel's impolitic remarks, for "There are no people who have more right than the Jewish people to oppose Hitler and all he has done, and they have a perfect right to use their influence in favor of war if they so wish." But they must rely upon "fact and logical argument, not merely . . . the cry of anti-Semitism."[77]

William Castle wrote Stuart, "You can't blame them for wanting to destroy Hitler after what he has done to the Jews in Germany but they would show more wisdom if they made it clear that their first interest was the U.S.A."[78]

Oswald Garrison Villard, who had left the National Committee in pacific protest against the AFC's endorsement of a strong defense, found Lindbergh's speech magnificent. Samuel Hopkins Adams, the crusading liberal novelist and muckraker of Owasco Lake, wrote General Wood on September 29, 1941, "Now, when the attacks upon the committee are becoming more virulent and unfair, is the time, as it seems to me, when we must stand together and not let any side issue, such as Col. Lindbergh's unfortunate and ill-timed utterance, divert us from the main purpose."[79]

Kathleen Norris defended her friend, who "in placing the Jews in the category of those desiring to have us enter the war, put them in the same company as the President, the administration, and the pro-British element, surely not [a] group in which inclusion of the Jews need cause them either shame or anger. This categorical grouping cannot possibly be interpreted except by deliberation and misconstruction as either an attack or an insult."[80]

At Cornell, a student columnist and chemistry major named Kurt Vonnegut came to Lindbergh's defense in the *Cornell Daily Sun.* (Which side in the war debate was literary and which reeked of the poetaster? I'll take Sinclair Lewis, e.e. cummings, Vidal, Vonnegut, Frost, and Edmund Wilson and give you Archibald MacLeish and Robert Sherwood, and your side can't sharpen my side's pencils.)

I quote Vonnegut's column of October 13, 1941, nearly in full, for I have never seen it published elsewhere:

Charles A. Lindbergh is one helluva swell egg, and we're willing to fight for him in our own quaint way. Several sterling folk, *Sun* members not excluded, have been taking journalistic pot-shots at the Lone Eagle, effectively, too. The great work is spreading. Give the stout, red-blooded American—the average mental age is fourteen, we're told— a person to hate, tell him to do so often, and he and his cousin Moe will do a damned fine job of it, providing there are plenty of others doing the same.

The mud-slingers are good. They'd have to be good to get people hating a loyal and sincere patriot. On second thought, Lindbergh is no patriot—to hell with the word, it lost it's [sic] meaning after the Revolutionary War.

What a guy! Look at the beating he takes. Why on God's green earth (we think He's sub-let it) would anyone lay himself open for such defamation if he wasn't entirely convinced that he must give the message to his country at any cost? To offer an obstacle to the premeditated Roosevelt foreign policy is certainly to ask for a kick in the face. . . .

Crusades, not that they're not worth twice the cost, cost about five million men these days. It's America's purpose to defend it's [sic] way of life, to bankrupt itself rather than let Hitler take our South American trade—a farce which ends in red ink every time—and to send the best crop of young technicians the country has known, who could make this fabulously wealthy nation self-sufficient within itself, into battle.

Charles A. Lindbergh has had the courage at least to present the conservative side of a titanic problem, grant him that. The United States is a democracy, that's what they say we'll be fighting for. What a prize monument to that ideal is a cry to smother Lindy. Weighing such inconsequential items as economic failure and simultaneous collapse of the flaunted American Standard of Living (looks good capitalized—it'll be fine for chuckles in a decade), and outrageous bloodshed of his countrymen, the young ones, is virtual treason to the Stars and Stripes—long may it wave.

Lindy, you're a rat. We read that somewhere, so it must be so. They say you should be deported. In that event, leave room in the boat for us, our room-mate, Jane, mother, that barber with the moustache in Willard Straight, and those two guys down the hall—you make sense to us.[81]

Four years later, infantryman Kurt Vonnegut, a POW held by the Germans, witnessed the destruction of Dresden and eventually memorialized its madness in *Slaughterhouse Five* (1969).

A Cornell classmate of Vonnegut's and fellow America Firster was Barber B. Conable, Jr., who became the Republican ranking member of the House Ways and Means Committee. Conable, who represented my home district in rural western New York, was by most bipartisan reckonings the finest member of Congress in the 1970s. Leading congressional scholar Richard Fenno called him "the best of the breed"[82]; Woodward and Bernstein gushed that "he was regarded by his colleagues as almost puritanical in his standards of personal and political conduct, a man of unquestioned integrity."[83] Conable was the son of a Republican pacifist judge in Warsaw, New York, birthplace of the abolitionist Liberty Party; undergraduate Conable organized the Cornell branch of the America First Committee.

Another student AFC leader was young Gene (later Gore) Vidal, who organized the America First chapter at Exeter. Vidal's future foil, William F. Buckley, Jr., championed America First at his prep school, Millbrook. Vidal is the link, the bridge, the blood that runs between the Old Republic antiwar isolationists and the new; he has written of Lindbergh, "it might be a pleasant gift to the new century and the new millennium to replace the pejorative 1812 caricature of a sly, treacherous Uncle Sam with that of Lindbergh, the best that we are ever apt to produce in the hero line, American style."[84] In a letter to me, Vidal called Lindbergh "the true white knight through and through" who "could not believe that anyone could twist his disinterestedness into such vileness."[85] But they did, and at times it seems that this twisting can never be righted. (As an example, Vidal wrote his essay on Lindbergh for the *New York Review of Books*, of which he has been the most distinguished contributor for more than thirty years. The *NYRB* refused to publish the piece, thus ending a long and rich relationship. From beyond the grave, the Reverend Birkhead gleams.)

The Jewish presence in America First has not been much noticed; the assumption, one gathers, is that these men and women were either deluded or self-hating, as the Establishment take on Noam Chomsky goes. The previously mentioned publicity director Sidney Hertzberg, perhaps the AFC's most prominent Jewish staffer, was a stalwart of the committee's left flank. He had earlier edited *Uncensored* and directed the Writers' Anti-War Committee for the Keep America Out of War Congress. He was the father of Hendrik Hertzberg, who later edited *The New Republic* and served as senior editor of *The New Yorker*.

New York lawyer James Lipsig was a prominent Jewish staffer whose name appears frequently in Ruth Sarles's papers. Sarles encouraged Stuart to hire Lipsig as a reseacher in June 1941. He did so through Pearl Harbor; thereafter, Lipsig contributed research to "A Story of America First." Sarles wrote Senator Robert A. Taft in February 1942, asking Taft if he could help this "unusually competent" and "imaginative researcher" find a job. "I am very much afraid he is going to have difficulty," confided Sarles. "His race and his views are against him. He spent about ten days in Washington early in January and found that his views made him persona non grata to some of the Jewish people in government who might have helped him, and his race makes him unacceptable in other quarters. He is in a tight spot."[86]

The only Jewish member of Congress—ex-member, actually—to serve on the AFC national committee was Representative Florence Prag Kahn (R-Calif.), a daughter of Polish Jews who succeeded her deceased husband, Julius Kahn, and represented a San Francisco district from 1925 until 1937. Congresswoman Kahn had a quick and irreverent wit. Appointed to the Committee on Indian Affairs, she complained, "The only Indians in my district are in front of cigar stores." When Representative Fiorello La Guardia taunted her for "following that reactionary, Senator George H. Moses of New Hampshire," she riposted, "Why shouldn't I choose Moses as my leader? Haven't my people been following him for ages?"[87]

Kahn was not among the more active members of the board, and she eventually resigned, as did the other Jewish member of the National Committee, Sears Roebuck director Lessing Rosenwald.

Most of America First's political leadership had been regarded before 1940 as friendly not only to Jewish political interests but, more importantly, to Jewish people themselves, and a man's private acts remain the best measure of his character. For instance, Senator Gerald Nye (R-N. Dak.), the populist firebrand who led the 1941 Senate investigation of "alien"—read: British—influences in Hollywood, was consistently libeled as an anti-Semite by interventionist and British front groups. (These attacks were meant "to cover the tracks of those who have been pushing our country on the way to war with their propaganda,"[88] the senator charged.) Nye "had a good record on religious toleration,"[89] as Wayne S. Cole wrote in his book-length study of the senator. More importantly, Nye's best man at his 1940 wedding had been Fargo banker William Stern, who was Jewish. This would be exceedingly odd behavior for an anti-Semite. Like Lindbergh, Nye acknowledged that American Jews had cause, qua Jews, to favor U.S. aid to the Allies; but as he wrote his friend Stern, the responsibility of the American statesman was to prevent "our entry into another futile foreign war."[90]

The force of the anti-isolationist assault in the popular media still stuns the reader. But then, the goal of some influential interventionists was nothing less than the removal of the antiwar voice from American politics. As a January 30, 1943, advertisement in the *New York Times* sponsored by Freedom House read, "First, we must win the war. Second, we must destroy isolationism forever."[91]

The extent to which the War Party would Nazi-bait at the drop of a hat is illustrated by the decline of Philip La Follette, son of Wisconsin Senator Robert M. La Follette, Sr., and brother of the Senator La Follette who assisted America First. Philip La Follette, animated by "the vitality and liberalism of the middle west,"[92] won two-year terms as his state's governor in 1930, 1934, and 1936. He won the first race as a Republican and the latter two as a Progressive. In 1937–38, La Follette sought to organize a progressive third party as an alternative to the "tweedledum and tweedledee politics [which] will destroy America."[93] With appealingly amateurish fanfare, he and 3,500 Progressives auspicated the National Progressives of America with a raucous rally in the University of Wisconsin livestock pavilion on April 28, 1938. Like his father, Philip La Follette envisioned a coalition of farmers, laborers, shopkeepers, and small merchants pitted against the corporate and bureaucratic powers of the East Coast. The economic program of the National Progressives was neither New Dealish nor laissez-faire: government ought to spend freely "to restore to every American the opportunity to help himself. After that he can sink or swim,"[94] declared the governor. This was an echo of the old Populists, who saw the state as the one institution that could tame the corporation yet still harbored a Jeffersonian fear of the state rampant. After all, said La Follette, "no government on earth can successfully manage, regulate, and direct the numerous details that make for healthy families or successful business."[95]

Within a year the National Progressives had expired, victim of . . . well, symbolism. You see, La Follette had designed a cross and circle emblem in red, white, and blue; this symbolized "the unity of the nation, the power of the ballot, equality, and the need for multiplication of wealth and organized social action."[96] To the smear-bund, it was "a feeble imitation of the Swastika,"[97] in the words of President Roosevelt. A compliant corporate media concurred—La Follette's sin, it seems, was hailing from the Germanic state of Wisconsin—

and another dissident of the Left was silenced. (Philip La Follette helped organize the America First Committee and sometimes served as General Wood's
representative to AFC headquarters. He spoke under AFC auspices but never
joined the National Committee. In one radio address of February 1941, he
pleaded with the president to cease the vilification of the peace party: "Instead
of smearing or wrecking, let us encourage and build character, in ourselves and
others. Argue—hit as hard as you please *on the issues*, but refuse to vilify
individuals simply because they do not agree."[98] As Harold Ickes might have
said . . . Sure, Phil. La Follette's brother, Senator Robert La Follette, Jr., voted
with the AFC but made only a single speech for the organization. The senator
vainly encouraged America First not to close shop after Pearl Harbor.)

Politicians were not the only ones to lose careers as a result of taking a stand
for America First. Lillian Gish was Hollywood's most prominent America Firster (Edward Everett Horton was another, though he was much less active).
Gish's visibility on the National Committee contributed to her invisibility on
the nation's movie screens—though none dared call it blacklisting.

Richard A. Moore of the AFC dictated this confidential memo on August 28,
1941:

> General Wood was in the office today and related a conversation he had just had with
> Miss Lillian Gish here in Chicago. Miss Gish stated that since her active association
> with the America First Committee, she has been "black-listed" by movie studios in
> Hollywood and by the legitimate theater.
>
> She has been seeking employment in Hollywood during the past several weeks, and
> her agent has finally notified her that he can now obtain a movie contract which will
> bring her $65,000. This contract, however, has been offered upon the condition that she
> first resign from the America First Committee and cease all her activities on behalf of
> the Committee; and upon the further condition that in resigning, she refrain from
> stating this reason for her resignation.
>
> Miss Gish has not had employment for a long time. She is supporting her Mother
> and is helping to support her sister.[99]

The movie, curiously enough, was probably John Farrow's forgotten wartime
propaganda effort *The Commandos Strike at Dawn* (1942). Gish makes no
mention of America First in her autobiography, *The Movies, Mr. Griffith, and
Me* (1969). Other artistic America Firsters would face the blacklist, the censor's
pen, the letter of rejection. For writing the antiwar novel *The Adventures of
Wesley Jackson* (1946), William Saroyan was threatened with a court-martial
by agrarian-turned-superhawk Herbert Agar of the Office of War Information.
Bennett Cerf and Random House refused to publish ten antiwar and anti-FDR
poems by Robinson Jeffers in what became his volume *The Double Axe* (1948).
Samuel Hopkins Adams's *The Incredible Era*, a popular history of the Harding
years, did not go into the expected paperback edition "because of Adams's
incorrect assessment that Americans should and could avoid involvement in
the war,"[100] as his biographer claims.

For more than half a century, the Birkheads in our midst have libeled any American who expresses even the most mild reservation about the wisdom of U.S. involvement in the Second World War. Not only could four-fifths of the American people be wrong in 1941, apparently, but the sentiments that motivated them must be forever locked away in the dungeon of unacceptable opinion.

When in the 1976 vice presidential debate the Republican candidate, Kansas Senator Robert Dole, cracked, "I figured up the other day, if we added up the killed and wounded in Democrat wars in this century, it would be about 1.6 million Americans, enough to fill the city of Detroit,"[101] he was flogged by the media for an implicitly antiwar worldview. Dole spent the rest of his odd career as a truculent compromiser apologizing for this gaffe. (Recall Michael Kinsley's memorable definition of a gaffe as an inadvertently true statement by a politician.) That the head of Dole's ticket was a founder of the America First Committee, opponent par excellence of "Democrat wars," was not noted by the lapdog press.

Being deceased is no defense against the thought-crime of isolationism. When in 1991 the diaries of the coruscatingly brilliant newspaper columnist and joyful libertarian H.L. Mencken were published, his diaristic assaults on FDR and the War Party were treated as the most abhorrent of hate thought. "Mencken was Pro-Nazi, His Diary Shows," blared the *Los Angeles Times*, though his diary showed no such thing. The single example adduced by the *Times* was this excerpt of October 24, 1945: "The course of the United States in World War II . . . was dishonest, dishonorable, and ignominious, and the Sunpapers, in supporting Roosevelt's foreign policy, shared in this disgrace."[102] (He goes on in this entry to ridicule "the preposterous Truman, perhaps the cheapest and least honest man ever to sit in the White House."[103] Mencken, like many America Firsters, saw the cold war as the logical extension of the Second World War, and a grave threat to what remained of American liberties and the republican form of government.)

Mencken's most eloquent defenders against this cowardly posthumous defamation were Jews. Joseph Epstein, writing in *Commentary*—which regards isolationists with the same good humor and solicitude as John Roy Carlson/ Avedis Derounian did—called the imputation of anti-Semitism to the Semitophiliac (at least judging by his personal friendships) Mencken "meshugga."[104] Epstein noted Mencken's prewar denunciations of the "intolerable brutalities" and "extraordinary imbecility"[105] of Hitler and the Nazis. In *Chronicles*, Murray N. Rothbard, the ebullient, yea, Menckenesque, libertarian economist, damned the diary's editor, Charles A. Fecher:

Fecher's purported shock and amazement at Mencken's hatred of FDR and his opposition to World War II is simply beyond belief. You don't have to be steeped in Mencken's published essays and letters to know that he hated Roosevelt and opposed U.S. entry into World War II. . . . Fecher panders to the notorious historical amnesia of most Americans by acting as if anyone with such outlandish views must have been a lone nut and, at least implicitly, pro-Nazi. Fecher conveniently ignores the fact that millions of Americans hated FDR with equal intensity (though not with Mencken's sparkling wit), and that a majority of Americans strongly opposed U.S. entry into World War II.[106]

So it's out to Coventry for poor Mencken, and down the memory hole for the tens of millions of Americans whose thought-crime was adhering to the classic advice bequeathed his American posterity by George Washington in his Farewell Address: "Observe good faith and justice toward all nations. Cultivate peace and harmony with all. . . . Europe has a set of primary interests which to us have none or a very remote relation. Hence she must be engaged in frequent controversies, the causes of which are essentially foreign to our concerns."[107] A useful idiot of Nazism, no doubt.

The indignities that America Firsters suffer, even beyond the grave, make for a dispiriting read. When Bill Regnery, grandson and namesake of the man who paid Ruth Sarles to write this book, visited the Northwestern University Library's Special Collections to view material from "the America First Committee" and "other American groups with similar goals," he found that these "other American groups with similar goals" included vile Jew-haters and outright Nazis. As the Special Collections Department guide says, the "materials reflect the anti-Semitism, racism, and anti-Communism masquerading behind the respectable front of association with the America First Committee itself and Charles Lindbergh."[108]

Patrick J. Buchanan, twice an insurgent Republican candidate for the presidency and in 2000 the nominee of the populist Reform Party, defended the America First Committee with great panache in his 1999 book *A Republic, Not an Empire*. Buchanan was the first politician since the noble Senator William Fulbright to use the "e"-word in political discourse; for his courage he was traduced as a nut, an anti-Semite, a crypto-Nazi, and other smears right out of Harold Ickes's handbook. As Mr. Vonnegut might write, And so it goes in the land of the free. . . .

But let us be optimists. Slowly, perhaps, some of the anathemas are being removed. One of the hoariest smears against the Peace Party focused on Representative Hamilton Fish (R-N.Y.), descendant of the Revolution, grandson of Grant's secretary of state, husband to a Stuyvesant, Bull Mooser turned reactionary Republican. Fish represented President Roosevelt's hometown of Hyde Park in Congress, and FDR's increasingly bitter attacks on his former friend may have owed to the president's relative unpopularity on their home turf. (FDR carried his hometown only three of the nine times he ran for office.)

Unlike the armchair admiral Roosevelt, Fish (1888–1991), a Walter Camp All-America football player, won a Silver Star and the French Croix de Guerre in the First World War while commanding the Harlem Hellfighters, a segregated unit of black soldiers. In Congress, he became a sort of national ombudsman for the often disenfranchised black citizens of these United States, but his personal aversion to racism did not lead him to crusade for its eradication by war in places distant. He told a nationwide radio audience in 1939, "As much as American citizens abhor racial and religious persecution and ruthless militarism, it is none of our business what form of government may exist in Soviet Russia, Fascist Italy, Imperial Japan, or Nazi Germany, any more than it is their business what form of government exists in our own country. We have our own problems to solve in America without becoming involved in the rotten mess in Europe or in the eternal wars of both Europe and Asia."[109]

Fish, the ranking Republican on the House Foreign Affairs Committee, never joined the America First Committee, though he did speak frequently on AFC platforms. ("Fish is erratic," John T. Flynn told Robert E. Wood, "but when his eye is clearly on the objective and he is in agreement with his colleagues . . . he is a good fighter."[110]) His reputation was done irreparable harm by a campaign orchestrated by British Security Coordination (BSC)—made famous by William Stephenson's *A Man Called Intrepid* (1976).

The scope of this mendacious and utterly illegal activity by foreign intelligence operatives to destroy an American politician is revealed in Thomas E. Mahl's groundbreaking *Desperate Deception: British Covert Operations in the United States, 1939–44* (1998), which confirms, sixty years after the fact, John T. Flynn's belief that "The plain and terrifying fact is that this great and peaceful nation is in the grip of one of the most subtle and successful conspiracies . . . to embroil us in a foreign war."[111] Suffice to say here that Hamilton Fish's defeat in 1944 was the culmination of a four-year campaign of character assassination by British intelligence, working with American fifth columnists, in which Fish, who for decades had been a leading friend of Jewish and Zionist causes in the U.S. Congress, metamorphosed overnight into a Nazi fellow traveler. A leading American collaborator in this extraordinary political crime was Christopher T. Emmett, Jr., who was active in countless front groups both before and after the war, when he lent his cloak and dagger services to the cold war. In 1940, Emmett, writes Mahl, "pronounced the essence of the entire British intelligence campaign against the isolationists: 'If . . . we can defeat Fish, who has been considered invincible for twenty years, we will put the fear of God into every isolationist senator and congressman in the country.'"[112]

In 1952, Fish looked back at his actions without regret: "I was never even a member of the America First organization, but I was for America first, and am still for America first and always will be. If that be treason, make the most of it."[113] Fish never did mellow. Upon turning 100, he told a reporter of FDR, "I know he hated me, but I really don't believe in hate. So now I don't hate Roosevelt—but frankly I despise him."[114]

Fish had company. And cause. It will take many years to restore a reputation tarnished by foreign operatives—but the restoration has begun.

THE STORY OF "A STORY OF AMERICA FIRST"

Had things gone according to Ruth Sarles's plan, the book you are about to read would have been published in 1943. It was not; nor did Sarles publish any other book in her lifetime.

Sarles did not bequeath her papers to any institution, but she did turn over what material she had from her America First days to historian Wayne S. Cole, who in turn deposited it with the Herbert Hoover Presidential Library in West Branch, Iowa. The America First collection of the Hoover Institution at Stanford University has a much smaller sheaf of Sarles's materials.

Ruth Sarles saved much of her correspondence from March 1941 until her work on "A Story of America First" was completed. The paper trail almost ends before it begins; on March 26, 1941, we find Sidney Hertzberg, who had recently hired Sarles for America First, warning Sarles that he is leaving the committee and that, moreover, "Finances are low and there will probably be other cuts. . . . There is a strong possibility that they may decide to get along without your services, and I want to warn you."[115] But not to worry: by April 2, national director Stuart assured her that "certain funds have become available during the last few days,"[116]—probably from William Regnery—and no more do we read of the dole imminent.

Sarles "conceived my job to be one of making myself as useful as possible to the Senators,"[117] though that may be overstating matters, for she was known to ward off the passes of the more lecherous solons.

She did write speeches and background papers, met with members of Congress (particularly senators) and their aides, clipped articles from the newspapers, monitored the *Congressional Record,* and remained "on call" to antiwar senators, "cramming my head with facts"[118] useful in debate.

She assisted Senator Gerald Nye in the preparation of his resolution providing for an advisory referendum before war is officially declared. The war referendum first became popular in the teens as a project of such populist statesmen as William Jennings Bryan and Senators Robert La Follette and Thomas P. Gore (D-Okla.), the grandfather of Gore Vidal; in January 1938, a binding war-referendum proposal sponsored by Representative Louis Ludlow (D-Ind.) was defeated in a procedural vote in the House 209–188. Sarles lobbied the AFC leadership to officially endorse the Nye resolution, which would give antiwar activists "something positive to work for—and we're usually anti-something or the other."[119] She envisioned a broad pro-Nye front encompassing the National Council for Prevention of War, the Women's International League for Peace and Freedom, and the Keep America Out of War Congress. Bob Stuart noted that such conservatives as Senator Robert Taft and Hanford MacNider "don't like the idea too well because it is inconsistent with representative government."[120] The AFC National Committee would not endorse a Ludlow-like binding war referendum, but it did endorse the milder advisory referendum embodied in Senator Nye's resolution.

Kendrick Lee, the Chicago-based AFC research director, requested that Sarles write him a memo every Sunday with enough insider information to enable Lee to send out a newsletter with an "authentic 'smell.'" Make it "a kind of gossip letter which you might write to some girl friend in Chicago giving her little tidbits of interest."[121] She did so, with rather less gossip than the moderately prurient reader might like, but this promising effort at chatty history was ended after just two months when the newsletter was killed by AFC headquarters. She did continue to file occasional memos to Bob Stuart.

"Working on the Hill is full of frustrations and aching feet," she wrote Kendrick Lee in April 1941. "You find people not in; you wait for an hour; you come to the end of a long day and wonder how it could possibly have taken so long to see only three people."[122] Yet the letters of these youngish America First staffers brim with the excitement of youth working for a cause: they are always writing at 1 A.M., 2 A.M., 3:41 A.M., galvanized by coffee and cigarettes and peace. One day all is drear and gloom; on the next, "the stay-out-of-war group is certainly beginning to stage a comeback."[123] On May 9, "I can find almost no one here who thinks we shall stay out,"[124] but on May 18 "the conviction is growing that the country is hardening against war."[125] On August 9, "we are getting in fast."[126] Rumors of war are bellowed and then muted, sometimes within a day, until December 7, 1941.

On December 9, 1941, Jimmie Lipsig informed Sarles, "Things are blue here [in Chicago headquarters], and everyone is discouraged as hell, and it's difficult to get anything done."[127] Lipsig reported that among those favoring a continuation of America First in some form were Charles Lindbergh, Amos R.E. Pinchot, Robert Hutchins, and Colonel Robert McCormick; Ruth Sarles told Bob Stuart on December 10 that Senators La Follette, George Aiken, Hiram Johnson, and D. Worth Clark thought that "America First should go on in some form or other."[128] As for Sarles, "I wish America First could dissolve. My understanding was that the organization was founded to keep the country out of war." She urges the committee to make its lists available to Frederick J. Libby, whose NCPW dedicates itself to "prevent[ing] a spread of intolerance and hate toward our racial and other minorities, and toward other peoples from growing, either in ourselves or in our communities."[129]

On December 11, the National Committee issued a statement. "The period of democratic debate on the issue of entering the war is over; the time for military action is here." The committee expressed its will-o'-the-wisp hope that the United States would abjure "imperialistic aims" and defend "the fundamental rights of American citizens under our Constitution and Bill of Rights,"[130] but the game was up, and America First had lost.

Within that same December, Sarles closed the Washington AFC office and started outlining "A Story of America First." She was to be assisted by Harry Schnibbe, the AFC's assistant director of organization, who agreed to write chapters on the founding and general setup of the AFC. The U.S. Navy had other plans, though, and Mr. Schnibbe was soon Ensign Schnibbe. Schnibbe said in a later letter that he had completed "the running story of the Committee from May 1940 to January 1941,"[131] and he suggests that his writings are larded with colorful anecdotes that did not, alas, survive. He is an amusing epistolary hysteric, dreading his inevitable naval assignment and confessing, "Sometimes despair overtakes me. Then, I laugh—a-ha-ha!! For relaxation I stand on my head in a corner—hours at a time. While I am working I am sorry I ever was a non-interventionist; like on Fridays when I am sorry I am a Catholic."[132]

William H. Regnery agreed to subsidize Sarles; she went off the AFC payroll and onto Regnery's payroll on January 10, 1942. He agreed to pay her $3,000 for the job, including expenses and funds for the temporary employment of others. By May 1942, $3,597.23 had been spent, but Regnery instructed Sarles that "As to the cost of the project, it is my opinion that this is very much of a secondary matter"[133]—he replenished the coffers. Frederick Libby let her have a desk, telephone, typewriter, and office for a song ($20 a month).

Regnery, the aforementioned Chicago manufacturer and vice chairman of the National Council for Prevention of War, was something of an almoner for peace causes. (He was "the largest financial backer"[134] of America First, according to Wayne S. Cole.) Typically, Sarles wrote him on April 21, 1942, forwarding Senator Nye's worries about "his chance for re-election in 1944." Nye "is handicapped by lack of money,"[135] Sarles hinted, and two weeks later a check (amount unspecified) arrived in a Regnery letter to Sarles. He was simply doing "the duty of those citizens who feel this way," and it is characteristic of the modest Regnery that he had crossed out "good" before "citizens."[136] Regnery believed it was his duty to give away his fortune to those who sought to preserve the republic, according to his grandson and namesake, and if the republic perished anyway, it was not for lack of effort on Regnery's part.

Sarles went through the files of Bob Stuart and General Wood in Chicago; she used John T. Flynn's files from the New York chapter. She hoped to finish the manuscript by May—a herculean task worthy of Samuel Hopkins Adams—but come April 26, she joked to Wood that "I have a mental picture of myself going down the years, still writing the America First story!"[137] Regnery reassured her that "this is just another one of those jobs that inevitably consumes more time and effort than any one can estimate at the beginning."[138]

From the beginning, the war intruded. Bob Stuart was shipped to Fort Sill, and she spent "less than two hours"[139] with the man she had assumed would be her primary source.

"Both Harry Schnibbe and I are more and more impressed with the drama of this story. In our rash moments we even talk about putting in dialogue!"[140] In a letter to Schnibbe, Sarles gently chided him for his "somewhat journalistic" approach in writing the Washington part of the story. He had executed "quite frankly a personal story, with adjectives etc. and lots of the author's slant."[141] Schnibbe's departure for the navy left Ruth scrambling for anecdotes; as she explained to Richard Moore, "I need some recollections of the human interest side of AF. Bill Jones probably had to wait until he got the beans picked before he could work up a meeting. I'll bet Mrs. Osterfeather sold Grandma's Paisley shawl in order to make a contribution. ETC. ETC. Incidentally, Harry Schnibbe was going to do this angle but the Navy got him in its toils before he was able to finish it."[142]

Among the most valuable artifacts from Sarles's papers is a letter of March 31, 1942, from Charles Lindbergh. It is remarkably, if characteristically, dispassionate, and I quote at length:

I have been turning over in my mind our discussion in regard to the history of the America First Committee. It seems to me that it would be a mistake to attempt too much "explaining." No amount of explaining you could do would satisfy our opposition, and I think very little explaining is necessary for others. I should think the best procedure would be to state facts and to quote directly from addresses, articles, etc. I believe the record of what we stood for and what we did is more effective and satisfying than even the most eloquent interpretation of motives could be.

For instance, when I was in Washington you spoke about the charges of anti-Semitism resulting from my Des Moines address. It is useless for me or for you to claim that that address was or was not "anti-Semitic." Different people would reach different conclusions in regard to this, based upon their view-point of life. I have never regarded myself as "anti-Semitic" but I have no intention of arguing this point with those who disagree with the content of my Des Moines address. I stand upon the statements made in that address, and I have little interest in the names attached to it by various factions. In other words, my suggestion is that you quote whatever portions of this and other addresses you feel desirable, and allow your readers to make their own interpretation.

If your history of the Committee is based primarily upon factual statements, letters, addresses, etc., it will constitute a permanent record of the pre-war period, and be referred to in the future by responsible historians and research workers. On the other hand, if you attempt to do too much explaining, you will immediately label your book with such partisanship that responsible writers will be hesitant to refer to it in the future.[143]

For better and worse, Sarles took Lindbergh's advice, and few writers, responsible or otherwise, have ever had a chance to refer to the book. The Olympian detachment counseled by Lindbergh, the refusal to scrap, to defend, to explain, may suit a hero, but it does not always behoove an author. Sarles's book *is* a valuable compilation of facts and speeches—this is what America First sounded like—but it might have benefited from a dash of partisanship.

In her response to Lindbergh, Sarles wrote, "I believe I agree with your point of view most of the way. . . . I have conceived my job to be one of reporting—not only activities and events but also to try to paint the picture of the mental climate (if I may be permitted a mixed metaphor) in which America First functioned. . . . However, I believe that can be done without going into the merits and demerits of these considerations, and your comments have done much to clarify the method for me."[144]

Why was "A Story of America First" never published? The evidence is fragmentary. The first caution against anything "that would promote disunity" on the home front comes from Sarles's old beau, Samuel B. Pettengill, who had seen an early version of the manuscript. In an August 1, 1942, letter to William H. Regnery, Pettengill—who switched parties and was now chairman of the Republican National Finance Committee—counseled, "The necessity of the preservation of national unity at this time is so great that outside of possibly one or two hundred copies for private circulation, I do not think the book should be published at this time."[145]

Whether Regnery regarded Pettengill as sage statesman or self-important fool is not known. By September 22, a note of resignation had crept into Regnery's correspondence with Sarles. "I hope to live long enough to see it published for the benefit of those interested in the many happenings of the years 1940 and 1941,"[146] he wrote the author, disabusing her of the usual auctorial hopes of immediate publication followed by best-sellerdom.

Sarles finished the manuscript in October 1942. The tone of her letter to Regnery apprising him of its completion suggests that all the initial buckram, the stiffness, is gone (though her salutation still reads "Mr. Regnery"; as his son Henry recalled, everyone addressed him "Mr. Regnery"):

Here is the formula for dwelling on Olympia—even if it's only occasionally:

Live a very active life for twelve years, in a milieu where exciting things are happening and your contacts are with people who are "doing things." Then suddenly—at the moment the world has cracked wide open, and you are trying to dope it out—allow yourself to be catapulted into a project that requires enough solitude for real thought, and separation from the exciting things that heretofore have made up your life because they interfere with the sense of detachment the project requires. You struggle, as if torn between two loves. Then, to save your reason, you accept the ivory tower existence. And once you accept it you find the discipline is excellent insulation against the anguish any person of sensitivity feels at the news of these times; a sense of history helps.

But, ah me, it's very lonesome up here sometimes. I think I shall go back to the world in about two weeks—but taking the aura of Olympia with me if I can.[147]

Regnery replied, plaintively, "How does one reach the Olympian heights these mornings or at any other time of day in times like these? I should like to know." And "I seem to be unable to make use of your formula for rising above mundane things and dwelling among the 'gods' if only because I still do not know how to ascend the ivory tower and, also, because I fear that if I could ascend it I would soon fall with a crash. In any event, I seem doomed to valleys even though I hope to avoid the fox holes."[148]

On March 2, 1943, Willam H. Regnery delivered the bad news to Ruth Sarles. "My own opinion is that this is not the time to publish the book—but for reasons other than the one mentioned by your friend. [An 'interventionist friend' of Sarles had suggested that the public appetite for isolationist works was greatly diminished.]"[149] And that is it. Regnery did not give the reasons for his unwillingness to pursue publication, and Sarles dropped the matter.

Regnery, in offering congratulations to Sarles on her job with the Washington *Daily News,* extended an invitation to return at any time to the National Council for Prevention of War, for "I shall be very glad to make proper arrangements . . . for your compensation."[150] She thanked him, but her peace work was done.

There seem to have been at least seven extant copies of "A Story of America First." Sarles kept one, sent four to Regnery, and two to General Wood, who was to keep one and pass the other around to interested America Firsters. A Bureau of Internal Revenue agent named Mr. Nevius got a glimpse of Sarles's copy during a 1943 audit of the committee, and Sarles—by now Mrs. Benedict—allowed the handful of interested researchers access as well. Wayne S. Cole did not have access to the manuscript for his definitive *America First,* but Justus D. Doenecke did use the copy in the Hoover Institution collection for his valuable *In Danger Undaunted.*

In 1999, Bill Regnery, grandson of the man who commissioned this work, asked if I would be interested in editing the manuscript for publication. I had published *America First! Its History, Culture, and Politics* (1995), which was not about the AFC but rather a cultural history of twentieth-century American isolationism. I was interested, and it is owing primarily to Bill's generosity and determination to see Sarles's book between covers that "A Story of America First" is now published. Sixty years after she descended from Olympus, Ruth Sarles is finally a published author.

Sarles said when she took her leave of Regnery, "The project must have cost you much more than you expected, as it took more of my time than I wished. I hope that between us we have produced something in which we find satisfaction."[151]

Finally, readers may judge for themselves.

A NOTE ON EDITING

The most common response I got to the news that we intended to publish "A Story of America First" was, "Fine—as long as you cut it." I have done so. The entire manuscript, which may be inspected at the Herbert Hoover Presidential Library in West Branch, Iowa, or the Hoover Institution Archives at Stanford, runs 759 pages. It includes many lengthy quotes and a good deal of padding, some of it added at the request of Sam Pettengill—who of course turned around and advised William H. Regnery not to publish the damn thing. I have omitted chapters IV through VIII, X, XIV, and XVI in the original manuscript, which are devoted largely to statement-laden accounts of the congressional debates over Lend-Lease, convoys, an Allied Expeditionary Force, and military preparedness. These subjects are treated better in many other accounts of the era. I have also omitted most of Chapter III, which describes in tedious detail the organization of the America First Committee. I wish these chapters had been chockful of Sarles's accounts of legislative maneuvering or contained candid appraisals of such figures as Senators Wheeler, Taft, Johnson, and others; alas, they did not. Instead, they consist primarily of testimony before various committees and vote counts that are easily obtained elsewhere. Chapter X is a lengthy compendium of profiles of interventionist groups; again, it offers nothing not found in other sources. I have also shortened the introduction and, where necessary, corrected obvious typos and omissions. I have renumbered the chapters. The endnotes to the chapters are part of Sarles's original work; the footnotes appearing in this volume are my original commentary.

What I have included is the pith of the manuscript: Sarles's knowledgeable accounts of the America First Committee's founding, its work with congressional allies, its popularity as measured in public opinion polls, the difficulties of being a loyal opposition as the war clouds descend, and the central role played by Charles A. Lindbergh.

The article in the title is significant. This is *a* story of America First, not *the* story of America First. Wayne S. Cole's *America First* remains the standard history; Justus D. Doenecke's *In Danger Undaunted* provides rich documentary evidence from the Hoover Institution's files. Sarles's book is a valuable supplement to those books, and to the others that will—I trust, despite the evidence of sixty years—follow.

Bill Regnery is the man most responsible for the appearance of this volume. I thank him, and so does the shade of Ruth Sarles. Dale C. Mayer of the Herbert Hoover Presidential Library was tremendously helpful, as were Sarah Connatser and Kim Molloy of the Norwood Branch of the Public Library of Cincinnati and Hamilton County and Cara Gilgenbach of the Denison University Archives. Thanks also to Wayne S. Cole, Gore Vidal, Robert D. Stuart, Jr., Hendrik Hertzberg, Olga Papach, Linda McNicol, Jeff Nelson and Elaine J. Pinder of the Intercollegiate Studies Institute, Ralph Raico, Wendell Tripp, Pat Buchanan, Geir Gundersen of the Gerald R. Ford Library, Karl Zinsmeister, Brandon Bosworth, Paula Meyer and Shelley Balonek of the Richmond Memorial Library in Batavia, New York, Greg Kaza, J. Garry Clifford, Justus D. Doenecke, R. Russell Maylone of Northwestern University Library, Ronald M. Bulatoff of the Hoover Institution Archives, Susan Fagan of the Newberry Library, Lesley Martin of the Chicago Historical Society, Leanne Dobbs, Justin Raimondo, and Lucine and Gretel Kauffman, of course.

NOTES

1. Michele Flynn Stenehjem, *An American First: John T. Flynn and the America First Committee* (New Rochelle, NY: Arlington House, 1976), p. 121.

2. Oswald Garrison Villard, "Valedictory," *The Nation* (June 29, 1940), p. 782. Those who expect the antiwar side to get a fairer historiographical shake once the self-proclaimed "Greatest Generation" dies off might consider the example of the antiwar

Northern Democrats of the Civil War. Copperheads and Peace Democrats were almost universally reviled by historians as traitors for at least eighty-five years after Appomattox. Not until the 1950s was it safe for historians to suggest that perhaps Fernando Wood, Clement Vallandigham, and their antiwar brethren might have been motivated by Jacksonian politics, agrarian or anti-industrialist preferences, or a concern for civil liberties. Even then, the task of revision fell largely to one man, the University of Wisconsin–trained historian Frank L. Klement, whose *Copperheads in the Middle West* (Chicago: University of Chicago Press, 1960) has attained classic status. For a good overview of Klement's lifework, see his posthumously published *Lincoln's Critics: The Copperheads of the North* (Shippensburg, PA: White Mane Books, 1999), which Klement called "a Copperhead Bible." For an examination of how historians have treated the foes of America's first "good war," see Richard O. Curry, "The Union as it Was: A Critique of Recent Interpretations of the 'Copperheads,'" *Civil War History* 13 (1) [March 1967], pp. 25–39.

3. See Stenehjem, *An American First*, p. 23.

4. Radio Address by Col. Hanford MacNider *Congressional Record*, 77th Congress, 1st session, p. A258.

5. Gilbert C. Fite, *George N. Peek and the Fight for Farm Parity* (Norman, OK: University of Oklahoma Press, 1954), p. 235.

6. Milton Mayer, *Robert Maynard Hutchins: A Memoir*, edited by John H. Hicks (Berkeley: University of California Press, 1993), pp. 216–217.

7. Alfred L. Castle, "William R. Castle and Opposition to U.S. Involvement in an Asian War, 1939–1941," *Pacific Historical Review* 54 (1985), p. 345.

8. John Roy Carlson, *Under Cover: My Four Years in the Nazi Underworld of America* (New York: Dutton, 1943), p. 249.

9. Joan Hoff Wilson, "'Peace is a woman's job . . .' Jeannette Rankin and American Foreign Policy: The Origins of Her Pacifism," *Montana: The Magazine of Western History* 30 (Winter 1980), p. 35.

10. Norwood (Ohio) High School yearbook, 1923, p. 38.

11. *The Adytum* (Denison University yearbook), 1928, p. 100.

12. Ruth Sarles to Harry Schnibbe, May 8, 1942, Mobilization Folder, Box 1, Hoover Presidential Library.

13. Wayne S. Cole note on an interview with Ruth Sarles Benedict, December 28, 1978, Cole-Sarles Folder, Box 3, Hoover Presidential Library. See also Ruth Sarles Benedict, "The Anti-War Warriors," *Chronicles* 15, 1 (December 1991), p. 23.

14. "Bertram Benedict, Retired Author, Editor of Research Reports, Dies," *Washington Post*, June 21, 1978, obituary page.

15. Ruth Sarles Benedict, "Application for Federal Employment," August 30, 1954, Civil Service Commission Form 57.

16. Wayne S. Cole note on an interview with Ruth Sarles Benedict, December 28, 1978, Cole-Sarles Folder, Box 3, Hoover Presidential Library. Wayne S. Cole is the dean of isolationist historiography. A son of Iowa, as so many of the critical figures in American isolationism and populism have been, Cole flew airplanes during the Second World War and came home to take his Ph.D. at the University of Wisconsin. His books include the first important study of the America First Committee (*America First: The Battle Against Intervention, 1940–1941*), a perceptive examination of Charles A. Lindbergh's role in the opposition to U.S. intervention in the Second World War (*Charles A. Lindbergh and the Battle Against American Intervention in World War II*), and his mag-

isterial *Roosevelt and the Isolationists, 1932–45.* He spent the majority of his teaching career at the University of Maryland in College Park, from which he retired in 1992. In 1994, the Society for Historians of American Foreign Relations honored Cole with the Norman and Laura Graebner Award as the senior historian who had contributed most significantly to the fuller understanding of American diplomatic history.

17. Letter from Wayne S. Cole to the editor, June 4, 1999. "No sense of guilt" from Wayne S. Cole note on an interview with Ruth Sarles Benedict, December 28, 1978, Cole-Sarles Folder, Box 3, Hoover Presidential Library.

18. Ibid.

19. Letter from J. Garry Clifford to the editor, January 2, 2000.

20. Sarles Benedict, "The Anti-War Warriors," p. 24.

21. Justus D. Doenecke, *In Danger Undaunted: The Anti-Interventionist Movement of 1940–1941 as Revealed in the Papers of the America First Committee* (Stanford, CA: Hoover Institution Press, 1990), p. 8.

22. Gerald R. Ford, *A Time to Heal: The Autobiography of Gerald R. Ford* (New York: Harper & Row, 1979), p. 61.

23. Doenecke, *In Danger Undaunted*, p. 17. John F. Kennedy's friend Torbert Macdonald later said, "I can recall distinctly at one stage that Jack thought that the people whose motto then was 'America First' were correct, and that we were just going to get, needlessly, entangled in what was basically a European war, or seemed to be at that time. He held these views for a while." Nigel Hamilton, *JFK: Reckless Youth* (New York: Random House, 1992), p. 287.

24. Chester Bowles, *Promises to Keep: My Years in Public Life, 1941–1969* (New York: Harper & Row, 1971), p. 5.

25. Howard B. Schaffer, *Chester Bowles: New Dealer in the Cold War* (Cambridge: Harvard University Press, 1993), p. 28.

26. Bowles, *Promises to Keep*, p. 9.

27. Ibid.

28. Schaffer, *Chester Bowles*, p. 27.

29. Ibid., p. 31.

30. Ibid., p. 26.

31. Justus D. Doenecke, "Edwin Montefiore Borchard," *Dictionary of American Biography*, Supplement Five: 1951–1955 (New York: Scribner's, 1977), p. 81.

32. Ibid., p. 82.

33. Edwin Borchard and William Potter Lage, *Neutrality for the United States* (New Haven: Yale University Press, 1940 [second edition]), p. v.

34. "George Washington's Farewell Address," in *Two Centuries of U.S. Foreign Policy: The Documentary Record*, ed. Stephen J. Valone (Westport, CT: Praeger, 1995), pp. 4–8.

35. Edwin Borchard to Robert E. Wood, September 24, 1941, in Doenecke, *In Danger Undaunted*, p. 105.

36. "Edwin Montefiore Borchard," *DAB*, p. 82.

37. Borchard and Lage, *Neutrality for the United States*, p. 423.

38. Castle, "William R. Castle and Opposition to U.S. Involvement in an Asian War, 1939–1941," p. 349.

39. Ibid., p. 345.

40. Charles A. Lindbergh, *The Wartime Journals of Charles A. Lindbergh* (New York: Harcourt Brace Jovanovich, 1970), p. 478.

41. R. Douglas Stuart, Jr., to Fred Burdick, May 27, 1941, Mobilization Folder, Box 1, Hoover Presidential Library.

42. Robert E. Wood to Ruth Sarles, October 17, 1942, Mobilization Folder, Box 1, Hoover Presidential Library.

43. Ruth Sarles to Page Hufty, December 5, 1941, Mobilization Folder, Box 1, Hoover Presidential Library.

44. Frederick J. Libby to R. Douglas Stuart, Jr., November 8, 1941, Mobilization Folder, Box 1, Hoover Presidential Library.

45. Frederick J. Libby, *To End War: The Story of the National Council for Prevention of War* (Nyack, NY: Fellowship Publications, 1969), p. 2.

46. See Millicent Bell, *Marquand* (Boston: Little, Brown, 1979), pp. 295–8 for Marquand's ambivalent relationship with the AFC.

47. Justus D. Doenecke, "Frederick Joseph Libby," *Dictionary of Modern Peace Leaders* (Westport, CT: Greenwood, 1985), p. 562.

48. Libby, *To End War*, p. 161.

49. Ibid., p. 160.

50. Henry Regnery, "William H. Regnery: An Account of My Family," in *Perfect Sowing: Reflections of a Bookman* (Wilmington, DE: ISI Books, 1999), p. 24.

51. Ibid., p. 31.

52. Ibid., p. 27.

53. Lawrence S. Wittner, *Rebels Against War: The American Peace Movement, 1933–1983*, (Philadelphia: Temple University Press, 1984 [revised ed.]), p. 25.

54. Ibid., p. 28.

55. R.E. Wood to Morris Stanley, undated, Mobilization Folder, Box 1, Hoover Presidential Library.

56. Samuel B. Pettengill to W.H. Regnery, August 1, 1942 (this letter is dated August 3 on pages two and three), Mobilization Folder, Box 1, Hoover Presidential Library.

57. Joseph Stromberg, "Anti-War Heroes," posted on www.mises.org (February 10, 2000).

58. Samuel B. Pettengill to W.H. Regnery, August 1, 1942 (this letter is dated August 3 on pages two and three), Mobilization Folder, Box 1, Hoover Presidential Library.

59. Samuel B. Pettengill to Ruth Sarles, August 3, 1942, Mobilization Folder, Box 1, Hoover Presidential Library.

60. Ruth Sarles to R. Douglas Stuart, Jr., June 3, 1941, Mobilization Folder, Box 1, Hoover Presidential Library.

61. Frederick J. Libby to R. Douglas Stuart, Jr., November 8, 1941, Mobilization Folder, Box 1, Hoover Presidential Library.

62. Ruth Sarles to Page Hufty, December 5, 1941, Mobilization Folder, Box 1, Hoover Presidential Library.

63. Mayer, *Robert Maynard Hutchins*, p. 231.

64. Wilson, "Peace is a woman's job . . . " p. 49.

65. Ibid., p. 41.

66. Stenehjem, *An American First*, p. 130.

67. Patrick J. Buchanan, "The Man Who Spits on Patriots' Graves," syndicated column, January 8, 1999, from www.buchanan.org.

68. Cole, *America First*, p. 136.

69. Ibid., p. 124.

70. Michael Sayers and Albert E. Kahn, *Sabotage! The Secret War Against America* (New York: Harper & Brothers, 1942), p. 203.

71. R.E. Wood to John T. Flynn, February 25, 1941, America First Collection, Box 291, Hoover Institution.

72. Lindbergh, *The Wartime Journals of Charles A. Lindbergh,* p. 271.

73. Quoted in Mayer, *Robert Maynard Hutchins,* p. 221.

74. Kathryn Lewis to R. Douglas Stuart, Jr., October 10, 1941, America First Collection, Box 291, Hoover Institution.

75. Melvyn Dubofsky, "John L. Lewis and American Isolationism," in *Three Faces of Midwestern Isolationism,* ed. John N. Schacht (Iowa City: Center for the Study of the Recent History of the United States, 1981), p. 28.

76. Norman Thomas to General R.E. Wood, September 17, 1941, America First Collection, Box 291, Hoover Institution.

77. Sterling Morton to R. Douglas Stuart, Jr., September 22, 1941, America First Collection, Box 291, Hoover Institution.

78. William Castle to R. Douglas Stuart, Jr., September 15, 1941, America First Collection, Box 291, Hoover Institution.

79. Samuel Hopkins Adams to R.E. Wood, September 29, 1941, in Wayne S. Cole research notes, Samuel Hopkins Adams Folder, Box 1, Hoover Presidential Library.

80. Kathleen Norris to R. Douglas Stuart, Jr., September 24, 1941, America First Collection, Box 291, Hoover Institution.

81. Kurt Vonnegut, "We Chase a Lone Eagle and End Up on the Wrong Side of the Fence," *Cornell Daily Sun,* October 13, 1941, editorial page.

82. Richard Fenno, quoted in Bill Kauffman, "The Power Broker Who Came Home," *The American Enterprise* 10, 6 (November-December 1999), p.32.

83. Bob Woodward and Carl Bernstein, *The Final Days* (New York: Simon & Schuster, 1976), p. 154.

84. Gore Vidal, "The eagle is grounded," *Times Literary Supplement,* October 30, 1998, p. 6. For Buckley as a youthful America Firster, see John B. Judis, *William F. Buckley: Patron Saint of the Conservatives* (New York: Simon & Schuster, 1988), p. 42.

85. Letter to Bill Kauffman, May 22, 2000.

86. Ruth Sarles to Senator Robert A. Taft, February 22, 1942, Mobilization Folder, Box 1, Hoover Presidential Library. Jimmie Lipsig was retained to do $60 worth of research for this book. Ruth Sarles to W.H. Regnery, February 20, 1942, Mobilization Folder, Box 1, Hoover Presidential Library.

87. Nancy J. Weiss, "Florence Prag Kahn," *Dictionary of American Biography* Supplement Four, 1946–1950 (New York: Scribner's), p. 446.

88. Wayne S. Cole, *Senator Gerald P. Nye and American Foreign Policy* (Minneapolis: University of Minnesota Press, 1962), p. 189.

89. Ibid., p. 188.

90. Ibid., p. 189.

91. Justin Raimondo, "Tale of a 'Seditionist': The Story of Lawrence Dennis," *Chronicles* (May 2000), p. 21.

92. Donald R. McCoy, "The National Progressives of America, 1938," *Mississippi Valley Historical Review,* 44 (June 1957), p. 80.

93. Ibid.

94. Ibid., p. 83.

95. Ibid., p. 84.

96. Ibid., p. 82.

97. Ibid., p. 87.

98. Cole, *America First*, pp. 113–4.

99. Confidential memo dictated by Richard A. Moore, August 28, 1941, America First Collection, Box 287, Hoover Institution.

100. Samuel V. Kennedy III, *Samuel Hopkins Adams and the Business of Writing* (Syracuse: Syracuse University Press, 1999) p. 196.

101. "Dole and Mondale Clash over Inflation and U.S. Foreign Policy," *New York Times*, October 16, 1976.

102. "Mencken Was Pro-Nazi, His Diary Shows," *Los Angeles Times*.

103. *The Diary of H.L. Mencken*, ed. Charles A. Fecher (New York: Knopf, 1989), p. 389.

104. Joseph Epstein, "Mencken on Trial," *Commentary* (April 1990), p. 39.

105. Ibid., p. 37.

106. Murray N. Rothbard, "That Infamous Diary," *Chronicles* (April 1990), p. 31.

107. "George Washington's Farewell Address," in Valone, *Two Centuries of U.S. Foreign Policy*, pp. 5–6.

108. "America First Movement," March 28, 1995, Northwestern University Library Special Collections.

109. Theodore Pappas, "Hamilton Fish in Perspective," *This World* 28 (1993), p. 12. For a slanderous fictive depiction of Fish that relies on John Roy Carlson's long-discredited *Under Cover*, see Scott Spencer's *Secret Anniversaries* (New York: Knopf, 1990). Spencer is best known for writing the Brooke Shields vehicle *Endless Love*. For more on the way that American novelists and poets have viewed our never-ending wars, see Bill Kauffman, "His Country's Own Heart's-Blood: American Writers Confront War," in editor John V. Denson's landmark *Costs of War: America's Pyrrhic Victories* (New Brunswick, NJ: Transaction, 1997).

110. John T. Flynn to Robert E. Wood, Doenecke, *In Danger Undaunted*, p. 138.

111. Stenehjem, *An American First*, p. 143.

112. Thomas E. Mahl, *Desperate Deception: British Covert Operations in the United States, 1939–44*, (Washington, D.C.: Brassey's, 1998) p. 107.

113. Pappas, "Hamilton Fish in Perspective," p. 17.

114. Eric Pace, "Hamilton Fish, in Congress 24 Years, Dies at 102," *New York Times*, January 20, 1991.

115. Sidney Hertzberg to Ruth Sarles, March 26, 1941, Mobilization Folder, Box 1, Hoover Presidential Library.

116. R. Douglas Stuart, Jr., to Ruth Sarles, April 2, 1942, Mobilization Folder, Box 1, Hoover Presidential Library.

117. Ruth Sarles to R. Douglas Stuart, Jr., April 4, 1941, Mobilization Folder, Box 1, Hoover Presidential Library.

118. Ruth Sarles to Kendrick Lee, April 8, 1941, Mobilization Folder, Box 1, Hoover Presidential Library.

119. Ruth Sarles to R. Douglas Stuart, Jr., June 13, 1941, Mobilization Folder, Box 1, Hoover Presidential Library.

120. R. Douglas Stuart, Jr., to Ruth Sarles, June 11, 1941, Mobilization Folder, Box 1, Hoover Presidential Library.

121. Kendrick Lee to Ruth Sarles, April 11, 1941, Mobilization Folder, Box 1, Hoover Presidential Library.

122. Ruth Sarles to Kendrick Lee, April 12, 1941, Mobilization Folder, Box 1, Hoover Presidential Library.

123. Ruth Sarles to Kendrick Lee, April 20, 1941, Mobilization Folder, Box 1, Hoover Presidential Library.

124. Ruth Sarles to R. Douglas Stuart, Jr., May 9, 1941, Mobilization Folder, Box 1, Hoover Presidential Library.

125. Ruth Sarles to Kendrick Lee, May 18, 1941, Mobilization Folder, Box 1, Hoover Presidential Library.

126. Ruth Sarles to R. Douglas Stuart, Jr., August 9, 1941, Mobilization Folder, Box 1, Hoover Presidential Library.

127. Jimmie Lipsig to Ruth Sarles et al., December 9, 1941, Mobilization Folder, Box 1, Hoover Presidential Library.

128. Ruth Sarles to R. Douglas Stuart, Jr., December 10, 1941, Mobilization Folder, Box 1, Hoover Presidential Library.

129. Ibid. NCPW goals from Ruth Sarles to Evelyn Palmer, December 12, 1941, Mobilization Folder, Box 1, Hoover Presidential Library.

130. Minutes of the National Committee, December 11, 1941, Doenecke, *In Danger Undaunted*, p. 469.

131. Harry Schnibbe to Ruth Sarles, April 23, 1942, Mobilization Folder, Box 1, Hoover Presidential Library.

132. Ibid. According to Sarles, Schnibbe worked on four chapters: brief ones on the New York, Chicago, and Washington AF chapters, and a lengthier one "dealing with the founding and activities up to January, 1941." Ruth Sarles to R.E. Wood, June 25, 1942, Mobilization Folder, Box 1, Hoover Presidential Library. Sarles also itemizes Schnibbe's contribution in a July 29, 1942, letter to W.H. Regnery, Mobilization Folder, Box 1, Hoover Presidential Library.

133. W.H. Regnery to Ruth Sarles, June 16, 1942, Mobilization Folder, Box 1, Hoover Presidential Library.

134. Cole, *America First*, p. 32.

135. Ruth Sarles to William H. Regnery, April 21, 1942, Mobilization Folder, Box 1, Hoover Presidential Library.

136. W.H. Regnery to Ruth Sarles, May 6, 1942, Mobilization Folder, Box 1, Hoover Presidential Library.

137. Ruth Sarles to R.E. Wood, April 26, 1942, Mobilization Folder, Box 1, Hoover Presidential Library.

138. W.H. Regnery to Ruth Sarles, June 29, 1942, Mobilization Folder, Box 1, Hoover Presidential Library.

139. Ruth Sarles to W.H. Regnery, unsent and undated letter, Mobilization Folder, Box 1, Hoover Presidential Library.

140. Ruth Sarles to W.H. Regnery, February 20, 1942, Mobilization Folder, Box 1, Hoover Presidential Library.

141. Ruth Sarles to Harry Schnibbe, May 8, 1942, Mobilization Folder, Box 1, Hoover Presidential Library.

142. Ruth Sarles to Richard Moore, July 7, 1942, Mobilization Folder, Box 1, Hoover Presidential Library.

143. Charles A. Lindbergh to Ruth Sarles, March 31, 1942, Mobilization Folder, Box 1, Hoover Presidential Library.

144. Ruth Sarles to Charles A. Lindbergh, April 30, 1942, Mobilization Folder, Box 1, Hoover Presidential Library.

145. Samuel B. Pettengill to W.H. Regnery, August 1, 1942 (this letter is dated August 3 on pages two and three), Mobilization Folder, Box 1, Hoover Presidential Library.

146. W.H. Regnery to Ruth Sarles, September 22, 1942, Mobilization Folder, Box 1, Hoover Presidential Library.

147. Ruth Sarles to W.H. Regnery, October 6, 1942, Mobilization Folder, Box 1, Hoover Presidential Library.

148. W.H. Regnery to Ruth Sarles, September 30, 1942; October 17, 1942; Mobilization Folder, Box 1, Hoover Presidential Library.

149. W.H. Regnery to Ruth Sarles, March 2, 1943, Mobilization Folder, Box 1, Hoover Presidential Library.

150. W.H. Regnery to Ruth Sarles, December 12, 1942, Mobilization Folder, Box 1, Hoover Presidential Library.

151. Ruth Sarles to W.H. Regnery, March 9, 1943, Mobilization Folder, Box 1, Hoover Presidential Library.

America First Creed

I believe in an impregnable national defense.

I believe that we should build it thoroughly, soundly, and immediately, but not hysterically.

I believe we should keep our country out of the Old World's everlasting family quarrels. Our fathers came to America because they were sick of them. Let's not stick our necks back into them.

I believe in the preservation of this Republic. Embroiled again in European affairs, we shall lose it. We shall be destroying the heritage our fathers fought for and sacrificed to leave us. In an effort to destroy totalitarianism, we shall be forced into totalitarianism ourselves. George Washington warned us of this day. His advice is better today than when he gave it.*

I believe that no man nor group of men—no foreign power nor group of powers—will ever attack a prepared America.

I believe that our job is clear before us. Let's not give our defenses away, nor destroy the best defense we possess—plain, ordinary American common sense. Hysteria and fear are poor substitutes. They have no place in our history.

I believe that no man here, nor any group of perhaps sincere, but obviously propaganda-bewildered citizens, should be permitted to divert us from our first

---

* The relevant portion of Washington's Farewell Address of September 17, 1796, reads:

The great rule of conduct for us in regard to foreign nations is, in extending our commercial relations to have with them as little *political* connection as possible. So far as we have already formed engagements let them be fulfilled with perfect faith. Here let us stop.

Europe has a set of primary interests which to us have none or a very remote relation. Hence she must be engaged in frequent controversies, the causes of which are essentially foreign to our concerns. Hence, therefore, it must be unwise in us to implicate ourselves by artificial ties in the ordinary vicissitudes of her politics or the ordinary combinations and collisions of her friendships or enmities.

See "George Washington's Farewell Address," *Two Centuries of U.S. Foreign Policy: The Documentary Record*, ed. Stephen J. Valone (Westport, CT: Praeger, 1995), pp. 4–8.

For the genesis of the Farewell Address, see Felix Gilbert, *To the Farewell Address: Ideas of Early American Foreign Policy* (Princeton, NJ: Princeton University Press, 1961).

duty to our country and our children—the defense and preservation of America and all that it represents.

I believe that our job is right here at home. It's big enough for all our energies. Sympathetic as we all may be with unfortunate nations overseas, we must remember that we stand alone. Europe and Asia cannot be expected to fight our battles. They never have and they never will. No nation will survive which depends on another to fight its battles.

I believe that our best contribution to a sorry, troubled world is an America to which men and nations can repair for help, guidance, and inspiration for the restoration of civilization—an America strong and unafraid.

—Creed subscribed to by the members of the governing body of the America First Committee

Statement of Principles and Objectives: Preamble

The America First Committee is unalterably opposed to our entry into wars now raging in Europe, Asia, and Africa. In that stand we have the support of formal declarations made by both of the major political parties. The national Democratic and Republican party platforms, adopted in June 1940, solemnly pledged to the people of America that this nation would not send troops abroad. During the campaign, both presidential candidates promised that American troops would not be sent to foreign soil. Passage of the Lend-Lease Bill was obtained through pledges of congressional leaders that the legislation would be a bulwark against our becoming involved in war.

Freedom of religion, freedom of speech, the right of peaceful assemblage, and the right to petition the government are prerogatives of a free people. These rights inevitably will be sacrificed if we enter this war. With them will perish most of the social gains achieved during the last two decades.

If the United States is to remain at peace, it is not enough for us to avoid formal declaration of war. We must also refrain from acts which would plunge us into war without declaration, and we must scrupulously forgo participation in European politics.

The primary objective of all patriotic Americans must be to achieve the high promise of democracy, and to this end, we must endeavor to improve the lot of the nation's underprivileged so that they may enjoy greater economic opportunity, improved standards of living, and, above all, opportunities for educational and spiritual development.

Only in this way can we further the aims of true democracy. And to do these things, we must have peace, not war.

PRINCIPLES

1. Our first duty is to keep America out of foreign wars. Our entry would only destroy democracy, not save it. "The path to war is a false path to freedom."

2. Not by acts of war abroad but by preserving and extending democracy at home can we aid democracy and freedom in other lands.

3. In 1917 we sent our American ships into the war zone and this led us to war. In 1941 we must keep our naval convoys and merchant vessels on this side of the Atlantic.

4. We must build a defense, for our own shores, so strong that no foreign power or combination of powers can invade our country, by sea, air, or land.

5. Humanitarian aid is the duty of a strong, free country at peace. With proper safeguard for the distribution of supplies we should feed and clothe the suffering and needy people of England and the occupied countries and so keep alive their hope for the return of better days.*

MEMBERSHIP

Membership in the America First Committee is open to all patriotic American citizens. We exclude from our rolls Fascists, Nazis, Communists, and members of the Bund.

---

* Sixth and seventh principles were added in May and November 1941.

The former read, "We advocate an official advisory vote by the people of the United States on the question of war or peace, so that when Congress decides on this question, as the Constitution provides, it may know the opinion of the people on this gravest of all issues."

The latter read, "The Constitution of the United States vests the sole power to declare war in Congress. Until Congress has exercised that power, it is not only the privilege but the duty of every citizen to express to his Representatives his views on the question of peace or war—in order that this grave issue may be decided in accordance with the will of the people and the best traditions of American democracy."

Introduction

This story of the America First Committee has been written in the months immediately following the attack on Pearl Harbor. When it will see the light of day in book form events will have to determine. Publication of the limited edition that had been planned for two or three hundred of the committee's friends has been abandoned. The Department of Justice and the Democratic Party have made it clear in the first nine months of the war that opposition to administration foreign policy before the country went to war is now subject to charges of lack of patriotism and worse as [if] it had been expressed [in] wartime. Although the America First story is an account of a great popular movement whose legitimacy in the prewar period during which it existed could not be questioned, even limited circulation at this time would be misconstrued and would probably lay the name of America First open to further smearing.

The sponsors of this book believe that a record of the committee's activities, written down while the experience is still fresh in memory, will aid the writers of the inevitable now-it-can-be-told period after this war* in analyzing the forces that played on the prewar struggle between those who believed Hitler must be crushed at all costs, and those who believed that our full participation in the war would only lengthen and intensify the sufferings of the peoples caught in the theater of war without solving their problems and with incalculable harm to our own country.

The purpose of this story—aside from recounting what the committee did— is to describe from the point of view of committee leaders the mental climate

---

* It was all too evitable. The revisionist spirit that animated post–World War I historiography did not take hold after the Second World War, perhaps because certain atrocities, the Nazi Holocaust among them, were without question real. For a survey of postwar revisionism, see Henry Regnery, "Historical Revisionism and World War II (Parts I and II)," *Modern Age* (summer and fall 1976), pp. 254–65, 402–11. Henry Regnery, whose book publishing imprint bore his surname, was the son of W.H. Regnery. For an account of the sad decline of a premier revisionist historian of both world wars, see Justus D. Doenecke, "Harry Elmer Barnes," *Wisconsin Magazine of History* 56 (summer 1973), pp. 311–23.

in which they functioned, to give enough of the background to show why the committee acted as it did under certain circumstances. Such an approach should be of assistance to those who will one day evaluate the motivation of those who led America First and of those who led the drive for opposite policies, in order to determine the proportion of idealism and self-interest that impelled them.

Analysts could do no better than to start with General R.E. Wood, who as acting chairman was the heart and soul of the committee to the end. More than any other one person he represented in himself the medley of purposes that animated the millions who gave their support to America First.

General Wood was America First's greatest asset. His reputation was unassailable. His record of integrity in his personal and business relationships ruled out any question regarding the leadership of America First. He was known as a soldier, and a patriot in the finest sense of the word.

General Wood was one of the builders of the Panama Canal, a veteran of the Philippine Insurrection, and during the First World War was director of purchases and storage in charge of all army supplies except ordnance and aircraft. He was awarded the Distinguished Service Medal and the Order of St. Michael and St. George (British), and was made a Knight of the Legion of Honor (French). Since 1928 he has served as vice president and chairman of the board of Sears, Roebuck and Co.

In the elections of 1932 and 1936, he supported President Roosevelt. He was one of the group of businessmen who believed that industry had become too powerful; he was in sympathy with the president's domestic reforms and split with him on foreign policy in 1940.

General Wood would be a particularly good study in motivation because he was a man who bestrode two ways of life. A firm believer in the system of free enterprise but aware of its failures, he understood and believed in the original vision of the New Deal. That the promise of a new day was blurred when those who assumed the responsibility for its delivery resorted to a methodology that seemed to him dangerous to realization of the ideal was a matter of profound regret to him.

The America First Committee owes its existence to R. Douglas Stuart, Jr., founder and director of activities. "Bobby" Stuart, son of the vice president of Quaker Oats Company, doggedly acted on the conclusions he and his circle of friends at Yale Law School had reached regarding the necessity for bringing together the antiwar elements in the country, until he had an organization. He stuck until the end, directing with rare judgment and tact the activities of an organization whose mushroom growth created sometimes overwhelming problems for solution. Bob Stuart gave up his third year of study at Yale Law, at the age of twenty-four, in order to give full time to America First. He had hoped at the conclusion of his law course to work with the National Labor Relations Board.*

_____

* See Appendix B for an interview with Mr. Stuart conducted in February 2000.

There are other individuals who would be mentioned by name and tribute paid to their individual contributions to the work of the committee, particularly in shaping the form of the organization. A few of them are Chester Bowles, Janet Ayer Fairbank, Philip La Follette, Hanford MacNider, Samuel T. Pettengill, W.H. Regnery, and Senator Burton K. Wheeler.*

It is too early to draw permanent conclusions about the whole effect of the committee's impact on the American public. It is not too early to draw conclusions about the policies against which America First fought: they have run their course and the country is now at war.†

There are important questions stemming from the "Great Debate of 1941" that ought to be asked about the practice of democracy. Does democracy, by providing an atmosphere in which all people—no matter how well informed—are encouraged to speak their minds, force government into the hands of a cabal of experts who, on the basis of facts available only to them, must scheme to accomplish what the people do not support and must always be propagandizing to make the people catch up with them? (One had only to live in Washington in the months before the country went to war to hear the view expressed freely that the tragedy of the times was that the men who knew what to do were handicapped by the slowness of the people to recognize reality.) Is our representative system, with its emphasis on sectional interests, adequate for the world of today?

If these questions are unwarranted what recourse do the people have against secret government?

America First showed that it was possible for individuals and groups of diametrically opposed political, social, and economic views to work together in the interests of social action. This was in a sense a rebellion against the label ideology that has colored the American scene for the last fifteen years; it was in effect a declaration of individualism against the growing American habit of classification.‡

America First taught millions of people who had never before exercised their right of petition to use that privilege freely.

In preparation for the writing of this story, General Wood's personal files dealing with America First matters have been read, as have those of R. Douglas Stuart, Jr., with the assurance from both of them that their complete files were available. All the literature of the organization has been perused, including

---

* The introduction and appendix by Bill Kauffman contain capsule biographies of many of these figures. For a fascinating look at Senator Wheeler through the eyes of his wife and daughter, see Elizabeth Wheeler Colman, *Mrs. Wheeler Goes to Washington* (Helena, MT: Falcon Press, 1989).

† I have here omitted a not terribly interesting discussion of the Lend-Lease debate.

‡ For a thought-provoking examination of this "label ideology," including a look at the evolution of the term "isolationism," see David Green, *The Language of Politics in America: Shaping Political Consciousness from McKinley to Reagan* (Ithaca, NY: Cornell University Press, 1987).

some 700 bulletins issued to the chapters. Access was possible to the more than 100 drawers of files accumulated at the national headquarters and sent in by the chapters on dissolution. Obviously, it was impossible to search them thoroughly.

The most serious omission from this story is the failure to include a detailed record and evaluation of the chapters and their leaders. The prolonged research necessary and the personal consultations with the hundreds of local leaders the country over were impossible at this time. But perhaps that is not a job for America First sponsors anyhow. Dr. Peter Friederich, professor of political science at Harvard University, has already launched a group of his seminar students on a study of the local activities of members of the interventionist and of the noninterventionist organizations. Other academic researches on various aspects of the America First story will no doubt be made in the years to come. The conclusions of an impartial scientific evaluation would have more permanent value than those of raconteurs biased on the committee's behalf.

The files have been sent to the Hoover Memorial Library on War, Peace and Revolution at Leland Stanford University, where they may be consulted by future historians.

One handicap has been the impossibility of extended consultation with the men and women who directed the activities of America First in the frantically busy days immediately following our country's entry into the war. General Wood immediately became consultant to the Chicago District Army Ordnance office, at the same time taking over many of Donald Nelson's duties at Sears Roebuck to enable him to come to Washington as head of the War Production Board. Bob Stuart enlisted shortly after Pearl Harbor and left for Fort Sill in January. Harry Schnibbe, who as assistant director of organization probably knew more about the chapters than any other member of the staff, started to compile the record of chapter activities, but was hardly able to dot the i's and cross the t's on the first hundred pages of manuscript before his enlistment in the navy took him to Annapolis.

Ruth Sarles
October 1942

1

Why America First?

The America First Committee made its public debut in the fall of 1940 to provide leadership for the steadfast 76–83 percent[1] of the American people who believed the country should stay out of war, and to establish an effective rallying point in opposition to the organizations that were conditioning the public mind for full participation in the war.

The committee had been founded in the summer of 1940 by a small group of students at Yale University who began with a mailing list of two hundred, working in their after-school hours. When Pearl Harbor closed its doors a year and a half later, it had outgrown its collegiate beginning and had become a nationwide organization with millions of adherents among the rank and file. Its roster of supporters included such distinguished citizens as ex-President Herbert Hoover, former ambassador to Belgium John Cudahy, and President Robert M. Hutchins of the University of Chicago. Serving on its governing body were a number of the most respected men and women in the country. Behind it was a record—admitted by proponents and opponents alike—of having exerted an influence that made possible full consideration by the public and by Congress of the momentous foreign policy questions confronting them in the year before the country went to war.

America First was a native American product from the word go, in spirit and in principle. The impulse for its organization and its leadership came from typical Americans—slightly right of center, wary of any "radical" tinge, believing in the American system of opportunity for all, devoted to the Stephen Decatur philosophy: "My country, right or wrong." Its basic principles of impregnable defense and staying out of war were rooted deep in American tradition; they expressed the traditional American distrust of foreign entanglements and the traditional American confidence in the ability of the country to defend itself against enemies from within and from without. Its methods were those guaranteed by the Bill of Rights—the right of assembly, of free speech, of petition through elected representatives.

America First was wholly indigenous. It was as American as the hot dog.

The committee came on the scene when it was clear that the contradictory nature of the president's foreign policy would precipitate all-out debate, American-style, and that the public was choosing sides.

The president's 1940 campaign speeches had given the impression that keeping the country out of war had been and would continue to be an overall boundary that circumscribed his decisions on foreign policy.* But the rapidly intensifying search for means to keep up the British resistance against Germany was resulting in methods that to many observers carried the seeds of eventual full U.S. participation.

The fact that both major presidential candidates had to make antiwar pledges showed the intense preoccupation of the people with staying out of war; they had not insisted that the contenders for the presidency guarantee the defeat of Hitler.[†]

The summer had been grim. Dunkerque and the fall of France had inoculated the country, by and large, with the hopeless sense that the best that could be hoped for England was stalemate. Many opened their morning newspapers expecting daily to read that England had been invaded. That Germany was "invincible" was privately feared by many ordinary citizens and privately submitted by a sizeable group of military and naval experts in Washington.

Those who from the beginning had believed that U.S. aid to nations fighting the Axis should not reach the point of military involvement, that the effects of full U.S. participation in the war would be infinitely more detrimental to the welfare of the country than a Hitler-dominated Europe, became more entrenched in their conviction that the country should stay out. These were the noninterventionists.

On the other hand, those who believed that the United States' position of power and its well-being could be preserved only by the defeat of Hitler, who held that the requirements of a twentieth-century interdependent world made the moral issue involved in the Hitlerian aggressions as much our business as Britain's, were pressing the president to hasten and expand the material aid that was to ensure Britain's victory. These were the interventionists.[‡]

The division was over what constituted real U.S. interests, over putting "first things first." To the interventionists, the first thing was the defeat of Germany,

---

* The most famous such Roosevelt utterance, ghostwritten by Robert Sherwood, came on October 30, 1940, in a pledge to the "mothers and fathers" of America: "I have said this before, but I shall say it again and again and again: Your boys are not going to be sent into any foreign war." Quoted in Kenneth S. Davis, *FDR: Into the Storm, 1937–1940* (New York: Random House, 1993), p. 621. Sherwood later conceded that he knew this to be a lie when he scripted the line.

[†] For a superb muckraking examination of the 1940 Republican convention, which nominated the Wall Street interventionist Wendell Willkie, see Mahl, *Desperate Deception*, pp. 155–176.

[‡] This is a fair-minded precis of the interventionist case; one can search for years through the interventionist literature for a similarly fair presentation of the antiwar position.

which required that Britain win even if we went to war to assure her victory. To the noninterventionists, it meant surrounding our aid to the nations fighting the aggressors with tried safeguards against full involvement, even though Britain went down.

The St. Louis *Post-Dispatch* thus summed up the difference:

Interventionists	Noninterventionists
We favor extensive American aid to Britain, while avoiding steps that will get this country into the war.	We favor avoidance of steps that will get this country into the war, while sending extensive aid to Britain.

In between the extremists was a sizeable section of the population that was not "bitter-ender" on either side. The aggressions of Hitler, whatever their basic cause, had violated every decent human impulse. There were few besides the outright pro-Nazis who did not ardently prefer a British victory to German triumph. Millions pinned their faith for the future on the hope and belief that President Roosevelt's world prestige, originality, and imaginativeness were such as to carry through the daring policy of throwing the United States' weight against German totalitarianism as a nonbelligerent ally of Britain without actually involving the country in war.

Both the antiwar and the preserve-Britain proponents could claim Roosevelt leadership. The noninterventionists had the frequent and unequivocal promises of the president through the summer of 1940 that we would not participate in foreign wars. The manner and occasion of their giving seemed to make them all the more binding because they were reassurances given in response to the expressed fears of a troubled people deciding on a president in time of crisis; they were not statements of policy gratuitously given.

The interventionists had the president's "stab-in-the-back" speech of June 10 in which for the first time he had committed the country to all-out material aid to the "opponents of force," and his statements over a period of years, beginning with the quarantine speech in 1937, committing the United States to the upholding of international morality, law, and order.

The noninterventionists had the chore of making the president's antiwar promises more binding than his commitment to aid the "opponents of force," of convincing the interventionists who were against going to war that the ultimate end of aid unlimited in advance was war.

The interventionists assumed the task of encouraging the president in furnishing ever-expanding aid to the nations fighting the aggressors, of convincing the antiwar public there was no hope for the future without the defeat of Hitler.

From the beginning the interventionists had the edge, because it was clear they had administration support; the noninterventionists were tolerated because this was a free country. The interventionists had also the advantage that the channels of public information—press, radio, movies—were inclined to the interventionist side* and showed the same attitude to noninterventionists the administration did—toleration. Another advantage was the fact that the "intellectuals"—the group that speaks most often on public controversial questions—were largely interventionist. The advantage of emotional appeal lay with the interventionists—Hitler's aggressions outraged the fundamental decencies.

From the beginning the noninterventionists had a priceless asset in the rock-bottom reluctance of the great mass of the plain people of the country to become involved in a war abroad.

It was this bred-in-the-bones conviction against foreign war on which America First's strength was built.

When America First became a full-fledged organization in the fall of 1940, there was no effective noninterventionist organization of national scope competent to match swords with the leading interventionist organization, the Committee to Defend America by Aiding the Allies.† The antiwar organizations already in existence, whose education of the public since World War I had done much to create the antiwar will to which America First offered leadership, could not capture widespread support chiefly because of their many years' opposition to large armaments.

The Committee to Defend America by Aiding the Allies had been organized in the spring, the latest incarnation of a long procession of organizations devoted to one aspect or another of world organization. It had made rapid headway in local organization, in capturing prominent spokesmen and headlines, in establishing a fruitful working relationship with government officials. A month before America First's advent it had tasted conspicuous success in its successful advocacy of the famous destroyer deal, by which fifty overage U.S. destroyers were turned over to England in exchange for the right to lease naval and air bases on eight British possessions in the Western Hemisphere. By its own admission, the Committee to Defend America had "sold" the country on the deal.

"The purpose of the [America First] Committee," General Wood told a Senate committee, "was essentially to counteract the so-called William Allen White Committee [Committee to Defend America by Aiding the Allies]."[2]

---

* One study by the antiwar College Men for Defense First found that of 553 defense-related newsreels shown in early 1941, only seven presented isolationist views. See Mark Lincoln Chadwin, *The Hawks of World War II* (Chapel Hill: University of North Carolina Press, 1968).

† The chairman of the Committee to Defend America by Aiding the Allies, the Emporia, Kansas, newspaperman William Allen White, was one of the few Midwesterners active in the leadership of the interventionist cause. White resigned as chairman in early 1941, when it became apparent that "aid" meant U.S. troops. Wayne S. Cole, *America First: The Battle Against Intervention 1940–1941* (Madison: University of Wisconsin Press, 1953), pp. 7–8.

Before the "great debate" was over, America First was to find itself striving valiantly to "counteract" also the *official* drive to get the country solidly behind the kind of policies advocated by the Committee to Defend America.

Thus America First's opposition was not confined to public opinion groups like the Committee to Defend America, led by private individuals. Its real opposition was a coalition of private organizations and government officials.

The America First Committee constituted the greatest *aggregate* revolt against war in history. Its aggregate quality—which made it vulnerable to attack on many fronts—has never been matched in the history of the popular movement against war. Not one of the antiwar organizations in existence before America First came on the scene had ever nourished such a conglomerate mixture of group and class interests, such varying political philosophies and loyalties, such a wide range of income levels. There were isolationists who saw in military involvement in war abroad a wholly unnecessary setback to the progress of a country they believed to be economically, politically, and socially self-sufficient. There were "continental Americans" who believed that war would not solve the old issues in new dress that were splitting Europe. There were internationalists who held that full military participation by the United States would weaken the United States's unique position of power in international collaboration after the war. There were Democrats who believed the Roosevelt administration had betrayed the party. There were Republicans who saw in a return of Republicanism the only hope for the country. There was a sprinkling of Socialists who saw the social gains of the last decade threatened by war. There were military men who privately gave their support because of the country's desperate state of unreadiness for war. There were a few pacifists who were willing to overlook America First's "impregnable defense" plank for the sake of the stay-out-of-war plank. There were the die-hard anti–New Dealers, the "big business" men who hated government regimentation and big taxes. There were New Dealers in government service and without who looked with alarm on the growing assumption of power by the executive. There were those who believed the threat of the kind of totalitarianism inherent in modern war more serious than the threat of a Nazi-dominated Europe.

The deep underlying motive, the adhesive force that for over a year kept together these antithetical elements whose close association for any less compelling reason would have been the signal for combustion, was the anti-foreign* war will.

After the steady procession of popular political movements wrapped around the dollar motive that had paraded across the last quarter of the American century, the impulse that moved America First was in comparison a fresh, clean

---

* At General Wood's insistence, "foreign" was inserted before "war" in this instance and elsewhere throughout the text.

wind sweeping through American politics. The bonus army, ham and eggs, every man a king, forty acres and a mule, $30 every Thursday, $200 every month—practically every mass movement except the prohibitionist had been stimulated by a pecuniary motive.

The anti–foreign war mood, which had been deepening its roots since the first disillusionment following World War I, had grown through the following years to such proportions that by 1935 the Congress passed neutrality legislation which if followed would have surrounded the United States with restrictions in dealing with nations at war that would have made full involvement in war for any reason other than actual attack practically impossible. That the president was admittedly not in harmony with the spirit of the neutrality laws and applied them or withheld their application as his judgment dictated for the "maintenance of peace"[3] did not in any sense diminish the public pressure for application of the noninvolvement safeguards provided in the neutrality laws.

It was to this existing anti–foreign war will that America First furnished direction and an outlet for active expression.

Many of those who accepted its leadership publicly took an active part. There were many more never openly associated with the committee—a group that would otherwise have been mute—who were encouraged by the fact of the committee's existence to express their opposition to policies they feared would end in war.

These were the people who for fear of social or economic pressures could not or would not associate with an organization that was openly opposing the policies of the administration in power. These were the men and women who as individuals and not as organization members would express their opposition, once they felt they were neither alone nor futile. The mere existence of a powerful antiwar organization, headed by responsible individuals of such prestige and influence that their leadership commanded respect, made it impossible to brush aside as fanatical, sincere opposition to war.

When the committee was publicly announced in the papers of September 5, 1940, its principles were

The United States must build an impregnable defense for America.
No foreign power, nor groups of powers, can successfully attack a *prepared* America.
American democracy can only be preserved by keeping out of European war.
"Aid short of war" weakens national defense at home.

On December 9, 1940, a fifth plank was added to the America First platform:

America must provide humanitarian aid for Britain and the Continent within the limits of our neutrality and with proper safeguards in the distribution of the food and supplies.

Early in 1941, the statement of principles was reworded:

Our first duty is to keep America out of foreign wars. Our entry would only destroy democracy, not save it. "The path to war is a false path to freedom."

Not by acts of war abroad but by preserving and extending democracy at home can we aid democracy and freedom in other lands.

In 1917 we sent our American ships into the war zone and this led us to war. In 1941 we must keep our naval convoys and merchant vessels on this side of the Atlantic.

We must build a defense, for our own shores, so strong that no foreign power or combination of powers can invade our country, by sea, air, or land.

Humanitarian aid is the duty of a strong, free country at peace. With proper safeguard for the distribution of supplies we should feed and clothe the suffering and needy people of England and the occupied countries and so keep alive their hope for the return of better days.

In May 1941, a sixth principle was added:

We advocate an official advisory vote by the people of the United States on the question of war or peace, so that when Congress decides this question, as the Constitution provides, it may know the opinion of the people on this gravest of all issues.*

In November, a seventh principle was added:

The Constitution of the United States vests the sole power to declare war in Congress. Until Congress has exercised that power, it is not only the privilege but the duty of every citizen to express to his representatives his views on the question of peace or war—in order that this grave issue may be decided in accordance with the will of the people and the best traditions of American democracy.

The two basic principles undergirding America First policy from beginning to end were impregnable defense and keeping the country out of war. That the committee's unrelenting adherence to the national defense principle was constantly pushed into the background[4] was due largely to the practice of its opponents of insisting that ensuring the survival of Britain was a defense measure, and that opposition to any aid measures proposed was ipso facto detrimental to the national defense.

Every measure that America First opposed as taking the country further along the road to war—Lend-Lease, convoys, allowing U.S. ships in combat zones—was advocated as a defense measure by its proponents.

The advocates of expanding aid to Britain did not distinguish between aid to Britain and national defense. As Congressman Shanley (D-Conn.) put it during his questioning of Administration witnesses at the Lend-Lease hearings: ". . . absolute and speedy aid to the British is a part of our defense . . . it bears so on that, it is melted into defense."[5]

---

* For the history of the war referendum idea, see Ernest C. Bolt, Jr., *Ballots Before Bullets: The War Referendum Approach to Peace in America, 1914–1941* (Charlottesville: University of Virginia Press, 1977).

The America First Committee always distinguished between aid to Britain and U.S. defense: they were two separate nations with two separate sets of interests. America First did not oppose aid to Britain. It favored aid to Britain within the limits of the neutrality law, but it opposed giving or selling or lending materials needed for our own defense.*

In a letter, General Wood wrote,

I am in favor of giving such aid to England as can be given within the limits of the Neutrality Law—to sell planes and such other articles as they have the cash to pay for and can carry away in their own ships. Beyond that aid, I am opposed, and I feel certain that if we do go beyond that aid, it means entering the war. If we enter the war, I see the end of our present economic system.†

What did America First accomplish?

The verdict of history takes time for the writing. At close quarters—six months after Pearl Harbor closed America First's doors—it can be said that the committee was a powerful force in delaying during the period of the country's most desperate unreadiness for war the full development of the policies that if challenged might have forced a choice between war or loss of prestige. While America First lost in every major battle—Lend-Lease, convoys, entering combat zones—it was instrumental in evoking such an outpouring of popular antiwar sentiment as to tighten the brakes on the execution of those policies by men whose eagerness to stop Hitler was likely to becloud their judgment as to the country's readiness to take on a war.‡

Whatever time America First bought by delaying U.S. entry into war was a gift of incalculable value to the country.[6]

NOTES

1. See chapter 4 for Gallup figures.

2. Hearings before the Senate Committee on Foreign Relations, 77th Cong., 1st sess., on S.275, p. 346.

3. See President Roosevelt's statement of August 31, 1935, on approving the Neutrality Act of 1935. For a record of the president's impatience over the slowness of public opinion to "catch up" with him, see *The American White Paper* by Joseph Alsop and Robert Kintner (New York: Simon & Schuster, 1940).

4. Typical of America First's constant advocacy of strong defense were (1) In a message to the chapters following the Lend-Lease vote, the National Committee said, "We must reiterate our support of the defense program—since a prepared America cannot be invaded." (2) The committee's statement of May 28 following the president's national

---

* I have deleted a Wood letter.
† I have deleted several Wood letters and memoranda.
‡ I have deleted a discussion of wartime production.

emergency proclamation said, "The America First Committee urges the carrying out of the defense measures contained in the president's proclamation."

5. Hearings before the House Committee on Foreign Affairs, 77th Cong., 1st Sess., on H.R. 1776, p. 214.

6. [I have saved this footnote from omitted material.] A friend of General Wood's, corresponding with the editor of a nationally known daily newspaper about a projected article explaining the general's views, wrote on February 25, 1941,

The basis of the General's non-interventionism is his deep conviction that the United States has a unique opportunity to achieve necessary and inevitable social changes peacefully. He believes that our entry into war would destroy that opportunity and ultimately bring about violent social upheaval in the United States. The General is primarily a builder and a doer. He is more interested in a work sheet than a balance sheet although he believes that the right kind of work sheet will always bring the right kind of balance sheets. You will find that he personifies to perfection one side of the broad division on foreign policy among men of means. This division seems to me to be between the eastern financier and the mid-western industrialist and businessman. I know that this division may appear to be over-simplified, but after close observation I am convinced it is valid. I am not saying that one side is more idealistic in its motives than the other; I think approximately the same amount of idealistic and economic motivation can be found in both camps. But the division is there and very much worth noting.

There is another side of the general I think illustrates another generality. Though he is not primarily a military man and certainly not in the shooting sense, the General's views do represent what I believe to be the reluctance of most military men to go along with the President's foreign policy.

Another thing about the General strikes me as noteworthy. The country is full of Republican and anti–New Deal Democrats who are now vigorously supporting the President's foreign policy. General Wood, on the other hand, is a New Dealer on all domestic problems who now opposes the President's foreign policy. The General supported President Roosevelt in 1932 and 1936. He was, you remember, one of the few really important businessmen who openly supported the New Deal. He broke with the President last year on the foreign policy and third term issues.

There is one other point worth mentioning. The General believes that our entry into war will let loose one of the most violent anti-Semitic campaigns in history. I have come across no one except those whose war hysteria has reduced them to a state of imbecility who has directly accused the General of being anti-Semitic. But there is much vague talk going around. He is pretty hard shelled, but accusations that he is anti-Semitic affect him more deeply than any of the other numerous slanders now being peddled about him. I happen to be one of the Jews—and I know many others who dare not say so—who believe that our entry into war will ultimately mean greater torture for the Jews than even the victory of Hitler in Europe. So few people have the courage to state this particular conviction. I think the General would.

2

Laying the Foundations

In the spring of 1940, the American people for the most part were not yet deeply concerned with the war in Europe. There was general sympathy for Britain and France, and pity for the overrun people of Europe. But there was also an underlying confidence that this was one war we would not have to fight. Whether or not Franklin Roosevelt would seek a third term was the favorite topic of conversation.

There was a comparatively small segment of the public, and a growing number of businessmen and of that group known as "leaders of thought," who believed that U.S. foreign policy was headed in the direction of war.

In New Haven, Connecticut, a handful of Yale college undergraduates and law students gathered almost nightly at 1175 Whitney Avenue to discuss the future of an America they would some day inherit. They were generally agreed that the country was ambling straight for the precipice, and that most of the people were unaware of it.

As they talked, they found themselves saying with growing frequency that "something ought to be done about it." The people ought to be told what was happening; they ought to be shown that there was an alternative. Since the people do the fighting and the dying in war, since they pay the bills, the people should decide whether or not the country goes to war.* And if the drift toward war was to be stemmed, only the people could do it.

In the appraisal of these young men, whose ages barely averaged twenty-three years, no one as yet had offered leadership sufficiently appealing to the people to resist effectively the dangerous list in the noninvolvement policy adopted by Congress.

---

* Sarles echoes Populist Georgia Senator Tom Watson, who asked of the Spanish-American War: "What do the people get out of this war? The fighting and the taxes. What are we going to get out of this war as a nation? Endless trouble, complications, expense. Republics cannot go into the conquering business and remain republics. Militarism leads to military domination, military despotism. Imperialism smooths the way for the emperor." Quoted in C. Vann Woodward, *Tom Watson: Agrarian Rebel* (1938; reprint, New York: Oxford University Press, 1972), pp. 334–35.

Dispensing with the frivolities of springtime in college, these dozen students laid the foundation for one side of the "great American debate" that was to stir and occupy millions of Americans until the Japanese created a single purpose in the nation by their attack on Pearl Harbor, December 7, 1941.

These young men were planting the acorn from which would spring the greatest oak tree of opposition of entrance into a war this nation has ever seen; an oak that was to be nourished and strengthened by the healthy sentiment of 80 percent of the American people.

The young men who were determined that spring to organize a crusade of their own designed to preserve for them the democracy they cherished and would inherit were members of the student body at Yale University. They were not pacifists. Most were reserve army officers. They were not of any one political party. They were concerned with the catastrophic effects on democracy that were inevitable with involvement in modern war. They knew there was opposition to war. But a rallying point was needed for this potential opposition, a vehicle which would ride in Paul Revere fashion through town, city, and countryside, awakening the people and warning them they might have a voice in the decision.

The America First Committee was not born until months later, but in this setting and by these young men, the seed was planted.

One man more than any other was responsible for guiding the discussions and decisions of the small group at Yale. He founded it, stimulated it, and with dogged persistence (and at times with discouraging lack of cooperation) directed it until it finally emerged as the America First Committee. He was R. Douglas Stuart, Jr., graduate of Princeton University in 1937, second-year law student at Yale and lieutenant in the reserve army.* It was at his home in New Haven that the students met. Stuart, whose father, R. Douglas Stuart, was then vice president of the Quaker Oats Company in Chicago, became national director of the America First Committee at twenty-four years of age and piloted that organization to the effectiveness it had attained at the time of Pearl Harbor.

From Stuart's Whitney Avenue home, plans were formulated for a nationwide organization of college graduates who would lead the opposition to war in their respective cities.

The simplest method of organization was employed. The group elected an executive committee made up of Yale Law School men, representative of different sections of the country. They were Eugene Locke, of Dallas, Texas, a graduate of the University of Texas in 1937; Gerald Ford, Grand Rapids, Michigan, a graduate of the University of Michigan in 1935; Potter Stewart of Cincinnati, Ohio, Yale 1937†; and Bob Stuart. Stuart was chosen secretary.

---

* See Appendix A for an interview with Stuart conducted in February 2000.
† Ford served as a Republican congressman from Michigan from 1949 to 1973, acting as minority leader from 1965 on, and president of the United States from 1974 to 1977. Stewart served as an

A statement of policy for the embryo group was drawn up. It demanded first that the United States expend all energy on building an impenetrable hemisphere defense. It warned that democracy here would be endangered by involvement in a European war and opposed further aid to England beyond the limitations of the "cash and carry act" (the Neutrality Law) in the belief that it would lead to war.

Following is the exact text of the first set of four principles as agreed upon by the Yale students:

We believe that the United States must now concentrate all its energies on building a strong defense for this hemisphere.

We believe that today our American democracy can only be preserved by keeping out of war abroad.

We oppose any increase in supplies to England beyond the limitations of cash and carry in the belief that it would imperil American strength and lead to active American intervention in Europe.

We demand that Congress refrain from war, even if England is on the verge of defeat.

A petition blank was mimeographed, topped by the statement of principles and describing, beneath the space for names and addresses, the purpose of the blank. "The national group of graduate students who initiated this petition," it asserted, "are unsubsidized, nonpacifist, and without political affiliation. Its efforts are confined to the one issue outlined above."

The petition was circulated among friends, acquaintances, suggested sympathizers, and every obtainable list of college names. Two were sent to each person. They were asked to obtain as many signatures as possible of people in accord with the stated principles. Bundles of petitions and letters were shipped to contacts at Princeton and Harvard. The signed petitions were to be returned to Stuart.

A letter accompanying the petition listed the Executive Committee and explained their purpose. The letter disclosed that men in eight states, including several former college editors and All-American football players, had already agreed to devote their summer to the work of organizing the opposition to war.

In a few weeks the signed petitions were rolling in, and to the new names listed additional petitions were sent. The framework for an organized opposition to war was being hastily thrown up around young college graduates in important centers of the nation.

The hundreds of letters that came in along with the petitions showed that there was latent interest waiting to be harnessed. This letter from a young man in Detroit is typical of the response received:

---

associate justice of the United States Supreme Court from 1958 to 1981. Eugene Locke became a prominent Dallas attorney and U.S. ambassador to Pakistan.

Without a doubt, I am as intensely interested in keeping a good head on my shoulders as you. But like most young men harvested in recent college crops, I have found no constructive method of expressing my objections to fighting someone else's scrap (I still think that's what it is) every time a score of years roll away.

The program you outline sounds like the thing we need. The situation today is obviously horribly confused. But of one thing I am sure; if we younger people fail to take long strides toward organizing ourselves now, the day will not be far to seek when any attempt to make our voices heard will be quite futile.

I want to help you do this job. Tell me how you plan to spread your program; how you plan to make it work. Let me hear from you soon.

As the idea caught and spread, fed by hunger for a means of expressing sentiment against participation in the war that was neither too radical nor too conservative, young Stuart brushed the amazement from his eyes. There was urgent need not merely for college graduate opposition but for a nationwide crusade including citizens of all ages, races, creeds, and political and social beliefs that would force the nation back from the precipice of war. He enlarged his vision, [and] began to change his plans of organization.

BUILDING A NATIONAL COMMITTEE

The original student group, realizing the publicity value in "big names" and knowing that through them there was an assurance of popular support, listed men in the public eye believed to be in sympathy with the principles set down by them. These they prepared to approach with the request that they serve as members of a National Committee for the new noninterventionist organization. These men were to be chosen from all fields of endeavor: writers, educators, industrialists, businessmen, labor leaders, all to be united in promoting a two-point program—impenetrable defense for the United States and staying out of war.

Stuart could now count eighty active leaders in twenty five states who had signified their willingness to enter the lists for the new organization. Now that the necessity for a tremendous effort on a vast scale had been impressed upon him, he instructed them to "crystallize local sentiment," begin community enrollment, secure the sponsorship for "substantial citizens of influence and respect," pool contributions to finance newspapers and radio announcements stating the aims and activities of the new local group, and get letters flowing to congressmen and senators.

All operations were being conducted from the Stuart household on Whitney Avenue in New Haven, and as correspondence increased, Stuart's wife was drafted from domestic duties. The directing group at Yale were amateurs in a strange environment, and they were frank about it. Their letters apologized awkwardly for lack of experience. The lawyers, journalists, doctors, businessmen, and others with whom they corresponded replied hesitantly that they too were unfamiliar with the organizing of public opinion on a large scale.

Thus without professional organizing advice, minus political affiliation, without adequate funds, they rushed ahead, stumbling here and there, propelled by the consciousness that time was short.

Summer was coming on and the colleges were emptying. A sketchy program of action had been constructed and the executives were prepared to carry on until fall. The most important step was the formation of a sound National Committee.

There were a few nationally prominent men and women known to be against involvement in war. These—Bob Stuart, Gene Locke, Gerry Ford, Potter Stewart, Kingman Brewster, Jr. (president of the Yale *News*)*, Bill Ford (staff of Yale *News*)—and others of their group set out to enlist in support of the new organization, which as yet had no name.

Colonel Charles A. Lindbergh had spoken out against intervention, and Gene Locke was dispatched to seek his assistance. Bob Stuart and King Brewster sped to Washington and consulted Senators Robert Taft (R.-Ohio), Burton K. Wheeler (D.-Mont.), and Henrik Shipstead (R.-Minn.). General Hugh Johnson contributed his encouragement and advice. Merle Thorpe, editor of *Nation's Business*, suggested prominent businessmen who could be approached. The Yale troubadours were hopeful of securing the cooperation of John L. Lewis, president of the United Mine Workers, and outspoken noninterventionist and critic of the administration.[†] They wanted Robert M. Hutchins, president of the University of Chicago, who in his convocation address to the university on June 11 had vigorously objected to the warlike moves in Washington and warned of the dangers to democracy if the United States became involved. They sounded out Norman Thomas, presidential nominee of the Socialist Party.

These men were to contribute in various ways to the vast program of the America First Committee within the next year and a half.

Late in June, Bob Stuart received a letter that was to begin an association that later provided the committee with its greatest asset. It was from General Robert E. Wood, chairman of the board of directors of Sears, Roebuck and Co. The note said simply,

Dear Bobbie:
In talking with your father over the phone this morning, he told me of the action you had taken at New Haven. I want to congratulate you on it. I think you showed a great deal more sense and judgment than the president of your university did.[‡]
With best regards, I am
Sincerely yours,
(signed) R.E. Wood

---

* Brewster later served as president of Yale University.

† For more on Lewis and his opposition to war, see Melvyn Dubofsky, "John L. Lewis and American Isolationism," in *Three Faces of Midwestern Isolationism*, edited by John N. Schacht (Iowa City: Center for the Study of the Recent History of the United States, 1981), pp. 23–33.

‡ The president of Yale was Charles Seymour.

Stuart was attending the Republican National Convention in Philadelphia. When he returned to New Haven and read the letter he was delighted. In the endorsement of General Wood the struggling organization had the approval of a man who had served with distinction as quartermaster general of the U.S. overseas forces during World War I and who was now recognized as one of the most respected business executives in the country.

Stuart wired General Wood immediately:

Greatly appreciate your support. People throughout the country are responding enthusiastically. Am forwarding our complete program by mail. We hope very much that you will serve as a member of our Advisory Committee. We need your help.

There was an exchange of letters and long distance telephone calls. Stuart reported on the response to his group's appeal—"not everybody but good enough to reassure us that the majority share our conviction." He pointed out what was quite evident—that his group [needed]* the experience and prestige that General Wood's name could give it.

A few days later Stuart left New Haven for Chicago and the Democratic National Convention. In Chicago, he conferred with General Wood. On July 15, the General agreed to become acting chairman[1] of the new committee, which it was decided would be called the Emergency Committee to Defend America First. Stuart was appointed national director.

The Quaker Oats Company,[†] in Chicago's skyscraper, the Board of Trade Building, had just shut down its Coupon Department. Offices along the east side of the eighteenth floor were vacant. Stuart dickered with his father for the rent-free use of one of these. Room 1804, which was large enough for three desks, a file cabinet, and a telephone, became the national headquarters of the America First Committee. (Before the committee was dissolved, it had rented eighteen additional offices).

With new headquarters, an acting chairman, a national director and new stationery, a new plan of action was adopted.

The objectives of the committee were to "give sane leadership to the desire of the American people to stay out of the European War; to promote the interests of America First" through advertising, radio addresses, public meetings, magazine articles, literature, etc.; "to register this opinion on Congress"; and to be prepared to "coolly analyze and counteract" hysteria and propaganda with realism rather than emotion. It was to organize a means of expression for all American people who opposed intervention "regardless of differences on other matters."

---

* Illegible in original.

† The America First connection with Quaker Oats was sweetly apposite. "Quaker" suggests America's oldest peace tradition, and "oats" the agrarian basis of the old America that America First was defending.

From the beginning, committee literature stated that Fascists and Communists were excluded. Pacifists were at first also excluded but later the restriction [on] them was withdrawn when it drew objections from such men as Oswald Garrison Villard, Dr. Albert W. Palmer, and Frederick J. Libby.

There was to be an Executive Committee presided over by General Wood, whose duty would be to formulate policy, enlist a National Committee (two prominent people from each state), and oversee and advise the national director's operations.

The national director would execute the program, decided upon by the Executive Committee, [and] direct national headquarters and the administrative work it involved, including publicity and organization of local committees. Local committees were to be patterned after the national arrangement.

Early in July the Emergency Committee encountered a situation which was to crop up many more times, in different guises, during the coming campaign to keep the country out of war. A resignation from a member of the original student Executive Committee was tendered. Jerry Ford, the Michigan University graduate, was employed by the Yale Athletic Association as assistant football coach. His salary assisted him through law school. He was advised that his connection with the antiwar organization might jeopardize his job in the fall. His name was removed from the petitions and letterheads.*

Wood and Stuart, aided by King Brewster and Bill Ford in the East, Gene Locke in the South, and Franklin "Dyke" Brown in the far West, settled down to spend their energies for the remainder of the summer in securing a representative National Committee that would give the group prestige.

On July 22 a luncheon for a few prominent Chicagoans was arranged. They discussed the new committee and its chances of solidifying the national sentiment against participation in the war. Each man contributed names of persons of national prominence whom he believed to be in accord with the committee's principles. Among those who had already offered their names to be used on the National Committee were General Thomas R. Hammond, president of the Whiting Corporation, and Sterling Morton, president of the Morton Salt Company.

When the names contributed during the luncheon were totaled, there were twenty-nine prominent Americans. Invitations to join the committee were sent to the twenty-nine, over the signature of General Wood.

Some immediately accepted. Among these were Louis Taber, master of the national Grange, [a] farmers' federation with 800,000 members; Eddie Rick-

---

* A wise move. In 1948, Arthur Vandenberg, Republican senator from Michigan and zealous convert from isolationism to internationalism—a conversion that seems to have been effected by a trio of foreign spies and courtesans, including one named Mitzi, thus Vandenberg's nickname in the Senate cloakroom: "the senator from Mitzigan"—sponsored Ford in his challenge to isolationist Congressman Bartel J. Jonkman. A career was born. For more on Vandenberg's seduction, see Mahl, *Desperate Deception*, pp. 137–54.

enbacker, World War I flying ace and president of Eastern Air Lines; James G.K. McClure, president of the Farmers Federation, Inc.; General Charles G. Dawes, chairman of the board, City National Bank & Trust Company Chicago, former vice president of the United States and ambassador to Great Britain; Mrs. Alice Roosevelt Longworth, daughter of "Teddy" Roosevelt and wife of the late Speaker of the House Nicholas Longworth*; Mrs. Burton K. Wheeler, wife of the senior Democratic senator from Montana; Colonel Hanford MacNider, past national commander of the American Legion, former assistant secretary of war and minister to Canada; and General Hugh S. Johnson, newspaper columnist and former director of the NRA [National Recovery Administration].

A short while later McClure and Dawes withdrew their names. McClure, while reasserting that he was "one hundred percent in favor of immediate and constructive measures for defending America," explained that additional responsibilities would prevent his serving. General Dawes withdrew after differences with the committee on the extent of aid to Britain.

Taber in accepting summed up the sentiments of the majority by stating, "I want immediate and adequate national defense, not to get us into war, but to keep us out of the conflict."

Robert M. Hutchins, president of the University of Chicago; Merle Thorpe, editor of *Nation's Business*; Dr. Alexander Ruthven, president of the University of Michigan; and Joseph Pulitzer, publisher, while expressing sympathy with the principles and objectives of the committee, declined the invitation to serve.

Edward L. Ryerson, Jr., president of the Inland Steel Corporation, was on his way to South America. Previously he had waived the need for a new committee by contending that the William Allen White Committee had done more harm than good to its own cause. Stuart tried again. He wrote Ryerson in Chicago on July 30, pointing out the hysteria fires it had started smoldering. On August 2, Ryerson, then in Miami Beach, wrote Stuart, "I do think it is desirable to develop some sound thinking along these lines in order to offset some of the other propaganda that has been broadcast so much by other groups," and agreed to serve on the National Committee.

By the end of July it was obvious that the sponsoring board was top-heavy with conservatives. This was the substance of criticism from several quarters. On this account King Brewster was finding it difficult in the East, and on July 30 wrote Stuart, "The National Committee should be substantial and prominent, but not stuffy or corporate. You need laborites and progressives. It would be awful if the Committee turned out to be the instrument of one class." Stuart agreed. Stuart had already spoken with a number of labor and farm leaders, among them Alexander V. Whitney, president of the Locomotive Engineers,

---

* For an examination of Alice Roosevelt Longworth as isolationist wit, see Bill Kauffman, *America First!: Its History, Culture, and Politics* (Amherst, NY: Prometheus, 1995), pp. 103–15.

and David B. Robertson, president of the Brotherhood of Railroad Trainmen. Both were in accord with the aims of the committee but felt they could not serve on the National Committee. Each suggested Philip La Follette, then Progressive governor of Wisconsin.

Phil La Follette, son of the late "Fighting Bob" La Follette, antiwar senator during World War I and later presidential candidate, and brother of Wisconsin's Senator Robert La Follette, had been governor of Wisconsin for three terms. He was a close friend of General Wood. They had frequently discussed the pro-war tendencies of the administration. During the Democratic National Convention in Chicago the General and Mrs. Wood entertained Governor and Mrs. La Follette, and the two men had speculated on the effectiveness of the new antiwar organization. It was La Follette's suggestion at the time that a fast practical means of warning the public would be through radio. He proposed that network time be obtained for speakers and that recordings of other speakers be made and distributed widely to local stations. General Wood arranged tentatively for a luncheon at the Chicago Club on August 8, at which time La Follette, William Regnery, president of the Western Shade Cloth Company*, and he would discuss the project. In the meantime the general had become acting chairman of the Emergency Committee and was taking a few days' vacation with young Stuart's father at the Stuart ranch in Red Lodge, Montana.

Stuart went up to Madison, Wisconsin, on August 1 to enlist Governor La Follette as a member of the National Committee. La Follette felt that because of his political affiliations (even though he would not campaign for reelection in the fall) it would be unwise for him to serve on the National Committee. But he agreed to incorporate his antiwar radio campaign under the banner of the Emergency Committee to Defend America First. From then on La Follette was to become an increasingly vital force in the committee, and contributed immeasurably toward crystallizing sentiment of the progressive middle-class group behind the objectives of the committee.

On Sunday, August 4, 100,000 Chicagoans flooded into Soldier's Field to hear Colonel Charles A. Lindbergh warn against the nation's unprepared condition and the moves that were putting us closer to participation in the European conflict. The rally was sponsored by the Citizens Keep America Out of War Committee, a local Chicago group formed for that purpose. The Committee was organized by World War I veterans, and its chairman was Avery Brundage, president of the National Amateur Athletic Association.[†]

Following the rally a dinner was given in honor of Colonel Lindbergh. Bob Stuart and his wife were invited. They discussed their committee with the flyer.

---

* Regnery subsidized the composition of this book; see the editor's introduction.

† Brundage was later kicked off the America First National Committee for his suspected Nazi sympathies. Justus D. Doenecke, *In Danger Undaunted: The Anti-Interventionist Movement of 1940–41 as Revealed in the Papers of the America First Committee*, ed. Justus D. Doenecke (Stanford, CA: Hoover Institution Press, 1990), p. 15.

He told them he would be glad to cooperate in an advisory capacity with the committee but preferred not to be identified with and bound by the objectives of any one organization. Anticipating even at that early date the fulfillment of Mark Twain's prophetic utterance that the people who oppose war will always be smeared, Lindbergh warned Stuart to choose his National Committee from persons who could not even remotely be smeared as pro-Fascist or pro-Communist. He himself was already beginning to feel the barbs of the interventionists.

Bill Ford (later editor of the Yale *News*) came on early in August to assist with national headquarters duties. Stuart was helplessly bogged down with mail. Hundreds of letters were coming in daily, the writers eagerly demanding "something to do." King Brewster, in the East, was spending a good deal of time pursuing the historian Charles Beard, to persuade him to serve on the committee. Beard declined but did agree to write a manifesto or statement of objectives which the committee could use in its printed publicity and literature.* It was printed in the *New York Times* of September 9:

The party of non-intervention represented by the America[1] First Committee includes no "appeasers," no "ostrich isolationists," no foreigners of any nationality in letter or spirit, and no pacifists.

It believes that the foreign policy of the Untied States should be directed to the preservation of the peace and security of this nation in its continental zone of interests; that the United States should not resort to any more measures verging in the direction of war outside its continental zone of interests, that measures should be adopted for the adequate defense of this continental zone of interests.

On August 8, General Wood, William Regnery, Phil La Follette, and Stuart met at the Chicago Club for lunch and La Follette's proposal for a vast radio program was adopted, to be directed by him.

In a sketchy, clumsy fashion, local organization was struggling along. There were few local committees. Stuart and the others had little time or energy to give to this phase of the work. Shorthanded as they were, virtually all their attention had to be devoted to building a suitable National Committee. In [the] face of this necessary neglect the college men who organized the movement were not making great headway in the country. Cleveland was further advanced than most others. Under Con Ewyer, a Princeton graduate who had been on the Cleveland United Press staff for six weeks, a number of club women, clergymen, professors, some labor leaders, and a few newspaper men formed a nucleus. He was having difficulty in getting businessmen to take a stand on the question. Businessmen thought immediately of potential pressure and reprisal. His group was small and lacking in influence with the mass of the people

---

*For more on Beard as an isolationist, see Ronald Radosh, *Prophets on the Right: Profiles of Conservative Critics of American Globalism* (New York: Free Life, 1978), pp. 17–65.

the committee was later to represent. The same situation existed in San Francisco, where Dyke Brown was working, and in Dallas with Gene Locke. Brewster in the East was having trouble, and Stuart and Ford in Chicago. The real organization period of the committee did not come until the early months of 1941.

National Committee invitations were being dispatched as fast as probable sympathizers of prominence could be proposed. The rate of acceptance was about one out of four. To the directors of the movement this was a far cry from the immediate, wholehearted open support they had anticipated. True, almost all they queried were in sympathy, but the one-to-four average stood when it came to public admission of this fact.

By the end of August, Oswald Garrison Villard; Bishop Wilbur E. Hammaker, Methodist bishop of the Rocky Mountain states and Methodist bishop of China from 1935 to 1939; John T. Flynn, author and economist; and Thomas N. McCarter, president of the New Jersey Public Service Company, had become members of the National Committee.

Sterling Morton had approached a number of his close friends, two of whom later joined the National Committee. They were Jay C. Hormel, president of Hormel Meat Packing Company, and William R. Castle, career diplomat, former ambassador to Japan and undersecretary of state. Both heartily endorsed the program as outlined by Morton. Castle hesitated to join the committee because he believed he would be active in politics during the presidential campaign. Hormel took active interest immediately.

They were black days for the committee in August. Discouraged by the reluctance of prominent people publicly to declare their opposition to war, and burdened with the responsibilities of a large business, General Wood said he would have to resign from the chairmanship of the committee. He would remain on the National Committee but would have to be relieved of the chairman's duties.

Stuart knew the Emergency Committee to Defend America First could not afford to lose General Wood's chairmanship, and he fought the resignation with all his strength. He appealed strongly and bluntly. Phil La Follette's persuasive powers were drafted, as were those of William Regnery and members of the National Committee. Hanford MacNider came to Chicago from Mason City, Iowa, and Jay C. Hormel from Austin, Minnesota. They all pled with the general to remain.

In the end General Wood agreed to carry on, but not until after two harrowing weeks during which time new chairmen were seriously proposed and discussed. The general did make clear, however, that before he would allow the committee to be officially announced there would have to be twenty influential persons on the National Committee.

Stuart again set to work. By the end of August, he had seventeen.

Noticeable progress was being made in the preparations for publicity. Phil La Follette had got fourteen U.S. senators to agree to make fifteen-minute radio transcriptions under the auspices of the committee, to be distributed to selected radio stations.* Sample newspaper ads were composed by a Chicago agency, and copies were sent to members of the National Committee. Since the ads accented the emotional approach, they were unanimously discarded. In Hanford MacNider's comment on the advertising he said: "If we are right, and I know we are, surely there are enough sound arguments which can be advanced in plain strong, dignified English to convince anyone who can be convinced."

Late in August the Blue Network of the National Broadcasting Company offered Stuart fifteen minutes [of] free airtime for the evening of September 5, covering 100 network stations.

Stuart saw at once an imposing "first night" for his committee. (By that time he lacked but a few names of the necessary twenty for the National Committee and was virtually assured of those.) He planned for a radio speech by General Hugh Johnson, broadcast from a stately inaugural dinner at the Blackstone Hotel in Chicago. General Johnson agreed to speak, but on condition that the program originate in Washington. The banquet was relinquished.

On Wednesday, September 4, the first publicity release of the committee was prepared and sent to newspapers and the news services. It announced the formation of the committee, its principles, objectives, names of National Committee members, and supplied General Johnson's inaugural speech. Jay C. Hormel had campaigned vigorously for a shorter name; it was now announced to the public as the "America First Committee."

The National Committee as announced was General Robert E. Wood, Brigadier General Thomas S. Hammond, Avery Brundage, Edward L. Ryerson, William H. Regnery, Sterling Morton, Mrs. Alice Roosevelt Longworth, John T. Flynn, Jay C. Hormel, Eddie Rickenbacker, Louis Taber, Hanford MacNider, Bishop Wilbur E. Hammaker, Thomas N. McCarter, Oswald Garrison Villard, Mrs. Burton K. Wheeler, and General Hugh S. Johnson. The new additions to the committee, which made a total of twenty-one, were Mrs. Janet Ayer Fairbank, author and former National Democratic Committeewoman from Illinois; Dr. Albert W. Palmer, president of the Chicago Theological Seminary; Dr. George H. Whipple of the University of Rochester, famed pathologist and joint winner of the Nobel Prize for medicine in 1934; and Ray McKaig of Boise, Idaho, master of the Grange for that district.

The principles of the committee, as they appeared in newspapers on the morning of September 5, were

1. The United States must build an impregnable defense for America.

2. No foreign power, nor groups of powers can successfully attack a *prepared* America.

---

* See Appendix C for Sarles's list of senators and representatives who spoke under America First Committee auspices.

3. American democracy can only be preserved by keeping out of the European war.

4. "Aid short of war" weakens national defense at home.

At 9:30 p.m. Eastern Standard Time, General Johnson spoke, not from Washington as he had wished, but from the studios of WFIL, Philadelphia. The title of his speech was "America Faces No Danger of Invasion."

Activities of the new committee surged at increased tempo in the fall of 1940, as people returned to normal living following vacations. There was immediate interest in the new organization from many directions. More National Committee members were added; promotion and publicity were developed; an intense program of activity was drawn up; congressmen and senators cooperated; organization of local committees was begun; financial contributions were made; other noninterventionist groups sought affiliation; and the first low-aimed firing of the opposition was heard.

General Wood, William Regnery, and Bob Stuart signed the committee's incorporation papers on September 12. The incorporation papers stated that "this corporation is organized not for pecuniary profit." Its objectives: "to encourage and maintain in the United States of America (1) peace and democratic ideals; (2) a program of adequate defense." In accordance with the laws of the state of Illinois, seven directors were named in the charter. They were Wood, Regnery, Stuart, MacNider, Hammond, Hormel, and Clay Judson, prominent Chicago attorney. A statement similar to the incorporation charter was later registered with the Chicago Better Business Bureau by Judson.

Following the incorporation of the committee on September 19, the first meeting of the directors was called for September 21. The incorporation certificate and bylaws were presented and approved, and it was agreed that all material printed or published should first be presented to a drafting committee consisting of Wood, Regnery, and Judson. A program of radio speeches and newspaper advertising was outlined.

While the general membership of the committee began to soar, more persons of influence were attracted. Bob Stuart had heard that the two Richardson brothers, H. Smith and Lunsford, of Vicks (Vapo-Rub) Chemical Company were interested. He wrote them on October 1. They immediately responded, and continued to give enthusiastic assistance to the committee to the end.*

The National Committee announced on September 5, 1940, numbered twenty-one. Of the original group Oswald Garrison Villard had resigned because of the conflict between his pacifist principles and the committee's program for "impregnable national defense." He resigned, however, over the protests

---

* The Smith Richardson Foundation has since subsidized the work of cold war liberals and internationalists, in a perfect example of why such foundations should be euthanized. For a general discussion of this topic, see Martin Morse Wooster, *Should Foundations Live Forever? The Question of Perpetuity* (Washington, DC: Capital Research Center, 1998).

of Stuart and other members of the National Committee. Dr. Albert W. Palmer, president of the Chicago Theological Seminary, resigned in October 1940 because the early ruling of the committee excluding pacifists, as well as Fascists and Communists, he wrote, "obviously read me out of the Committee."

Henry Ford consented in September 1940 to have his name used on the committee. Since he answered no communications addressed to him on America First matters and gave no help in any way, financial or otherwise, his name was dropped by action of the committee less than three months after he joined.*

John L. Lewis, president of the United Mine Workers, declined to serve. But his daughter Kathryn became a member in September and remained on the committee until the following September. William Green, president of the American Federation of Labor, invited at the same time, found it "inadvisable" to accept.

Lessing J. Rosenwald, retired chairman of the board of Sears, Roebuck and Co., distinguished philanthropist and close friend of General Wood, served only a few months.

William R. Castle, former U.S. ambassador to Japan and former undersecretary of state, who had previously hesitated to join for political reasons, decided just before the 1940 election to concentrate his energies on preventing intervention in the European war, and became a member. He frequently advised Stuart on policy and program. It was through him that the initial negotiations for establishment of the important New York and Washington chapters were conducted.

Clay Judson joined the National Committee and later assumed the duties of legal adviser to the committee, a position he held until dissolution of the organization. Under his guidance, America First weathered its course without stumbling into the many potential legal pitfalls that beset any organization dedicated to so controversial a purpose.

In October, November, and December of 1940, the energies of the committee were being concentrated on organization and publicity. The search for new members was relaxed. But at that, six important men were added. They were George N. Peek, Major Al Williams, Irvin S. Cobb, Chester Bowles, Amos R.E. Pinchot,[†] and Frank O. Lowden.

Peek began corresponding with General Wood shortly after the committee was announced. In November, before he left for his winter home in California, he agreed that if his name would be useful in rallying the farm population against participation in the war, he would serve. Peek was former New Deal

---

* This is only part of the truth. Ford's anti-Semitism, as revealed, for instance, in his publication of the anti-Semitic hoax *The Protocols of the Elders of Zion*, made him unfit for the committee. Cole, *America First*, pp. 132–33.

† For more on the colorful Pinchot, see Kauffman, *America First!*, pp. 27–67.

AAA administrator and during 1934–35 had been special adviser to President Roosevelt on foreign trade. He was, at one time, president of the government Export-Import Bank.

Peek was a regular consultant of Stuart's on matters of policy. Later he authored "Can Hitler Cripple America's Economy?," a critique of the theory popularized by Douglas Miller and many interventionists that Hitler could destroy American economic standards when he chose to do so.

Peek also devoted intense effort that fall to persuading Bernard Baruch, who directed the national war effort under Woodrow Wilson, to lend his support to the new committee. Baruch became interested and corresponded with Stuart and his friend Peek concerning the project to keep America out of war, but declined to serve on the committee.

Major Al Williams, renowned World War I flying ace and columnist for the Scripps-Howard papers, read a speech General Wood delivered at the National Association of Manufacturers convention in New York early in December 1940. He immediately made it the theme of one of his columns. He called for "more stout, courageous spirits and voices to demand first consideration for my country—America first." On December 26, Williams joined the committee.

The same day Williams agreed to serve, Frank O. Lowden, former governor of Illinois (who had once refused the Republican nomination for vice presidency of the United States),* accepted the invitation previously extended to him by the committee, which he had at first declined because of his participation in the presidential election campaign.

Late in November, Irvin S. Cobb, famous humorist, author, and lecturer, added his name to the group.

J. Sanford Otis, vice president of the Central Republic bank of Chicago, joined the committee and was elected treasurer.

Mrs. Bennett Champ [Miriam] Clark, wife of the U.S. senator from Missouri and chairman of the Washington chapter, became the fourth woman on the executive body, with her husband's picturesque admonition ringing in her ears: "I'm telling you, anybody that goes into this fight on the stay-out-of-war side will be played up as on the lap of and in the arms of Adolph Hitler before it's over."

On December 30, the National Committee of America First for 1940 was completed with the addition of Chester Bowles, New York advertising executive, and Amos R.E. Pinchot, New York lawyer, publicist, and Spanish-American War veteran.

For a few weeks in late 1940, Charles Francis Adams, chairman of the board of the State Street Trust Company, Boston, former secretary of the navy, was

---

* Lowden, who had served as governor of Illinois from 1917 to 1921, refused the Republican nomination for vice president in 1924. The presidential nominee, Calvin Coolidge, won the general election.

a member of the committee. An embarrassing conflict in his bank, whose president was prominent in the Boston William Allen White Committee, determined Adams's resignation from America First.

At the end of 1940 the National Committee numbered thirty-two.

On November 26, 1940, Dr. Henry Noble McCracken, president of Vassar College, sent the *New York Times* a public repudiation of the objectives of the William Allen White Committee, of which he had been an active executive member. Stuart invited him to join America First. McCracken explained that while he was in sympathy with the purposes of America First, he preferred not to be bound again by the principles of an organization. In the following year, however, he was to speak for and represent the committee on several occasions.*

Other men who in the fall of 1940 agreed with the principles and objectives of the committee but who preferred not to join were His Eminence Cardinal William O'Connell, dean of the Catholic hierarchy in the United States; Wesley Winan Stout, editor of the *Saturday Evening Post;* C.B. Wrightman, president of the Standard Oil Company of Kansas; J.F. Owens, president of the Oklahoma Gas and Electric Company; Will Durant, philosopher and author; M.S. Sherman, editor of the oldest newspaper of continuous publication in America, the Hartford *Courant;* and Dr. Alan Valentine, president of the University of Rochester, New York.

On October 4, the day the America First Committee's initial full-page newspaper advertisement appeared in the *New York Times,* Stuart and Charles Lindbergh met in Chester Bowles's office on Madison Avenue in New York to discuss the progress of the committee and in particular the organization of a New York chapter.

In the middle of October, Stuart, on the advice of General Wood, wrote a long letter explaining the committee to Samuel B. Pettengill of South Bend, Indiana. Pettengill had retired undefeated after eight years in Congress to practice law and write a newspaper column. He had the respect of members of the House and Senate, and for the period of the committee's existence was its chief political adviser, although his ability as consultant was not confined to the political field.

In the first week in December Boake Carter, noninterventionist newspaper columnist and radio commentator, wrote General Wood, suggesting that Carter's close friend Joseph P. Kennedy, former U.S. ambassador to Great Britain, be invited to serve on the committee. Carter said of Kennedy, "It is my humble opinion that he has done more than any other single man in this country in the last four or five months to drive a splinter into the public consciousness of this nation and start people thinking on more realistic lines."

---

*For more on McCracken, see Joseph L. Jaffe, Jr., "Isolationism and Neutrality in Academe, 1938–1941" (Ph.D. diss., Case Western Reserve, 1979, pp. 348–88).

Kennedy was at Palm Beach, Florida. On December 13, Stuart and Hanford MacNider flew to Palm Beach to urge Kennedy to come on the committee. Kennedy explained the obstacles. He had withdrawn as British ambassador, but the president had requested that he retain his position until a successor could be appointed. Officially he was still ambassador. Kennedy further explained that he could make a greater contribution to the antiwar fight if he were to speak and write for himself, and not as the representative of an organization. Stuart's and MacNider's mission was a failure, but at that they were deeply indebted to Kennedy, a short time later, when he wrote General Wood imploring him to carry on as chairman of the committee in [the] face of pressing obligations and difficulties. He wrote, "You are doing a great job in this country and people feel much more hopeful with what you are saying and doing than with anybody else."

The general replied to Kennedy that he would continue as chairman.

In August, Bob Stuart had obtained the use of one small room on the eighteenth floor of the Board of Trade. His staff consisted of himself and a secretary, his wife, Barbara, and Bill Ford (who returned to Yale in the fall).

By October 9, the committee had five paid employees. On November 4 it signed a lease with the Board of Trade Realtors and began paying rent on four offices.

Up to late fall, little attention had been paid to organizing in local communities. The shorthanded staff had concentrated on building up a sound National Committee, and on national publicity. The founders had had no idea of a complicated organizational scheme reaching out into local communities.

The thousands of letters that poured into the small office forced them to enlarge their vision: "Can't we join?" "Give us something to do!" "Send us a speaker." "Provide us with literature." "We want to organize a local group."

Thus the America First Committee was literally forced to provide the structure for a large organization.

Following the election, the *New York Times* (November 13, 1940) carried Bob Stuart's announcement that the America First Committee would now begin forming local units (it already had eleven).

Before the New Year came in, Stuart had enlarged his department directors and staff members to twenty-four. An Organization Department had been set up to handle the needs of the fast-forming local chapters. A radio and advertising executive was functioning at top speed. A general director of public relations was employed and a speaker's bureau was organized.

By January 1, the America First Committee was in fine fettle for the arduous campaigns of 1941, beginning with the Lend-Lease bill.

THE NEW YORK CHAPTER

The national headquarters of America First nestled in the heart of its support, the noninterventionist Middle West, from which was drawn its greatest strength. But America First was engaging a problem that concerned the whole nation; it could not rest with strong organization only in the area that by instinct and tradition was opposed to "European entanglements."

The Eastern states were closest, geographically and in sympathy, to the European conflagration. The interventionists were strongly organized in the East. It was important for America First to be solidly established in the East. If a strong organization could be set up in "enemy territory," there would be evidence that the noninterventionist pressure had more than traditional sectional roots.

Organization of a New York office had been coveted and anticipated from the earliest days of the committee. Action had been delayed while a strong National Committee was being recruited. Finding the right leadership in the embattled East was not an easy task.

Bob Stuart began to think seriously about New York development late in September 1940. He consulted Colonel Lindbergh and William Castle. Both knew many reputable men of noninterventionist persuasion in that city. Between the three of them, they cautiously sounded out possible leaders.

The three men who first set out to crystallize the organization in the East squeezed through some narrow escapes before the command was placed in the capable hands of John T. Flynn, writer and economist.* Representatives of the New York State Economic Council, the League for Constitutional Government, and *Scribner's Commentator* sought and worked to gain control of America First activity in the East. They were bowed off the scene while General Wood and his coworkers were reaching the conclusion that John Flynn was the right man.

Flynn had been on the National Committee of America First since August 28, 1940, but had taken little part in its activities. Typically, he swung into immediate action once full reliance was placed in him. He called a special luncheon for a few reliable men for Friday, November 29, to design a plan of organization. Bob Stuart and Hanford MacNider represented national headquarters. The following day, in an enthusiastic message to General Wood, Stuart announced that the New York chapter of America First was at long last on its official way.

Flynn's series of New York luncheons after that brought together impressive groups of men. The first open organization meeting for sponsors was held on December 6, a luncheon at the Town Hall Club. Those who attended, in addition to John Flynn, were Bruce Barton; Avery Claflin, French-American Bank; John Elting, General Motors Overseas Corporation; F. Abbot Goodhue, Bank of Manhattan; Robert M. Harris, Harris & Vose (cotton brokers); Ran-

---

*For a franker discussion of the problems in organizing the New York chapter, see Michele Flynn Stenehjem, *An American First: John T. Flynn and the America First Committee* (New Rochelle, NY: Arlington House, 1976), pp. 121–141.

dolph Phillips; Allen Pope, First Boston Corporation; Harold Sprout, Princeton University; Douglas Stewart, *Scribner's Commentator;* H. Dudley Swim, National Investors Corporation; Robert Upjohn Redpath, Jr.; and Robert R. Young, Allegheny Corporation.

The following week, while General Wood was in New York for conferences whose conclusion was the decision that America First could not work with Verne Marshall,* Flynn arranged another of his meetings with the general as a guest. (On this same trip to New York, the general also received an invitation to lunch with Louis H. Brown, president of the Johns-Manville Corporation, and some of his friends, for the purpose of discussing the new committee.)†

John Flynn was concentrating on building a strong sponsoring group for the New York chapter. It was to be made up of "respectable" names that would give the public confidence, with strong representation from businessmen. But Flynn was soon to find out that, because in New York no businessman works alone but is enmeshed in a network of corporative connections, the budding committee would have to struggle along without the open support of the sizeable number of businessmen who were by their own private avowals in sympathy with its aims. A well-known official of a prominent Eastern bank‡ agreed to serve as chairman provided that Flynn secured a businessman as executive secretary and enlisted five heads of three leading businesses in New York as sponsors. The conditions were fulfilled, but the man found he could not serve.

One by one the businessmen who had so enthusiastically offered their support in the beginning dropped out. Business connections were paralyzing their participation in the antiwar effort, while interventionist businessmen were free to take an active part openly in the activities of the interventionist organizations.

---

* Marshall, editor of the Cedar Rapids *Gazette,* was viewed by his contemporaries as a volatile, unpleasant, and probably anti-Semitic man. Even the equable Lindbergh could not abide him. See Justus D. Doenecke, "Verne Marshall's Leadership of the No Foreign War Committee," *Annals of Iowa* 41 (Winter 1973), pp. 1153–72. For the rapid evolution of Lindbergh's attitude toward Marshall—from "I like Marshall personally" on December 12, 1940, to "He is quick to form impressions and has a violent temper" on December 15 to his disavowal of any connection with Marshall on January 16, 1941—see Charles A. Lindbergh, *The Wartime Journals of Charles A. Lindbergh* (New York: Harcourt Brace Jovanovich, 1970), pp. 426–440.

† According to Sarles, "At this larger gathering were present: Mrs. J. Howland Auchincloss, W.H. Bennett (Bowery Savings Bank), Richard E. Berlin, Graham B. Blaine, Thomas W. Bowers, Avery Claflin, Mrs. W. Shippen Davis, John T. Flynn, F. Abbot Goodhue, John P. Grant, Robert M. Harriss, Robert Haydock, Joseph F. Higgins, Hugh Knowlton, William C. Lengel, W.L. Momsen, J.L. Montgomery, Mr. and Mrs. Cecil J. North, Randolph Phillips, Allen M. Pope, Bayard F. Pope, Robert R. Redpath, Jr., H.S. Richardson, Lunsford Richardson, Daniel Rockford, Archibald Roosevelt, Theodore Roosevelt, C.R. Scheaffer, Willard Simpkins, Benjamin Strong, H. Dudley Swim, Alfred J. Talley, and Robert R. Young."

‡ This "well-known official" was Colonel Allen Pope, president of the First Boston Corporation of New York. Stenehjem, *An American First,* p. 43.

As the first of the New Year of 1941 dawned, the America First Committee in New York City was just struggling out of its swaddling clothes. But it was strong and eager. By the time the Lend-Lease fight reached its peak in February, it was well on its way to full growth and power.

In the melting pot city, America First encountered the most persistent attempts at infiltration and domination by undesirable elements. John Flynn steered the committee with an experienced hand through the reefs and shoals of the ideological differences that find their most passionate expression in New York.

Early in 1941, Flynn was to share his responsibilities with Edwin S. Webster of Stone & Webster and senior partner of Kidder, Peabody & Company. Webster met General Wood in Chicago in January and agreed to relinquish his own business duties and devote full time to the fight to keep America out of war. He assumed direction of all the New York details, i.e., organization, finances, office management, etc. By December 1941, Flynn and Webster had forged in New York a barricade against intervention that touched millions. In a city that had at first been feared "lost," they fashioned by far the strongest chapter of the America First Committee.

THE WASHINGTON CHAPTER

It was only logical that America First should have a sturdy bastion amidst the confusion of foreign and national pressure politics in the nation's capital.

Concerned as the committee was with the administration's foreign policy, and intent as it was on impressing Congress with the popular antiwar will, it needed a reliable liaison group to interpret the patch-quilt formations of events and deeds which were being inauspiciously woven together toward one tangible objective—war. Thus it set about to establish its position in Washington, D.C.

Washington offered a particular problem and would have to be approached in a particular manner. It was evident that it would require two separate committee organizations. The first would be the Washington chapter of America First, whose function would be the same as any other subsidiary branch, namely, to crystallize and energize the antiwar sentiment in the area into an effective bloc. The second group would be a research bureau, the purpose of which would be to supply Congress, investigating committees, and publications with facts and data supporting the point of view of the noninterventionists, and to serve as a listening post on Capitol Hill for the national headquarters of America First.

The Washington chapter began to take shape shortly after the America First Committee was publicly announced. Miriam Clark, wife of Missouri's Democratic Senator Bennett Champ Clark, had joined the National Committee on October 27, 1940. On November 17 she wrote to Bob Stuart, "Does the Committee have a working organization in Washington? I would like to pitch in if there is a committee functioning here."

Stuart and William R. Castle, who had been communicating in an effort to obtain a suitable working committee in Washington, were elated at Mrs. Clark's interest. (She later became chairman.) Castle called the senator's wife a few days after her offer of help. A meeting of a selected few was arranged for at Mrs. Clark's Washington home on November 29.* Methods of acquiring substantial and prominent support for the organization of a local chapter were discussed. The group decided to call an open meeting for December 11 at the home of William R. Castle, and invite Bob Stuart to come from Chicago to explain the purpose and procedure of subsidiary committees.

About a hundred people gathered at the Castle home. Stuart was there and spoke to them. They were, for the most part, a genteel gathering, interested but not fired with enthusiasm to the point of immediate and dynamic action. The Washington chapter was starting in the leisurely, sophisticated Washington manner; it never quite released itself from that tempo.

From its inception, the Washington chapter was considerably constrained by the lack of "social roster" names in a city that abounds in big names; that was important in Washington, where the "cause" organizations that hit the headlines did so through their social connections. Drawing most of its support from a colony of persons who depended directly upon the government for livelihood (to them that meant the administration), the Washington chapter could call for open, active support from a definitely limited number of Washington residents. During the months of its existence, the Washington chapter encountered many instances of petty pressures on some of the few courageous federal servants who dared publicly assert their attitudes on foreign policy by openly working with America First. Even the Quaker meeting, which extended its hospitality to the Washington chapter for weekly meetings, was later subjected to detailed questioning regarding its connection with America First.

THE CHICAGO CHAPTER

It might be said that the Chicago chapter of America First comprised the readers of the Chicago *Tribune* (noninterventionist daily and the world's second-largest newspaper) who agreed with its editorial policy. The *Tribune* and America First were usually focusing their efforts on the same legislation, and the voice of the people of Illinois was always one of the loudest heard in Washington protesting steps toward war.

Stuart was testing for Chicago leadership from the very birth of the committee. There was organization work to be done in the area around Chicago

---

* According to Sarles, "Among those who attended the meeting were William R. Castle, Mrs. Emil Hurja, Alice Roosevelt Longworth, Katrina McCormick (daughter of the former Congresswoman Ruth Hanna McCormick Simms), Maude Parker Pavenstedt, Nina Rogers, Mrs. Frank Simonds, Mrs. Frank West, Mrs. Burton K. Wheeler, and John T. Wilmarth."

which the national office could not undertake. Most of the original membership was from Chicago, and that was multiplied with the absorption of the Roll Call of American Women,* a predominantly Midwestern organization. In November 1940, Stuart met with a body of professors and students of Northwestern University in Evanston, just outside the Chicago city limits, and a branch of the committee got under way there.

On December 7 strides forward were made in the establishment of a self-sustaining Chicago chapter when Edward L. Ryerson, Jr., advised Stuart that although he himself would be unable to accept the chairmanship, he would press General Thomas Hammond, president of the Whiting Corporation, to assume this duty and urge Mrs. Janet Ayer Fairbank, former Democratic National Committeewoman, to become vice chairman. Both General Hammond and Mrs. Fairbank agreed.

Hammond, a member of the National Committee, was one of the originators of the America First Committee who had attended the early organization luncheons as far back as July. Cooperating with the two new Chicago executives was George Ranney, a close friend of Stuart's whose attention was to be devoted to rallying the support of the prominent young college graduates in Chicago. Among others who offered their support to the new chapter was Donald McGibeny, Columbia Broadcasting Company news commentator. Mrs. Fairbank and her assistant, Miss Cornelia Howe, devoted full time to America First without salary until the war. Mrs. Fairbank's political experience was an incalculable contribution in the meetings of the executive and national committees. The Chicago chapter set up chapters all over the state of Illinois and covered a sizeable portion of the state of Iowa.

NOTE

1. General Wood never wanted to remain as chairman. Several times he set a date for termination of his services but remained when no one could be found to take his place.

* The president of the Roll Call of American Women was Harriet E. Vittum, who had been active in the Chicago settlement house movement and the Progressive Party of Theodore Roosevelt.

3

America First under Fire

The America First Committee was not an exclusive organization. An applicant was subject to blackball only for the reason specified in the official statement of principles: "We exclude from our rolls, Nazis, Fascists, Communists, and members of the Bund"; any American could join who wanted to keep the country out of war. "We have tried," wrote General Wood on August 14, 1941, "to go on the premise that while we do not endorse the aims of other organizations, we would welcome their support and cooperation as individuals in our common objective—opposing our involvement in the European war."

The nonexclusive character of the committee furnished its detractors with a ready-made avenue for attack: associate America First in the public mind with organizations of questionable motives by implying that acceptance of their members meant embracing their principles, ergo, America First was also under suspicion. So, obviously, went the reasoning of the defamers who yapped at America First's heels from beginning to end.

The technique of attack by association is an old one in the history of causes; it was to be expected in the case of an organization taking a stand on an issue so close to the hearts of the people as the question of war and peace.

A simple analogy is the practice of groups or individuals who bring court suits when they have no intention of prosecuting, on the theory that a five-line squib on an inside page of a newspaper stating that suit has been brought will incite doubt in the minds of readers about the character of the sued.

Any organization that was effective would be attacked. If attack was to be avoided, the only alternative was not to furnish effective organized leadership to the popular American sentiment against involvement in the war.

The committee offered a golden opportunity for the groups and individuals whose *main motive* was not opposition to war to attempt to put on the cloak of respectability and prestige America First could supply. The question involved was whether the risks of the unwanted association with the undesirables who clung to the America First coattails for their own purposes were greater than the risk of war. The America First Committee took the position that the war transcended every other threat to the welfare of the country.

The committee took steps to provide full information regarding its organization and activities to responsible government agencies.

On January 17, 1941, a letter was written* to Congressman Martin Dies, chairman of the House committee investigating un-American activities, requesting examination of America First lists for names of those "having a background not in accordance with true American principles":

We want as members of the American First Committee no one who has an ulterior motive in joining our organization. We want no "isms." We want only those who see eye to eye with our objectives; to build an impregnable defense for America; to give humanitarian aid to the suffering and needy people of England and the occupied countries; to maintain the provisions of the existing Neutrality Act, aiding Britain within the limits of that Act; and to keep the United States out of foreign war.

Particularly during this last week we have been literally flooded with requests for membership in our group and, quite naturally, the majority of those who are requesting membership are not known to us personally. Our problem, therefore is this: possibly among the applicants are those people who should be known to the government as having ulterior motives or activities which we, of course, could not countenance.

It has been suggested that through your committee we might secure the help of someone to check our lists and in this way help us avoid any connection with any one who is known to you at least as having a background not in accordance with true American principles. Thus, any assistance you can give us will be appreciated.

On March 13, 1941, a letter† was addressed to the Federal Bureau of Investigation requesting aid in keeping the lists clear of subversive elements:

The America First Committee is [a] non-political, non-partisan organization of American citizens, who believe the preservation of American liberties and the advancement of American democracy depend upon keeping out of the present conflict abroad.

We are constantly on the lookout for any subversive element, who might attempt to affiliate themselves with our organization, which consists of some 600 chapters and affiliates throughout the country.

We expressly state in our manual "How to Organize Chapters of the America First Committee" our vigorous stand against such undesirable elements as follows:

Every American citizen is invited to join the America First Committee and work with us. We exclude from our ranks those who have ulterior motives—anything other than the welfare of our country. Those who are unwelcome include the Communists, who really desire to destroy our Government; the Nazis and members of the Bund, who put the interests of Germany above those of this country; those of the school of thought who call themselves or may be considered American Fascists; some ultra-pacifists who forget the interest of their country in their desire for peace at any price.

From time to time we may have occasion to have advice from you regarding the status or standing of individuals we are unable to readily check. Would it be possible to have your help in such instances?

---

* The letter was from General Thomas R. Hammond, president of the Whiting Corporation.
† The letter was from Robert L. Bliss, America First's director of operations.

Of course, our membership files are always open to you and we would like to have you go through them if possible so that you might advise us of any exceptions to our ruling who have escaped our strict scrutiny.

The agent in charge of the Chicago office replied as follows on March 27, 1941:

I wish to acknowledge receipt of your letter dated March 13, 1941.

I regret very much that due to the confidential nature of the files of this Bureau, I will be unable to be of any assistance to you in connection with the subject matter of your letter of reference.

Early in September, Congressman [Samuel] Dickstein [D-NY]* requested an investigation of the America First Committee on the ground that it was pro-fascist. Congressman Dies in a public statement said he had no evidence of pro-fascism in the committee and lacked reason to investigate. At this time, General Wood wrote to Congressman Dies:

It is needless to say that we will welcome an investigation at any time. As far as that is concerned, we would be very happy to have you come up and visit our headquarters in Chicago and have you meet the members of the Committee personally. We will gladly give you any information you may require or would like to have. In other words, everything is open to you.

When Congressman Dies announced early in November 1941 that his committee would investigate both interventionist and noninterventionist organizations, General Wood addressed the following letter to him:

I was glad to learn from your representative that the Dies Committee plans to investigate those organizations which are engaged in promoting or opposing American involvement in the European war.

As you know, the America First Committee, in public statements has repeatedly urged that such an investigation be conducted. At all times we have been ready and willing to submit our list of members and contributors and all our records to the Dies Committee or any duly authorized Government agency.

Certainly the American people are entitled to know if foreign or subversive elements are connected with any organization which purports to be American, and in this connection the Dies Committee can perform an important public service.

From the outset the America First Committee has made it a policy scrupulously to exclude all persons having, or suspected of having, un-American views or connections. We believe this policy has been carried out with complete success, but we welcome the opportunity of having your Committee make a further investigation.

The Dies Committee has rendered an important service in exposing the activities of un-American groups with the United States. You are especially to be congratulated on

* Congressman Dickstein was later revealed to have been a paid agent of the Soviet Union. Allen Weinstein and Alexander Vassiliev, *The Haunted Wood: Soviet Espionage in America—The Stalin Era* (New York: Random House, 1999).

making the American people aware of the extent of the Communist penetration in this country.

Now that the pro-war groups are urging an American alliance with Soviet Russia, they have the ardent and open support of the Communists. I do not know that the pro-war committees are necessarily welcoming the Communists to their ranks but the evidence adduced by your Committee in the past shows how adept the Communists are at insinuating themselves into organizations which claim to be American. One of the most important services your Committee can perform in its forthcoming investigation, therefore, is to reveal the extent to which propaganda for war is being spread by Communists and their fellow travelers.

I assure you that the America First Committee will give its full cooperation to your Committee in this investigation. In order to facilitate your work we will be glad to give your representatives full access to all our files without requiring any formal order or subpoena. I trust that the pro-war committees will take a similar attitude if, like America First, they have nothing to hide.

The Dies Committee investigation of America First was in process at the time of the Japanese attack on Pearl Harbor. Since it was dropped with the declaration of war and the subsequent dissolution of America First, the report (which must have been near completion) has no status before the committee. Presumably, the investigation of the interventionist organizations was continued since they did not disband.*

While the reputations of the members of the national committee were such that the policy-making body of the organization was impervious to attack on charges of un-Americanism, the umbrella of their respectability could not reach out to cover all the activities of local chapters, which enjoyed a large degree of autonomy.

It became apparent as the committee grew that local chapters needed safeguards against undesirable elements that deliberately tried to insinuate themselves into the organization for purposes other than those for which the committee was founded. They also needed protection against energetic individuals whose zeal for the cause exceeded their experience in organization, who were unaware of the complexity of forces operating in the antiwar struggle, or who failed to realize that assumption of the right to influence public opinion involved an obligation to proceed with a sense of proportion.

The National Committee exercised some control through its power to revoke charters, if local chapters or their chairmen were remiss in carrying out the committee purposes.

The National Committee also exercised supervision through the personnel of the Organization Department, which maintained constant contact with the chapters by correspondence and through its field staff. The correspondence shows that, in the daily scheme of this, the Chicago staff was constantly ad-

---

*I have omitted a brief discussion of America First's lack of legal obligation to register with the federal government.

monishing and correcting local chairmen, checking up to see that orders were being carried out. Field men checked on the chapters personally, as they went their rounds from state to state.

The field staff never numbered more than six men, and the office force at national headquarters handling organizational problems never more than four, a staff totally inadequate to check on the chapters as frequently and as thoroughly as was desirable.

The best protection a local chapter could have, General Wood felt, was a reliable, intelligent chairman. Prospective chairmen were investigated either by a member of the national staff or by persons in the vicinity known to the National Committee. When a chairman did not carry out the purposes of the committee, he was replaced.

The committee tried without success to secure the services of a business reporting agency that made a specialty of investigating individuals, with particular reference to antecedents, and statements or actions indicating patriotism. None of the firms consulted would undertake to investigate volunteers to America First.

As committee procedure took shape, what actually happened was that several substantial and influential individuals in various parts of the country came to exercise a supervisory function in their areas. People in whom the general and the National Committee had confidence, they became in a sense deputies for the National Committee. They became the eyes and ears of the National Committee in their regions; they advised the general on policies. They undertook the responsibility, with General Wood's encouragement, of reporting to the National Committee and of acting in cases where local attitudes and actions threatened to give the organization a bad name.

Among those who served as "area supervisors" were John Wheeler (son of the noninterventionist Senate leader from Montana) of Los Angeles, California; John T. Flynn, economist and writer of New York City; Mrs. Janet Ayer Fairbank, author and former Democratic committeewoman from Illinois, of Chicago; Walter Gosgriff, banker of Salt Lake City, Utah; Lansing Hoyt, brother-in-law of John Cudahy, Milwaukee, Wisconsin; and former Senator David Aiken Reed of Pennsylvania.

NEW YORK CITY

The situation of the New York chapter was in a class by itself. Located in the heart of the interventionist East, at the home base of most of the interventionist organizations, in a city in which ideological differences reached a violence and intensity unknown in the Midwest, the New York chapter became the spearhead of America First's fight to rid itself of undesirables.

The chairman of the New York City chapter was John T. Flynn, well-known writer, a veteran of many years' steering among the treacherous ideological reefs of "crusader" organizations. John Flynn knew and understood the forces with which the America First Committee had to contend.

In the early days of the committee's existence, the anti-Semitic tag had not been attached. There was no self-consciousness on the question. When the New York office was organized, Jews and Gentiles occupied key positions. Nathan Alexander was made office manager; Fice Mork became publicity director; Max Putzel was in charge of research; Abe Lasky handled the extensive clipping files. There were three Jews on the New York chapter's executive committee.

The first charges of anti-Semitism came from interventionist groups. The immediate result was to attract to the America First Committee disreputable groups that were anti-Semitic. The interventionists, by associating anti-Semitism with the committee, had wrapped anti-Semitism in the cloak of respectability. Naturally, the anti-Semitic groups took advantage of the opportunity handed to them on a silver platter, and thereafter were to make constant attempts to worm their way into committee activities.

Another result was that once the question of Jews versus Gentiles was injected into the fight between interventionists and noninterventionists, forces were unloosed that were to bring to the surface latent racial prejudices that thrive in the emotional atmosphere that is the inevitable accompaniment of war.

As the America First Committee struggled to weed out the undesirables, those who charged the committee with anti-Semitism attempted to link it with the Coughlinite movement and the Christian Front. Neither organization as such had any connection with the committee. Interventionist organizations and press claimed to find something sinister in the presence at America First rallies of persons known to be followers of Father Coughlin or members of the Christian Front. But these were public meetings. Anybody could attend these rallies just as they could and did attend the interventionist rallies. They were no more invited, nor was their presence as representatives of their organization any more welcome than that of some of the interventionist leaders who regularly attended America First rallies, or of the Communists, who were taken to interventionist bosoms when Russia and Germany went to war.

It was an interesting paradox that while interventionists were charging America First with Christian Front and Coughlinite connections, the committee was being attacked from the other side. Father Coughlin denounced John Flynn in *Social Justice*.* He was constantly threatened and attacked through the mail by Christian Fronters because of his efforts to bar committee doors to those who sought to use the committee for their own ends. Father Edward Lodge

---

*General Wood told a person distributing copies of *Social Justice* outside an America First meeting, "We don't want you people at America First meetings. You confuse the issue." Cole, *America First*, p. 136.

Curran, of the International Catholic Truth Society, made a personal call on General Wood to urge Flynn's removal.*

In the spring of 1941 America First leaders were discussing among themselves how best to handle the constant embarrassment and damage the committee was suffering from the unwanted support of members of these organizations. General Wood in a telephone conversation with John Flynn urged him to denounce the undesirables in a public meeting, feeling that since New York was the center of their gratuitous support, the denunciation ought to be made in New York.

At the Madison Square Garden rally on May 23, at which Colonel Lindbergh, Norman Thomas, and Senator Wheeler spoke, John Flynn, sighting in the audience Joseph McWilliams, active in Christian Front activities and at one time Bundist candidate for Congress, publicly buried the canard that America First sought the support of anti-Semitic, pro-Fascist groups:

The America First Committee is not crazy enough to want the support of a handful of Bundists, Communists, and Christian Fronters who are without influence, without power and without respect in this or any other community. Just because some misguided fool in Manhattan who happens to be a Nazi, gets a few tickets to this rally, this meeting of American citizens is called a Nazi meeting. And right here, not many places from me, is sitting a man named McWilliams. What he is doing here, how he gets in here, whose stooge he is, I do not know, but I know the photographers of these war-mongering newspapers can always find him when they want him.

In spite of such denunciations, anti-Semitic, pro-fascist persons continued individually to wriggle like termites into various committee activities, particularly into the New York neighborhood chapters, and into the Street Speakers' Bureau, which nightly sent out a dozen street corner orators. As fast as their presence was learned, they were weeded out by John Flynn and his lieutenants. Because of their persistence and because of the physical impossibility of checking on half a hundred speakers a week in the New York area, street speaking was finally abandoned altogether. Two of the seventy five chapters in the New York area were closed.

Life magazine, outstanding interventionist periodical, paid tribute to the America First Committee's efforts to keep itself free of undesirable elements. Roger Butterfield, in his Colonel Lindbergh article wrote, "From the start America First has worked hard and usually with great success to avoid Fascist or Red tinge."†

---

* Flynn had earlier "tried unsuccessfully" to prevent Curran "from offering the invocation at a chapter meeting." Cole, *America First*, p. 135.

† Roger Place Butterfield, "Lindbergh," *Life* (August 11, 1941), pp. 70+.

In general there were three main lines of attack on the America First Committee:

It was helpful to the Nazis.

It was anti-Semitic.

By its failure to publish a full list of contributors as did the Committee to Defend America by Aiding the Allies, it admitted it was guilty of accepting funds from questionable sources.

HELPFUL TO THE NAZIS

Because it was to Germany's advantage for the United States to stay out of the war, it was inevitable that the America First Committee would be accused of pro-Nazism. It was likewise inevitable that real pro-Nazis would attempt to get on the America First bandwagon. This provided an excellent opportunity for critics of America First willing to make use of the technique of smear-by-association.

The committee never bothered to deny or answer officially the charge that it was pro-Nazi; the answer to this charge rested with the men and women who made the policies and directed the activities of the committee, people whose records of public service and devotion to American ideals were not open to question. It was felt that the intellectual dishonesty of this smear-by-association technique would be apparent to responsible, thinking persons, whether or not they agreed with the America First point of view.

A National Committee member wrote to General Wood,

Great Britain wants us in this war. Germany of course wants us to stay out. Our committee believes that its policy should not be affected one way or the other by what other nations want, but that American interests demand that we stay out. If on that one point our objective happens to be the same as the German objective, it may be unfortunate, but it cannot logically be claimed to indicate any pro-Nazi tendencies. I presume that the writers of the enclosed pamphlet would have to call Christ a Nazi if Hitler happened to quote the Bible.

And another:

Hitler doesn't want America to get into the war. The non-interventionists don't want America to get into the war. Thus, the non-interventionists, represented by the America First group, and the Nazis are all one and the same, q.e.d.

It would be just as cockeyed to say, "Joe Stalin believes that the plight of the share-croppers is a poor testimony to the efficiency, from the social point of view, of the American economic system. Senator Norris* believes that the plight of the sharecrop-

---

* Senator George Norris (R-Neb.) served as U.S. senator from 1913 to 1943. He was among the most stalwart Senate foes of U.S. entry into the First World War; his antiwar zeal had moderated by the end of his career, though he remained a sharp critic of conscription.

pers is a disgrace to American democracy and should and must be corrected. Thus, it is obvious that Senator Norris is working hand and glove with Joe Stalin for the destruction of the American nation, q.e.d."

There were laws on the United States statute books providing punishment for those guilty of "aiding the enemy." If there had been ground for such charges, certainly the administration whose policies were constantly under fire from America First would have taken action to put the committee out of business without delay.

America First leaders went on the assumption that the two most likely ways in which grounds for charges of association with pro-Nazis might be established were through contributions from individuals or organizations of known Nazi sympathies, or through the attempts of such individuals or organizations to take part in local America First activities. It was impossible for them to find their way into positions where they could have influence in directing national policies or activities.

The National Committee had made the rule that all contributions of over $100 were to be investigated before acceptance. No contribution of over $100 was ever brought into question. One case involving a small sum was reported in the *Oregon Journal*, August 7, 1941. It was alleged that the America First Committee of Oregon had accepted and cashed a check for $20, contributed by the German War Veterans.

General Wood's letter of August 12 to the editor of the Chicago *Daily News* tells the story:

My attention has been called, by a representative of the Chicago *Daily News*, to an article appearing in the *Oregon Journal* of Thursday, August 7th, supported by a photostat of a check for $20 payable to the America First Committee and cashed by Dellmore Lessard, Oregon State Chairman of the America First Committee. The photostat of this check was shown to me in June by a representative of the B'nai Brith.

Our National Director of Field Organization, Mr. Earle C. Jeffrey, was to go to the Pacific Coast at that time, and I asked him to visit Mr. Lessard at the earliest possible moment and get the actual conditions of the offering and acceptance of this check. Mr. Jeffrey conferred with Mr. Lessard on July 5th when Mr. Lessard presented evidence that to be a member of the German War Veterans required either full United States citizenship or the completion of the first steps of naturalization under our laws. Mr. Jeffrey ruled that this contribution was from American citizens, but because of the attitude of the National Committee in avoiding all controversial contributions requested that the contribution be returned by the Oregon chapter to the German War Veterans. This was done. We have been able to find no evidence indicating that this group includes in its members Nazis or Bundists.

At the same conference with Mr. Jeffrey, Mr. Lessard presented his chapter financial records which were approved. It was noted that Mr. Lessard had acted in the dual capacity of both Secretary and Treasurer in the interim between the resignation of the original Treasurer and the acceptance of his successor, and that his financial records were entirely in order.

Local chapters are largely autonomous, but they must follow the rules of National Headquarters in refusing all donations from any source which would be open to honest criticism, and we, of course, bar from membership persons who place the interests of any foreign nation ahead of the United States, such as Nazis, Bundists, Fascists, Advocates of Union Now,* and Communists.

Our chapters have been asked to refund any contribution which is accompanied by any letter or literature abusive of our elected officials or expressing or indicating racial or religious intolerance. Upon our invitation the FBI has examined the National Committee's records.

The reference in General Wood's letter to an FBI investigation of America First files had to do with an investigation of the German-American Alliance, functioning in the Chicago area. Since the alliance had recommended that its members support the America First Committee, the FBI asked if it might examine the America First list of contributors. No names known as questionable to the FBI investigator were found on America First lists. As a result of this inquiry, the staff kept a list of persons in the Chicago area suspected of pro-Nazi sympathies, with the order that any correspondence from them was to be turned over to the director for special action.

The following news story, copied from the *New York Times* of May 19, 1941, tells the story of America First's prompt rejection of support gratuitously recommended by a Bundist paper:

ANTIWAR GROUP SPURNS BUND AID

German Organ Prints Flynn's Letter Saying its Readers Are
'Not Eligible' Members

Had Urged Them To Join

But America First Committee Declares Hitler Supporters
Are Not 'Good Americans'

The America First Committee required and obtained yesterday the publication in full on the front page of The Free American and Deutscher Weckruf und Beobachter, a letter rejecting the support of this organ of the German-American Bund, which has long proclaimed its devotion to the Nationalsozialistische Weltanschauung, otherwise known as the Hitler philosophy.

The officers of the Bund are also officers of the newspaper: G. Wilhelm Kunze, president; August Klapprott, vice president; Gustave A. Elmer, treasurer; and Willy Luedtke, secretary.

The letter, signed by John T. Flynn, chairman of the New York chapter of the America First Committee, was printed in full as follows:

---

* Union Now was the brainchild of former *New York Times* correspondent Clarence Streit, who advocated a formal merger of the United States and Great Britain.

May 2, 1941

Editor,
Free American and Deutscher Weckruf und Beobachter,
175 East Eighty-fifth Street, New York City.
Dear Sir:

A copy of your newspaper has been mailed to me and my attention called to an article in which you ask your readers to join the America First Committee. Let me say to you that not only does the America First Committee not solicit their membership, but that they are not eligible for membership. The America First Committee is against America's entry into the war not because it approves of the philosophy, the government, the aggression or the methods of Hitler's Germany, but because it wishes to protect this nation from involvement in Europe's wars.

We do not want in our organization men who support the philosophy of Hitler's government because we do not believe them to be good Americans. The very first and one of the indispensable qualifications for membership in our organization, as stated in all our literature, is that it is not open to those who are members of the Communist or Fascist parties or the German Bunds in this country, or those representing any foreign power which desires to involve us in this war.

May I suggest that you give this letter the same publicity in your newspaper as you gave to the article to which I have referred.

Yours very truly,
John T. Flynn

The three confidential memoranda sent to local chapters from the national office printed below are samples of attempts to keep the local chapters "clean":

There is one menace that usually is not considered ahead of time and is only apparent when a public meeting is under way.

We refer to the practice of other organizations handing out literature to people attending America First rallies. These other organizations customarily station their people on the sidewalk outside the building.

There is apparently no effective way of combating this except to tell these people that they are not wanted. Try to get police protection to avoid such an unfavorable impression as that made by some of the objectionable literature distributed.

The implication is that the point of view is that of the America First Committee, or that of the meeting in progress. Very often it represents the literary outburst of groups that are anti-British in sentiment. Many times people selling *Social Justice*—Father Coughlin's Newspaper—are the trespassers.

We suggest that you will know the most effective means of preventing this in your community. We bring it to your attention believing that forewarned is fore-armed.

The America First Committee does not presume to dictate the beliefs or convictions of any individual. But we cannot permit the effectiveness of our work to be jeopardized by the introduction of extraneous issues of any sort.

What any person thinks, writes or says as an individual is his own business, but it is strictly understood that no one can commit either a local chapter or the National Committee to any position not explicitly detailed from these headquarters.

If you prepare and distribute handbills and flyers for your senatorial meetings and other public rallies, you should protect yourself in every way possible to be rid of all undesirable elements who may attend such open meetings.

We suggest a line similar to the following printed at the foot of the leaflet page—set off by a rule or box:

"The America First Committee reserves the right to refuse admittance or eject any members of Communist, Nazi, Bundist or Fascist groups."

Perhaps the most notorious of the pro-Nazi charges was the pamphlet issued by L.M. Birkhead, national director of the Friends of Democracy, Inc., entitled "The America First Committee, the Nazi Transmission Belt."*

The gist of the pamphlet, which was carefully written to avoid libelous statements, was contained in the following paragraph:

We do not question the integrity of the leadership and membership of the America First Committee nor the sincerity of its program. But we do seriously question the wisdom of the policy makers and the soundness of a policy which has the unqualified approval of Adolf Hitler, Benito Mussolini and their agents in the United States.

Obviously the logical procedure, if the thinking behind Mr. Birkhead's statement were accepted, was entire cessation of any activity to keep the country out of war.

There was unconscious—or conscious—irony in the spectacle of an organization dedicated to *democracy* expressing a point of view which, if carried to its logical conclusion, meant abandonment of the principle of freedom of expression.

This must have been apparent to several members of Friends of Democracy, who expressed themselves as opposed to the statements of their director.

John T. Flynn, chairman of the New York chapter, wired the national committee members of the Friends of Democracy, asking their views on the "Nazi Transmission Belt" pamphlet. The following replies were released to the press and were published in the *New York Times:*

Albert Edward Wiggam, writer, replied: "Have not seen or heard of document by Friends of Democracy denouncing the America First Committee. I could not approve violent accusations and denunciations against any organization that works openly for national interest because as never before we must win opponents in thought and opinion by the fellowship of tolerant discussion and thus demonstrate democracy in action if we are to achieve what we need now above everything else, namely unity of national faith and purpose."

Orday Tead, chairman of New York City's Board of Higher Education, replied: "Had no knowledge Birkhead release before seeing newspaper story today. Am not in sympathy with that kind of attack and was in no way party to it."

Cyrus Leroy Baldridge, artist, wired: "Brochure was completely unauthorized by national committee. I only saw it in the papers. People who issue such statements should be held legally responsible to prove them.†

* For more on Friends of Democracy as a front group of the BSC (British Security Coordination), see Mahl, *Desperate Deception,* pp. 23–45.

† I have omitted a paragraph that is partly illegible in the original.

A.J. Carlson of Chicago wired: "Have neither seen nor approved Birkhead statement. I am interested enough in America First to be one of its members."

Will Durant wired: "I certainly would not want to share in any attack upon the patriotism of such men as General Wood. The notion that every opponent of America's entry into the war is a Nazi agent is a disgrace to the American reputation of fair play."

Walter Russell Bowie, Baker Browell, and Paul Douglas declared that they had not seen the attack on the America First Committee sent out under the support of their names. Only two of those we reached seemed to approve it—Louis Bromfield and David Cushman Coyle.

In this case the National Committee followed its customary policy of not replying to attacks, after General Wood had written to the members of the committee, to find out if they wished to break their silence. The general commented as follows on the incident in a letter to a friend:

Birkhead himself is a rather disreputable character; he is practically an unfrocked clergyman. His Unitarian Church in Kansas City was used for Communist meetings and he was finally forced out of the church. He did not consult the members of his organization (among whom are many reputable citizens) about sending out his brochure, and a majority of his own committee has repudiated the statement he made. We felt that it would just play into his hands to dignify such a communication with a reply, because all that he wants is publicity.

Another attempt to identify the America First Committee with Nazi sympathizers occurred in connection with the grand jury investigation in Washington of the activities of Nazi agents. The committee came into the picture at two points, both of them dealing with the distribution of the franked speeches of members of Congress, reprinted from the *Congressional Record.* The first occasion was late in September 1941, when the executive secretary of the Washington chapter was called before the grand jury to explain why the chapter had accepted several bags of franked speeches by noninterventionist senators and congressmen that had been delivered by a House of Representatives truck from the office of Prescott Dennett, under suspicion as a Nazi agent.* The second occasion was about a month later when several partially burned copies of franked speeches were found at the back of the America First chapter's premises.

The America First Committee's amateur standing was well established in these two cases! What amounted to a series of minor errors was responsible for the committee's connection with both. In the first incident, no one in the local Washington chapter had requested the franked speeches; delivery had been accepted by a stenographer who assumed the chairman had ordered them, while the responsible heads of the organization were out to lunch.

---

*Dennett's Islands for War Debts and Make Europe Pay Committees were financed by George Sylvester Viereck, a Nazi agent. Cole, *America First*, p. 123.

As for the affair of the charred remains, after the September incident, when the publicity attached to franked speeches by the grand jury investigation had made them "hot stuff"—even though they were available in the *Congressional Record*—the Washington chapter chairman gave orders that franked speeches were no longer to be distributed. When the chapter moved its offices, staff members discovered a box of such speeches in the process of unpacking. A member of the local chapter, found to be the owner of them, was asked to dispose of them. He promptly took them out into the small alley at the rear of the office, put them in a metal container, and burned them. The following morning the *Washington Post* carried front-page headlines and pictures, the implication of which was that the committee was involved in a sinister plot and was attempting to destroy the evidence.

A second time the executive secretary journeyed downtown and told her story before the grand jury. No action was taken against America First.

But damage had already been done through the headline treatment given the story by the Washington papers, particularly the *Washington Post*. The explanation of what had actually happened was never given as much prominence as the initial smear.[1]

It seemed apparent to some Washington newspaper readers that the *Washington Post*, interventionist paper, dealt more enthusiastically with America First's part in the case than handling of the story from a strict news point of view warranted. The *Post* reporter assigned to cover the case appeared to have "inside" information. The *Post* gave far more space to the story, day after day, than any other Washington paper. *Post* photographers seemed, mysteriously, to be on the spot—cameras poised—with each new development in the case.

It also seemed to noninterventionist observers in Washington who knew something about the case that the federal lawyers handling the case were going out of their way to link the committee with questionable activities. Comments in private from two responsible Department of Justice officials suggested that committee supporters were not the only ones on whom this impression was forced. An illustration was the attempt of one federal lawyer, in a private conversation with an America First staff member, to establish that a congressman's clerk later convicted of perjury in the grand jury investigation and thereby implicated with Nazi agents, had influenced decisions of the committee in connection with the four congressional district polls.*

The mailbag incident and the backyard burning had significance apart from the hunt for unauthorized Nazi agents. They brought into the limelight, in such a way as to reflect only on noninterventionists, the practice of senators and congressmen of allowing individuals and organizations to buy (at cost) reprints of speeches printed in the *Congressional Record* and to mail them out under the frank of the members who inserted them in the *Record*. It was a

---

* On the polls, see Chapter 4.

time-honored practice, indulged in by interventionists and noninterventionists alike, Republicans and Democrats, conservatives and liberals. When Senator Barkley* on the floor of the Senate sought to take Senator Wheeler to task for following the precedent, Senator Bennett Clark reminded him that when the Kentucky senator had been a candidate for reelection, one of his most widely used pieces of campaign literature was his own (Barkley's) speech that had been put into the *Record* by Senator Clark, and distributed in the state of Kentucky under the Missouri senator's frank.

The America First name was linked with the Flanders Hall Publishing Company, reported to be a German-supported propaganda organization and so registered with the State Department, through the company's publication of a book by Congressman Stephen A. Day that carried on the title page the description "A Flanders Hall—America First book," without the knowledge of the committee. General Wood wrote to the president of the company, S.H. Hauck:

> I understand that you have just put out a book called "We Must Save the Republic" by Stephen A. Day, which is described on the cover as a "Flanders Hall—America First book."
>
> We must ask you to refrain from using anything on the cover or anywhere in the books you bring out, which infers that the book is sponsored by the America First Committee. We do not sponsor books unless we are first consulted.

John Flynn was asked by Flanders Hall to assist in distribution of the book. He refused.[2]

In their philosophical moments, America Firsters addicted to comment on life's small ironies took note of the propensity of interventionists for openly consorting with Communists (after the German attack on Russia made them our allies), while stretching the truth to implicate noninterventionists with Nazism.

Of an interventionist rally held in Madison Square Garden in the summer of 1941, *Uncensored*[3] commented,

> The rally's principal speakers will be labor leaders Sidney Hillman, Frederick Umhey, and Matthew Woll. Its chairman will be Wendell L. Willkie. And running the meeting behind the scenes will be the new factotum of the labor divisions of both the CDA [Committee to Defend America by Aiding the Allies] and FFF [Fight for Freedom]— Jay Lovestone.† Until 1929, Lovestone was general secretary of the Communist party.

---

* Senator Alben Barkley (D-Ky.) served as vice president under President Harry Truman (1949–1953).

† Lovestone, the Communist, became the revered elder of a later generation of cold war liberals and neoconservative socialists. From 1944 to 1974, he ran the foreign-policy shop for the AFL-CIO. For an excellent history of the American labor movement's collaboration with the bureaucratic state, see Paul Buhle, *Taking Care of Business: Samuel Gompers, George Meany, Lane Kirkland, and the Tragedy of American Labor* (New York: Monthly Review Press, 1999).

He was succeeded, on instructions from Moscow, by Earl Browder. Lovestone opposed the Communist trade union policy of "dual unionism" in favor of "boring from within." As head of his own political faction, he bored quite successfully. His men were accepted as legitimate progressive unionists. He earned a reputation as a smooth operator among the smooth operators in the New York labor movement. Lovestone replaces Alfred Baker Lewis, who obviously was not a smooth operator. Lewis had tried to use the CDA influence to defeat non-interventionist candidates in union elections.

Among those who spoke at the "national emergency" rally were Rear Admiral Richard E. Byrd (who had received a two months' leave from active duty so that he might "arouse the nation"); Justice Owen J. Roberts, United States Supreme Court; former Warden Lewis E. Lawes of Sing Sing prison; Samuel Shore, vice president of the International Ladies' Garment Workers Union; and Carl Sandburg. An observer at the meeting reported,

The larger portion of the audience appeared to be Communistic from the ovation which was given each mention of the Soviet. There were at least 100 people selling "New Masses," "Daily Worker" and a new pamphlet called "Soviet Power," of which the Communist Party has printed 1,000,000 copies. A great many copies of the "Daily Worker" were being read in the audience. When Warden Lawes spoke the people began shouting "Free Earl Browder!"

None of the interventionist papers in New York, naturally, carried such observations, although they had been known in the past to comment on the makeup of the crowds at noninterventionist rallies.

On April 24 (also reported by *Uncensored*) Charles A. Lindbergh addressed a non-interventionist rally in New York. The *New York Times* reported that Father Coughlin's *Social Justice* was sold outside this meeting, that "German accents were numerous," and that the audience cheered remarks unsympathetic to Britain.

On July 17, the Committee to Defend America and Fight for Freedom Inc. held a pro-war rally in the same hall presided over by Wendell L. Willkie. Outside the meeting Communists distributed copies of the *Daily Worker,* the *New Masses,* and the latest statement of the Communist Party. Inside the hall Communists revealed their presence by applauding references to the Soviet Union. Most of the speakers emphasized their hope that the peoples of the dictator countries would be freed, and mentioned specifically Germany, Italy, and the conquered territories. But they failed to mention Stalin's people. None of these aspects of the meeting were reported by the *New York Times.*

Before the Communists had become "respectable," the New York chapter of the Committee to Defend America by Aiding the Allies, in a statement commenting on Nazis and Communists at America First mass meetings, had said,

If these Nazis and Communists came to mass meetings of the Committee to Defend America by Aiding the Allies and cheered what our speakers said, we would be sure there was something wrong—with us. What Hitler, Mussolini, and Stalin and their friends in this country applaud cannot be good for America.[4]

Exactly thirty-four days later, after Communist Russia had suddenly become one of the "Allies," the same committee, asserting that it was having a good laugh watching the antics of the Communists in this country as they did a "flip-flop" to keep in step with the party line, made the following incomprehensible comment:

But the followers of the Nazi Party Propaganda line (presumably including the America First Committee) still working the same side of the street the Commies so abruptly deserted, have taken their flip-flop in stride. Seemingly they blush at nothing, but do they think they can take the American people in with such talk?[5]

ANTI-SEMITISM

Charges that the America First Committee was anti-Semitic grew out of the facts that Henry Ford, who years before had circulated the notoriously false *Protocols of the Elders of Zion*, had at one time been a member of the National Committee; that individuals and members of organizations known to be anti-Semitic joined the committee and attended meetings; and that Colonel Lindbergh had made a speech at Des Moines, Iowa, on September 11, 1941, which was widely interpreted as anti-Semitic.

During the period of the committee's existence there had been two Jewish members of the National Committee: Lessing Rosenwald, former chairman of the board of directors of Sears, Roebuck, who helped to organize the America First Committee in the fall of 1940, and Mrs. Florence Kahn, former member of Congress from California. Mr. Rosenwald resigned in December 1940, and Mrs. Kahn in May 1941.*

Dr. Charles Fleischer, former editor of Hearst's *New York American*, was a member of the New York chapter until late November 1941. Mrs. Paul [Greta] Palmer stuck with the New York chapter until the end. Two able Jews served on the staff: Sidney Hetzberg was national publicity director from December 1940 to April 1941. James Lipsig was head of research in the Research Bureau in Washington until the committee was dissolved.

Attempts were made by America First leaders to secure Jewish leaders to speak for those Jews who opposed the policy that appeared to be taking the country into war. These efforts were made particularly in the spring of 1941, when several of General Wood's Jewish friends had come to him privately and said they were on his side.

The most significant Jewish support came voluntarily from Dr. Hyman Lischner, prominent physician of Los Angeles and former president of B'nai B'rith at San Diego, who in September 1941 wrote an unsolicited letter of appreci-

---

* For more on Congresswoman Kahn, see the editor's introduction.

ation to the America First Committee.[6] Dr. Lischner's letter was released to the press and attracted wide attention.

Henry Ford's membership on the National Committee had been solicited in the early days of the organization. The following letter, written by Mr. Stuart on November 15, 1940, to a prominent Jew in New York City, furnishes the explanation:

> This Committee is endeavoring to establish a rallying point for every point of view. Mr. Henry Ford does not agree with Kathryn Lewis. Kathryn Lewis does not agree with Henry Ford. I think, quite frankly, they are immediately skeptical of one another, but this does not prevent their serving together on a committee which they both feel is controlled by persons working in the best interests of America.
>
> I hope you will see what I mean by this. Mr. Lessing Rosenwald shares your skepticism of Henry Ford, but feels that it is so important that we work together on this job that he has put aside his worries.

But less than a month later, on December 11, 1940, Mr. Stuart wrote to the same man,

> At a meeting of the America First Committee last Thursday a resolution was passed requesting Mr. Henry Ford to withdraw from the Committee.[7]
>
> As you know, Mr. Ford was asked to join the America First Committee in good faith by men who abhor race antagonisms. I am now convinced that we made a grave mistake.

The extent of Mr. Ford's connection with the committee was described by General Wood in a letter to the head of the Washington *PM** bureau under date of December 21, 1940:

> I think probably the most logical basis for the accusation of anti-Semitism came from the fact that Henry Ford was on the Committee. I might say, however, that Mr. Ford has never contributed a penny to the Committee nor has he even communicated with the Committee since it was formed. He has had absolutely nothing to do with passing on the policies or acts of the Committee.

Charges of anti-Semitism among those active in the America First Committee never touched members of the National Committee: those who made the policies and directed the activities of America First were not anti-Semitic; at no time, so far as can be discovered, was the direction of the organization in the hands of persons who on the basis of any reasonable definition could be called anti-Semitic.

There is no doubt that there were anti-Semites among the rank-and-file members. There is evidence that some passionately anti-Semitic individuals

---

* *PM*, the New York City–based interventionist newspaper edited by Ralph Ingersoll, was backed by Marshall Field, owner of the *Chicago Sun*. Although Field was technically a Midwesterner, he was educated at Eton and Cambridge.

deliberately sought to further anti-Semitism by working through the America First Committee.

The committee disavowed any connection with the organization [by those] whose disreputable objectives [included] the promotion of anti-Semitism. It was constantly weeding from active positions in local chapters individuals who spread anti-Semitism by publicly blaming the Jews for the trend toward war, or who were suspected of having been planted for the purpose of promoting anti-Semitism. When it came to disavowing individuals with anti-Semitic bias, it would have been impossible to draw the line without a private Gestapo.

How the committee dealt with anti-Semitic charges is revealed in the two following cases:

On July 24, 1941, H.A. Hollzer, United States district judge in Los Angeles, wrote to General Wood,

Supplementing our conversation over the telephone this morning, I am herewith submitting certain data which in my judgment substantiate the complaint to the fact that meetings held in this vicinity under the auspices of the America First Committee are being used to spread bigotry and intolerance.

It is because of my confidence in your sense of fairness and because I feel that you desire to rid the Committee of those elements engaged in these un-American activities that I am bringing this information to your attention. I do believe, however, that it is essential that you give public expression respecting your position on this matter before anything can be accomplished in this area toward ridding the Committee of its seeming association with these subversive elements.

I am most appreciative of the sympathetic hearing that you have accorded my presentation of this problem.

There was enclosed with the letter a four-page typed report on America First meetings held in the vicinity, and on at least twenty-five individuals who had taken part in America First activities as speakers, as members of groups making arrangements for America First meetings, or simply as observers at America First meetings. They were individually charged with such complaints as anti-Semitism, connections with the German Propaganda Ministry and with the Japanese Consulate, [and] membership in the Bund.

General Wood replied that he had asked John Wheeler, Southern California chairman and a trusted friend, to look into the charges and report to him.

On August 19, John Wheeler wrote as follows:

As a result of my reading the report, while you were here I called Judge Hollzer and told him I would like to talk with him. He was reluctant to see me, suggesting that I talk with Mr. Leon Lewis, counsel for the News Research Bureau, which had prepared the report. I talked at length with Mr. Lewis, explaining our position and some of the difficulties. He emphasized the subversive phase of some of our members. I took their names and have carefully checked each individual with local police and Federal authorities, and none of the statements which Mr. Lewis made to me have any foundation, according to these sources. As you know, we have a very extensive department for the study of subversive activities in the Police Department here and we have made arrangements to clear all people active in our organization through these channels. However, as a result of my conversation with Mr. Lewis, I received the enclosed letter. I plan to talk with Judge Hollzer further.

The enclosure from Leon Lewis to which he referred was a memorandum from Mr. Lewis addressed "To All NRS Correspondents" under [the] date of July 28, 1941, regarding America First. It read:

The chairman of "America First" in Southern California is John Wheeler, a Los Angeles attorney, and the son of Senator Wheeler.

After a lengthy conference with him today, I am satisfied that the responsible heads of "America First" organizations in the various cities throughout the country are honest and sincere in their efforts to prevent subversivists from climbing on to the "America First" bandwagon. However, they are able to accomplish this only when sufficiently apprised of the background and activities of those anti-democratic elements who are trying to use the "America First" set-up for their own purposes.

Arrangements for interchanging information of this character have been made in Southern California. It is believed that where local "America First" organizations are headed by men of responsibility and integrity—as they are in most centers—that similar arrangements could be made and would be welcome.

General Wood had an extended correspondence with Dr. Sigmund Livingston, chairman of the Anti-Defamation League Jewish organization, regarding charges of anti-Semitism.

On December 16, 1940, Dr. Livingston asked that General Wood be told that one of the members of the America First national staff had been discharged from a prominent newspaper because of scurrilous remarks about the Jews. General Wood replied on December 31, 1940:

Mr. —— seems to be in the "doghouse" with all sides. A week ago I was approached by certain parties in New York City who desired to make a donation to the committee, but only on the condition that Mr. —— be discharged because he had been associated with *PM* and Mr. Ingersoll and, in their opinion, was a prominent Pro-Semite. I might say that I did not accept the contribution as I suspected these people of anti-Semitism.

We cannot control the various classes of people who, for one reason or another, support the objectives of keeping the United States out of war. We can, however, control the people on the Committee, none of whom are in the least anti-Semitic. In fact they are very much the other way with the possible exception of Henry Ford, who I might say has not contributed a penny to the Committee and has not communicated with the Committee since it was formed.

As you possibly know, Lessing Rosenwald has withdrawn from it. I personally feel that it was a great mistake. There is persistent propaganda all over this country to the effect that the Jews here are trying to get us into the war. For that reason I think it would be a very good idea to have a man of Mr. Lessing Rosenwald's standing and character on the Committee as he would be performing the very greatest possible service to the Jews of this country. We are most anxious, at the present time, to find a Jewish citizen of high standing to replace Mr. Rosenwald. Certainly there is not a single thing in the resolutions of the Committee to indicate anti-Semitism in any way, shape or manner, and if there were I would not be associated with it.

Dr. Livingston replied on January 10, 1941:

I can well appreciate how conflicting attitudes at this time produce difficulties which we are unable to avoid. In my particular post as Chairman of the Anti-Defamation League I have a constant burden to keep complaints within conservative limits.

It is frequently said that the Jews are over-sensitive. This may be true, but perfectly justified under present world conditions. Every Jew of true character necessarily feels the pang of barbaric persecution of the Jew inflicted by the Nazi regime. The victims of this persecution may be entire strangers to the American Jew; in fact, many of them are of different blood and without kindred relationship. The psychological question has been raised, why do we have such deep sympathetic fellowship? The answer is that every Jew in this country knows that if he happened to be a German citizen instead of an American citizen, he would himself be the subject of this persecution.

I agree with you to the fullest in all the statements you made. If Lessing Rosenwald had asked for my opinion, I would have advised against his resignation if such action did not conflict with his personal concepts of the large issue involved.* I have heretofore on several occasions answered correspondence from leaders of all Jewish organizations, in which I stressed the point that it was fortunate that men like you and Lessing Rosenwald were on this Committee; and also stated that if you were not the Chairman of this Committee, some other man would be, who would possibly not have the broad and comprehensive mental attitude that you possess.

I appreciate that you are at a great sacrifice giving this matter your unstinted time and energy because of your honest belief in that side of the issue sponsored by your Committee. . . .

The correspondence was resumed in May when Dr. Livingston wrote General Wood that anti-Semites were being selected as heads of local America First chapters; in particular, the chairman of a certain West Coast chapter was definitely anti-Semitic. With great consideration, Dr. Livingston wrote on May 15, 1941,

Unless something is done concerning this, they will bring it before the public. I have been able thus far to stop such procedure; in fact, the night before last, I sent a telegram to San Francisco to the end that such steps should be taken, and that I would take the matter up with you direct. . . . [I]f your national executives of the Committee deem it advisable to take corrective measures, it would be better to do so now rather than to do so after the matter has been brought into the public limelight.†

Accordingly, General Wood on May 21, 1941, wrote to Bob Stuart,

---

* It did not.
† The chairman referred to was a Dr. Parkinson of San Francisco. R.E. Wood to R.D. Stuart, Jr., June 3, 1941, America First Collection, Box 291, Hoover Institution.

I wish you would immediately check up the ——— situation and find out about this Dr. ———, whether he is anti-Semitic, and whether he is communicating with the people and organizations mentioned in Dr. Livingston's letter. If this information is correct he should be removed at once as chairman of the chapter.

On May 29, 1941, Dr. Livingston wrote to General Wood,

I can say to you positively that Dr. ———, the chairman of the downtown chapter in ———, is an anti-Semite, and that his record is quite well-known.

In his letter Dr. Livingston cited chapter and verse his reasons for believing that the chairman he complained of was anti-Semitic.

Therefore General Wood wrote to Bob Stuart on June 3, 1941,

I have received reliable information that there is no question about this Dr. ——— being a confirmed anti-Semite. I wish you would take it up with our people in California immediately and make arrangements to relieve him as chairman of the downtown chapter or, if that is not feasible, to dissolve the chapter.

General Wood, during a trip to the West Coast in August, talked with the man charged with anti-Semitism. When he returned to Chicago he thereupon wrote to Dr. Livingston that the man had resigned from the America First Committee while the general was in the West.

On June 11, 1941, Dr. Livingston wrote to the general that the suspected man had resigned as chairman but that the man who had taken his place was far more objectionable in his attitude concerning the Jews than his predecessor and that he had refused to resign.

General Wood had his West Coast field-worker investigate and found Dr. Livingston's complaint regarding the second chairman was fully justified; he was asked to resign. On August 15, 1941, the America First regional director for Northern California wrote to General Wood,

Mr. ———, who was the former chairman of ——— chapter, no longer holds office in that chapter, nor membership in this organization.

The Board of Directors ousted him from the America First Committee on July 18, 1941.

COLONEL LINDBERGH'S DES MOINES SPEECH

On September 11, 1941, Colonel Lindbergh, in a speech at Des Moines, Iowa, that was broadcast over the Mutual Network said,

The three most important groups who have been pressing this country toward war are the British, the Jewish and the Roosevelt administration. Behind these groups, but of lesser importance, are a number of capitalists, Anglophiles, and intellectuals who believe that their future and the future of mankind, depends upon the domination of the British empire.

. . . The second major group mentioned is the Jewish. It is not difficult to understand why Jewish people desire the overthrow of Nazi Germany. The persecution they suffered in Germany would be sufficient to make bitter enemies of any race. No person with a sense of the dignity of mankind can condone the persecution of the Jewish race in Germany. But no person of honesty and vision can look on their pro-war policy here today without seeing the dangers involved in such a policy, both for us and for them.

Instead of agitating for war, the Jewish groups in this country should be opposing it in every possible way, for they will be among the first to feel its consequences. Tolerance is a virtue that depends upon peace and strength. History shows that it cannot survive war and devastation. A few farsighted Jewish people realize this, and stand opposed to intervention. But the majority still do not. Their greatest danger to this country lies in their large ownership and influence in our motion pictures, our press, our radio, and our government.

I am not attacking either the Jewish or the British people. Both races, I admire. But I am saying that the leaders of both the British and the Jewish races, for reasons which are as understandable from their viewpoint as they are inadvisable from ours, for reasons which are not American, wish to involve us in the war. We cannot blame them for looking out for what they believe to be their own interests, but we also must look out for ours. We cannot allow the natural passions and prejudices of other peoples to lead our country to destruction.[8]

Immediately, there was a tremendous protest in the press and over the radio, charging Colonel Lindbergh and the America First Committee with anti-Semitism. The America First Committee could prove that it was not anti-Semitic, it was said, only if it repudiated Colonel Lindbergh's sentiments and, some insisted, Colonel Lindbergh himself. The White House took cognizance of the speech to the extent that the president's secretary, Stephen Early, said on September 12, "You have seen the outpourings of Berlin in the last few days. You saw Lindbergh's statement last night. I think there is a striking similarity between the two."

The National Committee was summoned for a meeting in Chicago on September 16.

Following the meeting, Mr. Stuart issued a statement:

The National Committee of the America First Committee met in Chicago today to discuss an intensified campaign in answer to the president's threat of an undeclared war in violation of the Constitution. Colonel Lindbergh's Des Moines speech was discussed and the National Committee will issue a statement within a few days.

On September 24, the National Committee issued the following statement:

Ever since the nationwide effort to keep America out of war began, the interventionists have sought to hide the real issue by flinging false charges at the America First Committee and at every leader who has spoken out against our entry into the European conflict. The present attack on Colonel Lindbergh is merely another case in point.

Colonel Lindbergh and his fellow members of the America First Committee are not anti-Semitic. We deplore the injection of the race issue into the discussion of war or peace. It is the interventionists who have done this. America First, on the other hand, has invited men and women of every race, religion, and national origin to join this committee, provided only that they are patriotic citizens who put the interest of their country ahead of those of any other nation. We repeat that invitation.

At least 80 per cent of the American people oppose our entry into the war. The America First Committee has supplied to those millions of citizens a leadership which has thus far helped to avert disaster. Consequently, the aim of the war makers is to destroy the America First Committee.

Behind a smokescreen of groundless charges this nation is being led to war in violation of the Constitution of the United States.

There is but one real issue—the issue of war. From this issue we will not be diverted. We will carry on the fight until it is won.

So much for the public record. What went on behind the scenes?

When within less than twenty four hours after delivery of the speech at Des Moines it became clear that this was a cause célèbre, the America First leaders decided to sit tight for a few days while the storm raged to study the public reaction and to issue no statement before the whole matter had been considered at length by the National Committee. The members of the National Committee who knew Colonel Lindbergh personally felt that he was not anti-Semitic. The problem was to handle the matter with the maximum of fairness to the antiwar cause, to the America First Committee, to Colonel Lindbergh, and to the truth.

A number of chapter chairmen wired or wrote to the Chicago headquarters asking for a lead from the National Committee. On September 15 the following wire was dispatched to all chapters:

It is possible that newspapers will request your views on Colonel Lindbergh's Des Moines speech.

It is important that America First Committee chapters throughout the country adopt a uniform attitude. Therefore urge you await statement of National Committee which will consider matter thoroughly meeting Thursday the 16th.

The full text of the Lindbergh speech was sent to all chapters with an urgent note that it is "of utmost importance that it be carefully read by all chapter officials and as many members as possible."

A careful record was kept of mail received at national headquarters commenting on the speech. Analysis showed that of those writing, 89 percent supported Colonel Lindbergh's views and 11 percent were in disagreement.

Tentative plans for a Washington mass meeting at which Colonel Lindbergh was to have been a headline speaker (which had got to the stage of hiring a hall) were canceled.

The National Committee met in Chicago on September 18 with the following members present: General Wood, Dr. A.J. Carlson, Mrs. Bennett Champ [Miriam] Clark, Mrs. Janet Ayer Fairbank, John T. Flynn, Clay Judson, Colonel Charles Lindbergh, Mrs. Alice Roosevelt Longworth, George N. Peek, Amos R.E. Pinchot, [and] R. Douglas Stuart, Jr.

Colonel Lindbergh had written the outline of the speech six months before
he delivered it, believing that sooner or later its subject must be brought out
in the open for frank discussion. To him, the question was not, "Are you or
are you not anti-Semitic?" but rather, "Is Jewish influence leading us toward
war?" He had made the speech on September 11 because he believed the country was close to war, and he felt he must issue a warning while it might still
be effective and before war clamped down on freedom of speech. At the September 18 meeting, he proposed to the National Committee that he issue a
public statement making clear that at Des Moines he had spoken for himself
alone and not for America First.

These were some of the considerations voiced by members of the National
Committee during the eight-hour discussion:

1. America First had never followed the practice of asking that its speakers
submit their manuscripts in advance—it was clear from the outset that men
and women who spoke on America First platforms would differ among themselves in their analyses of the problem of keeping the country out of war. The
situation would have been intolerable if every speech had to be approved in
advance. This tacit—if unspoken—agreement implied that if America First had
enough confidence in its speakers to sponsor them without prior approval of
their speeches, it would stand by what they said. No one of the National Committee or staff had been apprised officially or unofficially in advance of the
delivery of the Des Moines speech of its contents.

2. The text of Colonel Lindbergh's remarks was not anti-Semitic; he had not
criticized the Jews on grounds of race or religion; he had not advocated dis-
crimination of any kind against the Jews; his statement showed complete understanding of any Jewish desire for the crushing of the persecutors of their
race. There was no more impropriety in saying that Jewish people were interventionist than in applying the same term to the president or the British, or
the Dutch. No group in a democracy is entitled to immunity from criticism. It
was hard to believe that any group in America could be regarded as occupying
a position where its attitude on any public question should be unmentionable,
and that anyone who did mention them should be accused of trying to incite
prejudice. Colonel Lindbergh did not create anti-Semitism in the 1941 struggle
between interventionists and noninterventionists. He had described it and personally disavowed it.

3. The barrage of criticism of Colonel Lindbergh's speech in general was not
leveled at the colonel's statements of facts, but *at his saying them*. The colonel's
critics might have made a case on the basis of facts since there was disagreement
as to the proportionate number of Jews who were for intervention. On the one
hand, Dr. Jerome Frank, eminent Jewish author, in his *Saturday Evening Post*
article of December 6, 1941, declared that Jews in America were no more nor
no less interventionist than the United States population as a whole:

[T]he views of the overwhelming majority of Jews concerning intervention are not
Jewish. Their views on that subject are American. . . . [U]nder the impact of the amazing

Nazi victories the attitudes of many Americans have changed. Just so have those of many American Jews.

On the other hand, Dr. Anton J. Carlson, widely known, much-respected professor of physiology at the University of Chicago, said,

> I have seen no statistics on the question but of the Jews of my acquaintance 90 to 95 per cent are for United States participation in the present war, particularly since hostilities started between Russia and Germany. Before that time many Jews of Russian extraction were hardened opponents towards entrance into this war.

The one criticism of Colonel Lindbergh's speech on the basis of fact that cropped up more that once was his statement regarding "their large ownership and influence in our motion pictures, our press, our radio, and our government." It was noted that he had not dealt in percentages, that a distinction could be made between quantitative and qualitative influence.*

4. It was regretted that more Jewish people had not spoken out in opposition to intervention. America First had steadily believed that a sizeable proportion of the Jews were noninterventionist; it had sought Jewish spokesmen of the noninterventionist point of view. If the quarrel with Colonel Lindbergh's remarks was that their *effect* was anti-Semitic, in all fairness should it not also be said that the failure of Jewish leaders to speak out against intervention had the *effect* of implying that Jews were not against intervention?

Several times stories were recalled of Jewish patriots of 1776 like Robert Morris and Haym Solomon who had identified themselves for all time with the clear course of American independence. They had stripped themselves to finance the war of the Revolution so as to achieve an independence for America.

5. The interventionist press and organization leaders were making capital of the incident in order to discredit the entire noninterventionist movement. They were exploiting the Jews for the purpose of promoting the interventionist point of view.

A prominent interventionist lecturer was reported to have said privately in Washington, "You know this uproar on our side against Lindbergh on account of his Des Moines speech about the Jews is largely synthetic—a lot of our crowd has been saying the same thing as Lindbergh."

The belief that interventionists were taking advantage of the situation was encouraged by the knowledge of specific anti-Semitic actions[9] by individuals connected with interventionist organizations.

"One hundred clubs and hotel foyers," said the *Christian Century* editorially, "rang with denouncement of Lindbergh on the morning after his Des Moines speech—clubs and hotels barring their doors to Jews."†

---

* In fact, Jewish moguls were reluctant to make interventionist films; the British were far more responsible for propaganda films. See Kauffman, *America First!*, pp. 85–99; and Gore Vidal, *Screening History* (Cambridge, MA: Harvard University Press, 1992).

† "Forbidden Theme," *Christian Century* (September 24, 1941), pp. 1167–9.

Out of the day's discussion the National Committee members came to several conclusions:

1. They were completely satisfied that Colonel Lindbergh was not anti-Semitic; they believed that he had spoken out of his desire to save the Jews from postwar victimization exactly as he had stated. (Someone recalled that when he and Mrs. Lindbergh turned their Sourland Mountain, New Jersey, home over to an organization for the benefit of children in 1934, they wrote into the charter a provision that it should be used without regard to religion, race, or creed.) A Negro leader (member of a race always sensitive to evidences of race prejudice) wrote that he had had "several level-headed colored men" read Colonel Lindbergh's speech and they agreed that it "shows no hostility whatsoever for the Jews, but rather that he is their friend and is speaking frankly with them." The America First Committee was confidentially advised that at the meeting of a well-known liberal organization called to draw up a statement deploring the anti-Semitic effect of Colonel Lindbergh's speech (which was released to the press), the twenty-five people present, including four Jews, agreed without dissent that the speech itself was not anti-Semitic although they believed it had liberated anti-Semitic forces.

2. Loyalty to the purpose for which America First had been created—keeping the country out of war—and to Colonel Lindbergh demanded that the America First Committee and the colonel present a united front, regardless of any difference of opinion regarding the wisdom of referring to the Jews as a separate group.

3. If the America First Committee were to issue a "provocative" statement it would only furnish ammunition to the interventionists and prolong the altercation, dissipating the energies and attention not only of leaders of the America First Committee but of the general public on an issue that for the moment must be secondary to the transcendent imperative of keeping the country out of war.

4. Any reference to Jews as a group opened up a question that was too complicated for sane public evaluation in time of crisis. As Jerome Frank wrote, "A crisis like the present augments all the hates, fears, and suspicions latent in any society."

It was better to say nothing that would fan the flame of discussion because discussion only intensified feeling. The issue that Colonel Lindbergh touched, said the *Christian Century* editorially, "is so superheated with prejudice and fear that any articulation of it opens up an abyss of social possibility before which all but the stoutest or most callous will shrink."

"You see," wrote a friend of America First, a man of national prominence,

It isn't a question of merely the honesty and directness of one's motives, as they might be understood in normal times; it is a question of one's skill and willingness to face abnormal situations and to deal with them so as to do the maximum of good and minimum of harm for one's own cause.

So the America First Committee issued a statement that was recognized by those subscribing to it as a compromise, a statement that had been diluted to the point of weakness, because it was the best solution for all concerned.

It was felt by the members present that official action should not be taken on the matter without consulting the absentee members of the committee. The tentative statement agreed upon by those present was sent to absentee members. Within the week the statement had been revised along the lines suggested by absentee members and was issued to the press on September 24.

The following letter went to all chapter chairmen on September 23:

In one or more attempts to divert the attention of Americans from the issue of peace or war, the war promoters have sunk to a new low level. They have deliberately raised the false issue of anti-Semitism.

Let us nail down this false charge now for the willful fraud that it is.

In an effort to discredit Colonel Lindbergh, and through him the vast majority of American people opposed to our entry in the war, the war party by twisting and distorting what Colonel Lindbergh said at Des Moines, have tried to label that address as anti-Semitic. Although our speakers state their own views and not necessarily those of the committee, we challenge anyone to find one anti-Semitic sentence in it.

Though the charges are baseless, they are nevertheless dangerous. There are doubtless some members of the public who have been misled. It is not unlikely that certain elements which seek to promote racial and religious intolerance, may mistakenly conclude that they will now be welcomed in the ranks of America First.

Careful as we have been, we must now scrutinize each membership application with re-doubled care. We must continue to keep our membership rolls clear of those who seek to promote racial and religious intolerance. That is the American way—that is the America First way.

As in the past, we welcome to our ranks all patriotic Americans, whatever their race, color or creed.

The principles of the America First Committee remain unchanged. We believe that democracy and tolerance can best be preserved by staying out of Europe's war. Let no one distract us from that fundamental belief.

There was one resignation from the National Committee directly traceable to Colonel Lindbergh's speech, that of Kathryn Lewis, daughter of John L. Lewis. Merle Miller,* chairman of the Indianapolis chapter, and Herbert K. Hyde, chairman of the Oklahoma City chapter, both issued statements denouncing the speech.

PUBLICIZING CONTRIBUTIONS

On New Year's Day 1941, the *New York Herald-Tribune* invited the America First Committee, the Committee to Defend America by Aiding the Allies, and

---

* This is not Merle Miller the journalist who compiled the best-selling *Plain Speaking: An Oral Biography of Harry S Truman* (1974).

the No Foreign War Committee to publish the names of their financial backers so the public would know who was "putting up the cash" for their respective campaigns. The Committee to Defend America responded with a list on January 9; the No Foreign War Committee refused; the America First Committee took the position that it could not release the names of its contributors without first securing their permission, but that the records were open at any time to an authorized government agency.

During the period while America First was corresponding with its contributors to secure permission for publication of the list, it was criticized by the *Herald-Tribune* and challenged by the Committee to Defend America, the implication being that failure to produce the list without delay was tantamount to an admission that its contributors were open to suspicion.

At the first meeting (January 14) of the National Committee of America First following the *Herald-Tribune's* invitation to publish the list, the matter was discussed. The minutes of the meeting report,

The question of the release of names for a story for the *Herald-Tribune* on contributors to the committee was discussed. It was agreed that we should not release any such names, but that the Director should write to the contributors and if they consented, there would be no objection to the committee's releasing their names.

Accordingly, on January 30 Mr. Stuart wrote the following letter to all contributors of more than $100:

The *New York Herald-Tribune* has asked this Committee for the names of those persons who have made contributions of $100.00 or more and for the amounts contributed.

The Committee to Defend America by Aiding the Allies has made their figures available. It is good public relations for us to do the same.

After consideration, the Board of Directors, at a meeting on January 21, decided that these names should be released, upon securing the approval of the individual contributors.

However, since in some communities the issue of "war or peace" has become so surcharged with emotion, we felt that, in all fairness to our contributors, we should ask their individual permission for release of their names.

I would greatly appreciate securing your permission to use your name in the near future.

Within twenty-four hours after the letters had been mailed from Chicago, several anxious contributors telephoned the national office insisting that under no circumstances could their names be given out, that intolerable business and social pressure would be the result.

In the exchange of somewhat caustic statements with the Committee to Defend America over publication of the lists, one America First release had said that in some communities, interventionists "have hounded and smeared patriotic Americans who oppose a war policy. Business and social pressures are brought to bear within the communities. We will protect these contributors as best we can. Naturally, however, our complete list is always available and open to any authorized government group."

General Wood, in a letter answering the query of an America First member why the full lists could not be published, wrote,

As far as the National Committee and its members are concerned, we are perfectly willing to make this list open. However, any Committee such as ours, has an implied agreement with its subscribers that the names are not to be made public without their consent and a great many of them have written us informing us that they do not want their names published. Of course if an authorized Government Agent, acting under law would request the list, it would be furnished. In view of the smear campaign, particularly in the east, you can readily see it would be unjustified were we to give out this list. We have a few Jewish contributors who favor our cause, while most Jews oppose us, therefore, these contributors would be in an uncomfortable position if their names were made known. Then too, there are subscribers whose business partners and business associates are on the other side.

A letter from an active America First worker will indicate the type of pressure that prompted the committee's position in withholding the names of contributors who did not authorize their publication:

On or about April 24, the Chief Engineer called me into his office and told me he had a complaint regarding some literature of the Committee that I had mailed out a couple days previous; I assured him that none of this work had been done on company time.

On May 1, the Manager of Engineering and Operations, stopped to talk to me about design of one of the buildings that was awaiting his decision. He told me that he had something very serious to talk about—the pressure was being put on regarding my activity in the America First—Washington insisted that I must either give up the Chairmanship and drop out of the America First or resign from my position with the company. That it appeared that Lindbergh's resignation had made the Administration sore and they were after anyone who belonged to the America First Organization. The Chief Engineer, who was present, explained that he had spoken to me severely about it some days ago—but the Manager said this was something that had just come through from Official Army Headquarters, and they were putting on plenty of heat about it.

They hoped I would be wise and give up the organization as they were well pleased with my work, and would hate to lose me.

On March 12, the *Herald-Tribune* published the list furnished by America First, carrying the names of slightly fewer than two-thirds of its contributors of $100 or more. Forty-five names were withheld by request. The list showed that as of February 20, $118,906.21 had been contributed by 12,343 supporters, an average of $9.63. The Committee to Defend America list, released by the *Herald-Tribune* a few days earlier, showed total contributions up to January 8 of $324,459.39 from 14,619 donors, an average contribution of $22.20.

($60,463.38 more had been contributed to the Committee to Defend America by March 8.)

NOTES

1. Mrs. Bennett [Miriam] Clark, wife of the Missouri senator and chairman of the Washington chapter, was moved to make the following statement:

The smear of the America First Committee, undertaken by the Department of Justice will fade into nothing except a cheap trick on the part of the Department itself.

The rotten egg technique has finally reached Washington, with eggs at sixty cents a dozen.

The ordinary procedure accompanying a grand jury investigation is for the facts first to be ascertained in secret and press releases to follow. In this instance the story was given to certain newspapers before the facts were established, which procedure is actually illegal.

If the Department wishes to operate in such a manner that is the Department's business. In the last war the Department of Justice stubbed its toe and bids fair to be treading a devious path this time.

So far as the America First Committee is concerned, the government is welcome at any time to examine our files. The Committee has always been on the "up and up" and always will be. Since the government has never availed itself of this opportunity, it is assumed that the Government appreciates the integrity of this Committee.

The day will come when all propaganda—German, British, Russian and all kinds—will be investigated. The America First Committee will come out all in one piece and with a record that perhaps governmental agencies will envy.

The America First Committee desires at all times to cooperate with the Government in obtaining any information which will disclose the use of any foreign funds to influence public opinion. This goes for fascist, communist or any other subversive influences.

The Government preaches unity, the Attorney General talks free speech, while the Department of Justice lays a rotten egg.

(*Washington Times-Herald*, September 27, 1941)

2. Dear Mr. Hauck:

I have your letter of July 25 asking my support for distributing a book called "We Must Save the Republic" by Stephen A. Day.

I do not, of course have any knowledge of your organization save that I have seen its name on one or two pamphlets which have come to me. However, I am informed that your organization is a German-supported propaganda enterprise and that you are registered as such. While I do not deny the right of any country to present its case in America I have condemned the activities of all the warring countries—Great Britain and Germany—for their various kinds of propaganda to involve America one way or another in the existing European quarrel. The America First Committee is opposed to America entering the war, but purely upon grounds touching the interests of America and not because of any sympathy with the objectives of those nations against whom the British are fighting.

Of course I have no evidence that your concern can be justly charged with the criticism which I have named and I do not, therefore, wish to do you an injustice. I am told, however, that the facts about your organization have been printed in the newspapers. I feel, therefore, that before our Committee could collaborate with you in any way it would have to be assured of the falsity of these criticisms and of the complete American character of your organization.

Yours very truly,
John T. Flynn

Dear Mr. Flynn:

Thank you very much for your letter of September 4. Although we had no intention of having our books look as if they were sponsored by the America First Committee, our use of the motto "A Flanders Hall America First book" may have given a few people such an impression.

About four weeks ago we turned over all publication rights of WE MUST SAVE THE REPUBLIC to its author, Congressman Stephen A. Day,* and began withdrawing from the market all copies of the book bearing our imprint. I also wish to assure you that we shall not use the aforementioned motto on any of our future publications.

I again wish to assure you of my own Americanism and that of my firm.

Very sincerely yours,
S.H. Hauck, President
FLANDERS HALL

3. Weekly background news service edited by Sidney Hertzberg, published in New York.
4. New York *Daily News*, May 23, 1941.
5. New York *Daily News*, June 26, 1941.
6. The letter read,

Will you permit an humble American born in Russia, of Jewish parentage, to give expression of gratitude to the noble service your Committee is performing in holding up the light of reason and unbiased judgment amidst gathering clouds of emotion and passion. Those of us, and I believe there are millions, who feel that our trust and confidence was betrayed by "campaign oratory" must not allow ourselves to be again swayed and confused by the oratory and side quips of the hired "attorney for the defense." Let us read and re-read the farsighted words—aye, prophetic words of that courageous and robust American, Col. Charles A. Lindbergh. Where, in the name of American good sense, can we find even the slightest suggestion of race prejudice in all his talks or writings. There may be honest differences of opinion as to whether we should move toward or threaten to go to war, but can anyone with reason and good sight deny that the three groups' names are among those most important in "pressing this country toward war"? Why single out the Jewish group? Are they not classed equally with the very respectable British and Administration groups? As a matter of fact, Col. Lindbergh is sympathetic with the feelings and natural concern of the American Jews for their brethren in Germany. He holds that they, as also the British, have real cause to be concerned and are more consistent and sincere in the pursuit of their policies. The progressive war propaganda of the Administration, with its continually increasing governing power, stands alone apparently uninfluenced by any compunction of a violation of trust or by any natural feeling for the immediate welfare of its own people, particularly the youth of America. Col. Lindbergh but repeats wisely the lesson Israel ought to have learned through the teachings of her prophets and philosophers and in the experience she has gone through during the many centuries of persecution in various lands. Are the diseases, the materialistic concepts, the race and class prejudices in Europe today less contagious than the flu or the emotional and economic diseases carried over from Europe during the last war?

Mark well these classic words of Lindbergh: "Tolerance is a virtue that depends upon peace and strength. History shows that it cannot survive war and devastation." It is no discredit to the Jewish people that a large "ownership and influence in our Motion Picture Industry" is in their hands, but there is danger in the possibility of allowing their personal feelings and natural concern to influence their own judgment and the judgment of the American people as a whole. It is no discredit to the man in a jury panel who is eliminated from jury service because of personal interest in the case. (Incidentally, it is an old truism that increase of power for any party or group demands an

* Day was an Illinois Republican.

increased sense of moral responsibility to the whole. A little self-imposed timely house-cleaning along several lines may save some real embarrassment from the outside that is sure to come in the near future to our movie magnates and directors, and their pious defenders—Jews or Gentiles.)

Is it prejudice on the part of some of our representative men who see, for instance, self-interested bias in a labor group, capitalistic group, or a governmental group? As a nation, we have not yet overcome our European heredity of group bias—racial, religious, and economic. We are sick, suffering from lack of coordination economically, mentally and emotionally. We are going through a transitional period threatening the very heart of America. How dare we pursue steps that ultimately must lead us into the very maelstrom of hatred and passion? Our urgent duty now is to stabilize our emotions, to rationalize our thinking, to put our own house in order, to gather our moral, mental and physical strength, that our commanding voice may be heard and obeyed. How often have we witnessed one man with moral courage and strong voice stopping a panic-stricken mob from destroying itself and others?

It is the silent inner prayer of a hundred million Americans that the leaders of the America First Committee and others active in the effort to keep this country out of war, do not permit themselves to be confused by side issues and differences of opinion as to what Col. Lindbergh, Senator Wheeler, Clark, Nye or Johnson may or may not say, as individuals, but all continue perseveringly united on fundamental principles in the supreme effort now necessary to save this nation from impending disaster, holding it to its manifest destiny as a Republic of Brotherhood and a haven for the heavy laden and oppressed.

Yours for America as a Whole,
"One and Indivisible,"
(signed) Hyman Lischner

7. The resolution adopted December 3, 1940, by the National Committee read, "Resolved, that since Mr. Henry Ford has been unable to give any time or attention to the work of the Committee, and because the Committee could not be sure that from time to time Mr. Ford's views were consistent with the official views of the Committee, that from this date he should be dropped as a member."

8. The full text of the Lindbergh speech follows:

It is now two years since this latest European war began. From that day in September, 1939, until the present moment, there has been an ever-increasing effort to force the United States into the conflict. That effort has been carried on by foreign interests and by a small minority of our own people, but it has been so successful that, today, our country stands on the verge of war.

At this time, as the war is about to enter its third winter, it seems appropriate to review the circumstances that have led us to our present position. Why are we on the verge of war? Was it necessary for us to become so deeply involved? Who is responsible for changing our national policy from one of neutrality and independence to one of entanglement in European affairs?

Personally, I believe there is no better argument against our intervention than a study of the causes and developments of the present war. I have often said that if the true facts and issues were placed before the American people, there would be no danger of our involvement.

Here I would like to point out to you a fundamental difference between the groups who advocate foreign war and those who believe in an independent destiny for America. If you will look back over the record you will find that those of us who oppose intervention have constantly tried to clarify facts and issues; while the interventionists have tried to hide facts and confuse issues.

We ask you to read what we said last month, last year, and even before the war began. Our record is open and clear, and we are proud of it. We have not led you on by subterfuge and propaganda. We have not resorted to "steps short of" anything in order to take the American people where they did not want to go. What we said before the elections we say "again, and again, and again" today. And we will not tell you tomorrow that it was "just campaign oratory."

Have you ever heard an interventionist, or a British agent, or a member of the administration in Washington, ask you to go back and study a record of what they have said since the war started? Are these self-styled defenders of democracy willing to put the issue of war to a vote of our people?

Do you find these crusaders for foreign freedoms advocating the freedom of speech, or the removal of censorship here in our own country?

The subterfuge and propaganda that exist in our country is obvious on every side. Tonight I shall try to pierce through a portion of it to the naked facts which lie beneath.

When this war started in Europe, it was clear that the American people were solidly opposed to entering it. Why shouldn't we be? We had the best defensive position in the world; we had a tradition of independence from Europe; and the one time we did take part in a European war left European problems unsolved, and debts to America unpaid.

National polls showed that when England and France declared war on Germany in 1939, less than 10 per cent of our population favored a similar course for America.

But there were various groups of people here and abroad whose interests and beliefs necessitated the involvement of the United States in the war. I shall point out some of these groups tonight, and outline their methods of procedure. In doing this, I must speak with utmost frankness, for in order to counteract their efforts, we must know exactly who they are.

The three most important groups who have been pressing this country toward war are the British, the Jewish and the Roosevelt administration. Behind these groups, but of lesser importance, are a number of capitalists, Anglophiles, and intellectuals who believe that their future and the future of mankind, depends upon the domination of the British empire.

Add to these the communistic groups who were opposed to intervention until a few weeks ago, and I believe I have named the major war agitators, not those sincere but misguided men and women who, confused by misinformation and frightened by propaganda, follow the lead of the war agitators.

As I have said, these war agitators comprise only a small minority of our people; but they control a tremendous influence.

Against the determination of the American people to stay out of war, they have marshaled the power of their propaganda, their money, and their patronage.

Let us consider these groups, one at a time. First, the British. It is obvious and perfectly understandable that Great Britain wants the United States in the war on her side. England is now in a desperate position. Her population is not large enough, and her armies are not strong enough to invade the continent of Europe and win the war she declared against Germany. Her geographical position is such that she cannot win the war by the use of aviation alone, regardless of how many planes we send her. Even if America entered the war it is improbable that the Allied armies could invade Europe and overcome the Axis powers.

But one thing is certain. If England can draw this country into the war she can shift to our shoulders a large portion of the responsibility for waging it, and for paying its cost. As you all know, we were left with the debts of the last European war and unless we are more cautious in the future than we have been in the past we will be left with the debts of the present one.

If it were not for her hope that she can make us responsible for the war financially, as well as militarily, I believe England would have negotiated a peace in Europe many months ago, and be better off for doing so.

England has devoted and will continue to devote every effort to get us into the war. We know that she spent huge sums of money in this country during the last war in order to involve us. Englishmen have written books about the cleverness of its use. We know that England is spending great sums of money for propaganda in America during the present war.

If we were Englishmen we would do the same. But our interest is first in America and, as Americans, it is essential for us to realize the effort that British interests are making to draw us into their war.

The second major group mentioned is the Jewish. It is not difficult to understand why Jewish people desire the overthrow of Nazi Germany. The persecution they suffered in Germany would be sufficient to make bitter enemies of any race. No person with a sense of the dignity of mankind can condone the persecution of the Jewish race in Germany. But no person of honesty and vision can look on their pro-war policy here today without seeing the dangers involved in such a policy, both for us and for them.

Instead of agitating for war, the Jewish groups in this country should be opposing it in every possible way, for they will be among the first to feel its consequences. Tolerance is a virtue that depends upon peace and strength. History shows that it cannot survive war and devastation. A few farsighted Jewish people realize this and stand opposed to intervention. But the majority still do not. Their greatest danger to this country lies in their large ownership and influence in our motion pictures, our press, our radio, and our government.

I am not attacking either the Jewish or the British people. Both races, I admire. But I am saying that the leaders of both the British and the Jewish races, for reasons which are as understandable from their viewpoint as they are inadvisable from ours, for reasons which are not American, wish to involve us in the war. We cannot blame them for looking out for what they believe to be their own interests, but we also must look out for ours. We cannot allow the natural passions and prejudices of other peoples to lead our country to destruction.

The Roosevelt administration is the third powerful group which has been carrying this country toward war. Its members have used the war emergency to obtain a third presidential term for the first time in American history. They have used the war to add unlimited billions to a debt which was already the highest we had ever known. And they have used the war to justify the restrictions of congressional power, and the assumption of dictatorial procedures on the part of the President and his appointees.

The power of the Roosevelt administration depends upon the maintenance of a wartime emergency. The prestige of the Roosevelt administration depends upon the success of Great Britain to whom the President attached his political future at a time when most people thought that England and France would easily win the war. The danger of the Roosevelt administration lies in its subterfuge. While its members have promised us peace they have led us to war heedless of the platform upon which they were elected.

In selecting these three groups as the major agitators for war, I have included only those whose support is essential to the war party. If any one of these groups—the British, the Jewish, or the administration—stops agitating for war, I believe there will be little danger of our involvement. I do not believe that any two of them are powerful enough to carry this country to war without the support of the third. And to these three, as I have said, all other war groups are of secondary importance.

When hostilities commenced in Europe, in 1939, it was realized by these groups that the American people had no intention of entering the war. They knew it would be worse than useless to ask us for a declaration of war at that time. But they believed that this country could be enticed into the war in very much the same way we were enticed into the last one. They planned, first, to prepare the United States for foreign war under the guise of American defense; second, to involve us in the war, step by step, without our realization; third, to create a series of incidents which would force us into the actual conflict. These plans were, of course, to be covered and assisted by the full power of their propaganda.

Our theaters soon became filled with plays portraying the glory of war. Newsreels lost all semblance of objectivity. Newspapers and magazines began to lose advertising if they carried antiwar articles. A smear campaign was instituted against individuals who opposed intervention. The terms fifth columnist, traitor, nazi, anti-Semitic were thrown ceaselessly at any one who dared to suggest that it was not to the best interests of the United States to enter the war.

Men lost their jobs if they were frankly antiwar. Many others dared no longer speak. Before long, lecture halls that were open to advocates of war were closed to speakers who opposed it. A fear campaign was inaugurated. We were told that aviation, which has held the British fleet off the continent of Europe, made America more vulnerable than ever before to invasion. Propaganda was in full swing.

There was no difficulty in obtaining billions of dollars for arms under the guise of defending America. Our people stood united on a program of defense. Congress passed appropriation after appropriation for guns and planes and battleships, with the approval of the overwhelming majority of our citizens. That a large portion of these appropriations was to be used to build arms for Europe, we did not learn until later. (That was another step.)

To use a specific example; in 1939 we were told that we should increase our air corps to a total of 5,000 planes. Congress passed the necessary legislation. A few months later, the administration told us that the United States should have at least 50,000 planes for our national safety. But almost as fast as fighting planes were turned out from our factories, they were sent abroad, although our own air corps was in the utmost need of new equipment.

Today, two years after the start of war, the American army has only a few hundred thoroughly modern bombers and fighters, less, in fact, than Germany is able to produce in a single month. Ever since its inception, our arms program has been laid out for the purpose of carrying on the war in Europe far more than for the purpose of building an adequate defense for America.

Now at the same time we were being prepared for a foreign war it was necessary, as I have said, to involve us in the war. This was accomplished under that now famous phrase, "steps short of war." England and France would win if the United States would only repeal its arms embargo and sell munitions for cash, we were told. And then a familiar refrain began, a refrain that marked every step we took toward war for many months . . . " [T]he best way to defend America and keep out of war," we were told, was "by aiding the allies."

First, we agreed to sell arms to Europe; next, we agreed to loan arms to Europe; then, we agreed to patrol the ocean for Europe; then, we occupied a European island in the war zone. Now we have reached the verge of war.

The war groups have succeeded in the first two of their three major steps into war. The greatest armament program in our history is under way. We have become involved in the war from practically every standpoint except actual shooting. Only the creation of sufficient "incidents" yet remains and you see the first of these already taking place, according to plan—a plan that was never laid before the American people for their approval.

Men and women of Iowa: Only one thing holds this country from war today. That is the rising opposition of the American people. Our system of democracy and representative government is on test today as it has never been before. We are on the verge of a war in which the only victor would be chaos and prostration. We are on the verge of a war for which we are still unprepared, and for which no one has offered a feasible plan for victory—a war which cannot be won without sending our soldiers across the ocean to force a landing on a hostile coast against armies stronger than our own.

We are on the verge of war, but it is not yet too late to stay out. It is not yet too late to show that no amount of money, or propaganda, or patronage, can force a free and independent people into war against its will. It is not yet too late to retrieve and to maintain the independent American destiny that our forefathers established in this new world.

The entire future of America rests upon our shoulders. It depends upon our action, our courage, and our intelligence. If you oppose our intervention in this war, now is the time to make your voice heard. Help us to organize these meetings, and write to your representatives in Washington.

I tell you that the last stronghold of democracy and representative government in this country is in our House of Representatives and our Senate. There we can still make our will known. And if we, the American people, do that, independence and freedom will continue to live among us, and there will be no foreign war.

9. The following letter written by Dr. Gregory Mason, head of the Department of Journalism at the College of the City of New York and chairman of the Stamford-Greenwich-Norwalk America First chapter, to Thomas Chubb, chairman of the Greenwich Committee to Defend America by Aiding the Allies, revealed one instance of anti-Semitism on the part of the interventionists:

Replying to your letter of the 14th, I considered Lindbergh's whole speech as not anti-Semitic although small parts of it repeatedly quoted by the pro-war papers may sound so when lifted from their context. All fair-minded persons know that such emphasis on isolated parts of a speech without consideration of the whole is unjust.

In my opinion Lindbergh's mistake in his Des Moines address was a mistake of omission. Although he indicated that there are other groups in this country than "the British, the Jewish and the Roosevelt Administration" which are more pro-war than most Americans he did not name them. I should have named the Czecho-Slavak [sic], Polish, Norwegian, Danish, Dutch, Belgian, French, Greek, Chinese, Yugo-Slav, Russian (have I overlooked any?) as elements in our population which have more reason to hate Hitler than the majority of Americans because their brothers in Europe have been attacked by him or his allies. Of course the Jews, who have been specially singled out by Nazi cruelty, have the best reason of all. As Lindbergh rightly said, "No person with a sense of the dignity of mankind can condone the persecution of the Jewish race suffered in Germany."

I assure you that the Stamford-Greenwich-Norwalk Chapter of the America First Committee stands by its resolutions condemning anti-Semitism which were published in Fairfield County papers *before* Lindbergh spoke at Des Moines. I assure you that we believe that Lindbergh's Des Moines speech was not anti-Semitic, and that we believe that Lindbergh, and Hoover after him, were wise in begging Americans whose European relatives have suffered from Hitler's persecutions to try (swallowing their very understandable resentments) to be Americans first and Polish, French, Greek, Norwegian, Jewish or what-not second. Only so can we maintain the unity and equilibrium which our country sorely needs.

To me the most despicable of human failings is hypocrisy. A great deal of hypocrisy has been evidenced by smug citizens in our midst who sounded off to condemn Lindbergh on the basis of a hasty reading of two or three sentences lifted from his Des Moines address. Many such citizens *practice* anti-Semitism every day of their lives.

Many of the individual supporters of the Committee to Defend America by Aiding the Allies and of the Fight for Freedom Committee and of other interventionist organizations belong to exclusive social clubs from which Jews are strictly barred. Pick at random any local newspaper report of the attendance at a Bundling for Britain or Parceling for Pinks party, at a rummage sale for the R.A.F. or a Wavell Ball, and you'll find a very high percentage of names of wealthy snobs who would shun a Jew socially as they would shun a leper.

Inasmuch as it is people of this sort, many of them prominent supporters of your Committee, who have raised this unjust outcry against Lindbergh and the noninterventionists, let's have this whole despicable anti-Semitic issue thoroughly aired. I have plenty of ammunition but my space is short, so I'll specify only two organizations now.

1. The New Canaan Country Club is definitely anti-Semitic. Not long ago my father and mother, Mr. and Mrs. Daniel Gregory Mason, rented their New Canaan house to a Jewish refugee from Germany. This person bears a name famous in music, being descended from a composer whose works are played all over the world. The chairman of an important committee of the New Canaan Country Club went out of his way to warn my father and mother that their new tenant would not be allowed to enter that club. Influential members of this club support your organization, Mr. Chubb, and other interventionist organizations now calling Lindbergh "anti-Semitic."

2. Even though you have lived in Greenwich a very short time you must know that the Greenwich Real Estate Board opposes renting or selling houses to Jews in the "exclusive" part of Greenwich from which was subscribed in a few weeks enough money to buy England six ambulances (although these same "socialites" let Greenwich itself get along with a police wagon as an "ambulance" for years) and from which comes the loudest local denunciation of Lindbergh.

In conclusion, I hereby challenge you, Mr. Chubb, to a public debate at a time and place to be arranged at mutual convenience on this subject:

"Resolved, That the Committee to Defend America by Aiding the Allies is riddled with Anti-Semitism."

Following your example, I am releasing this letter to the newspapers. I am asking them in fairness to give it the same prominence they gave your letter to me, and if possible to publish all of it. If they garble its meaning by cutting or editing, as some of them garbled Lindbergh's speech, I shall notify my attorney, Morris L. Ernst, a Jew, and well known for his espousal of freedom of press and speech.

4

What the Polls Said

The rock-bottom reluctance of the American people to go to war, as over-whelmingly shown by the polls, was the strength of America First.

The nationwide, general public opinion surveys of the American Institute of Public Opinion (headed by Dr. George Gallup), best-known and probably the most influential polls of the time, for two years had shown a noninvolvement majority that never went below 76 percent and in August 1941 went as high as 83 percent.[1]

Editor and Publisher, a newspaper trade magazine, in a survey of the 1,878 daily newspapers listed in its 1941 International Yearbook, found 70.7 percent against immediate United States participation in the war, out of 871 replying.

The New York *Daily News,* taking a poll of every tenth registered voter in the area of its coverage, got 122,802 "no" to 51,507 affirmative answers on the question, "Shall the United States enter the war to help Britain defeat Hitler?"; a percentage of 70.5 opposed.

The *Chicago Tribune,* testing every tenth registered voter in its area on the same question, found 80.79 percent opposed (62,394 out of 76,570).

Polls covering only limited areas showed the same preponderance against involvement in war.

The Kokomo (Indiana) *Tribune,* circulating a blank ballot on the question, "Do you favor the United States entering the war and sending our troops abroad?" turned up 95.65 percent opposed.

The *Indianapolis News* showed 95 percent opposed.

A survey of the adult residents of Boulevard Gardens, private housing de-velopment of 960 families at Woodside, Long Island, revealed 89.3 percent in opposition.

There was evidence that as time went on, the country and the press were becoming more noninterventionist. Following the outbreak of war between Russia and Germany, Dr. Gallup found a 3 percent increase in sentiment against entrance into war, reaching a high of 83 percent in August 1941.

Time magazine, interventionist weekly, on July 14, 1941, reported that on the outbreak of war between Hitler and Stalin, the effect on the United States press was to make it considerably less interventionist. Said *Time,*

Last spring James S. Twohey Associates, analysts of newspaper opinion, calculated that upwards of 65 percent of the U.S. press plumped for more aid to Britain and attacked isolationists. Last week, presumably upset by the spectacle of Germany fighting Russia, some 20 percent of the press had not changed sides but gone to sit on the fence. This left only 53 percent of the press interventionist, against 27 percent definitely isolationist.

Equally striking was the indirect evidence of a new trend of press feeling. Also by the Twohey figures, the editorial comment on Secretary Knox's rip-roaring speech for using the Navy to clear the seas was 53 percent against to 25 percent for, but ex-President Hoover's speech saying that Germany's attack on Russia made the whole argument for the U.S. going to war a "Gargantuan jest" won applause from 50 percent of the press—more than has applauded him in years—and criticism from only 26 percent.

A confidential audience mail report from the National Broadcasting Company on the Town Hall radio debate (May 22, 1941) between President Robert M. Hutchins of the University of Chicago and Colonel William (Wild Bill) Donovan, U.S. Coordinator of Information, on the question, "Should we do whatever is necessary to insure a British victory?" said, "Letters favoring Dr. Hutchins' speech or his side of the debate were five times as numerous as those favoring Colonel Donovan's stand."

THE PUZZLE OF THE POLLS

Along with the public opinion surveys that showed the country overwhelmingly against war, there were polls on questions other than the specific question of war participation but closely related that seemed to contradict flatly Dr. Gallup's findings on the basic question of getting into war. Such polls—the 71 percent pro-convoy poll, for instance—were widely quoted by interventionists.

America First could not ignore the polls unfavorable to its position if it were to accept the favorable evidence. Furthermore, the polls were extremely influential, particularly with members of Congress. The public opinion surveys of the American Institute of Public Opinion (Dr. Gallup's organization) which had been "taking the pulse of democracy" for over five years, enjoyed especially high prestige with men in politics because of its accuracy in predicting election returns.* G.F. Lewis, Jr. found that while many congressmen denied the polls influenced their votes on foreign policy, not less than two-thirds of them probably took the results into consideration in making a choice. From daily asso-

---

* The Gallup Poll had been "penetrated" by British intelligence. See Mahl, *Desperate Deception,* pp. 69–86.

ciation with members of the Senate and the House, America First staff members learned that these men avidly followed the polls. Hardly a day went by that at least one was not quoted in a speech on the floor, or inserted in the *Congressional Record*.

America First was constantly faced with the necessity of interpreting the polls. If the 76 to 83 percent majority constantly turned up by Dr. Gallup on the fundamental question of getting into war was accurate, then the basic concept on which America First functioned—that a majority of the people wanted to stay out of war—was correct. If the evidence of the polls quoted by the interventionists was the whole truth, then America First was following a chimera and was needlessly stirring up the country.

An analysis of several apparently contradictory polls answered any questions America First leaders may have had regarding the soundness of the poll evidence on the basic question of staying out of war. Following is an illustration:

On April 21, 1941, the Public Opinion Institute used the question, "Do you think we should send some of our warships manned with American sailors to Europe to help the British?" Twenty-seven percent were reported favorable, and 67 percent opposed.

Just two days later, on April 23, the same institute reported on the question, "If it appears certain that Britain will be defeated, would you favor or oppose such convoys?" To that, an almost identical question, the report was favor, 71 percent; oppose, 21 percent.

It hardly seemed possible that public opinion shifted so swiftly that on April 21 the public was 67 percent opposed to convoys and two days later was only 21 percent opposed. It was incredible that 46 percent of the people had altered their conviction overnight. It was difficult to believe that 71 percent favored convoys at a time when the president's reported statement, "Convoys mean shooting and shooting means war," had been thoroughly drummed into the consciousness of the American people.

Obviously, they were one and the same question, with a hairline difference in phrasing. Sending "warships manned with American sailors to help the British" and "using part of our navy" (manned with American sailors) for convoys were identical statements. The difference was that once the whole story was spelled out for the voters in terms of the lives of American sailors, they saw it in a different light.

Besides, on April 26, three days following the 71 percent vote for convoys, the institute had reported on the question, "If you were asked today on the question of the United States entering the war against Germany and Italy, how would you vote—to go to the war, or to stay out of the war?" The vote showed 81 percent voting to stay out.

In the polls on the "periphery" questions such as arming merchant ships [and] convoys, there was a noticeable fluctuation. Over a period of weeks or months the conclusion was inescapable that the popular vote on such questions was at least partly dictated by the most recent events. For instance, on the question of convoys, opinion fluctuated with the number of ship losses: when losses were high, sentiment for convoys grew stronger; when they were low, the percentage for convoys diminished. It was the vote on the fundamental question of going into war or staying out of war that showed the greatest consistency.

In "interpreting" the polls, America First leaders also kept in mind several points raised in connection with the process of poll-taking by public opinion experts.

Dr. Ross Stagner, associate professor of psychology at Dartmouth College, made a special study[2] of all the Gallup poll questions relating to foreign policy from April 1937 to February 1941. His purpose was to discover whether the questions conformed to scientific principles of opinion measurement [and] whether the results agreed with each other and with outside measurements of opinion. He examined 59 questions, chosen because they related specifically to the problem of intervention against Germany.

Professor Stagner found 55 cases of "dubious practice" (introduction of prestige-bearing names or terms, presence of unjustified assumptions in the statement of the question, suggestion of a positive answer). Of the 55, 48 were biases in favor of an interventionist answer; 7 tended to elicit a noninterventionist reply.

THE POLLS AND FOREIGN POLICY

Careful reading of the polls for the pre–Pearl Harbor era is bound to bring up questions regarding the relationship of the poll evidence to the development of U.S. foreign policy. If the country was overwhelmingly opposed to getting into war as the polls showed, since this is a democracy where the majority is supposed to rule, why were the measures that involved increasing risks of war continually successful in Congress? Why did not the popular opposition to involvement in war, consistently expressed in responsible polls, restrain the president—in those areas of action where he could exercise his executive powers without legislative approval—from identification of the United States's interest with the outcome of the war?

The answers are probably to be found in two comments on the "educational" techniques of administration spokesmen and of spokesmen for interventionist groups: (1) Major policy moves proposed or taken by the administration had all been publicized as safeguards to peace, as measures through whose adoption the country was less likely to become involved in war than by failure to adopt them. The Lend-Lease bill, "naval escorts" or convoys, arming merchant ships, were all said to be "peace measures"; there were interventionist spokesmen who went so far as to claim that allowing U.S. merchant ships to go into combat zones was a "measure for peace." Obviously, untold numbers accepted these assurances at their face value. (2) The polls showed clearly that the public wanted to aid Britain to the point of defeating Hitler, and at the same time, to stay out of war. So completely contradictory were these aims, so undeniably antithetical on the basis of any known experience, that the expedient was adopted of telling the public that both were possible: It was maintained over and over again, by official spokesmen and others, that the way to stay out of war was to become a semi-active belligerent; "aid short of war" was the answer.

Thus America First leaders found in the interventionist method of appealing to the public confirmation of their fundamental belief that the country was overwhelmingly against war: If the *interventionists* recognized the preponderance of the stay-out-of-war sentiment over the defeat-Hitler sentiment to the point where they had to represent as peace measures actions that past experience had shown to be war-inciting, then the committee was justified in offering leadership to so large a body of public opinion.

AFC GOES IN FOR POLL-TAKING

Since the results of public opinion polls had great influence with the public and with legislators, the America First Committee early considered moving into the field of public opinion sampling with a great national referendum. As early as February 1941, before the Lend-Lease bill had been written on the statute books, the committee leaders were studying the record of the great English peace ballot of 1935, when 11,500,000 British voters (38 percent of the total electorate) had registered in a gigantic peace ballot overwhelming support for the League of Nations–sanctions point of view.

The essence of the plan, as adapted to this country, was to "let the people speak." The Committee to Defend America by Aiding the Allies would be invited to join in conducting the vote. Dr. Gallup or Elmer Roper, public opinion experts, would be invited to serve as consultants. Contributors who were hesitant about aiding a pressure group might be willing to show their faith in the democratic process by supporting such a project.

The question would be one that dealt with the fundamental issue of peace or war, leaving aside such secondary questions as "aid short of war."

It would give the great mass of individuals a job to do; it would energize the thousands who promoted circulation.

It would accomplish the same results, if conducted on a truly large scale, as the enactment of the Ludlow proposal for a constitutional amendment providing a popular referendum on war,* and as the Nye resolution for an advisory referendum on war; at the same time it avoided the insurmountable opposition to the two proposals—the impossibility of securing congressional approval on strategic grounds.

The ballot-taking process would be organized by cities and by congressional districts. It would be launched in several states representing various shades of opinion, probably in Massachusetts, Illinois, and California.

---

* See Bolt, *Ballots Before Bullets.*

The plan had gone so far that on April 15, Bob Stuart was writing, "At present we are working out a plan to try it in Illinois. We are hoping to get it under way in the very near future."

It was, perhaps, the one project—short of a march on Washington—that aroused the greatest amount of enthusiasm among the greatest number of those who were doing the planning for the organization. And it had to be discarded for practical reasons.

It was clear that to be at all effective the ballot would have to be carried out on a gigantic scale. A ballot that was only semi-successful, that was not really representative, would have been worse than no ballot. Such an undertaking would have been expensive—it was estimated on the basis of the British ballot that it would cost around $200,000. There was nowhere near that amount of money in sight.

There was a question as to whether the country would accept as reliable the results of a ballot circulated in a high-pressure campaign by a crusading organization, and yet if it were turned over to a professional poll-taking organization, not only would it have been very expensive but it would have defeated what was perhaps the most important purpose—offering a task that would energize the noninterventionists. So, regretfully, the project was abandoned.

THE CONGRESSIONAL POLLS

Late in the spring of 1941, America First needed a project. It was hard-pressed for a challenging activity to recommend to its chapters. There was no immediate legislative issue on the horizon. And yet there was an uncomfortable sense that the country was moving closer to the brink of war through actions over which the Congress and the people had no control. While an outpouring of antiwar sentiment had prevented a legislative test on the convoy question, and had resulted in administration assurances that convoys were not being used, many people had a queasy feeling in their bones when they thought of "naval escorts," "naval reconnaissance," [and] "naval patrols."

The polls were showing that when a question was so worded as to make clear the effect of foreign policy moves on individuals, the answers were likely to be preponderantly noninterventionist. At the same time, a growing number of people felt the British were doomed to defeat without our aid. In other words, the "dual personality" aspect of what the public wanted was more pronounced than before.

Something was needed to register the undiminished popular will against involvement in the war. America First needed a job it could get its teeth into.

About this time, General Wood, Bob Stuart, and Richard Moore* had been turning over in their minds and exploring in conversations a plan to urge

---

* Richard Moore later became a broadcast executive and public-relations adviser to Richard Nixon.

congressmen and senators to take polls. Possibly the thought was stimulated by Congressman [Bernard John] Gehrmann's [P-Wis.] poll of his district. The Wisconsin congressman had had reprinted from the *Congressional Record* his brief speech in which he expressed the desire to know what his constituents thought about convoys. He had sent this out over his own frank to thousands of individuals and to most of the newspapers in his district. The response had been excellent; within a short time he had over 6,000 replies.

Late in May, Bob Stuart and Richard Moore made a flying visit to Washington, [and] consulted with several senators and congressmen about the advisability of congressional polls. One of them appeared at a meeting of the noninterventionist bloc on May 28 and outlined the plan.

Several members of Congress were immediately interested and offered to make the experiment in their districts.

The first poll would be taken in the Twenty-sixth District of New York, it was decided, largely for publicity reasons. This was the district in which Franklin Delano Roosevelt voted. This was the district whose most distinguished citizen's foreign policy views were "misrepresented" in Congress by Hamilton Fish.

The plan was to send a ballot to every registered voter in the district, asking him to vote on the following question:

The United States should
Enter the war __
Stay out of the war __

The question was chosen as the simplest, most free from bias, [and] least loaded, and as the question that posed the real issue that faced the people. It was an attempt to steer fairly between the prejudice against British defeat and the prejudice against personal loss if we got into war.

The ballot, which was to be returned to Mr. Fish's office for counting within five days, was accompanied by the following letter, sent in Mr. Fish's franked envelopes with return postage enclosed:

TO THE PEOPLE OF THE TWENTY-SIXTH CONGRESSIONAL DISTRICT:

We are on the brink of war. Congress alone, under the Constitution, may declare war. An undeclared war is an invention and creation of totalitarian nations, and a negation of democratic processes and of our constitutional form of government.

The issue of war or peace is clear-cut. It should be discussed and debated throughout the Nation. It is the greatest issue with which the American people have been confronted since the birth of the Republic. It transcends all political, social and family affiliations.

I have no quarrel with any American citizen who wants to go in or stay out of the war. That is his or her right as a free sovereign American.

As your Representative in Congress, I want to be guided by the thoughtful opinion of my constituents. I am conducting a poll or referendum to the enrolled voters of my District to find out the sentiment of the people on this greatest of all issues, and would appreciate your cooperation by returning the enclosed postcard ballot to me within three days after you receive it.

While the addressing of the ballot was going on in Washington, an America First field man went into the district to arrange for publicity, and to work with a local committee in setting up a rally at which Mr. Fish and some of his colleagues were to speak and to announce the final results.

A group of interventionists, said to be members of the Committee to Defend America by Aiding the Allies and of Bundles for Britain, attempted to force the board of education to withdraw its permission for use of the high school auditorium by an "anti-government organization," but the board voted three to two to allow the meeting to proceed. General Wood promptly wired a telegram of commendation to the board:

I sincerely congratulate the Board of Education of Poughkeepsie upon their insistence that free speech in America shall remain unimpaired. As the President made clear in a recent press conference, we have not yet reached the tragic stage where patriotic Americans are denied their right to be heard.

The voters of the 26th Congressional District of New York, which includes Poughkeepsie, are presently being invited by their Congressional representative, Honorable Hamilton Fish, to express to him through a referendum their views on the question of peace or war. At a time when a splendid democratic experiment like this is being conducted in the area, it would be ironic, indeed, if the President of a great College and the distinguished members of the United States Senate and the House of Representatives should be silenced by a small war minded group.

I sincerely hope that the Poughkeepsie meeting will contribute to the success of Mr. Fish's referendum, and that it will encourage those on both sides to cooperate with his statesmanlike effort to make democracy work at home.

Dr. Henry Noble McCracken, president of Vassar College, who had resigned from the Committee to Defend America, presided. Senator David I. Walsh of Massachusetts and Mrs. Bennett [Miriam] Champ Clark, wife of the Missouri senator and chairman of the Washington America First chapter, spoke. Mr. Fish announced that 90.1 percent had voted against entering the war.

Nationwide publicity resulted when the president, asked by reporters in his press conference if he had received a ballot, indicated "that he would place little reliance on the outcome of such polls." Mrs. Roosevelt also drew attention to the poll by devoting a full "My Day" column—critical, of course—to it.*

Following the successful outcome of the poll in Mr. Fish's district, arrangements were made with three other congressmen to take similar polls in their districts: Congressmen Knute Hill [D] of the Fourth District in Washington,

---

*Eleanor Roosevelt, "Shall There Be a Referendum on War?" ("My Day," June 28, 1941), reprinted in *Courage in a Dangerous World: The Political Writings of Eleanor Roosevelt*, edited by Allida M. Black (New York: Columbia University Press, 1999) pp. 104–5.

Harry Sauthoff [P(rogressive)] of the Second District of Wisconsin, and Paul Shafer [R] of the Third District of Michigan.

The America First Committee was particularly eager for the results of the poll in Congressman Hill's district since the West Coast states were said to be interventionist.

The lead given in Congressman Fish's district was followed by the other three. The results were

Congressman Knute Hill—85.2 percent opposed

Congressman Harry Sauthoff—94.2 percent opposed

Congressman Paul Shafer—93.1 percent opposed

To Congressman Fish's district, 106,000 ballots had been sent; 28 percent were returned. Mr. Hill sent 90,000 and had a 30 percent return. Mr. Sauthoff sent 157,500 and received a 43 percent return. Mr. Shafer sent 135,000, and 34 percent of them came back.

The America First Committee paid the expenses of printing the ballot and letter, of addressing the envelopes, and of return postage. Altogether it spent $10,694.10 on the polls in the four districts.

As interest grew in the congressional polls, America First chapters in various parts of the country began campaigns urging their congressmen to take polls in their own districts. The National Committee had no more funds for poll-taking. Among others, the chapters in Appleton, Wisconsin; Butte, Montana; Greenfield, Massachusetts; Albuquerque, New Mexico; Wittenberg, Wisconsin; Hartford, Connecticut; and in the state of Idaho worked for district polls. So far as is known, none of the congressmen accepted the suggestion.

The America First Committee was particularly hopeful that Representative [Herman Paul] Kopplemann [D], of the First District of Connecticut, would respond favorably to the request from his America First constituents. Mr. Kopplemann, in his first period of service in the House, from 1932 to 1938, had been numbered among the staunch noninterventionists. But when he returned to the House in 1940, he had become an interventionist.

The following letter was addressed to Representative Kopplemann by the Hartford America First committee with signatures of persons representing eighteen towns:

We of the America First Committee desire unity as much as any group of citizens. In a democracy, however, we believe that unity means unity of the people, not merely unity among cabinet officers. We seek unity now in the face of an issue affecting American lives, resources and liberties—the issue of war. Consequently, we believe that our representatives should and will want to know today, more than ever before, how their constituents stand on the war issue which confronts the United States.

They have not had a chance to vote on this issue and no prospect of having a chance to vote has been suggested.

A method of finding out how they feel has, however, been devised, by at least one of your colleagues, Representative H. Fish of New York.

To all the registered voters in his district, he has sent a letter reminding them that only the Congress can declare war in this country and with each letter he sent a postcard with the following statements, giving the voters a chance to check one.

The United States Should

Enter the war

Stay out of the war

We think this constitutes a patriotic, useful and necessary service to the people concerned, and we respectfully suggest that you do the same in your district.

Will you please let us know whether you are willing to do so?

Representative Koppleman never replied.

THE HUTCHINS POLL

One of the most significant and influential polls of the last few months before the country went to war was the survey of public opinion sponsored by a group of educators and ministers whose chairman was Robert M. Hutchins, president of the University of Chicago, taken by a professional public opinion organization, and financed by America First.

Based on answers to six questions, this poll showed that seven out of ten citizens did not want the United States to participate in European affairs. To the question, "Do you believe that the United States should enter the war as an active belligerent at this time?" 79.7 percent of those with an opinion replied "no," and 20.3 percent said "yes."

By a ratio of about twelve to five, the country believed that the Congress and not the president should decide whether the United States should take any action likely to involve the nation in a shooting war.

This poll was of especial interest because, unlike most surveys of the kind, it probed the thinking behind the basic question, "Do you or do you not believe the country should enter the war as an active belligerent at this time?" Those who said they did not believe the United States should enter the war as an active belligerent at this time were asked the question, "Under what circumstances do you think the United States should go to war?" Attack or invasion of the country was given by 41.1 percent as sufficient for war; 18.7 percent regarded attack on the Western Hemisphere as such a circumstance; 15.6 percent so regarded attack or sinking of American ships; 14 percent accepted attack on United States property, citizens, or possessions as cause for war; 6.6 percent were for war if England was being defeated.

Thus as late as July 1941, 59.8 percent of the American people believed that the only circumstances under which the country should go to war were attack or invasion of the country or of the Western Hemisphere.

The sponsors who conducted the poll under the chairmanship of Dr. Hutchins were the Reverend Harry Emerson Fosdick, President Raymond Kent of the University of Louisville, President Henry Noble McCracken of Vassar College, the Reverend Albert W. Palmer, president of the Chicago Theological Seminary, [and] President Alan Valentine of the University of Rochester.*

The survey was made by the Samuel E. Gill organization of New York, which has conducted public opinion studies for such clients as Columbia Broadcasting System, *Time, Look,* and the Crowell Publishing Company. The investigation was made in the period of June 28 to July 3, following the declaration of war by Germany on Russia. [A total of] 5,031 individuals (relatively a large sample under modern methods: Dr. Gallup bases his polls on 600 interviews) covering every income class, geographic section, age, race, etc. of the adult population over twenty-one years were interviewed.

The America First Committee made an unconditional grant of $3,500 (the fee charged by the Gill organization for making the survey) to the sponsoring committee.

For the benefit of those who would like to analyze the results of the survey, detailed data from the Gill report are included:

TABLE 1 *Question 1*

Who do you think should decide whether or not the United States should take any action that is likely to involve us in a shooting war?

	No.	% of Choices	% of Total Interviews
Congress	2,820	70.4	56.0
The President	1,186	29.6	23.6
Total Choices	4,006	100.00	
No Opinion*	1,025		20.4
Total Interviews	5,031		100.0

*Those respondents who had no opinion regarding a choice between Congress and the president break down in their answers as follows:

	No.	% of Total Respondents
Both the president and Congress should decide	195	3.9
Neither the president nor Congress should decide but the people of the U.S. should make the decision	221	4.4
Don't know who should decide	609	12.1

* See Jaffe, "Isolationism and Neutrality in Academe, 1938–1941," for an assessment of Hutchins, Valentine, and McCracken.

TABLE 2 *Question 2a*

Do you believe that the United States should use its armed force to occupy any part of Africa, the Azores, or the Cape Verde Islands?

	No.	% of Opinions	% of Total Interviews
Yes	1,302	33.7	25.9
No	2,560	66.3	50.9
Total Opinions	3,862	100.00	
Undecided	1,169		23.2
Total Interviews	5,031	100.0	

TABLE 3 *Question 2b*

If the answer is yes, who do you think should decide whether such action should be taken?

	No.	% of Choices	% of Total Responses
Congress	633	53.6	48.6
The President	549	46.4	42.2
Total Choices	1,182	100.0	
No Opinion*	120		9.2
Base	1,302		100.0

Based on total "yes" answers to question 2a. (See preceding table.)

*Those respondents who had no opinion regarding a choice between Congress and the president break down in their answers as follows:

	No.	% of Total Respondents
Both the president and Congress should decide	62	4.8
Neither the president nor Congress should decide but the people of the U.S. should make the decision	9	.7
Don't know who should decide	49	3.7

TABLE 4 *Question 3*

If our navy or any part of our armed forces engages in armed hostility against Germany, do you believe we can avoid full participation in the war?

	No.	% of Opinions	% of Total Interviews
Yes	984	23.0	19.6
No	3,285	77.0	65.3
Total Opinions	4,269	100.0	
Undecided	762	15.1	
Total Interviews	5,031	100.0	

TABLE 5 *Question 4*
Do you believe that the United States should offer to mediate between England and Germany?

	No.	% of Opinions	% of Total Interviews
Yes	1,381	30.6	27.4
No	3,127	69.4	62.2
Total Opinions	4,508	100.0	
Undecided	523		10.4
Total Interviews	5,031		100.0

TABLE 6 *Question 5*
Do you believe that the United States should enter the war as an active belligerent at this time?

	No.	% of Opinions	% of Total Interviews
Yes	959	20.3	19.1
No	3,758	79.7	74.7
Total Opinions	4,717	100.0	
Undecided	314	6.2	
Total Interviews	5,031		100.0

TABLE 7 *Question 6*
If no, under what circumstances do you think the United States should go to war? (Answer specifically.)

	No.	% of Total Responses
If U.S. attacked or invaded	1,545	41.1
If Western Hemisphere attacked	703	18.7
If our ships attacked or sunk	858	15.6
If U.S. property, citizens, or possession attacked	527	14.0
If England is being defeated	248	6.6
When prepared for war	145	3.9
Under no circumstances	124	3.3
If any part of North America attacked	84	2.2
Miscellaneous reasons	63	1.7
If enemy is placed in threatening position	50	1.3
If Germany defeats Russia	23	0.6
Don't know	148	3.9
Duplication	487	
Base	3,758	

Based on those respondents who answered "no" to question 5.

Note: [A total of] 3,758 respondents gave 4,245 circumstances under which they think the United States should go to war. Any one of the duplicate reasons would, on the part of those who gave such duplicate reasons, be sufficient cause for entering the war.

TABLE 8 *Occasions for United States Entry into War As an Active Belligerent*

	Cumulative	
	No.	%
Believe U.S. should enter war as an active belligerent at this time (cuml)	959	19.1
Undecided whether U.S. should enter war as an active belligerent at this time (cuml)	1,273	25.3
Believe U.S. should not enter war as an active belligerent at this time but:		
When prepared (cuml)	1,418	28.2
If Germany defeats Russia (cuml)	1,441	28.6
If enemy is placed in threatening position (cuml)	1,491	29.6
If England is being defeated (cuml)	1,732	34.4
If our ships attacked or sunk (cuml)	2,288	45.5
If Western Hemisphere attacked (cuml)	2,919	58.0
If any part of North America attacked (cuml)	2,995	58.5
If U.S. property, citizens, or possessions attacked (cuml)	3,404	67.7
If U.S. attacked or invaded (cuml)	4,711	93.6
Miscellaneous occasions (cuml)	4,759	94.6
Don't know (cuml)	4,907	97.5
Total Interviews*	5,031	100.0

The above counts and percentages are cumulative and eliminate duplicate answers progressively.

*[A total of] 124 respondents would have United States enter war as an active belligerent under no circumstances.

CATHOLIC CLERGY POLL

A poll of all Roman Catholic clergymen in the country (except cardinals, archbishops, bishops, and army and navy chaplains) in which America First cooperated showed 91.5 percent against the United States entering a shooting war outside the Western Hemisphere.

The poll was conducted by the Catholic Laymen's Committee for Peace through the office of the Official Catholic Directory.

Two questions were asked of the 34,616 clergy on the mailing list. To the first, "Do you favor the United States engaging in a shooting war outside the Western Hemisphere?" of the 13,155 replying, 12,038 voted "no." In answer to the second question, "Are you in favor of the United States aiding the Communistic Russian government?" 11,860 replied "no." The returns on this poll were exceptionally high, reaching approximately 40 percent.

The America First Committee financed the taking of the poll.

NEOSHO POLL

The May 26, 1941, issue of *Life* magazine carried a two-page spread with pictures reporting on the visit of a *Life* reporter to Neosho, Missouri, where he declared he had found a "unanimity of interventionist sentiment that surprised me."

An America First field man who lived near Neosho and knew the town was also surprised—and frankly skeptical. According to his findings Neosho was 80 percent for staying out of war.

The America First Committee asked the Springfield (Mo.) papers to take a poll of all citizens of Neosho listed in the city directory, and agreed to pay the costs.

[A total of] 3,152 ballots were mailed out asking a yes or no answer to the question, "Do you favor United States entry into the European War?" [A total of] 994 legitimate ballots were returned, 692 marked "no," 276 marked "yes," and 26 marked "uncertain." [A total of] 69.6 percent had voted against intervention.

The following letter written by R.E. Wood to Henry Luce, editor of *Life*, tells the rest of the story:

June 16, 1941
Dear Mr. Luce:
In an article in the May 26th issue of *Life* magazine titled "Neosho" there appeared the following statement . . ." Visiting this small and peaceful town in Missouri, *Life*'s reporter investigates its feelings on the war and finds most of its citizens are for intervention."

The America First Committee, surprised at this statement, invited the Springfield (Mo.) Newspapers, Inc. to conduct a fair and impartial poll to decide the question.

On Saturday, May 31st, the Springfield Newspapers, Inc. mailed postcard ballots to the 3,153 Neosho citizens listed in the latest City Directory.

The question on the ballot was simply stated, "Do you favor United States entry into the European War?"

Ballots were returned directly to the office of the newspaper, counted and filed by their employees that there might be absolutely no criticism of the manner in which the poll was taken.

One hundred and ninety-eight (198) cards were returned which might have been of another printing than those mailed by the Springfield Newspaper, Inc. These were all voted "no" and likely an attempt to discredit the poll. They were not counted.

On Sunday, June 8, the Springfield *News and Leader* printed the final results of the poll, proving that 69.6% of those voting do not favor the United States entry into the European War.

In view of this result, we feel in all fairness that *Life* should retract the statements and publicize the true conviction of the residents of Neosho as they have expressed them in this poll.

To date, Mr. Luce has not replied.

COLLEGE POLLS

Time magazine for October 13, 1941, carried a report that undergraduate students had changed their minds about war, that they had become interventionist.

The America First College Department, having read the October 22 news story reporting that 76 percent of the students at Columbia University—whose president, Nicholas Murray Butler, was known as one of the country's ranking interventionists—were opposed to declaring war; the October 25 report that a "majority of student editors attending the Rocky Mountain Intercollegiate Press Association convention declared themselves against an American expeditionary force to Europe to aid Great Britain and Russia"; and others, therefore initiated a poll of 800 colleges that turned up a 64 percent majority against U.S. entrance into the war.

The poll was conducted by the Yale *News,* with America First paying the expenses of approximately $100. The four-point questionnaire was sent to the editorial boards of 800 colleges and prep schools in all sections of the country. The poll results were as follows:

		Yes	No
1.	Weighing carefully the factors for and against intervention, do you think the United States should enter the present European war?	56 (36%)	99 (64%)
2.	Do you favor revision of the neutrality law which will permit American merchant ships to enter the war zone?	81 (52%)	76 (48%)
3.	Do you believe that such revision will result in our entry in the war?	132 (87%)	20 (13%)
4.	If the United States enters the war, do you believe that we should send an American expeditionary force to Europe?	56 (36%)	100 (64%)

The geographical breakdown on answers to question 1 was as follows:

	Yes	No
Northeast	17 (39%)	27 (61%)
Southeast	9 (38%)	15 (62%)
North Central	12 (43%)	16 (57%)
Northwest	6 (30%)	14 (70%)
Southwest	10 (26%)	28 (74%)
Women's colleges	8 (44%)	10 (56%)
All other colleges	48 (35%)	89 (65%)
Prep schools	7 (58%)	5 (42%)

The America First Committee was in the midst of correspondence with those schools and colleges that had shown a majority against participation in war, urging them to take separate polls of their student bodies, when Pearl Harbor put an end to all committee activities.

THE CAMPAIGN PROMISE POLL

At the request of the America First Committee, the Wabash (Indiana) *Plain Dealer* in June 1941 took a poll on the question, "President Roosevelt and Mr. Willkie both promised last fall not to send American boys to fight in Europe unless the United States is attacked. Do you think the circumstances today have so changed as to justify a departure from these pledges?"

Over 88 percent (88.4) answered no.

APPENDIX

Here are the appended Gallup polls that were most interesting to America First leaders in evaluating public opinion. Readers who wish to read all the polls for the period covered here will find them in the *Public Opinion Quarterly* (published at Princeton University, Princeton, N.J.), from which this record is taken. The *Quarterly* gives also the complete *Fortune* polls:

October 24, 1941

What persons or groups do you think are most active in trying to keep us out of war? (October 24, 1941)

(Ranked in order of mention)

1. Lindbergh, Wheeler, Nye.

2. America First Committee.

3. Roosevelt administration.

4. Nazi agents and fifth columnists.

5. Church groups and organizations.

What persons or groups do you think are most active in trying to get us into war?

(Ranked in order of mention)

1. Roosevelt administration and Democratic Party.

2. Big business, industrialists, profiteers.

3. British organizations and agents.

4. American organizations with pro-British sympathies.

5. Jews.

Should the United States enter the war? (This question was sometimes worded, "Would you vote to go into the war or stay out of the war?")

	Go in	Stay out		Go in	Stay out
June 2, 1940	16%	84%	March 20	17%	83%
June 14	19%	81%	April	19%	81%
July 7	14%	86%	May 16	21%	79%
Oct. 13	17%	83%	June 19	21%	79%
Jan. 9, 1941	12%	88%	June (late)	24%	76%
Feb. 2	15%	85%	July 19	21%	79%
Feb. 13	14%	86%	Oct. 4	21%	79%

Poll of Who's Who   July 19, 1941   45%   55%

(May 1941)

	Go in	Stay out		Go in	Stay out
Wis.	14%	86%	N.M.	24%	76%
Minn.	15%	85%	Nev.	24%	76%
Iowa	15%	85%	Del.	25%	75%
Ind.	15%	85%	Okla.	25%	75%
Ohio	15%	85%	La.	26%	74%
Mass.	17	83	Tenn.	26	74
N.H.	17	83	Mont.	26	74
Ill.	17	83	Utah	26	74
Mich.	18	82	Md.	27	73
Nebr.	18	82	W.Va.	27	73
S.Dak.	18	82	Ky.	27	73
Conn.	19	81	Idaho	27	73
Kan.	20	80	Ore.	27	73
N.Dak.	21	79	Ga.	28	72
Me.	21	79	Ark.	28	72
R.I.	22	78	Va.	28	72
Pa.	22	78	Miss.	28	72
Wash.	22	78	Colo.	28	72
Vt.	23	77	N.C.	29	71
N.J.	23	77	Ala.	29	71
Mo.	23	77	Tex.	29	71
S.C.	23	77	Wyo.	29	71
Calif.	23	77	Ariz.	33	67
N.Y.	24	76	Fla.	35	65

It has been suggested that Congress pass a resolution declaring that a state of war exists between the United States and Germany. Would you favor or oppose such a resolution at this time?

Favor 26%   Oppose 63%   Undecided 11%

Which of these two things do you think is the more important for the United States to try to do—to keep out of the war ourselves, or to help England win, even at the risk of getting into the war?

	Stay out	Help England
May 1940	64%	36%
June	64	36
July	61	39
Aug.	53	47
Sept.	48	52
Nov.	50	50
Jan. 9, 1941	40	60
Jan. 23	32	68
April	33	67
Oct.	30	70
Nov.	32	68
Dec. (before war)	32	68

Do you think our country's future safety depends on England winning this war? (Jan. 2, 1941)

Yes   68%   No   26%

If it appeared certain there was no way to defeat Germany and Italy except for the United States to go to war against them, would you be in favor of the United States going into the war?

April 27, 1941	Favor war	68%	Would oppose war	24%	Undecided	8%
May 7		66%		34%		

Do you think the United States will go into the war in Europe sometime before it is over, or do you think we will stay out of the war?

	Go in	Stay out
Oct. 1939 (outbreak of war)	46%	54%
Feb. 1940 (war's quiet phase)	32	68
May 1940 (invasion of France)	62	38
June 1940	65	35
Sept. 1940	67	33
Dec. 1940 (Greek-British successes)	59	41
Jan. 1941	72	28
Feb. 1941	74	26
Mar. 1941	80	20
April 1941 (Balkan invasion)	82	18
May 1941	85	15

If Germany defeats the Allies, should the United States fight, if necessary, to keep Germany out of the British, French, and Dutch possessions located in the area of the Panama Canal? (July 21, 1940)

Yes   84%   No   16%

Do you think Britain will ask for help from the American army before the war is over? (May 2, 1941)

Britain will call for help of United States Army	57%
Britain already doing so	14%
Don't think Britain will call	20%
Undecided	9%

Do you think the United States should send part of our army to Europe to help the British? (April 19, 1941)

Yes   17%   No   79%   Undecided   4%

Do you think the United States should send part of our air force with American pilots to Europe to help the British?

Yes   24%   No   69%   Undecided   7%

Do you think the United States should send some of our warships manned by American sailors to Europe to help the British?

| Yes | 27% | No | 67% | Undecided | 6% |

Do you think Congress should give the army power to send drafted men to points outside the Western Hemisphere? (July 29, 1941)

| Yes | 37% | No | 50% | No opinion | 13% |

If the United States does enter the war against Germany and Italy, do you think we would send our army to Europe to fight before the war is over? (Aug. 16, 1941)

| Yes | 65% | No | 24% | No opinion | 11% |

The army has asked Congress to change the law which says drafted men cannot be sent to fight outside of North or South America or this country's possessions. Do you think Congress should give the army the right to send drafted soldiers to any part of the world? (Nov. 7, 1941)

	Yes	No	Undecided
July	37%	50%	13%
Aug.	35%	59%	6%
Today	42%	53%	5%

Which side do you think will win?

	England	Germany	Undecided
Sept. 1939	82%	7%	11%
May 1940	52	17	28
June	32	35	33
Sept.	43	17	40
Nov.	63	7	30
Sept. 1941	69	6	25

(July 12, 1941)

Russia	22%
Germany	47%
Undecided	23%
Stalemate	8%

Do you think we are giving enough help to England, or do you think ways should be found to give England more help than we are at present, but short of going to war? (July 18, 1940)

	Total
Give more help	53%
Enough help now	41%
Give less help	6%

If it appears that England will be defeated by Germany and Italy unless the United States supplies her with more food and war materials, would you be in favor of giving more help to England? (Nov. 19, 1940)

Yes   90%   No   10%

If the British are unable to pay cash for war materials bought in this country, should our government lend or lease war materials to the British, to be paid back in the same materials and other goods after the war is over? (Jan. 21, 1941)

	Total
Approve	68%
Disapprove	26%
Undecided	8%

Do you think Congress should pass the president's lease-lend bill?

	Yes	No	Qualified	Undecided
Feb. 9, 1941	54%	22%	15%	9%
Feb. 14	58%	21%	14%	7%
Feb. 28	55%	20%	11%	14%
March 8	56%	27%	8%	9%

If the lease-lend bill is passed, do you think it will result in sending an American army abroad to fight? (March 11, 1941)

Yes   31%   No   47%   Qualified or don't know   22%

Has the new war between Germany and Russia changed your attitude toward helping Britain? (July 10, 1941)

Yes   12%   No   83%   Undecided   5%

Some people say that since Germany is now fighting Russia, as well as Britain, it is not so necessary for this country to help Britain. Do you agree or disagree? (July 31, 1941)

Agree   20%   Disagree   72%   No opinion   8%

Some people say that since Germany will probably defeat Russia and then turn new full strength against Britain, it is more important than ever that we help Britain. Agree or disagree? (July 31, 1941)

Agree   71%   Disagree   19%   No opinion   10%

The Johnson act prevents any country which has stopped paying interest on its debt of the last world war from borrowing money in the United States. Would you approve of changing this law so that England could borrow money from our government? (Dec. 19, 1940)

	Yes	No
May 1940	35%	65%
Nov. 1940	54%	46%
Dec. 19, 1940	55%	45%

Should the Neutrality Law be changed so that American ships can carry war supplies to England? (Dec. 7, 1940)*

Yes   40%   No   60%   No opinion   14%

Since the English have lost many ships, they may not be able to come and get the war materials we make for them. If this proves to be the case, should American ships with American crews be used to carry war materials to England? (Jan. 16, 1941)

Yes   46%   No   45%   Undecided   13%

(Asked of person who favored sending American ships)
If American ships and American crews are used to carry war materials to England, should these ships be guarded by our navy while crossing? (Jan. 16, 1941)

Yes   82%   No   12%   Undecided   6%

* Total is more than 100 percent for this and the next question.

If American merchant ships with American crews are used to carry war materials to Britain, and some of them are sunk by German submarines on the way over, would you be in favor of going to war against Germany? (Feb. 16, 1941)

Yes   27%   No   61%   Qualified or undecided   12%

If it appears certain that Britain will be defeated unless we use part of our navy to protect ships going to Britain, would you favor or oppose such convoys? (April 22, 1941)

Favor   71%   Oppose   21%   Undecided   8%

If the United States Navy is used to guard merchant ships crossing the Atlantic and some of our warships are sunk by German submarines, would you be in favor of going to war against Germany? (May 1, 1941)

Yes   40%   No   50%   No opinion   10%

Do you think the United States Navy should be used to guard (convoy) ships carrying war materials to Britain? (June 14, 1941)

	Yes	No	Undecided
April 1941	41%	50%	9%
May 6–16	52%	41%	7%
May 22–30	52%	40%	8%
June 14 (following F.D.R. speech)	55%	38%	7%

Do you think the American navy should be used to convoy ships carrying war materials to Britain? (Sept. 2, 1941)

Yes   52%   No   39%   No opinion   9%

In general do you approve or disapprove of having the United States Navy shoot at German submarines or warships on sight? (Oct. 2, 1941)

Approve   62%   Disapprove   28%   No opinion   10%

Should the Neutrality Act be changed to permit American merchant ships with American crews to carry war materials to Britain?

	Yes	No	Undecided
April 1941	30%	61%	9%
Sept.	46%	40%	14%
Early Oct.	46%	40%	14%
Mid-Oct.	54%	37%	9%
Nov. 5	61%	31%	8%

Should the Neutrality Act be changed to permit American merchant ships to be armed?

	Yes	No	Undecided
Mid-Oct. 1941	72%	21%	7%
Nov. 5	81%	14%	5%

Do you think drafted men should be kept in service for longer than one year, or should they be released at the end of one year? (July 29, 1941)

Should be kept 51%   Should be released 45%   No opinion 4%

Should a vote of the people be required before Congress can send men to fight overseas?

	Yes	No
Feb. 4, 1941	52%	48%
June 19	56%	44%

Do you think President Roosevelt has gone too far in his policies of helping Britain, or not far enough?

	Too far	About right	Not far enough
May 23, 1941	21%	59%	20%
June 14	21%	59%	20%
July 19	23%	55%	22%
Oct. 18	27%	57%	16%

Do you think our country's army, navy, and air force are strong enough so that the United States is safe today from attack by any foreign powers? (June 2, 1940)

Yes   15%   No   85%

Are you satisfied with the progress that the present administration is making in rearming our country? (Aug. 18, 1940)

Yes   61%   No   23%   Don't know   16%

Are you satisfied with the present rate of production of airplanes, tanks, warships, and guns for our national defense program? (Aug. 18, 1940)

	Yes	No	Don't know
Aug. 18, 1941	32%	40%	28%
Sept. 21	40%	41%	19%

(Asked of the 41% who were dissatisfied) Whose fault do you think it is?

Administration, Roosevelt, the government	14
Congress, the politicians	11
Industry and business	3
Public apathy, the people themselves	2
All others	3
No reply	8
	41

Do you think it was a mistake for the United States to enter the last war? (April 5, 1941)

	Yes	No	Undecided
April 1937	64%	28%	8%
Nov. 1939	59%	28%	13%
Dec. 1940	39%	42%	19%
April 1941	39%	43%	18%

Do you think the United States should have joined the League of Nations after the last war? (Aug. 22, 1941)

Should have	37%
Should not	37%
Undecided	26%

Do you think the United States should risk war with Japan if necessary in order to keep Japan from taking the Dutch East Indies and Singapore?

	Yes	No	Undecided
Feb. 23, 1941	39%	46%	15%
March 13	40%	39%	21%

Should the United States take steps now to prevent Japan from becoming more powerful, even if this means risking war with Japan?

	Yes	No	Undecided
July 1941	51%	31%	18%
Sept.	70%	18%	12%
Nov. 14	64%	25%	11%
Dec. 7	69%	20%	11%

Do you think the United States will go to war against Japan sometime in the near future? (Dec. 7, 1941)

Yes   52%   No   27%   Unready to guess   21%

NOTES

1. The Gallup Poll of people listed in *Who's Who* showed only 57.2 percent opposed. The Gallup Poll of opinion by regions revealed a low percentage—as compared with the percentage for the nation—opposed in the Southern states. Without discounting the evidence of these polls, it was known that intellectuals and individuals in the upper-income brackets—who made up the *Who's Who* roster for the most part—were inclined to be interventionist. It was also known that since many persons in the South were disfranchised by the poll tax, and Dr. Gallup queried only registered voters, his survey of Southern opinion must have been weighted somewhat on the side of those in the upper-income brackets.

2. *Congressional Record*, May 9, 1941, p. 3924.

"He was my hero": 24-year-old America First Committee National Director R. Douglas Stuart, Jr., with Charles Lindbergh. © Bettmann/CORBIS.

Senator Gerald Nye (R-North Dakota), scourge of the "merchants of death." © Bettmann/CORBIS.

Charles Lindbergh confers with General Robert E. Wood, acting chairman of America First, before speaking to a St. Louis audience. They are flanked by Charles P. Muldoon (left) and Senator Bennett Champ Clark (D-Missouri, right). © Bettmann/CORBIS.

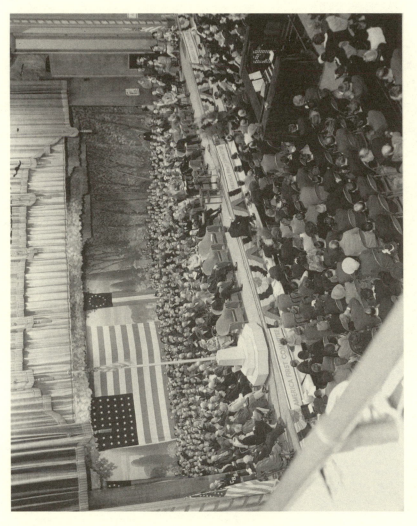

Charles Lindbergh addresses an America First rally in Minneapolis. The aviator's father, Minnesota Congressman Charles A. Lindbergh, had been smeared as "the Gopher Bolshevik" for his opposition to U.S. entry into the First World War. © Minnesota Historical Society/CO.

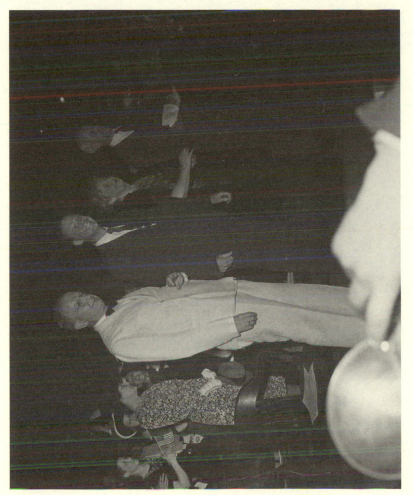

The diversity of the America First movement is on display in Madison Square Garden. From left to right, speakers include Senator Burton K. Wheeler (D-Montana), Charles Lindbergh, novelist and pacifist Kathleen Norris, and Socialist Party leader Norman Thomas. © Bettmann/CORBIS.

Anne Morrow Lindbergh, writer and wife of the famed aviator, greets the crowd at a "No Foreign War" rally in Philadelphia. © Bettmann/CORBIS.

Charles Lindbergh speaks to an August 1941 America First rally in Cleveland. Anne Morrow Lindbergh is framed by the table legs. © Bettmann/CORBIS.

A crowd of between 20,000 and 30,000 listens to antiwar Senator Burton K. Wheeler address the St. Charles, Illinois, fall festival in September, 1941. One day earlier, fewer than a thousand people had turned out for a pro-intervention speech by Kentucky Senator A.B. Chandler.

Antiwar Americans packed Madison Square Garden on October 30, 1941, to hear (left to right) Senator Gerald Nye, Senator Burton K. Wheeler, Charles Lindbergh, and John Cudahy, former U.S. ambassador to Belgium.

A somber General Robert E. Wood arrives at La Guardia Field on December 7, 1941, hours after the Japanese attack on Pearl Harbor. © Bettmann/CORBIS.

Congresswoman Jeannette Rankin (R-Montana) explains her lone vote against the U.S. declaration of war on Japan. Between the world wars, Rankin worked with Ruth Sarles at the National Council for Prevention of War. © Hulton-Deutsch Collection/CORBIS.

—For war wishers to pave the way for—

THE BIG PARADE

THE HIGH COST OF FOREIGN ENTANGLEMENTS

UNCLE SAM'S PARTIAL EXPENSES FOR "MAKING THE WORLD SAFE FOR DEMOCRACY"

Loans to War Associates	$11,000,000,000
Unpreparedness Costs	13,000,000,000
"Ships, Ships & More Ships" for Hard Pressed Allies	4,000,000,000
Credits to Europe after War	5,000,000,000
Supplies sold to France (about)	403,000,000
Pay for transporting American Soldiers to France on British Ships	500,000,000
Rental of French trenches during training period	100,000,000
Cost of National Prohibition (outgrowth of War Prohibition)	10,000,000,000
Cost of Crime in the U.S. resulting from Violations of Prohibition Law	20,000,000,000
Loss of Revenue (same cause)	

Fleeting Storms
Veterans Expenses
Bonuses
Pensions
Loss in U.S. Naval Construction (resulting from Washington Naval Conference)
Moral Slump caused by War
Ethical Slump
Stock Speculation (result of Reduction of rediscount rate to help England protect her financial position)
Stock Crash
Unemployment

RUSSIAN DICTATORSHIP
DEPARTMENT-ERSHIP
DEFAULT-ERSHIP
KINGDOM
TURKISH DICTATORSHIP
GERMAN DICTATORSHIP
AUSTRIAN DICTATORSHIP
ITALIAN DICTATORSHIP
BRITISH DEFAULTERSHIP
BELGIAN DEFAULTERSHIP
FRENCH DEFAULTERSHIP
SPANISH DICTATORSHIP
EUROPE

McCUTCHEON
Copyright, 1934, by The Chicago Tribune.

When Charles Pinckney, John Marshall, and Elbridge Gerry were sent as American ambassadors to protest to France against unjust treatment on the high seas, Ambassador Pinckney used these ringing words to Foreign Minister Talleyrand.

Today the overwhelming majority of American mothers will paraphrase those historic, undying words.

—let the 86 per cent go over and join the 14 per cent?

THE WAY THE AMERICAN PEOPLE ALWAYS HAVE VOTED

and the way they would undoubtedly vote today if given the chance.

When the American voter in 1916 had a chance to express himself on getting into the war in Europe.

When the United States senate voted on entangling our country in an Anglo-French-American alliance.

When the United States senate voted on the ratification of the Versailles treaty.

When the country voted on the league of nations issue in 1920.

When our Interventionists tried to entangle the U. S. still further in Europe by keeping American troops on the Rhine.

5

Colonel Lindbergh and America First

Colonel Charles Lindbergh's close association with the America First Committee began in the spring of 1941. Up to that time, he had cooperated with the committee while avoiding a direct connection. His policy was to force the opposition to divide its fire against various noninterventionist movements.*

By the spring of 1941 he felt that conditions had changed sufficiently to make close association advisable. He did not have time to organize the meetings at which he spoke and did not want to accept speaking invitations without knowing in detail the character of the organizations extending them. He had confidence in America First's National Committee, and the organization was in position to set up his meetings.

His interest in the committee grew to the point where he accepted membership on the National Committee, spoke at twelve America First rallies, and became one of the committee's trusted friends who frequently consulted with General Wood and his staff members on policy and program.

Following his radio addresses, the colonel's testimony against the Lend-Lease bill† before the House and Senate committees dealing with foreign affairs in January and February had identified him in the public mind with the militant opposition to Administration foreign policy headed by America First, then waging an anti-Lend-Lease campaign. It had enhanced the esteem in which he was held on Capitol Hill by interventionists and noninterventionists alike. Interventionist members of both committees had grilled him with that intensity

---

* Lindbergh wrote in his diary on October 1, 1940, "[Bob] Stuart phoned and I told him it was essential to avoid friction between antiwar groups. I told him I thought they should all be able to look to his committee in Chicago for leadership." Charles A. Lindbergh, *The Wartime Journals of Charles A. Lindbergh* (New York: Harcourt Brace Jovanovich, 1970), p. 394.

† Lindbergh testified before the House Committee on Foreign Affairs on January 31, 1941. Chairman Sol Bloom (D-N.Y.), an interventionist, said, "You have made one of the best witnesses that this committee could possibly ever hear. You answered all the questions only as a Colonel Lindbergh could answer them." Quoted in A. Scott Berg, *Lindbergh* (New York: Putnam's, 1998), p. 415.

which has been developed to a fine art in congressional committees. But his handling of the crackling inquisition had made an excellent impression on committee members, on the press, and on the audience. When he left the stand in the House hearing, the largely hostile audience and the overwhelmingly hostile committee stood in tribute, led by Chairman Sol Bloom.[1]*

In the period following passage of the Lend-Lease bill, America First was in a blue funk. There was no immediate issue sufficiently appealing to rally the country. Contributions were slow. General Wood's pressing business and personal obligations made him feel he ought to resign; he wanted Colonel Lindbergh to take the chairmanship.

Several of the colonel's greatest admirers—among them Bob Stuart—were doubtful of the wisdom of making him chairman. If he were to take the leading position in the committee, America First would then be the target not only for the attacks the *committee* drew to itself, but also of all the animus that had been generated against the colonel personally. However, Bob Stuart conquered his doubts and went east to lay the matter before Colonel Lindbergh.

The flyer was reluctant to undertake the job. Although he did not give a categorical answer, the understanding was that if the general—for whom Colonel Lindbergh had great admiration and affection—insisted, he would seriously consider accepting the chairmanship.[†]

At a lively meeting of the executive committee on March 28, the members threshed out the matter. The minutes report that

General Wood told the Directors of the heavy pressure under which he was working. He was having to spend more and more time on the work of the Committee. In view of his tremendous responsibility with Sears, Roebuck & Company, he was more than ever anxious to secure a full-time chairman for the Committee[2]. He had come to the conclusion that Colonel Lindbergh was the best possible man for the job. Colonel Lindbergh would be able to give the Committee's work his full time. Also, he had emerged

---

*His harshest treatment came from Senator Claude Pepper (D-Fla.), who was put in his place by a deadpan Lindbergh.

"Colonel," asked Pepper, "when did you first go to Europe?"

"Nineteen twenty-seven, sir," replied Lindbergh, to "laughter and applause," according to Scott Berg.

Berg, *Lindbergh*, p. 415.

†Lindbergh wrote in his diary on March 30, 1941, "Ed Webster [senior partner in Kidder, Peabody & Company and leader of the New York AFC chapter] came for lunch. He wants me to take the national chairmanship of America First. Says I will receive a letter from General Wood shortly, asking me to do this. I told Webster I would gladly work with America First and assist the committee in any way possible, but that I felt it would be a mistake for me to take the national chairmanship at this time, if at all. I told him that if I took the national chairmanship, I would have to give up the type of work I am now doing, that I could not write and make addresses on the war and at the same time carry on the executive duties that would be required." Lindbergh, *Wartime Journals*, p. 471.

as the real leader of our point of view, with a tremendous following amongst the people of this country.

This matter was discussed at length pro and con.

After discussion it was decided that General Wood would write to Colonel Lindbergh to inquire as to whether or not he would be willing to serve as Chairman of the Committee, with the understanding that an appointment as Chairman would be subject to the approval of the majority of the members of the National Committee.

The day after the meeting General Wood wrote to Colonel Lindbergh, urging him as the "head of all the elements that are opposed to our entry into this European conflict" to become chairman of America First:

In my opinion, there is only one man in the United States who should head the Committee, and that is your good self. Your patriotism, your courage, your intellectual honesty have made you stand out as the head of all the elements that are opposed to our entry into this European conflict.

I would like to ask you if you would accept the chairmanship in the event it were tendered to you. Before formally tendering it to you, I would want to consult all the members of the National Committee. I am confident that the majority of them will heartily approve, but I would not want to do so unless you would be willing to accept.

A few days later General Wood was in New York and the two men talked the matter over by telephone. Colonel Lindbergh could not bring himself to the point of feeling that the interests of the antiwar cause or of the committee would best be served by his acceptance of the chairmanship. He feared that it would intensify differences within and without the committee at a time when "our only hope of success is in exercising all possible influence immediately." He proposed an alternative, that he become a member of the National Committee, speak at America First meetings, and in his public addresses urge those who wanted to stay out of war to join the committee. Confirming this conversation, he sent the following letter to General Wood:

During the weekend I received information that members of the New York America First Committee had knowledge of the fact that I was being considered for National Chairman. This information was in their possession last week even before our meeting at the Waldorf. By "members," I refer in this instance to members of the organization who are not on the main New York Committee.

Aside from the possibility that a story may be carried in the press before we are ready for an announcement, I would attach little importance to this situation if it were not that I find divergence of opinion arising in regard to my becoming Chairman, and the effect it would have upon the Committee. Possibly the most serious problem in this respect lies in the apparent friction which exists within the National Committee, within the New York Committee, and between various members of the National Committee and local Committees.

It seems obvious to me that it would be a great mistake, from every standpoint, for me to take a leading position in the America First Committee at a time when internal friction may come to a head. Our opposition would seize upon this immediately in an attempt to discredit the Committee and to nullify, as far as possible, the unifying effect we are striving for among anti-interventionist forces. Since the major crisis of the war now seems at hand—both in the Balkans and in the Atlantic—a division of our forces would be multiply unfortunate. It is vital for us all to exercise our utmost influence during these weeks, and it would be impossible to do this and, at the same time, straighten out an internal committee conflict.

In view of this situation, I suggest the following plan as one which would bring the greatest effect while involving the least vulnerability:

I would (if satisfactory to your Committee, of course) accept membership on the National America First Committee. As soon as possible after the announcement was made, I would speak before one of your meetings (wherever convenient and advisable) requesting everyone opposed to war to join America First in a unified effort to counteract the trend of intervention. I believe that I could help to increase the membership and influence of the Committee in this way without precipitating the friction and argument which apparently would be involved in my taking a leading position at this moment.

Please let me have your reaction at your earliest convenience so that I may lay my own plans accordingly. Personally, I believe it is essential for us to act with the utmost rapidity in whatever we do. This country's decision on intervention must, I believe, be made in the very near future.

In closing this letter, I want to tell you again how greatly I appreciate the honor of your suggestion that I take the Chairmanship of the National Committee. I would like nothing better than the opportunity of working with you in this cause, and I know of no one in whom I have more confidence. I hope you fully understand that my hesitation lies in the knowledge that our only hope of success is in exercising all possible influence immediately, and in my feeling that we must avoid the appearance of friction and division at all costs.

At the April 11 meeting of the Executive Committee, Colonel Lindbergh was elected a member of the National Committee. He agreed to speak at a rally at the Chicago Arena on April 17, at which time his membership on the committee was to be announced.

The announcement of his membership and his "plea for unity among the forces and people in America who stand against our intervention in this war" were received with tremendous enthusiasm by the 11,000 persons in the hall (and 4,000 outside). He told the audience that "whether or not America enters the war is within our control," that the "claim that our participation is inevitable is simply propaganda by those who want to get us in. If we can be forced into a foreign war against the opposition of more than four-fifths of our people, then the idea of representative government and democracy will be proved such a failure at home that there will be little use fighting for it abroad."*

---

* Lindbergh wrote in his diary on April 17, 1941, "Arrived at auditorium at 8:00. Songs. Then General Wood introduced Mr. Pettengill, who made a forceful but slightly too long extemporaneous speech. General Hammond spoke next. Then General Wood introduced me, and I spoke for

The antiwar forces now had a popular hero, and the America First Committee was incalculably strengthened by the addition of a man who not only drew thousands of new members,[3] but gave valuable service in the less glamorous give-and-take of hammering out policy and program behind the scenes.

Late in March, [4] Colonel Lindbergh's much discussed "Letter to Americans" appeared in *Collier's* magazine, advocating the building of

a military and commercial position on this continent that is impregnable to attack, and which will force other nations to trade with us, if through expediency alone. . . . We, in America, should not be discussing whether we will enter the war that England declared in Europe. We should not be wasting our time arguing about whether it is cheaper to defend someone else than to defend ourselves. We should not be conscripting our youth for a foreign war they do not wish to fight. We should all be marching together toward one clear and commonly accepted goal—the independent destiny of America. . . . It is by building our own strength and character at home—not by crusading abroad—that we can contribute most to civilization throughout the world.

He urged readers who agreed with him to organize and attend mass meetings against U.S. entry into the war, [and] to write to congressmen and senators and to newspaper editors.

According to a North American Newspaper Alliance story, *Collier's* had reported that public response to the article was the largest ever expressed spontaneously to the magazine about an article. Over 700 letters had been received. "Of those addressed to the editor, 233 favored Lindbergh and 120 opposed him. About 400 additional letters were received, addressed to Colonel Lindbergh personally, which were said to be overwhelmingly in agreement with him, with only about one in twenty arguing with him."[5]

Colonel Lindbergh's second appearance for the committee was at the Manhattan Center rally in New York on April 23. It was before this meeting that the colonel, in a statement to the press, made clear his attitude toward the "subversives" who were said to be attending America First meetings. He said that "pro-Nazis, pro-Fascists and pro-Communists or any group favoring un-American theories are certainly not for the America First Committee."[6]*

---

about twenty-five minutes. Well received; enthusiastic crowd. Had expected considerable opposition, but there was practically none. (In fact, I had thought there might be some fighting and was surprised by the orderliness of the crowd. Was also surprised by the amount of anti-British feeling in Chicago.)" Lindbergh, *Wartime Journals*, p. 475.

* Lindbergh wrote in his diary on April 23, 1941, "The hall was decorated with American flags everywhere. Mrs. Marquand [Adelaide, wife of novelist John P.] opened the meeting. Flynn presided. Senator [Walter] George [D-Ga.] spoke for forty minutes. Mrs. [Kathleen] Norris for fifteen minutes, and I spoke for twenty-five minutes. The crowd seemed one hundred percent with us. It was courteous and good-humored and, I think, represented an unusually good cross section of New York. As in Chicago, there was considerable anti-British feeling. I think it is due to pent-up emotion and a feeling of frustration—a feeling that we are being pushed into war regardless of how the people feel about it, and that England is largely responsible for the mess we are being dragged into. It results from resentment against British interference with American life and affairs." Lindbergh, *Wartime Journals*, pp. 476–7.

Colonel Lindbergh had made four addresses[7] at America First rallies in May. At the St. Louis rally (May 3) he described his surveys of air strength in Germany, Italy, and Russia before 1939, and his fruitless attempts to convince the British that for Britain's "own safety it was essential for England to increase the strength of the Royal Air Force greatly." He told of his conclusion that the United States led the world in the development of commercial aviation but that Germany led in the development of military aviation, and that this situation was filled with the utmost danger if we intended to take part in a European war:

Briefly and bluntly . . . we in America are not in a position to wage war abroad successfully at this time. Not only is the performance of some of our vital types of service aircraft inadequate, but our total Air Force in the United States today, including both Army and Navy, both modern and obsolescent types, is not more than Germany can produce in a few weeks. It is a small fraction of her present Air Force. To enter a European war today with our Air Force would be almost as great a folly as that committed by France when she declared war on Germany in 1939. . . .

. . . [W]ith every point I make, and with every argument I use, I keep wanting to say, again and again: Why must our people be divided over this question of European war? Here in America, we *are* prepared to win a victory. Here, we can defend our own nation—our own hemisphere. Here, we can develop a civilization as great or greater than any the world has ever known. We have every geographical advantage for defense. We have unlimited natural resources. We have the most highly organized industry in the world. And we have another advantage in defending our own country—the most important of all. It is unity of purpose. Every true American is ready to fight to preserve our nation.

In the Manhattan Center speech of April 23, the colonel said,

[T]he United States is not prepared to wage war in Europe successfully at this time. We are no better prepared today than France was when the interventionists in Europe persuaded her to attack the Siegfried line. . . .

[The British] hope that they may be able to persuade us to send another American Expeditionary Force to Europe, and to share with England militarily, as well as financially, the fiasco of this war. I do not blame England for this hope, or for asking for our assistance. But we now know that she declared a war under circumstances which led to the defeat of every nation that sided with her from Poland to Greece. . . . [W]e cannot win this war for England, regardless of how much assistance we extend.

I charge [the interventionists] with being the real defeatists, for their policy has led to the defeat of every country that followed their advice since this war began . . . Every nation that has adopted the interventionist policy of depending on some one else for its own defense has met with nothing but defeat and failure. . . .

We have been led toward war by a minority of our people. This minority has power. It has influence. It has a loud voice. But it does not represent the American people.

Two days after the speech, the president in a press conference compared Colonel Lindbergh with the "Copperheads" of the Civil War period. The New York *Times,* summarizing the president's statements, said,

Col. Lindbergh's name was brought into the press conference when a reporter asked why the flier had not been called into service, although he held a commission in the Army Reserve. In answer to the question . . . Mr. Roosevelt said that during the Civil War numerous foreigners, liberty-loving people, fought on both sides and that at the same time both sides let certain people go, that is, did not call them into service.

The people who were thus ignored, he added, were the Vallandighams.* The President explained that the Vallandighams were people who, from 1863 on, urged immediate peace, arguing that the North could not win the war between the states. . . . The President said, too, that there were many appeasers at Valley Forge trying to persuade George Washington to quit and arguing that the British could not be defeated. He urged that the newsmen read what Thomas Paine wrote at that time on the subject of quitting.

"Are you still talking about Colonel Lindbergh?" a reporter asked. A simple and emphatic affirmative was the answer.

America First released a statement to the press supporting the colonel:

President Roosevelt's remarks about Colonel Lindbergh today do not exhibit the spirit of tolerance or the respect for freedom of conscience and freedom of belief that the American people have admired in him.

The President of course knows, and the American people know, that Colonel Lindbergh is an American first, last and always.

Colonel Lindbergh, left with "no honorable alternative to tendering my resignation," resigned his Air Corps Reserve commission[8†]:

My Dear Mr. President:

Your remarks at the White House press conference on April 25, involving my reserve commission in the United States Army Air Corps, have, of course, disturbed me greatly. I had hoped that I might exercise my rights as an American citizen, to place my viewpoint before the people of my country in time of peace, without giving up the privilege of serving my country as an Air Corps officer in the event of war.

But since you, in your capacity as President of the United States and Commander in Chief of the Army, have clearly implied that I am no longer of use to this country as a reserve officer, and in view of other implications that you, my President and my superior officer, have made concerning my loyalty to my country, my character, and my motives, I can see no honorable alternative to tendering my resignation as colonel in the United States Air Corps Reserve.

I am therefore, forwarding my resignation to the Secretary of War.

* Clement Vallandigham was an Ohio congressman and constitutional Democrat who was a leader of the antiwar forces in the early 1860s. See Frank L. Klement, *The Limits of Dissent: Clement L. Vallandigham & the Civil War* (Lexington: University Press of Kentucky, 1970).

† Lindbergh wrote in his diary on April 27, 1941, "Have decided to resign. After studying carefully what the President said, I feel it is the only honorable course to take. If I did not tender my resignation, I would lose something in my own character that means even more to me than my commission in the Air Corps. No one else might know it, but I would." Lindbergh, *Wartime Journals*, p. 480.

I take this action with the utmost regret, for my relationship with the Air Corps is one of the things that has meant most to me in life. I place it second only to my right as a citizen to speak freely to my fellow countrymen, and to discuss with them the issues of peace and war which confront our nation in this crisis.

I will continue to serve my country to the best of my ability as a private citizen.

Respectfully,

(signed) Charles A. Lindbergh

Secretary of War Stimson accepted the resignation, and the president's secretary, Stephen Early, commented to the press, "I understand from the press that Colonel Lindbergh is returning his commission to the Secretary of War. That leads me to wonder whether he is returning his decoration to Mr. Hitler."

The question of the German decoration (awarded in 1938 by General Goering), which was to dog Colonel Lindbergh from the beginning to the end of his speaking campaign, had been brought up by Senator Pepper in the Senate hearings on the Lend-Lease bill three months before, and Colonel Lindbergh explained the circumstances under which he had received the medal. But the press had never given his explanation the same prominence it gave the aspersions cast on his patriotism for accepting the medal. When Stephen Early once more used the story to discredit the colonel, several noninterventionist leaders believed the true and complete explanation should be given the public; Stephen Early was a White House mouthpiece.

Colonel Lindbergh and Senator Bennett Champ Clark were scheduled to speak at an America First Rally in St. Louis, May 3. Senator Clark was glad to tell the audience the story the colonel was unwilling to recount in his own defense. A few hours before the St. Louis meeting, the colonel dictated the story at Senator Clark's request, and sent it to the Missouri senator at his hotel. The letter read,

In accordance with our telephone conversation this morning, I will outline below the circumstances which surrounded the presentation of the German decoration at the American Embassy in Berlin in 1938.

I had accepted an invitation to attend the Lillienthal Conference. This is an aeronautical, scientific conference held each year in Germany, and attended by delegates from practically every major country in the world.

Before leaving France, where I was living at the time, I received a message from the American Ambassador in Berlin, Mr. Wilson,* asking if I would be willing to attend a dinner to be given in honor of General Goering, at the American Embassy, while I was in Berlin. Mr. Wilson said that he was anxious to create a better relationship between the American Embassy and the German Government. Since General Goering had given a luncheon for me on one of my previous trips to Germany, the Ambassador said that

---

* The U.S. ambassador was Hugh Wilson, who said that he "hoped to obtain at such a dinner Goering's support for certain measures especially desired by the State Department concerning the easing of the financial plight of the large number of Jews who were being forced to emigrate from Germany in a penniless condition." Berg, *Lindbergh*, p. 370.

he would like to use my next visit as a reason for inviting General Goering to the American Embassy. I replied, of course, that I would be glad to attend the dinner.

There were approximately thirty guests at the American Embassy that evening— about one-third American and two-thirds German, although I am not certain of the exact number. General Goering was the last to arrive. He went around the reception room shaking hands and when he came to me he handed me, unopened, a small red box; saying through an interpreter that he was giving me The Order of the German Eagle. He then passed on to the remaining guests.

I had no previous information in regard to the plan for presenting this decoration, and I understand that Ambassador Wilson was not previously informed either.

Aside from the political capital which has been made of it, there was very little difference between the presentation of the German decoration and the presentation of decorations which I received from other countries in years past. Frankly, I believe the German decoration was given with the utmost good will and with no more political background than is usual in the case of foreign decorations. I believe it was arranged by various friends I had made on previous trips to Germany.

Personally, I believe the importance attached to decorations of this kind demonstrates an entirely false sense of values. I can see nothing constructive gained by returning decorations which were given in periods of peace and good will. The entire idea seems to me too much like a "child's spitting contest." Even though we eventually [may] enter war against Germany, there is nothing to be gained by indulging in such a contest before the war begins. The entire matter seems to me to be beneath the dignity of this Nation.

Incidentally, if I were to return the German decoration, it would bring up the question of what I should do with the decorations I received from Italy, France, Belgium, Rumania, Japan, England and other nations. From first to last, these decorations were given in connection with my activities in aviation. I have presented all of them to the Missouri Historical Society. Many are in showcases in the Jefferson Memorial Building and others are in storage.

I believe I have covered the important facts involved, in this outline, but if there is anything else you would like to know, please do not hesitate to telephone. As I believe I told you in Washington, there is no detail of my activities abroad or in this country that I am not entirely willing to have brought out.

P.S.—As a matter of background, I would like to recall to your attention, the fact that the German decoration was presented in an atmosphere which prevailed in Europe after Munich. As you know, a great effort was made to bring about a peaceful re-adjustment of the problems there. At about the same time I received my decoration, the French Ambassador to Germany was also given one. There was no resentment of this in France. On the contrary, such gestures were met with hope rather than any disapproval at that time.

Had the press carried Senator Clark's explanation in behalf of Colonel Lindbergh as fully as it had carried the charges against him, the matter might have been dropped at that point: A fair-minded public would not have tolerated perpetuation of the canard that Colonel Lindbergh had been guilty of lack of patriotism in accepting the medal, once the true facts were made known. But Secretary of the Interior Ickes once more revived the charge in a speech[9] characterized by the *New York Times* as "one of the most bitter attacks ever made on Mr. Lindbergh by any member of the Roosevelt Administration."* Colonel Lindbergh then took steps to have *officially* disposed of a charge that had been *officially* made. He wrote the following letter to the president:

I address you, sir, as an American citizen to his President. I write concerning statements made by an officer of your Cabinet, the Secretary of the Interior.

For many months, and on numerous occasions, your Secretary of the Interior has implied in public meetings that I am connected with the interests of a foreign government, and he has specifically criticized me for accepting a decoration from the German government in 1938.

Mr. President, is it too much to ask that you inform your Secretary of the Interior that I was decorated by the German government while I was carrying out the request of your ambassador to that government? Is it unfair of me to ask that you inform your secretary that I received this decoration in the American embassy, in the presence of your ambassador, and that I was there at his request in order to assist in creating a better relationship between the American embassy and the German government, which your ambassador desired at that time?

Mr. President, if the statements of your Secretary of the Interior are true, and if I have any connection with a foreign government, the American people have a right to be fully acquainted with the facts. On the other hand, if his statements and implications are false, I believe that I, as an American citizen, have a right to an apology from your secretary.

Mr. President, I give you my word that I have no connection with any foreign government. I have had no communication, directly or indirectly, with any one in Germany or Italy since I was last in Europe, in the Spring of 1939. Prior to that time, my activities were well known to your embassies in the countries where I lived and traveled. I always kept in close contact with your embassies and your military attaches, as the records in your State Department and War Department will show.

Mr. President, I will willingly open my files to your investigation. I will willingly appear in person before any committee you appoint, and there is no question regarding my activities now, or at any time in the past, that I will not be glad to answer.

Mr. President, if there is a question in your mind, I ask that you give me the opportunity of answering any charges that may be made against me. But, Mr. President, unless charges are made and proved, I believe that the customs and traditions of our country give me, as an American citizen, the right to expect truth and justice from the members of your cabinet.

To date, Colonel Lindbergh has had no reply.

---

* In this particular slinging of mud, Ickes, once described by Clare Boothe Luce as having "the soul of a meat axe and the mind of a commissar," discoursed on "what a menace [Lindbergh] and those like him are to this country and its free institutions." Ickes added, "I have never heard this Knight of the German Eagle denounce Hitler or Nazism or Mussolini or Fascism." Berg, *Lindbergh*, p. 423.

The series of public addresses in the spring of 1941 continued, with a speech in Minneapolis on May 10.* He told his audience,

[T]he question is whether we have learned enough [in the years since World War I] to withstand the barrage of propaganda to which we have been subjected ever since this war began; and whether, if we can withstand that barrage, we will be able to impose our will upon the government in Washington. . . .

There was once a time in America when we could impose our will by vote. Candidates brought political issues before us, and stated clearly their stand. After an election was over, responsibility to the voters remained . . . but it now seems doubtful that we had even two parties last November, at least as far as the Presidential candidates were concerned.[†] The people of this nation were not given the chance to vote on the greatest issue of our generation—the issue of foreign war. And yet we are told now that we must go to Europe to fight for the very principles of democracy that were denied to us in our own nation last November. . . .

The future of democracy depends on our ability to govern our own country. It rests in the character of our own people, in the welfare of our farmers and our workmen. What happens in Europe and Asia is of secondary importance to what is happening to us here in our own land. It is far more essential for this country to have farms without mortgages, workmen with their own homes, and young people who can afford families, than it is for us to crusade abroad for freedoms that are tottering in our own country.

The Madison Square Garden meeting in New York on May 23 heard Colonel Lindbergh define an "independent destiny for America":

We are assembled here tonight because we believe in an independent destiny for America. . . . An independent American destiny means, on the one hand, that our soldiers will not have to fight everybody in the world who prefers some other system of life to ours. On the other hand, it means that we will fight anybody and everybody who attempts to interfere with our hemisphere, and that we will do so with all the resources of our nation. It means that we rely on our own strength, our own ability, and our own courage, to preserve this nation and to defeat anyone who is rash enough to attack us. It means that we have faith that these United States of ours can compete in commerce or in war with any combination of foreign powers; and that we are no more afraid of the Europe of Germany than our forefathers were afraid of the Europe of France or England or Spain.

We in America should have no reason to fear. With adequate leadership we can be the strongest and most influential nation in the world. No other country has as great

---

* Lindbergh wrote in his diary on May 10, 1941, "After supper we drove to the meeting hall a few blocks away. It was already jammed with about 10,000 people when we arrived. . . . Senator Shipstead [R-Minn.] spoke first; then Hanford MacNider introduced me. This time I kept well within my half hour. The crowd came up onto the stage after the meeting and made it rather difficult for us to get our party together and into the cars. The people seemed to be one hundred percent behind our stand on the war, and they averaged a very high type of American." Lindbergh, *Wartime Journals*, p. 485.

† For a brilliant analysis of the Coke-Pepsi "choice" presented by the parties in 1940, see Gore Vidal's novel *The Golden Age* (New York: Doubleday, 2000).

resources. None is as easily defended. We lack only a leadership that places America first—a leadership that does for one hundred and thirty million people what Washington did for us when we were only three million people—a leadership that tells what it means and means what it says. Give us that and we will be the most powerful country in the world. Give us that, and we will be so united that no one will dare to attack us.
. . .

I opposed this war before it was declared because I felt it would be disastrous for Europe. I knew that England and France were not in a position to win, and I did not want them to lose. I now oppose our entry into the war because I do not believe that our system of government in America, and our way of life, can survive our participation.

The May 30* speech delivered in Philadelphia summarized the records of the interventionists in the countries of Europe—encouraging the smaller nations to fight on the strength of promises of help that were never carried out, knowing that no nation was in any sense prepared to fight against a prepared Germany.

[The interventionists] say that the only way we can defend democracy is by adopting the policies of a totalitarian state ourselves. They tell us it is undemocratic for us to question the type of leadership that has taken to defeat every nation in the world that followed it. They shout to us, as they shouted at England and France; they say: Never mind realities, the moral effect will make up for our lack of preparation. Their prophecies have been false, their policies have failed, and their promises have been worthless. They have a record of utter failure behind them—Poland, Finland, Norway, Holland, Belgium, France, Yugoslavia, Greece. Yet now they demand that we too enter the greatest conflict in history, unprepared. I ask you, is our nation to follow them further? Is it not time for us to turn to new policies and to a new leadership?

The America First Committee stands for leadership of a different type. We have constantly opposed the interventionist philosophy. We believe that the security of our country lies in the strength and character of our own people, and not in fighting foreign wars. . . .

I tell you it is time for our people to ask where we are going, to consider where our course will end. We are not children to be coddled into unpleasant situations. We are not the blind followers of a totalitarian regime. We are the citizens of a free country, a country governed by the people and for the people. We demand the truth from our leaders. We demand that they stop all this vagueness and confusion, and tell us, as free men should be told, what their intentions are about this war. We demand a philosophy and a policy that will lead to strength and success; not to confusion and failure as in the past.

The colonel's appeal for "new leadership" drew forth widespread charges that he was advocating impeachment of the president or revolution. Queried by the editor of the Baltimore *Sun* as to his exact meaning, the colonel asserted

---

*Actually May 29; Lindbergh wrote in his diary, "In some ways the audience was the most enthusiastic we have had yet. . . . This country is not ready for war, and the people who are against it do not intend to be intimidated into silence." Lindbergh, *Wartime Journals*, p. 498.

that he had directed his statement not at the president's office, but at "the leadership of the interventionists which the Nation has been following in recent months." He explained further that "neither I nor any one else in the America First Committee advocates proceeding by anything but constitutional methods." The exchange follows:

From William E. Moore, managing editor of the Baltimore *Sun*, to Colonel Lindbergh:*

Since you recently began using the phrase that the America First organization is "seeking new leadership in Washington," it has been noted that other foremost speakers for the America First cause are using the same phrase. Governor La Follette used it here in his speech last night. The Sun would be glad to print your explanation of the meaning of this phrase, and how a new leadership could be set up under our constitutional form of government before the next election.

From Colonel Lindbergh to Mr. Moore:

In reply to your telegram of June 6, my reference to the need for new leadership applied to the leadership of the interventionists which the nation has been following in recent months.

This is obvious if you read the paragraph of my Philadelphia address in which I asked, "Is it not time for us to turn to new policies and to new leadership?" In many press reports my question was removed entirely from its context.

Neither I nor any one else on the America First Committee advocate proceeding by anything but constitutional methods. It is our opposition (the interventionists) which endangers the American Constitution when it objects to our freedom of speech and expression.

Under the Constitution, we have every right to advocate a leadership for this country which is non-interventionist and which places the interests of America first. This is, in fact, the primary objective of our committee. We believe that a non-interventionist and fundamentally American leadership is of vital necessity to the security and welfare of our country.

In a personal letter to General Wood, Colonel Lindbergh wrote frankly of his attitude toward the criticism directed at his statement:

Thank you very much for your June 2nd letter in regard to the Philadelphia meeting. I am enclosing a copy of my address so that you can read the full paragraph in which my question, "Is it not time for us to turn to new policies and to a new leadership?" appeared. This paragraph was in regard to the "interventionists." As usual, my reference to a "new leadership" was taken completely out of context by the newspaper reports of the address. They made it appear that I suggested "Revolution or Impeachment" which was not in any way the case.

My entire address was wound around the "Intervention" leadership we have been following in recent months. That President Roosevelt is among our arch interventionists

* June 6, 1941.

is obvious, but to advocate a "new leadership" in place of the "interventionist" leadership we have been following does not in any way imply that we should impeach the President or go through a revolution.

I do not believe there is any way of preventing an antagonistic press from removing sentences from their context. One can only attempt to avoid giving our opposition the opportunity to do this more than is necessary. As you know, I spent considerable time analyzing my addresses with this in view—so much so that many of our friends criticize their infrequency. As I reread the paragraph in question, however, I am inclined to the belief that its meaning cannot be misunderstood, if read with even reasonable care; and that if our opposition had not selected this sentence for attack, they would have selected some other sentence. As a matter of fact, the New York *Herald Tribune* did select another sentence for their headline which read approximately as follows: "Lindbergh says Roosevelt desires world domination—not Hitler." This was taken from the following portion of the paragraph ending on page 8 of the enclosed copy: "Mr. Roosevelt claims that Hitler desires to dominate the world. But it is Mr. Roosevelt himself who advocates world domination when he says that it is our business to control the wars of Europe and Asia, and that we in America must dominate islands lying off the African coast."

The question of interpretation or misinterpretation which has arisen in these instances shows how essential it is for me to use the utmost care in writing my addresses. You are one of the few people in America First who realize this. I am under constant pressure to speak more frequently; but some of the very people who told me a few days ago that it made very little difference what I said as long as I said it often enough, were among the first to be disturbed by the opposition's criticism of the "new leadership" portion of my Philadelphia address.

The Philadelphia address was bound to bring this concentrated criticism of our opposition because it followed so closely the President's "Unlimited Emergency"* Proclamation. Obviously, the Administration was anxious to silence us by that Proclamation as far as possible. The question arose as to what attitude it was best to take. I felt the time had come to attack. It seems obvious to me that Roosevelt always uses support as one more stepping stone to war.

As I have said, I believe it is impossible to guard completely against willful misquotation. But possibly the most significant element in the present situation lies in the rather subconscious attitude in America which caused the (even willful) implication that my reference to the need for "new leadership" was a suggestion of revolution or impeachment. That suggestion, apparently, was not so much in my address as in a feeling that is beginning to appear among our people—unrecognized as yet, but extremely serious. The President, knowingly or unknowingly has been nursing this feeling for many years. How far it rises depends more upon him than upon his opposition. In this respect, it is interesting to note that the question of impeachment has arisen through the fear of Administration supporters rather than through the attacks of their opposition.

Please do not hesitate to write about any question which arises in your mind concerning my addresses. It is of great help to me and I know of no one for whose judgment I have more respect.

---

* President's speech of May 27, 1941.

The popular reception to Colonel Lindbergh's first half-dozen speeches had been such that General Wood felt it was time once more to urge the colonel to take the chairmanship of the committee, and so wrote him on May 23:

I feel more strongly than ever that you are the one logical man to take the chairmanship of the America First Committee. Your courage, your patriotism, your clear thinking—the way you have carried the banner in the last six weeks, and the trust your fellow citizens repose in you, make you the logical man.

As I told you at the time, I feel the committee is handicapped by not having a full time chairman. While I have done everything I possibly could, it is impossible for me, as head of a great business, to give the time and thought to the Committee that it ought to have and that I would like to give it. My idea is that you should take the chairmanship on July 1st. I, of course would remain on the Committee as honorary chairman and as a member of the executive committee. I would give you every ounce of assistance I could.

Colonel Lindbergh again refused, because he believed his lack of training in executive work would require his taking too much time from speaking to learn organizational work:

I would have to discontinue making addresses and, for several weeks or months, concentrate upon the duties required of the National Chairman. I could not carry on both adequately until I learned each thoroughly.

He believed there was a tactical advantage to the noninterventionists in presenting two fronts to the interventionist opposition—the committee and himself. He could take a more advanced position on issues as an individual than as chairman of the committee:

I have put off answering your May 23d letter: first, because I was working on my address for the Philadelphia meeting; and second, because an adequate reply requires more time than I have had up to this moment.

I have considered very carefully the question of taking the Chairmanship of the America First Committee, and have come to the conclusion that such a move would be inadvisable from many standpoints. I shall look forward to discussing these with you in New York next week; but, meanwhile, I would like to outline some of the reasons upon which I base my feeling.

First I want to tell you again how greatly I appreciate the confidence you place in me when you suggest that I take the Chairmanship. Coming from you, this means more to me than it would coming from anyone else, and I mean this literally.

My arguments against taking the Chairmanship fall into two classifications—one concerns the effectiveness of the Committee, and the other is personal. Both are, of course, somewhat interrelated. Since my personal arguments are the least important in view of the magnitude of our objective, I shall mention them first.

My experience, ability and interests have always lain in fields which are not primarily executive. I could, I believe, learn to carry on executive work, but it would mean at least the partial abandonment of other efforts. In this instance, if I were to take the Chairmanship of the National Committee, I would have to discontinue making addresses and, for several weeks or months, concentrate upon the duties required of the National Chairman. I could not carry on both adequately until I learned each thoroughly.

To be specific, if I were to take the Chairmanship of the America First Committee, every local Committee and every member and every outside individual who has ideas of reform or criticism or salvation would descend upon me as soon as my Chairmanship were announced. There would be the internal conflict of Committeemen, the reconsideration of appointments and decisions and all the confusion which comes when people see a new opportunity of getting their particular ideas across. The handling of the resulting situation with reasonable tact and courtesy would require weeks of time and, as I have said, the temporary abandonment of everything else. As you know, if I disregarded the requests which arose, it would lead to terrific criticism and to increased friction within the Committee and its branches.

There is another personal consideration which I believe I should mention here. It is that I have no desire to enter political life, or to continue political activity after this war crisis has passed. I believe that every man has an obligation to his country in time of real crisis, but I do not follow the argument that the greatest contribution one can make to his country is by permanently entering the political field. I find it very difficult to explain this to my friends, and know that it would be still more difficult to explain if I were to take the Chairmanship of America First. I am most anxious to hold myself in a position where I can return to non-political interests and activities as soon as the war crisis has passed and do so without appearing to "let down" the people with whom I have been working in this emergency. I realize that America First is not a political organization, but my acceptance of the Chairmanship would have a political appearance which I am anxious not to create.

Now I will argue my position from the standpoint of the America First Committee's welfare: it is of vital importance to force our opposition to spread their fire. At present they strike America First only indirectly when they strike at me, and vice versa. If I were National Chairman, whenever they strike at me, they would strike directly at America First. This would greatly weaken our position. Also, we now have two sources of striking power whereas, if I were Chairman, we would only have one.

Under the present relationship, I feel free to take a far more exposed stand than I could take as Chairman. If some of the members of the Committee do not agree with all that I say, they are less likely to take active issue or to resign than they would if I spoke as National Chairman. On the other hand, I can advance ideas that the Committee might, in some cases, wish to support after some time has passed.

My last, and possibly my most important, argument is that no man in this country is as well qualified to be Chairman of the America First Committee as you yourself. Here again, I speak literally and not simply in order to pass a compliment. You have exceptional executive experience and ability, you hold the title of General in the American Army, you served in the last war, you are the head of a great commercial organization with world-wide interests, your name is well known throughout America, you are liked and respected by every person I have ever met who knows you personally. It would be impossible for me or anyone else to adequately replace you as Chairman of the America First Committee.

On the other hand, the relationship we now hold is, I believe, ideal. I am in a position to assist the Committee in the field in which I have most background and ability, while you give the committee leadership and prestige that is absolutely irreplaceable. It seems to me that during these weeks of crisis—and I have always felt the spring and summer would bring the period of great crisis for America—it is vital for us to operate with our maximum efficiency as an organization.

I know what sacrifice you are making to carry on the Chairmanship of the America First Committee in addition to all of your other obligations. But the entire future of our country, and even of our civilization, is at stake and I fervently hope you may find it possible to continue as Chairman until we can foresee the future more clearly. It seems probable that the next few weeks—possibly the next few days—will place us in a better position to lay plans and make decisions. I know that I voice the sentiment of the entire America First Committee and of many millions of Americans when I ask you to continue as our Chairman during this emergency.

Through the summer and early fall, Colonel Lindbergh made six more addresses at America First rallies.*

In San Francisco, July 1, Colonel Lindbergh discussed the "record of hypocrisy and confusion" of this war:†

The murderers and plunderers of yesterday are accepted as the valiant defenders of civilization today; and the valiant defenders of yesterday have become the wicked aggressors of today. Finland and France are now our enemies; Russia our friend. . . . When Germany was a republic, France and England refused her simplest requests. But when she turned into a Fascist state, they let her do as she pleased. When German troops marched into the Rhineland, France and England made no move, but after the Siegfried Line was built, they declared war. . . . One month we hear that England and France will fight to the death against the gangster tactics of Germany. The next month, we hear that the British Navy has turned its guns on the French fleet and that French aircraft are dropping bombs on Gibraltar. One year a war is declared without consulting America. The next year we are told that America is responsible for the war. . . .

Confusion is not an accidental fact in this war. It is the major weapon of the interventionists. . . .

The record of the interventionists has been a record of abject failure. . . . Intervention with sanctions in the war between Italy and Abyssinia didn't save Abyssinia; it simply threw Italy into Germany's open arms. Intervention by England and France in the war between Germany and Poland did not save Poland; it postponed the war between Germany and Russia, and brought the defeat of France and the devastation of England. The attitude of American interventionists toward Japan force that country, too, into the arms of the Axis. . . .

The real defeatist in America is the man who says that this Nation cannot survive alone.

---

*I have omitted an excerpt from Lindbergh's June 20, 1941, Los Angeles speech.

†Lindbergh wrote in his diary on July 1, 1941, "I spoke from 8:30 to 9:00. Then Mrs. Norris, Miss [Lillian] Gish, and Senator [D. Worth] Clark [D-Idaho], in the order named. I think the meeting was a little too long, but the crowd was responsive and apparently ninety percent or more behind us, if one can judge by the demonstration." Lindbergh, *Wartime Journals*, p. 512.

"Government by Representation or Subterfuge" was the subject of Colonel Lindbergh's Cleveland address on August 9:*

We are faced with the stark fact that we have been carried to the verge of war against the opposition of a majority of our people—a war not of defense, but of attack; a war not in America, but in Europe and Asia. We are faced with the realization that our President consults our representatives in Congress with less and less frequency, and that, while the direct attempt to pack our Supreme Court failed, its membership has now changed indirectly through retirement. We are faced with the knowledge that the most important issue of our generation—that of peace or war; that of defense or attack; that of whether or not the destiny of America is to be merged with the destiny of Europe—has not been placed before a vote of our people. . . . [T]he question arises whether we any longer have a representative system of government in this country, whether we any longer have the right to know about, and to vote upon, the fundamental policies of our nation. . . .

National polls show that from the time this war started in Europe, when Americans were asked whether or not we should enter it, the overwhelming majority answered "No"! National polls today show that the great majority of our people still stand opposed to entering the war. But step by step we have been carried towards it. . . . [I]nside of these sweetened promises of peace lay the deadly pills of war, and . . . we have been swallowing them one after another for many months. . . .

[Freedom for us] lies today in the question of whether or not the action of our Government in America is controlled by the will of our people. If we are represented in Washington, we are free men; but if we are ruled by Washington, we are not.

In his August 29 Oklahoma City address, Colonel Lindbergh discussed the effects of air power, as observed in his study of several years both in Europe and in the United States:†

I was forced to the conclusion that France and England were not in a position to win a war against Germany, and that the dominant position in Europe had shifted from England, as a sea power, to Germany, as a land and air power. . . . [W]hile aviation greatly strengthened our positon in America from the standpoint of defense, it greatly weakened our position from the standpoint of attacking Europe. . . .

It was obvious, even before this war started, that air power made it costly, if not impossible, for naval forces to operate within effective bombing range of an enemy coast adequately protected by aircraft. This meant that troops could not be landed and maintained on any coast where an enemy had strong supremacy of the air. . . .

It was obvious, before the war started, that Germany had by far the strongest air

* Lindbergh wrote in his diary on August 9, 1941, "It was an excellent meeting—enthusiastic crowd which, as usual, seemed to be eighty percent or more with us. No sensible person can attend these meetings without realizing that public opinion is *not* ready for war." Lindbergh, *Wartime Journals*, p. 525.

† The rally was held at a ballpark after the city fathers refused to permit an America First gathering in the civic auditorium.

force in Europe . . . that England lay within ideal bombing range of aircraft based on the continent of Europe, and that her sea lanes could be harassed both by submarines and bombing planes. . . .

It was just as obvious that the great distance across the ocean placed America outside the effective bombing range of European aircraft, and that even if it were possible to establish European air bases in South America, which I believe we can prevent, the United States would still be outside of their effective bombing range.

. . . I came to the conclusion that there were two, and only two, great and natural air powers in the world at this time—the United States, in the Western Hemisphere, and Germany, in the Eastern Hemisphere. I was convinced that neither was in a position to attack the other successfully across the ocean, unless an internal collapse preceded an invasion. It seems clear to me that the quickest way for Germany to lose a war would be to attack America, and that the quickest way for America to lose a war would be to attack Germany. . . .

Let us take advantage of the changes that aircraft and this modern era bring to nations and to men. Let us use these changes to our advantage, and not permit them to be used against us.

Colonel Lindbergh's September 11 address at Des Moines on the subject "Who Are the War Agitators?" is reprinted in full as footnote 8 in Chapter 3.

Speaking at an America First rally in Fort Wayne (Indiana) on October 3 "as though this were my last address," Colonel Lindbergh talked of "A Heritage at Stake." He expressed his fears of encroachments on free speech, his concern lest the next elections be abandoned:*

It is essential for us to realize that what we used to call representative government, American independence, and the American way of life, is rapidly becoming a thing of the past. We are approaching a point where we are no longer governed by the will of the people. We are, in fact, governed by one man who has consistently evaded the checks and balances on which representative government depends—a man who is drawing more and more dictatorial powers into his own hands.

Recently—no one will ever know the exact date—we began following a road which involved the abandonment of our most fundamental customs and traditions. And since we have been traveling that road, our leaders have rapidly burned the bridges behind us. We must face the fact that you and I and our generation have lost our American heritage. It is no longer simply a case of defending it. It is a case of re-building it. We are entering a period in America that can be compared only to the periods passed through by the nations of Europe during the last generation.

---

* Lindbergh wrote in his diary on October 3, 1941, "The opposition paper here is carrying a large advertisement in which statements are attributed to me which I never made. As far as the 'war party' is concerned, what I actually say seems to be of little importance. They quote me as saying what they *wish* or *think* that I said. . . . The result is that I am often quoted as saying things which I not only never said, but which I never believed." Lindbergh, *Wartime Journals,* p. 544.

Colonel Lindbergh's popularity increased with every speech, and the insistence of chapters from Maine to California that he speak at their rallies became a problem for national headquarters, through which all requests cleared, and for the colonel himself, who spent from two to three weeks in the preparation of every speech.

At the conference of chapter chairmen in Chicago in July, every one of the 118 chapters represented had indicated that a Lindbergh meeting was a "must" item on their programs for the next few months. The clamor for Colonel Lindbergh had been temporarily diverted during the summer by holding a membership contest among the chapters; the promised prize was that "first consideration for a future appearance of Charles A. Lindbergh" would be given to the winning chapter. The Fort Wayne (Indiana) chapter was the winner, and Colonel Lindbergh spoke there on October 3. But when the contest was over the pressure began again.

The problem created by more demands for addresses than he could fill was in process of solution by the colonel when the war broke. His letter to General Wood of October 27, concerning not only his connection with the committee but also the future of the committee itself, furnishes the explanation. It also explains his preoccupation with "belief and fact" in the preparation of his speeches, rather than "popularity and effect:"[10]

I have just finished writing my address for the Madison Square meeting Thursday evening, and plan on leaving for New York tomorrow afternoon.

During these days on Martha's Vineyard, I have spent a great deal of time considering the future of the America First Committee, and my own connection with it.

I know, from our conversations in Chicago, that your mind has been working actively along similar lines; and, therefore, I believe you will be interested in the conclusions I have reached.

The question which seems paramount to me, involves the length of life the Committee is to have. Several possibilities arise: We may be forced to adjourn in the near future because of our country's involvement in war. England may decide to negotiate a peace that will place the Committee in the position of having accomplished its objective. Unforeseen developments may cause the Committee to enter the field of domestic politics, and become a permanent political organization.

As you know, some of our members desire the Committee to dissolve as soon as the war issue ends, while others desire to see it continue indefinitely.

In view of trends now developing in this country, it seems to me there will be increasing need of an organization of the type that America First represents.

The very nature of our times, and of the Committee itself, makes it impossible to lay definite plans. This creates a problem in regard to my personal relationship with the Committee in the future.

As I have often said, I do not feel that I am suited, either by temperament or desire, to the field of active politics. I have entered this field, during the last two years, only because of the extreme wartime emergency which confronts our country.

For more than six months now, I have devoted the major portion of my time to America First meetings and other activities. From my standpoint, it has been time well spent. I believe the work of the Committee has been of great importance, and that it has had a very constructive effect in this country. But I now find myself headed toward a position which I do not wish to hold, and which I think would be inadvisable from the standpoint of the Committee itself, especially if it is to continue for many months into the future.

I am receiving letters and phone calls from Chapters all over the country, saying that my attendance as a speaker is essential to a major meeting in their section. I greatly appreciate the confidence that these invitations imply, and would be very pleased to receive them if I could devote all of my time in the future to America First activities, and if I did not see the danger involved for the Committee in the relationship which is arising.

It seems to me that it is advisable for the America First committee to avoid building up any one man to a position of too great importance in the organization. The Committee is made up of too many conflicting viewpoints, aside from the issue of intervention, to permit its membership to be satisfied with any single leader. The reaction to my address at Des Moines is an example of what I mean.

But if the Committee is to organize around a single leader, that man should be able to devote practically his entire time to America First activities, in which case, it would be perfectly normal to expect him to attend all the major rallies.

In a letter, one can never communicate more than a portion of his attitude and feeling. As I read back, over the preceding paragraphs, I feel that I have expressed myself inadequately. Possibly I can paint a clearer picture if I write from a purely personal viewpoint, not with the idea of shifting my burdens to your shoulders, but in order to clarify a mutual problem.

I have just finished an address which it has taken me many days to write. The best part of a week will be taken up with traveling, and arrangements connected with its delivery. As soon as I get to New York, there will be representatives of various chapters (there were seven at Fort Wayne) demanding that I set a date for a meeting in their community.

Frankly, I feel "written out" on addresses. It takes a great deal of time for me to write an address that I feel is worth giving, and I have too much sympathy for my audience, and respect for myself, to be willing to speak unless I have something that I think is worth saying.

The result of this situation is that I feel I am speaking much too often, while most of my friends on the America First Committee feel that I am speaking nowhere near often enough.

As things now stand, every meeting I attend increases the problem. Instead of building up new speakers, it makes Committee members feel that my attendance at the next rally is still more important, while it separates me farther from interests which I cannot indefinitely set aside.

It is not a case of being unwilling to sacrifice personal interests to the welfare of the nation, but of believing that my contribution, in the future, lies primarily along other lines than giving addresses at rallies.

Bearing these considerations in mind, I have tried to lay out fairly definite plans for my own action. Subject to developments of the war, I intend to withdraw gradually from participation in these rallies. That work should, I believe, be turned over to men who have a natural aptitude for politics and speaking.

In doing this, I want to assist the Committee as much as I can from the standpoint of a supporter, rather than from the standpoint of a committee leader.

This will accomplish two important objectives. From my standpoint, it will permit me to pick up the threads of other activities which I dropped in order to help build up the strength of the America First Committee. From the Committee's standpoint, it will, I believe, bring about a more practical organization; and it will largely absolve the Committee as a whole from feeling responsible for my personal views. (One of my greatest concerns at the moment lies in the fact that many members of the Committee feel more or less responsible for my personal views on matters which are outside of the war issue. Their primary interest often lies in popularity and effect, whereas I think my primary interest lies in belief and fact. We frequently disagree on the compromise that is to be made between these elements.)

In coming to any conclusion, one must allow much flexibility for unknown developments of the war. If a crisis arises in the near future, in which the America First Committee can be effective, our plans should certainly allow for concentration on that emergency. The collapse of the Russian armies may easily bring the demand in England for negotiation. If so, I think we should be ready to support that demand over here, and that I shall hold myself in readiness to assist in doing.

But in going on from month to month, the day may come when what we now call an emergency becomes rather normal life. Knowing that many of our members look forward to the America First Committee's (or a large portion of its membership, under another name) entering the field of domestic politics, I believe it will be advisable to follow out the plans I have outlined in this letter.

I write at this time because I believe it would be unfair to allow a false impression to arise among members of the Committees concerning my position and relationship, and because I want you to be the first to know of my plans. They involve a control over the situation I see arising, rather than any change in attitude. I intend to continue opposing American intervention as strongly as ever, and in whatever way I think will be most effective.

This letter does not require an answer. I will look forward to talking all these matters over with you when we meet again. I am convinced that the course I have outlined will prove the most constructive in the long run; but it necessitates no immediate decision, and, as I say, it is quite possible that war developments will sweep these problems entirely out of our control.

Colonel Lindbergh was to make one more speech for America First before war came. [It was] at Madison Square Garden in New York City on October 30.* There he told his hearers that as one of those "who have taken a leading part in opposing American intervention," he wished to lay his "motives openly before the millions of Americans who have stood at our side." Regarding his motives for opposing the war in Europe, he said,

---

* Lindbergh wrote in his diary on October 30, 1941, "This was in many ways the most successful meeting we have yet held. . . . The thing that I think pleased me most about the meeting was the quality of the people who attended. I studied their faces carefully while I was sitting on the platform, and they were *far* above the average of New York. Those people are worth fighting for." Lindbergh, *Wartime Journals*, pp. 551–2.

My estimate of the situation in Europe, and the best policy to follow, was different than that of most of my friends. After the Siegfried Line was built, I knew that the French and British armies were no longer in a position to attack Germany successfully. . . .

By 1938, I had come to the conclusion that if a war occurred between Germany on one side, and England and France on the other, it would result either in a German victory, or in a prostrate and devastated Europe. I therefore advocated that England and France build their military forces with the utmost rapidity, but that they permit Germany to expand eastward into Russia without declaring war.

As you know, the opposite school of thought prevailed. The men who were in control in England and France said that Germany was bluffing, that she was not strong enough to win a major war, that air power was no match for the British navy, and that the best way for England and France to defend themselves was to defend Poland. The idealists rushed forward with the cry that aggression must be stopped, and that war must be declared on Germany in order to preserve the peace and civilization of Europe.

Concerning his reasons for opposing U.S. intervention, he said,

I knew that no amount of intervention by the United States could change the basic fact that aviation weakened the military position of the British Isles in relation to the Continent. I believed that the future of England and France depended more upon their own birth rates and internal conditions than upon our assistance in winning another war. . . .

My opposition to American intervention was based upon many reasons; but I think that none was stronger than my belief that modern aviation made it impractical, if not impossible, for an expeditionary force to cross an ocean and land successfully on a hostile coast against a strong enemy air power.

I believed that history, and experience, and judgment, all showed that the destiny of America should not be tied to the outcome of European War.

The speech scheduled for a Boston America First rally on December 12 was never delivered. The war put an end to committee activities, and to Colonel Lindbergh's crusade to keep the country out of war.

Because the speech Colonel Lindbergh had prepared for the Boston rally dealt with a subject on which his views were frequently sought, "What Do We Mean by Democracy and Freedom?" a preliminary draft of the undelivered address is printed in full:

In the slogans and propaganda that have been hurled back and forth during these months of war, there has been much discussion of those qualities of American life called *Democracy* and *Freedom*. Committees have been formed to defend and to befriend democracy, and to fight for freedom. Our President says we must make this nation an "arsenal for Democracy," and that it is our mission to spread, by force if necessary, various forms of freedom throughout the world.

I believe it is time to define exactly what we mean by democracy and freedom. These are qualities too sacred to our country, to our traditions, and to our hopes, to be left to the irresponsible use of slogans and propaganda. It is meaningless to talk about fighting for freedom or defending Democracy unless we have first established, deep in our minds and hearts, what freedom and democracy really mean.

I believe in freedom and I believe in democracy, but I do not believe in the form of freedom and democracy toward which our President is leading us today. I say that *democracy* is gone from a nation when its people are no longer informed of the fundamental policies and intentions of its government. I say that the word *freedom* is a travesty among men who have been forced into war by a President they elected because he promised peace.

If democracy means anything at all, it means that the citizens of a democratic state have the right to be informed about, and to vote upon, the major policies of their government. If freedom means anything at all, it means that free citizens have the right to decide whether or not they send their men to die in foreign wars.

A democratic people must be an informed people, a trusted people. If we do not know what our government is doing or what it intends to do; if we have no right to vote upon the issue of foreign war; if our news is to be censored and mixed with propaganda, as in the totalitarian states; if our citizens are to be drafted, and our national economy upset, by a President who ran for his first term on promises of economy, and for his third term on promises of peace; then ours is no longer a free and democratic nation.

Men and women of Massachusetts: *Freedom* and *Democracy* cannot long exist without a third quality, a quality called *Integrity*. It is a quality whose absence is alarming in our government today. Without integrity, freedom and democracy will become only politicians' nicknames for an American totalitarian state.

What we need today is not a "Committee to Defend Democracy" by "steps short of war," but a "Committee to Defend Integrity" by steps that are not short of anything at all. We do not need a "Committee to Fight for Freedom" abroad, as much as we need a committee to fight for the freedom of American citizens to decide their own destiny at home. I think we need a "New Deal," but we need one that holds its cards above the table.

There is one word that describes better than all others our danger in America. It is not invasion; it is not intervention; it is not Germany or Russia or Japan; that word is subterfuge—subterfuge in our Government, subterfuge in our political campaigns. Subterfuge marked every step we made "short of war," and it now marks every step we are making "short of" a dictatorial system in America.

Our nation has been led to war with promises of peace. It is now being led toward dictatorship with promises of democracy. The battle cry of freedom is being used to regiment our people.

It is time to strip the masque from the leadership we have been following. It is time to find out what ideas and what beliefs march behind the words waving on its banners. Many of us are tired of listening to promises that are made "again, and again, and again," and then turn out to be nothing more than the "oratory" of a political campaign.

Have you ever stopped to think how ridiculous it is that this democratic nation has twice, within a generation, been carried to war by Presidents who were elected because they promised peace? Have you ever realized how absurd it is for us in America to have committees who claim, in one breath, to stand for freedom and democracy, when in the next breath they demand that the Government of this country declare war while the majority of our citizens are opposed to it?

Our President has spoken of four freedoms that should be spread all over the world. I believe it is time to ask him about other freedoms that he left unmentioned, freedoms that apply to us right here at home. For instance, let us address this question to our President:

Do you or do you not, Mr. Roosevelt, believe in the freedom of the American people to decide their own destiny by means of the vote? If you do believe in this freedom, how do you explain your thrice stated election promises of peace, in the light of your leadership to war? If you say that conditions have changed since the election, and if you still say you believe in democracy and freedom, why are you unwilling to submit the question of foreign war to a referendum of the people? And Mr. President, please give us credit for enough intelligence so that you do not reply that we are at war because American warships, attending to their own affairs in Icelandic waters, were, for no reason at all, attacked by the German navy.

And Mr. President, there is one more question we would like you to answer so that we may better know what you have in mind when you use such words as democracy and freedom. Mr. President: Iceland was a European island, belonging to Denmark. It was occupied by belligerent forces of Europe. It was in a war zone which was declared soon after the start of hostilities. It was in an area that you yourself recognized as a war zone by banning it to American shipping. There could be a no more momentous decision for this free and democratic nation than the decision whether or not to send American forces to occupy a foreign island, lying in the German war zone, off the European coast. Yet you made this decision upon your own initiative, as a dictator would have made it, without any warning to our people, and without even laying the matter before our Congress. Mr. President: Is this your idea of democracy and freedom? Is this your standard of integrity, after promising us again, and again, and again, that our boys would not be sent to fight in foreign wars?

The American people have a right to answers to those questions, Mr. President, and if they are not forthcoming, do not be surprised when you find among us a new movement, a movement for democracy and freedom of a different sort; a movement that has real democracy and real freedom as its foundation; a movement which has integrity as the ideal at its peak.

The record of the Roosevelt Administration has been a record of subterfuge masquerading as a crusade for freedom. "Cash and Carry," "Steps Short of War," "Aid to the Democracies," "Neutrality Patrols," "Lease and Lend"; every one of these slogans was used to deceive the American people; every one of them was a disgrace to the names of democracy and freedom.

First, we were subjected to a fear campaign, and told that America would be invaded if we didn't defend England. Then we were subjected to a greed campaign, and told that Germany would get some of our foreign trade if we didn't protect the British Empire. Now we are subjected to a hate campaign, and told that Germany may not be crushed if we don't enter the war ourselves. And in between, our ideals are appealed to. We are told that we must go to war to help the British Empire and the Soviet Union defend democracy and liberty and non-aggression. We democratic people are apparently considered such imbeciles that we can be told one year that France and Finland represent everything we would be willing to die for, and told the next year that France and Finland have changed and represent everything we should be willing to die against. One year Russia is a totalitarian monster, and the next year she is a democratic friend.

The United States is on the verge of war today. Our navy has already become involved in fighting. We are on the verge of war in Asia, in Europe, and in Africa; war on the Atlantic, war on the Pacific, on the Mediterranean Sea, on the Indian Ocean; war with

Germany, with Italy, with Japan; war, possibly, against France and Spain and some of the smaller countries of Europe as well. And what is our objective? Are we to die by the millions to make the world safe for ideals of freedom and democracy that are denied to us in our own country? Are we to spend unlimited American lives, throw American business into bankruptcy, and harness our children and our grandchildren with debt, in a crusade to make democracy safe among foreign nations who don't desire it?

Before we crusade for freedom and democracy in foreign nations and on foreign continents, let us decide how we intend to apply these terms at home, how they are to be applied to us, here, in what we have called the foremost democracy on earth. How are we to apply freedom and democracy to our right to vote on vital issues, to our right to determine our own destiny either in peace or in war, to our right to be accurately informed about the policies and the actions of our own government. Before we crusade for freedom and democracy abroad, let us decide how these terms are to be applied to the Negro problem in our southern states. Before we send our youth to die defending the freedom and democracy of the British Empire, let us decide how freedom and democracy are to be applied to British Imperialism in India. Before we send American soldiers to fight for Soviet Russia, let us inquire why a nation as brave and as respected as Finland, a nation that has fought for freedom and democracy with the utmost courage, let us inquire why such a nation has been fighting on the other side.

Before we spend unlimited billions for foreign war, before we crusade so blithely for four freedoms across the seas, before we send the spirit of America "to stand on foreign ground," let us make sure that the roots of freedom and democracy are firmly planted in our own country, and that these words, dear to the heart of every American, stand for more than the campaign slogans of politicians and the propaganda of foreign agents.

Men and women of Massachusetts: It is time for a new movement in this country, a movement with its roots in American traditions, and with its branches in American ideals, a movement which is not tied to political parties, and which says what it means, and which means what it says, a movement which carries on its banners the words— *Freedom, Democracy, Integrity.*

When war came, Colonel Lindbergh, with the committee, closed ranks in support of a united America. On December 8, he released a statement to the press:*

We have been stepping closer to war for many months. Now it has come and we must meet it as united Americans regardless of our attitude in the past toward the policy our government has followed. Whether or not that policy has been wise, our country has been attacked by force of arms, and by force of arms we must retaliate. Our own defenses and our own military position have already been neglected too long.

---

*Lindbergh wrote in his diary on December 8, 1941, "Phoned General Wood in Boston. His first words were, 'Well, he got us in through the back door.' . . . We have been asking for war for months. If the President had asked for a declaration of war before, I think Congress would have turned him down with a big majority. But now we have been attacked, and attacked in home waters. We have brought it on our own shoulders; but I can see nothing to do under these circumstances except to fight. If I had been in Congress, I certainly would have voted for a declaration of war." Lindbergh, *Wartime Journals*, p. 561.

We must now turn every effort to building the greatest and most efficient army, navy, and air force in the world. When American soldiers go to war, it must be with the best equipment that modern skill can design and that modern industry can build.

On December 14, the following message from Colonel Lindbergh went to all chapters:

Our country is now at war, probably the most serious war in all its history. We who opposed involvement in this war were, I believe, correct in our stand. We advocated building an impregnable defense for America, and leaving foreign wars to foreign peoples. The wisdom of our policy of building strong defenses has been clearly shown by developments in the Pacific. The final judgment of our policies must be left to the future and to more objective times; but in this final judgment, I have complete confidence.

Now, nothing is to be gained by arguing about who was right and who was wrong. Our political opinions may be expressed at the coming elections, but our primary attention must be devoted to prosecuting this war in the most constructive and intelligent manner. We have contributed the best we could give to our country in time of peace. Now, we must contribute the best we could give to our country in time of war. America needs our assistance, and that assistance will be forthcoming to the greatest ability of every one of us.*

NOTES

1. A brief colloquy in the House hearing furnished a clue to that impersonal approach characteristic of the colonel which was always a mystery and an irritant to his critics. Congressman Jarman† was beginning a line of questioning which obviously was designed to show that the colonel was qualified to speak on only one question—aviation. Colonel Lindbergh said,

We have been living in an era of experts and the position we have reached is under the leadership of experts, and therefore I think it is time for us to consider where that leadership is taking us and for all of us to begin to think a little bit about the fields of those experts who have been leading us, bar none.

Mr. Jarman asked, "Then I am wrong in feeling I ought to follow you on aviation?" The colonel replied, "Yes, sir; not without consideration." (Hearings before the Committee on Foreign Affairs, House of Representatives, 77th Cong., 1st Sess., on H.R. 1776, p. 406.)

2. On April 9 General Wood addressed the following memorandum to members of the Executive Committee:

I have been associated with the America First Committee since last September. When I agreed to serve as acting chairman, it was with the idea that a permanent chairman would be found. It seemed impossible to find a suitable chairman, and I have remained. I have given considerable money and a great deal of time to the cause. I abandoned the vacation trip I had planned to South

* I have omitted a brief coda about Lindbergh's experience in the first year of the war.
† Representative Pete Jarman (D-Ala.).

America this winter because of the fight on the Lease-Lend Bill and have done everything in my power to help the Committee.

My own business is crippled by the absence of our executive vice-president in Washington. I have a great responsibility to a very large business. With that responsibility, my other business interests, and, above all, my duty to my family, I feel that I cannot continue to give any further time as acting chairman. It places too great a burden on me. I will, of course, continue my support of the Committee and I am making a further substantial financial contribution to it, but I cannot contribute more time.

I, therefore, insist on my relief as acting chairman not later than June 1st. I had hoped to be relieved on April 1st but am giving the Committee another two months to find a successor.

Colonel Lindbergh has agreed to act as chairman of the Executive Committee, and I think can be prevailed on to take the chairmanship of the whole Committee. While he has many enemies, he is courageous and patriotic and has attracted a great following in the country. In my opinion, he should be selected as chairman of the Executive Committee with the understanding that not later than the middle of May he will become chairman of the America First Committee.

3. Nine thousand new members came to the New York chapter as the result of Colonel Lindbergh's April 23 speech. On all the trips he made to address America First rallies, Colonel Lindbergh paid his own expenses, and received no fees.

4. March 29, 1941.

5. *New York Times*, March 29, 1941.

6. *Washington Post*, April 24, 1941.

7. The summaries of and quotations from Colonel Lindbergh's addresses in this chapter are intended to convey the gist of each speech.

8. "A majority of the commercial airline pilots operating out of La Guardia Field support Charles A. Lindbergh's isolationist views and his action in resigning his commission in the Army Air Reserve, but at the same time hope that Britain can win, according to a canvass of more than 100 pilots made at the airport over a two-day period by the New York City News Association." (*New York Times*, May 3, 1941)

9. In New York on July 14, 1941.

10. An exchange with Senator Pepper in the Lend-Lease hearing throws light on Colonel Lindbergh's failure to include condemnation of the aggressors in his speeches:

Senator Pepper: I think it is only fair to say to you that a good many people have been puzzled by the absence of any indication on your part of any moral indignation at what they consider outrageous wrongs which have been perpetrated and are being perpetrated by the German Government. Do you care to make any comment on that?

Colonel Lindbergh: I believe very firmly that nothing is gained by publicly commenting on your feeling in regard to one side of a war in which your country is not taking part. For instance, I feel very strongly that the attitude of this country should be receptive to a negotiated peace. I have purposely attempted to avoid stating indignation publicly because I feel it would have no constructive result. I am not sure that I have been able to do this in each instance, but I have tried to.

As far as my attitude toward aggression is concerned, I personally would prefer not to see it happen ever again. However, I know that it always has taken place in history, and that unless conditions are created in the world or on the continents to prevent war, aggression will probably take place in the future. (Senate Hearing, ibid., p. 522.)

In a personal conversation, Colonel Lindbergh once said, "To damn Hitler won't do any good. Personal attack is a cheap way to fight and it won't get you anywhere."

6

The Antiwar Bloc in the War Congress

The leaven of the noninterventionist members—at work in Congress like a tireless conscience for more than ten years before Pearl Harbor—reached its highest efficiency in the war Congress.

Congress has never had an antiwar *bloc* in the sense of an organized group that could be counted on to function as a unit day in and day out. Noninterventionist members of the Seventy-seventh Congress, however, confronted with the threat of actual war, achieved a degree of organization that is worthy of record because it was unprecedented and because it was accomplished in the face of longstanding obstacles inherent in the "system." It was notable also because it cut a wide swathe through party lines; the members had no established discipline—other than self-imposed—to keep them in line.

The noninterventionist bloc was loosely organized; the carrying out of its decisions was entirely voluntary. Unfortunately, records were not kept of its meetings from April 1 through October 9. This account must rely on newspaper reports, on notes of conversations with members at the time, on the records of an America First staff member who assisted the Executive Committee of the bloc in the details of arranging for meetings, and on memory.

Just before the Lend-Lease debate, six of the noninterventionist senators met informally at dinner, and agreed that Senator [Burton K.] Wheeler [D-Mont.] should serve as their leader. With Senator [Robert A.] Taft [R-Ohio] as "speakers' chairman" for the Republicans and with Senator Wheeler performing the same office for the Democrats, a handful of men succeeded in filling more than half the time of a prolonged debate that stretched over three weeks, and in pressing their arguments against the bill with such vigor and effect that the proponents were forced to adopt as one of their leading talking points the claim that the bill was a measure for peace.

For three weeks following the Lend-Lease vote, the antiwar forces hardly raised their heads. Like the interventionist members, they were recuperating from the mental, physical, and emotional exhaustion of a debate that had demanded all their energies, and catching up on work that had been put aside during the debate. Several of the leading noninterventionists, believing that unless the antiwar forces were to concede final victory to the interventionists with passage of the Lend-Lease Act they would have to shake off their lethargy and rally their forces without delay, took steps to show that a "loyal opposition" still existed. On the assumption that the Lend-Lease bill was the decisive point at which the substance, as well as the letter and spirit, of our old neutrality policy had been abandoned, these men laid plans to organize a joint group among members of both Houses who had voted against Lend-Lease.

A small committee composed of senators [William John] Bulow [D-S. Dak.], [D. Worth] Clark [D-Idaho], [Robert] La Follette [P-Wis.], [Clyde Martin] Reed [R-Kans.], [Henrik] Shipstead [R-Minn.], and Wheeler wrote to every member of the Senate and the House who had voted "no" on Lend-Lease urging them to attend a meeting in the Senate Caucus Room on Tuesday evening, April 1. The letter said in part,

Throughout the debate on H.R. 1776, supporters of the legislation from the President on down repeatedly assured the country and the Congress that the bill was a "peace measure." Those of us who opposed this legislation did so largely because we felt it to be a war measure and one leading toward dictatorship. Now that the bill is a law fully supplied with the funds to implement it, those of us who oppose complete entrance into a shooting war *must not give up the fight*. We should unite in a great peace-protecting program of American effort to save our way of life in our sphere of influence and seek an "area of agreement" in which we can all work toward that end in keeping with the letter and spirit of the peace planks of both major party platforms.*

Seventy-one members (14 senators and 57 congressmen) attended an enthusiastic meeting. The release handed to the press after the meeting said,

Seventy [sic] Senators and Congressmen opposed to the involvement of the United States in foreign war met this evening in the Senate Caucus Room to consider methods of making impossible the use of convoys. Speakers emphasized the statement of President Roosevelt that "Convoys mean shooting, and shooting means war." The meeting was bi-partisan. All major political parties are pledged to keep America out of foreign wars. Since only Congress can declare war, Congressmen said they do not intend that the President shall involve the country in war indirectly through convoys or otherwise. Various groups are now advocating that the President send to Congress a bill authorizing convoys, but the meeting determined to raise the issue at once by pressing the affirmative resolution of Senator [Charles] Tobey [R-N.H.] and other resolutions introduced in the House which prohibit convoys. The meeting determined that in spite of the defeatist propaganda being promoted that war is now inevitable, those present

* The relevant portion of the 1940 Democratic Party platform read, "We will not participate in foreign wars, and we will not send our army, naval or air forces to fight in foreign lands outside of the Americas, except in case of attack." The 1940 Republican platform read, in part, "The Republican Party is firmly opposed to involving this Nation in foreign war." *National Party Platforms, 1840–1964*, compiled by Kirk H. Porter and Donald Bruce Johnson (Urbana: University of Illinois Press, 1966), pp. 382, 390.

would press the fight against any active involvement in war which would take American boys to foreign battlefields. Senator Wheeler, of Montana, who presided at the meeting, said: "I appeal to the overwhelming majority in America who are for keeping out of war to make their demands known in Washington both in Congress and the White House."

"The appealing thing to me about this movement and this statement," wrote one congressman afterward, "is that for the first time it gives those on our side a positive, active, affirmative approach to the problem. We can now urge our friends to ask their Congressmen to vote *for* these no-convoy resolutions in the House and Senate instead of once again having to urge them to write in to oppose some legislation. Psychologically, that places us in a much more advantageous position."

Within a few days after the meeting, fifteen resolutions dealing with convoys, some of them identical with Senator Tobey's, were introduced in the House.

In addition to the items covered in the release, the members discussed an affirmative action program which was never published but which served to clarify the most effective talking points. One draft of the program read as follows:

If all Americans who want peace will unite through their various organizations, through their representatives in Congress, and through individual expressions of personal opinion, in support of a specific program for Peace it will yet be possible to rescue this republic from involvement in war and to offset interventionist propaganda putting this Nation on the road to war.

(1) America must be rescued from the defeatist philosophy now sponsored by all interventionist groups in the country that "WE ARE ALREADY IN THE WAR." This is part of a cunning propaganda drive to condition the country to feeling that war is inevitable. We should renounce this fatal fiction. We are not in the war and will not be in unless we are attacked or unless we attack somebody. The country should be told the truth—*we are not in the war.*

(2) The use of convoys means sending boys to Europe. It means war. It violates every platform pledge and personal promise of the Administration. No man has a moral or legal right to order convoys without action by Congress—the people should know NOW that convoys means war.

(3) The President now has full responsibility for matters of foreign policy. He has pledged himself again and again not to involve this country in war. He must be held to this pledge.

(4) This is not our war. America is not in danger of military attack and America has not been attacked by any foreign foe. America must go to the war if we wish to become an active belligerent. The Administration recognizes this is not our war or it would not propose and support a program of sending materials but not men.

(5) The fearful consequences of actual participation in this war should be made clear to every citizen in terms of what it would mean to America morally, economically, politically, and in terms of the sacrifices of American youth. The war crowd has tried to frighten our people into believing that WAR is an easy escape from the consequences

of an unjust peace. The people have a right to know what war itself on foreign battle-fields would mean to them.

(6) We appeal to America to awaken before it is too late, to assert its desire for peace, and to demonstrate its immunity to the torrents of war propaganda now striving to becloud the thinking and muddle the conclusions of our citizens. NOW is the time to give articulate service to the cause of peace—leaders in every community should seize this opportunity to serve their country well by mobilizing for peace and preparedness.

(7) The terrific costs of our own defense plus the seven billions for other countries under the lend-lease bill must be raised by taxes. Substantial portions of those costs must be raised NOW if National bankruptcy and the destruction of the private profit system is to be averted. Citizens should be patriotic enough to insist that large new taxes be levied by this Congress and Congress should be courageous enough to tax all profit out of war and to add other taxes to raise every possible dime from current earnings of all in order to pay for these expenses. Our National Defense and our aid to others should not be financed by robbing the baby's bank or by mortgaging the lives of children yet unborn. All should pay something now toward this program and those with greatest ability to pay should be taxed accordingly to finance our multi-billion dollar spending, lending, leasing program.

Senator Wheeler as chairman of the group appointed as members of the executive committee Senators Bulow, Clark [D-Mo.], La Follette, and Taft; and Congressmen [John Martin] Costello (D-Calif.), [Hamilton] Fish [R-N.Y.], [Knute] Hill [D-Wash.], [Karl] Mundt [R-S. Dak.], [James F.] O'Connor [D-Mont.], and [James E.] Van Zandt [R-Pa.].

The next meeting of the noninterventionist bloc took place on April 29. The letter of invitation said, in part:

Reports will be heard from members who have been out in the hustings speaking against convoys and war, and important matters will be discussed and plans formulated which may have a vital influence in determining the future of America, the preservation of free government in this hemisphere and the destiny of millions of American boys. It is hoped that you will arrange your schedule so that you will be present at this probably historic meeting.

This letter is being mailed only to members of both Houses who voted against H.R. 1776. It is known, however, that a great many members who voted *for* lend-lease are *against* convoys and war, so you may bring with you any members you desire who are openly opposed to the use of United States convoys regardless of any prior vote.

As the members compared notes, they agreed that the statement attributed to the president—"Convoys mean shooting and shooting means war"—had made a deep impression on the country which would probably prevent open use of convoys for the time being. But, they said, the administration probably controlled enough votes in Congress to vote down any prohibition against the use of convoys. This discussion, and several informal conversations following it, resulted in Senator Tobey's decision not to insist on bringing in his anti-convoy resolution as an amendment to the ship seizure bill. Their best tactic, they agreed, was to continue speaking to the country in mass meetings and over the radio, to encourage a constant barrage of mail directed to the White House.

The day of the president's "unlimited emergency" speech, a committee of seven members of both Houses,* designated by the noninterventionist bloc, dispatched a letter to the president, giving him some pointers on the mood of the country:

The undersigned members of the Senate and House of Representatives designated as a committee by a larger group of members affiliated with all parties, realize the tremendous responsibility of your high office and your desire to act for the best interests of the people of America and in accord with the public opinion which must be conclusive in every democratic nation.

We therefore desire to inform you that we have tested our sentiment in our districts and throughout the country through direct conversations, extensive correspondence and public meetings and we find that over 80 per cent of the people are opposed to any course which will take this nation into the European War.

We call attention to the great hazard of bringing about a war, and the difficulty of conducting that war successfully, when public sentiment is so sharply divided. There is no question that under our Constitution war can only be declared by Congress, the direct representatives of the people. The purpose of this provision is to prevent a war of which the people do not approve. By every sound principle of government the same requirements must attend to acts which mean war, such as convoys and naval action.

We urge that in your radio address to the nation you will give renewed assurances that you will take no step likely to involve this country in war.

The day after the speech (May 28), the noninterventionist bloc held its third meeting. The thirty members present were impressed with the demonstration of the power of public opinion, in first, contributing to the postponement of the speech, and second, having prevented an announcement of convoys. Impressed also with the fact that the president had practically ignored Congress in the speech, they saw that the country would have to continue to speak. Much of the discussion at this meeting dealt with methods of eliciting further expressions of popular antiwar sentiment. This was the meeting at which America First representatives appeared to urge the taking of polls by congressional districts.

The statement released to the press following the meeting said,

The members of Congress who are opposed to our military or naval intervention in foreign war declare that we will redouble our efforts to keep America out of war in Europe, Asia or Africa.

We are encouraged to carry on the fight against war because the President has not yet been won over to the war party.

---

* According to Sarles, these seven were Senators La Follette, Taft, and Wheeler, and Congressmen Carl Curtis (R-Neb.), Frank Keefe (R-Wis.), James F. O'Connor (D-Mont.), and James William Robinson (D-Utah).

In his fireside chat he did not close the door on the millions of voters who believe his unequivocal promise of the presidential campaign—"We are arming ourselves not for any foreign war. We are arming ourselves not for any purposes of conquest or intervention in foreign disputes. I repeat again that I stand on the platform of our party: 'We will not participate in foreign wars, and we will not send our army, naval, or air forces to fight in foreign lands outside of the Americas except in case of attack.'"

The voice of the eighty percent of the American people opposed to war has been heard in Washington above the clamor of the "war now" spokesmen, including members of the President's cabinet. Public opinion still functions in the United States. War is not inevitable.

The proclamation of the President does not diminish the rights of the citizens of this country to voice their opposition to war by public meetings, use of the radio, the telegraph, and the mails to register their will with the president, and their senators and representatives in Congress.

We urge the people, who are with us in the struggle to preserve democracy at home against its enemies, both foreign and domestic, to carry on with renewed vigor and determination the campaign to keep our country out of shooting war.

The Russian-German war set the date of the next bloc meeting, held on July 1, with forty men in attendance. The letter of notification said,

In view of the entrance of Russia into the war, we consider it extremely important to bring together non-interventionist Senators and Representatives to discuss developments, analyze the new situation and decide on strategy.

It is now apparent to all that it is more necessary than ever for the United States to keep out of foreign wars due to (1) the ever changing alliances; (2) the need to concentrate on building an impregnable defense for the Western Hemisphere and (3) the advisability of protecting our half of the world from the insidious spread of Communism, Nazism and Fascism.

Since the whole Communist front has joined the interventionist camp, it is more important than before that all non-interventionist members of Congress work together with steadily increasing unison.

The men agreed that Russia's overnight change from an enemy to an ally was an important talking point for them. The country as a whole would be hesitant to become a "fellow traveler."

Secretary of the Navy Knox* was a major target of this day's discussion. He had just reached a new high in his career of incendiary statements with his declaration to the Conference of Governors at Boston that "the time to use our navy to clear the Atlantic of the German menace is at hand. . . . Now is the time to strike. . . . Now is the time to put in motion the huge machine we have been building since the war began."

---

* Secretary of the Navy Frank Knox of Illinois had been Republican presidential candidate Alf Landon's running mate in 1936.

The antiwar bloc voted "general condemnation" of Knox, but resisted suggestion that they call for his impeachment, on the ground that such action would divert them from their main job, which was to keep the country out of war. Senator [David] Walsh [D-Mass.], chairman of the powerful Naval Affairs Committee, was moved following the bloc meeting to issue a statement in which he said that Knox's Boston speech carried "shocking implications. If his utterances are in accord with the views of the president, then Congress and the country have been grievously misled. If his words are not consonant with the views of his Commander in Chief then surely he is subject to censure." He charged the navy head with counseling "open warfare, either with or without the formalities of a declaration of war."

Senator Wheeler and Congressman Fish also issued scorching statements. The Montana senator, asserting that Knox "should resign or be thrown out of office," charged that he had "intentionally deceived" the Senate when he told the committee before which he was seeking confirmation to his Cabinet post that he was opposed to intervention. "A man who will deceive the Senate of the United States in order to be confirmed to office is not fit to be Secretary of the Navy or to hold any public office," Senator Wheeler declared.

Congressman Fish flatly called for impeachment: "If Secretary Knox puts our Navy into a shooting war without the approval of Congress, which has sole authority to declare war under the Constitution, he should be impeached immediately."

With an administration move to extend the draft in the offing, sixty members of the noninterventionist bloc met on July 21 for what was probably their most enthusiastic meeting, twenty new men attending for the first time. There was virtual unanimity for fighting the extension of the draft on the ground that breaking faith with the selectees would destroy confidence in the government, and that an adequate army (based on General Marshall's previous testimony)* could otherwise be raised. The group determined to resist moves to get Congress to declare a national emergency (which the administration had requested rather than a measure specifically extending the draft), believing it a move to force Congress to commit itself to the whole foreign policy of the administration. It was agreed that despite the sudden change in the military situation that had overnight made Russia a "friend" of the United States, there would be no slackening in opposition to communistic influences in America. A committee of five senators and ten congressmen was appointed to analyze sentiment on the selective service problem and to work out floor strategy, particularly to prevent any moves designed to lift the ban on sending selectees outside the Western Hemisphere. The group agreed to oppose "joint action between the United States and Britain in Iceland."

---

* For instance, Marshall's testimony before the Senate Appropriations Committee on May 1, 1940.

It was shortly after this meeting, the scene of the most detailed planning to date for coordinated activities to resist war moves, that Samuel B. Pettengill, former member of the House from Indiana, agreed to come to Washington for a month to serve as liaison man among the members. As a former member, he had wide contacts in Congress, and the privilege of going on the floor of the chamber.

The final meeting of the noninterventionist bloc before Pearl Harbor took place on October 8. The last-ditch fight waged by members of both houses in the debates on Neutrality Law revision reflected the determination behind the decision of the sixty men at this meeting to "oppose in every way amendments to the Neutrality Act as being, in fact, an authorization to carry on war."

In between these called meetings there were innumerable informal meetings of small groups of the noninterventionists.

THE BEGINNING OF THE ANTIWAR BLOC

While under the stimulus of imminent war, congressional antiwar forces went further in *organizing* their activities than ever before. As far back as the early thirties they were acting upon the pressure that came from the postwar disillusionment of the public as a whole. The Graham Committee investigation in the early twenties had uncovered a sordid story of corruption and greed for profits in the war effort of 1917–18, to the point of wanton disregard for life. The War Policies Commission* in the early thirties had underlined the ugly world war story in an abortive attempt to "equalize the burdens of war." The sensational revelations of the Senate Munitions Investigating Committee, which began its prolonged hearings in the fall of 1934 with Senator Nye as chairman, fed the popular anger against huge war profits.[†]

Through the pressure of veterans' groups and others, the antiwar feeling of this period took the form of a demand to take the profits out of war, which emerged in Congress as the McSwain war profits bill. This measure (passed by the House but not by the Senate) provided for wartime commandeering of industrial plants and executives, for price freezing, for a 100 percent tax on profits "shown to be due to war time conditions," and for the regulation of business. The bill obviously was so full of loopholes that a real war profits control bill was introduced and endorsed by practically half the Senate, a measure designed to take all but $10,000 of individual earnings per year during

---

* The War Policies Commission, a joint commission of the Hoover Cabinet and Congress, convened its first meeting on March 5, 1931, and reported to Congress on March 7, 1932, on ways to "prevent profiteering" in wartime.

[†] For an excellent political biography of Senator Nye, see Wayne S. Cole, *Senator Gerald P. Nye and American Foreign Relations* (Minneapolis: University of Minnesota Press, 1962).

wartime. This bill was reported by the Nye Munitions Investigating Committee, then referred to the Senate Finance Committee and there interred.

No omnibus war profits control measure ever got through Congress. But the popular antiwar feeling had generated momentum for action by Congress. It created in a small group of members the determination that so far as legislation could prevent, profits-thirsty interests would not again increase the chances of United States participation in war. They had distinguished endorsement of their purpose in the president's Chautauqua statement of August 1936:

> If war should break out again in another country, let us not blink the fact that we would find in this country thousands of Americans who, seeking immediate riches—fools' gold—would attempt to break down or evade our neutrality. . . . If we face the choice of profits or peace, the Nation will answer—must answer—"We choose peace." It is the duty of all of us to encourage such a body of public opinion in this country that the answer will be clear and for all practical purposes unanimous.

Beginning with the ban on profits in excess of 10 percent on naval building contracts over $10,000 that was written into the Vinson-Trammell naval bill of 1934, these men steadily carried the torch of war profits limitation. The Vinson bill restriction was dropped in 1940 and the excess profits tax enacted, which captures 94 percent of all profits in excess of 95 percent of average earnings (based on earnings from 1936 to 1939) plus $10,000. The supplemental national defense appropriation bill passed in the War Congress provides for renegotiation of contracts in order to capture excess profits. There are other laws now in effect and measures pending that seek to keep war profits down.

It is not exaggeration to say that the congressional noninterventionist group kindled the light that today is illuminating some of the dark aspects of the war effort; excess of war profits is so generally accepted as a crime against the public welfare that in this war congressional investigation of the offenders does not have to await the armistice.

The Munitions Investigation had made a profound impression on the public. The disclosures of the international character of the munitions industry served to heighten public distrust of *international* dealings. The revelations of how United States policy with regard to credits, loans, and ships—and the incidents arising from our trade in war supplies with Europe—put the country in a position where it had no other recourse than war, led to the hope that a new interpretation of neutral rights, put on the statute books, could prevent repetition. The divulging by members of the investigation committee of propaganda operations of our world war allies in this country encouraged skeptical examination of motives in any international commitments.

The Munitions Investigation turned up a bill of particulars on how a country goes to war that popped up in practically every foreign policy debate up to Pearl Harbor. It also infused at least four members of the Investigating Committee—and a sizeable number of their colleagues—with a burning conviction that a second journey down the 1916–18 road to war must be prevented by legislative safeguards set up in peace-time, while unemotional discussion was possible.

The Munitions Investigating Committee had recommended an embargo on arms, ammunition, and implements of war to all belligerents, a ban on the floating of loans by belligerents, and on extension of credits to belligerents except for a limited time and a limited amount, a prohibition on travel of American citizens on belligerent vessels or vessels carrying contraband through war zones, refusal (when the United States was a neutral) of clearance to armed merchant vessels of any nationality where the vessel's armament is not exposed to easy view, and withdrawal of protection from American citizens serving on armed merchant ships.

Thus the committee laid the basis for the legislation whose abandonment was to constitute the last important debate in Congress before the United States went to war in 1941.

Out of the determination of a few senators and congressmen to take steps in peace-time to prevent a repetition of 1917–18, plus the increasingly non-interventionist temper of public opinion, grew the series of neutrality laws passed by Congress beginning in 1935. It should be added that the neutrality laws of 1935, 1936, and 1937 also had the support of members of Congress who later emerged among the most outspoken interventionists. In those days there was a lingering reluctance to serve as the base of supplies for the wars of other countries, probably due to the growing understanding that there was a price on staying out of war. Furthermore, it was not until the fall of 1937 when the president made his famous "quarantine" speech that important leadership was assured for those who claimed the privilege of passing moral judgments on disputes anywhere in the world, and backing them up with concrete assistance.*

THE 1940 CONSCRIPTION LAW

The conscription debate of 1940 provided the next congressional forum where opposing views on foreign policy were aired. Proponents had insisted that the adoption of conscription was the democratic way of providing the larger army that Dunkerque and the fall of France had made necessary. Opponents, claiming that competent testimony cast doubt on the necessity of conscription for defense, declared it was a step toward fascism and a move to ready the country for an eventual war abroad.† The clash on fundamental foreign policy showed

---

* I have omitted a lengthy recapitulation of the Neutrality Acts of 1935, 1936, 1937, and 1939.

† John T. Flynn invoked, unsuccessfully, the specter of our "robust individualist forefathers who would have chased the conscription officer in peacetime away from their doors with a squirrel gun." Flynn, *As We Go Marching*, p. 204. Flynn asked us to look for powerful men "who wish to commit this country to the rule of the bureaucratic state; interfering in the affairs of the states and cities; taking part in the management of industry and finance and agriculture; assuming the

such bitter opposition to fighting wars abroad, that a proviso was forced into the measure exempting draftees from service outside the Western Hemisphere.

The vote in the House was 263 to 149; in the Senate, 58 to 31.

WHAT THE VOTES MEAN

It was not until the [convening of] Congress that opened in January 1941 that the record votes give a truly accurate picture of the ayes and noes on the naked issue of basic foreign policy. Some members who were interventionist by conviction had voted for neutrality legislation because they were forced to it by public opinion. And they could vote for each neutrality law without violating their interventionist inclinations too seriously because the administration had forced discretionary features into every neutrality act, and no one act was a clear-cut triumph for the noninterventionists. Periphery considerations had not been chiseled away until the 1941 Congress, in the votes on the Lend-Lease bill and on revision of the neutrality law to permit opening combat zones to United States ships, got down to the rock-bottom issue. The votes on two important foreign policy debates in the War Congress—the draft extension and arming merchant ships—must be passed over because they were considered and voted upon by some members as defense measures and as such were not fair tests of attitude toward basic foreign policy.

The votes on the two measures that can be considered real tests of opinion on the fundamental issue show that between passage of the Lend-Lease Act in January 1941 and final action on the neutrality act, the noninterventionist ranks gained twenty-nine members in the House. In the Senate, six men were added to the noninterventionist bloc during the same period.

CRYING OVER SPILT MILK

A glance at the votes on the measures described shows that in the years 1935 to 1941 a sizeable number of members in both houses must consistently have voted "no" on war-trend measures. The antiwar vote represented a majority mood in the country. But those whose most sensitive nerve as public servants responsible for the people's welfare was the antiwar nerve did not carry to a logical conclusion the full purport of their votes. They did not go in for the

---

role of great national banker and investor, borrowing millions every year and spending them on all sorts of projects through which such a goverment can paralyze opposition and command public support; marshaling great armies and navies at crushing costs to support the industry of war and preparation for war which will become our greatest industry; and adding to all this the most romantic adventures in global planning, regeneration, and domination all to be done under the authority of a powerfully centralized government in which the executive will hold in effect all the powers with Congress reduced to the role of a debating society. There is your fascist." Recognize anyone? Flynn, *As We Go Marching,* p. 253.

long-range group planning with well-defined objectives that might have created an effective bloc. Through the formative years of the policy that was
operating when the country went to war—before it had jelled and when it
could have been cast in a different mold—the individuals in Congress whose
rock-bottom conviction was a conviction against war were for the most part
working against war in their separate ways, displaying unified action only in
spurts, in the flush of excited maneuvering that preceded important votes.
While a neutrality—or more accurately speaking, a noninvolvement—policy
had been adopted by Congress, those who brought about its adoption did not
at the same time offer to the executive the spectacle of responsible congressional leadership functioning consistently at all times. It allowed the neutrality
policy to be undermined while it was still on the statute books, so that its actual
abandonment became little more than ratification of a then inevitable course.
To this day no one can say whether the policy of noninvolvement advocated
by the noninterventionists in Congress would have kept the country out of
war because the spirit—and in some cases the letter—of the neutrality law was
not observed in its application.

Some of the reasons for this situation should be noted to round out this
quick view of Congress:

1. The patronage system—under which the party in power can allot jobs (including
   judgeships)—reduces the freedom of members in voting their own convictions or
   what they understand to be the wishes of the majority of their constituents. In a
   choice between "the people versus the party," the party has the edge unless the people
   are aroused and vocal.

2. The very system by which members are elected to Congress makes for the individualistic approach to legislative action.
   In the Senate particularly—the chamber that has the more influence in the conduct
   of foreign affairs—the members are inclined to be "prima donnas." Nothing short
   of the majority party whiplash can be wholly effective in bringing them together in
   a competent organization. Senators of like views working on issues that cut across
   party lines are most likely to function efficiently as a unit in floor debate; the Senate's
   zealous guarding of its most highly prized privilege—full and free discussion—as-
   sures opportunity for almost unlimited debate, of which minority as well as majority
   groups take advantage. But the real work of Congress is done behind scenes; unity
   in floor debate is not a basic unity. The inclination to be individualistic causes the
   members to hesitate about associating themselves with moves initiated by their colleagues unless they approve the colleague's skill and reputation as a tactician as well
   as the substance of his ideas.
   In the large, unwieldy House, where of necessity debate is limited, the members
   tend to gravitate to small groups outside of the party caucuses. But these groups
   rarely cross party lines (the short two-year term allows little time for functioning
   except as party members); until the day when peace becomes a party issue they would
   hardly lend themselves to organization for antiwar purposes primarily.

3. The antiwar view has usually been the expression of an idea rather than of an en-

lightened concern for self-interest. During peace-time, the practical men of affairs, even though fully aware that war would be harmful to their economic interests, left the antiwar movement to the "crusaders" of whom the "practical" people were slightly contemptuous. If those who were against war because they were anti–New Deal, anti–big taxes, or even plain anti–Democratic Party—in short, if those who were against war for reasons of self-interest—had used their prestige, influence, and money to organize, while there was yet time, a strong public opinion without which a real antiwar congressional bloc could not function, there might have been no occasion for this story.

4. On the reverse side of the medal, in peace-time the liberals outside of Congress assumed a virtual monopoly on expression of the antiwar view. Yet for the most part they were far more interested in keeping their records "clean" on a wide range of social questions than in an expedient compromise for the sake of a strategic gain on the antiwar front. Men of money and influence were likely to steer clear of people with whom they agreed on the war question but disagreed and feared on economic questions, and with whom they knew they could not work against war without accepting a brace of liberal principles. "Professional" liberals were looked upon as "impractical" by most of those who have power in public affairs. Members of Congress, aware of this, were afraid to "play ball" too closely with the people who by reason of their assumption of positions as spokesmen for the antiwar view, were identified in the public mind as *the* antiwar movement, and yet were without power.

Perhaps a simpler way of stating points 3 and 4 is to say that both liberals and conservatives recognized war as a basic threat to what each held most important, but did not act accordingly.

5. Except in time of crisis, it is difficult to hold people together for group action that is always in a position of opposition. Such a position depends on someone setting up an object for attack, and therefore rarely allows taking the initiative. Those who are against war are usually just that—not pro-peace. They have not planned beyond the absence of war to the dynamic state of peace which, to be enduring, requires constructive planning and action. This has been true of Congress as well as of the public in general.

AMERICA FIRST AND CONGRESS

The America First Committee enjoyed excellent cooperation from the men and women of Congress, ranging from speaking at America First rallies to advising the committee on its activities.

Twenty members of the Senate and thirty-four members of the House spoke at America First rallies or on America First radio programs. (The committee publicized the radio speeches of at least twenty more who spoke on the radio under other auspices.) A glance at the list (Appendix C) will indicate the catholicity of the group: it shows representatives of the major and minor parties, spokesmen for liberals and for conservatives.

America First usually asked the advice of leading noninterventionist members of Congress in making important decisions on committee activities. The initial plans for the series of rallies that proved to be America First's most important contribution in the antiwar drive were thoroughly discussed with a few senators and congressmen. Twice General Wood came to Washington for consultation at times when the committee was about to launch a new campaign. On at least one occasion America First literature was submitted to a few non-interventionist members for comment before publication. During important legislative fights when special action from the country was needed, congressional leaders several times telephoned Chicago headquarters and outlined the situation.

It was a two-way process: The noninterventionist leaders in Congress helped America First and America First helped them. At no time did "cooperation" reach the point where either party lost freedom of decision and action. While it was not possible to go through the hundreds of thousands of membership cards at national headquarters, nor the membership lists of local chapters, so far as is known to the headquarters staff or the Washington staff of America First, no member of Congress joined the committee.

7
On the Record: "What We Said"

The Most Reverend Francis L. Beckman, archbishop of Dubuque (Iowa), August 2, 1941

The present conflict is not a "holy war," least of all a just war; but a war of one imperialism against another, in which godlessness is incidental to all belligerents. Neither side is interested in God so much as in gold or its equivalent.

A long and horrible war will crush and distort the human spirit, deprave and bestialize it. And the spirit of whole peoples shattered by interminable warfare will prove fertile soil for the cockle of neo-Communism.

Senator Wayland C. Brooks, R-Illinois, October 31, 1941*

What are we considering here today? It is the destiny of America. What is the destiny of America? The destiny of America is to unite this country for her own national defense. The destiny of America is to build a defense so strong that no one will invade or attempt to invade the Western Hemisphere. The destiny of America depends upon her ability to produce the food and supplies upon her farms and in her factories, to produce and produce to the maximum of the ability of free men to defend their freedom.

The destiny of America is to renew her faith in her own form of Government, to govern and defend herself, to remain free and independent, owning her own soul, maintaining her own way of life and guaranteeing the dignity and freedom of her people.

The destiny of America depends upon her elected officials keeping their word to the people who believed them, to unite this country, to keep their pledge to the American people and to the allied peoples as well.

When, across the sea, the warring countries have finally bombed each other's cities, when they have destroyed their churches, when they have crushed to ashes their great works of art, when they have destroyed their institutions of learning, when their factories have been leveled to the ground, finally out of

---

* From *Congressional Record,* 77th Cong., 1st session, p. 8381.

the anguish of it all surely there will come a time when the starving people of the conquered lands and the distressed, weary, war-torn, and burdened people of the victors as well will cry out: "Isn't there a land somewhere on earth where there is a government truly of the people, where the people's wishes will be respected and observed?

"Isn't there a land somewhere where all the nationalities and all the creeds and all the colors can live in harmony with each other, and build and enjoy a real civilization?

"Isn't there a land somewhere where by living example men can preach, where men can live and can produce the foods and necessities of life—necessities for the body and for the spirit as well?

"Isn't there a land somewhere where there is freedom of speech and expression, freedom of worship, freedom from want, and freedom from fear?"

And if America is still solvent, still strong, still free, we can send the word back across the ocean that we are ready to feed and to clothe and to rebuild the homes of the distressed people of the world.

That is America's destiny.

Senator Bennett Champ Clark, D-Missouri*

There has been much said about mandates involved in the last election. If there was any mandate in that election whatever it was to the effect that the American people believed in the sincerity of the President more than they did in the sincerity of Mr. Willkie with respect to their pledges to keep the country out of war, and the fact that the Democratic platform went a good deal further in that regard than did the Republican platform I believe influenced many voters in making their decision.

I do not think anyone will stand on the Senate floor and challenge this proposition. If either candidate for the Presidency of the United States had advocated any such proposition as is embodied in this bill (Lend-Lease) that candidate would have been defeated. I know that as one supporter of the President in the last election I took his declaration, and I also took the declaration of the Democratic platform, in perfect faith. If I had not done so I should not have been able to vote for the reelection of the President of the United States.

Did we mean what we said or did we not? I am offering the flat naked pronouncement of the Democratic platform itself, a declaration of national policy upon which we appealed to the American people, which was unreservedly accepted by the President of the United States himself. As one who made speeches on behalf of the Democratic ticket I offer that as a declaration of principle in this bill.

* From *Congressional Record,* 77th Cong., 1st session, p. 2072.

Senator D. Worth Clark, D-Idaho, October 16, 1941

About two years ago, we repealed the Arms Embargo provision of our Neutrality Act. In doing so we took sides; we became un-neutral. We took the first step on the road to war. We had taken fifteen years of calm, sane, constructive work when we were thinking straight and building an edifice of neutrality and independent destiny. And then like a crazed architect who has run amuck, in a few short months we pulled our temple down upon our heads.

Incident after incident was devised with fearful rapidity. Belligerent act followed belligerent act. We set out, it would seem almost deliberately, to insult every powerful nation on earth. We will end up where we ended up twenty-three years ago, with just two friends left on this earth—the Atlantic and the Pacific. Destroyers were given England on a questionable trade. Then came the mis-called Lend-Lease Bill, giving away our substance and likely conferring upon the President power to conduct an undeclared war anywhere on earth. Despite everything that could be done, however, the American people themselves would not again be driven into Europe's war. And so, as a final result, we are now asked to repeal what is left of our Neutrality Act. There can be only one purpose in this, and that purpose is war. Send armed American merchant ships, loaded with contraband, into combat zones and you send American sailors to a certain death and your country to a certain war from which it may never recover. Of course, people of America, it won't be put to you so bluntly. It never is. They don't dare deal with you frankly or realistically on a matter of war or peace. Already you hear much of that glittering phrase "freedom of the seas." It's another catchword designed to conceal thought rather than to express it. But it's a useful phrase now because it diverts your attention from the stark realities of the slaughter pens of Europe. There is no such thing as freedom of the seas and there never has been since America became a nation. The British Navy has had control of the seas over most of the world for hundreds of years, and the commerce of the world has gone and now goes wherever the British Navy says it may go and nowhere else. Some of us have tried to send merchant ships loaded with food and medical supplies to the stricken countries of Europe, but the British Navy says, "No," and that means "No," and it means "No" to the United States of America. We talk about freedom of the seas, we rail at German submarines which have done us little harm, and yet we cringe before British guns. Let me repeat, Freedom of the seas is just another device of skilled propagandists to make you stop thinking and start feeling.

John Cudahy, former U.S. ambassador to Belgium, October 13, 1941

[T]here was, as all you Senators remember, a section set up in the Department of State concerned in ascertaining the causes which led us into the last war, and we found out that while there was a great dispute among the authorities, those causes were, first, the freedom of the seas, and it became clear by refreshing our recollection that this country would have gone to war, as

Senator Johnson* knows so well, in 1915–16, because of the high-handed manner in which England acted with regard to our shipping on the high seas—the
stopping of our ships, the enlargement of contraband in contradiction of and
ignoring the Declaration of London, the elimination of distinction between
conditional and absolute contraband, the placing of a blacklist on American
shippers, and other arbitrary, high-handed measures that simply denied the
rights of a free nation on the high seas to such a point that such a record was
made.

Then it became apparent that as a proud and independent Nation this country would have to proceed to force or else be denied the high seas. Then, of
course, as you all know the submarine campaign began and the dramatic features of the ruthless submarine campaign so superseded those actions of England in its arbitrary control of our shipping that the issue became focused on
Germany and we went to war. . . .

I think that if this country enters the war you will have a parallel with that
awful war which is called by historians the Thirty Year War, when such equal
forces were pitted against each other that the whole Continent was devastated,
and the effects were felt for two centuries in Europe. . . .

Now, for the last 250 years we have had the doctrine of the balance of power,
that is, pitting one nation after another, under British aegis. Unless there can
be a realization of some international organization that will really function and
that will have back of it the physical power of enforcing its decrees, as a sheriff
enforces those of a judge of a court, I cannot see any hope for peace in Europe.
. . .

. . . I cannot see how we can win this war except by an all-out effort that
will stagger the world and prostrate the world and will lead to eventual anarchy
and the worst depression, the economists tell me, that this country has ever
seen. It will make the last depression look like a zephyr compared to a Kansas
hurricane. I cannot see what we can do for the cause of democracy except by
staying at peace and using our great prestige to try to bring about some settlement.

Now, I have been subjected to a great deal of abuse since two weeks ago. I
engaged in a debate with some professors at Northwestern University and
suggested that now or very soon would be the time for this country to use its
great prestige and its great potential war power to try to bring about some
settlement in Europe.

---

* Senator Hiram Johnson (R-Calif.) was a battling Progressive who had fought every manifes-
tation of internationalism from U.S. membership in the League of Nations to, on his deathbed,
U.S. membership in the United Nations. Ironically, Johnson, then governor of California, had been
the running mate of 1912 Bull Moose presidential candidate Theodore Roosevelt, at whose foreign
policy a mature Johnson stood at antipodes. See Peter J. Boyle, "The Roots of Isolationism: A Case
Study," *Journal of American Studies* 6 (April 1972), pp. 41–50.

I am convinced that the Vatican would join in such an effort. I am convinced, and anyone would be convinced here who has ever read what the German generals had to say after the last war, that Germany deplores not having made peace in 1916, when Colonel House, you will remember, went over to Berlin and London and Paris and tried to bring about negotiations.

Why do I say that? Because I think that the German objective in this war was to get the resources of the southeast, and anyone will think that who has ever gone through the writings of Germany and the revealing of German ambitions since the Reich became a great international power. And I believe that Hitler would not dare to refuse to entertain such a proposal. It would become known to the German people, and more than that, more significant, it would reach the German generals, who are the real power in Germany today. The German generals, I believe, want to make peace.

Now, I was asked in the debate by your distinguished colleague here, Senator Pepper,* what would happen to the occupied countries of Europe. I did not think that that was primarily a question for American concern. It goes back to moral leadership of the world. Naturally, our sympathies are enlisted, and we would be very much distressed, and I would personally, to see countries like Holland and Belgium incorporated into the Reich, but I do not believe that Hitler has any such intention.

I believe that he realizes that these countries, with their recalcitrant nationalism, are more liability than an asset. Every day proves this to be true. Revolt is seething in these occupied lands, and I believe that Hitler would accept a restoration of these occupied countries, especially to the west. I do not think— and all the reading of German ambition shows this—that the German ambition was ever toward the west. I think it was always toward the east.

Of course, such a settlement would probably be at the expense of Russia, but I believe that the western nations would be accepted. That, of course, is speculation, but it is based upon a great deal of investigation on the subject. . . .

. . . I do not believe that Hitler has any designs on America, and it is not because I have any faith in his word. I regard him as an international criminal, and his record is just one of broken promises; but simply on the realities of the question I think it will take at least a generation for the Germans to consolidate and organize their victory in Europe.

John T. Flynn, economist and writer, October 23, 1941

When I am asked why I want to stay out of war and not arm merchant ships and create incidents that bring on war, why I do not want to repeal the Neu-

---

* Senator Claude Pepper (D-Fla.), in his dotage, as a member of the U.S. House of Representatives, was transmogrified by an adoring press into a lovable old codger and champion of Social Security.

trality Act and send merchant ships into belligerent ports and get into war, it is not because I want to help Hitler. I want to save the United States. . . .

By the way, gentlemen, I do not know whether you have noticed it or not, but what is going to happen when the war is over? I do not know what period that is. It may be a year from now, or it may be after we have discouraged the German people six months from now, or a year or two years from now, when we have bombed the Germans into submission, or five or ten years from now, or a decade from now, as Senator Pepper has suggested, or maybe 30 years from now. What are we going to do when the war is over? We are going to have a new order in America.

I submit this to you in all seriousness. To me this is the determining factor in this whole situation. We have fooled along with our domestic situation, and, as I say again, I am not blaming anybody. Our problem is so vast—take the farm problem—who knows what to do about it? Nevertheless, I think that, as strong and as rich as we are, if we work it out we will probably find some way out of it.

They are talking about a new order in the United States, which is nothing more or less than the extension of the defense program.

You remember a conference that was held here in Washington, probably seven or eight months ago—I do not have the date—at which a group of industrial economists, representing banks and colleges, had a conference, with economists representing the Government—Mr. Rexford Tugwell, Mr. Mordecai Ezekiel, and Mr. Leon Henderson, all of them known to you—and the question was how to pay for the defense program. That was a pretty knotty problem.

Senator, you had a program to pay for it at one time, but it was very much like the one I had, which went up in smoke.

They were discussing how to pay for it. Finally one of them said—I think it was Mr. Ezekiel—"Gentlemen, don't you realize that with this defense program we are going to give a demonstration of how abundance can be produced in the United States by spending money?"

One of the economists said, "You have spent a lot of money already. You are spending $3,000,000,000 a year. You have not produced abundance."

Then Mr. Tugwell said, "But $3,000,000,000 a year won't do it. That is ridiculous. That is chicken feed. What you have got to spend is $12,000,000,000."

I want to develop this point, and I will be through. I think it is very important. Now, the mayor of the city of New York,* who is a friend of mine and for whom I have great respect, and who has been a grand mayor, was making a speech at New York the other day, and he said, "We are going to have a new order in the United States when it is all over."

---

* Fiorello La Guardia.

What is the new order? He said, "We are going to spend as much on peace as we are spending on defense."

Saying all these things is not important. It is the desperation and despair which has finally brought these men to believe that this Nation is done as a great nation of free-operating businessmen, and that in the future there is going to be one great customer for the business of the Nation, and that is the United States of America.

Now, that is fascism, gentlemen. We talk about fascism, and we think of it in terms of its ugly aspects, the ugly Mr. Hitler and his nasty little mustache, and the marching song troopers, and the burning of holy books, and the persecution of the Jews. But they are only the ugly consequences of fascism. The individual ingredients of fascism are not, taken by themselves, morally or in any other [way] repulsive. This is one of them—that the capitalistic system is done; that it can be supported only by the government creating purchasing power, which will be done by vast taxation, exhaustive taxation, vast borrowing, and the creation of money in all kinds of fantastic ways, which the Government will pour out in the stream of business and keep it flooded. That is one of them.

The other is the system of intimate, comprehensive, minute bureaucratic control of every article of production, from the mine and farm into the retail shop and into the hands of the consumers.

Militarism is another one, and we are heading in that direction.[*]

When the war is over the seeds of all these things will be here, and when we go to war we will loose these ugly passions, these ugly hatreds, which have made their appearance all over. You will get us hating each other. You will get one set of citizens calling another set of citizens names. You will get them calling them transmission belts of the Nazis. You will get people denouncing the Jews. You cultivate and you bring into being and you nurture every base emotion in your society, and when the war is over you turn that society, thus emotionalized and loosed, on a bankrupt nation.

What do you think you will get out of this war? Do you think it will be calm, rational, reasoning leaders who will be leading us at that time? We are going in the same direction as Hitler's Germany. That is what disturbs me. I do not think we have any trusteeship in Europe. I do not think we know what to do about everything in Europe. We have not known what to do about it here.

Here is what Mr. Herbert Agar[†] says, and I have a great deal of respect for him. He is one of the most intelligent and one of the finest men I know on the other side of this question. He says:

---

[*] See Flynn's *As We Go Marching* (1944; reprint New York: Free Life, 1973) for a book-length exposition of this argument.

[†] Agar, once a leading publicist of the agrarian and distributist movements and editor of *Who*

Do not let us fool ourselves on one point. The war will do no positive good. It will do the negative good of getting rid of Hitler and the criminal system of politics which Hitler has built, but it may also get rid of the entire civilization it is intended to save.

Hitler is over in Europe; and I do not regard Hitler as the cause of the troubles of Europe. I regard Hitler as a consequence of this trouble, and fascism as a consequence of this trouble, and Europe did not know what to do about the economic and social problems.

Read the history of Italy in the last 20 years, before the present war. It was the same as this country, moving slower, because it was a slower economy.

Mussolini and Hitler and the consequences are the consequences of the seeds of decay in the systems that these nations were not courageous enough to deal with. We go over there and get rid of Hitler, and after we get rid of Hitler what are you going to do with that vast bankrupt nation in disorder and chaos, unless you set up some kind of order? You do not know what kind of order to set up because you do not know what kind of order to set up here.

You are going to go to war to make over Europe, to get vengeance on Hitler, this little, despicable creature that we hate with a blazing hatred, because we make him the semblance of this thing. We go to war to get rid of Hitler, and when we have got rid of Hitler we will have the continent of Europe on our hands to police for a hundred years.

What are you going to police? What kind of order are you going to police? You cannot police an order unless you make an order.

Now, gentlemen, I say that is my reason for saying the time has come to stop any further commitments.

*Herbert Hoover,** ex-president of the United States, June 29, 1941

I agree that the world would be vastly better if the whole totalitarian idea were extirpated. But those who still cling to this as the mission of America should ask realistically how much of a job it is. Especially in the face of this revolution in military weapons and this actual military situation.

Such a war means that Hitler must be defeated. It means Mussolini must be defeated. It means the War Party in Japan must be defeated. It means that Turkey, Spain, and Portugal must be defeated. It means that unless Hitler first disposes of Stalin we must defeat him also. Does any sane person believe that by military means we can defeat two-thirds of the military power of the whole world in even years and years? It would be another Children's Crusade.

Owns America? (1936), was a leading interventionist intellectual who, from his perch in the Office of War Information, threatened William Saroyan with a court-martial for Saroyan's antiwar novel *The Adventures of Wesley Jackson* (1946).

    * For a sympathetic consideration of Hoover as a Quaker pacifist, see William Appleman Williams, *Some Presidents: From Wilson to Nixon* (New York: Vintage, 1972).

We cannot slay an idea or an ideology with machine guns. Ideas live in men's minds in spite of military defeat. They live until they have proved themselves right or wrong. These ideas are evil. And evil ideas contain the germs of their own defeat.

Hitler's real weakness would be in peace. His invasions have won not the loyalty but the undying hate of two-thirds of the people under his control. They have known self-government and liberty for centuries. They are people of great spiritual and intellectual resistance. They cannot revolt in arms against tanks and planes but they will never accept a new order based on slavery. And these aggressions have won the fear and hate of all the rest of the world. Conquest always dies of indigestion.

The whole Nazi ideology and the Nazi economic system are based upon coercion of the individual, the group or the class. Those coercions can be held in preparing for war or during war. They cannot be held in peace. Even if Hitler got peace the Nazi system will begin to go to pieces. Therefore, we do not need to despair that these evil ideologies will continue forever on this earth. . . .

. . . Suppose we join the war. Suppose we have victory over Hitler. Suppose we should march down the Unter den Linden. What happens then? It is possible to say right now what would happen.

Within a week after Germany is defeated each one of twenty nations in Europe will necessarily declare its national independence. Each one will set up a government of its own. Within another week each will begin to organize an army. They will occupy their utmost boundaries. In order to get revenue and to protect jobs for their own people, each one will again set up their tariff walls. And these nations will at once coagulate into groups and combinations for power politics, intent on increasing their strength at the peace table. There will be reparations and territory to divide.

All this is what happened before the Peace Conference in 1919, and it will automatically happen again. Moreover, many nations will have suffered greatly. Hate and revenge will sit at that Peace Table again.

No responsible statesman on the democratic side has yet stated how or by what plan this inevitable result of victory is to be molded into permanent peace. We are asked to go in blind as to the ultimate purpose of this war.

If we stay out and retain our economic and moral resources we will be able to contribute to the rehabilitation of the world, and we may be able to make an affirmative contribution to a method to end war and bring about a better world.

And what happens in the United States during and after a war that must take years and years even if it were won? We must at once establish further centralization of authority amounting to practical dictatorship in the United States. We will disguise its name, but total war cannot be won without it. We must bring about unity by force. We must regiment industry and labor. Intellectual life and civil liberty must be shackled to the war machine.

The necessities of war organization require vast taking over and operation of industry by the Government. War organization creates vested personal power, vested economic interests, vested habits and vested ideas. We have a taste of all this already in organizing preparedness only.

It is easier to regiment a people than to un-regiment them. They can be deprived of their liberties by an ukase, a command, or by administrative order. It is a long and painful climb back to freedom. Does any American believe that these vast powers vested in government will be soon restored to the people if we join in world war?

When we came out of that last war our national debt was about 10% of our national wealth. Instead of that we will have a debt equal to 50% of our national wealth if we ever go into this one. The only answer is to inflate wages and prices by huge amounts in order to make it bearable. That would rob every present life insurance policy, every savings bank deposit, every college endowment of its buying power. That would be the ruin of the saving classes in the United States. No such event has ever happened in history without moral degeneration and the wreck of the whole form of government.

After this war is over it is certain that the forces pressing for continued economic dictatorship would be stronger than ever.

Lord Lothian in his last impressive address wisely remarked as to the dictatorships in Europe that these world evils "grew out of the despair . . . from long years of war, inflation . . . unemployment and frustration." What profit to us is it to destroy totalitarianism abroad and create it at home? . . .

. . . Let me propose for reasoning people a course for us at this time which avoids the most destructive forces and holds fast to the most constructive forces. And that program is neither defeatist nor isolationist nor interventionist.

1. Give every aid we can to Britain and China but do not put the American flag or American boys in the zone of war.

2. Arm to the teeth for defense of the Western Hemisphere, and cease to talk and to provoke war until we are armed.

3. Uphold Congress steadily in assuming the responsibility to determine peace or war.

4. Stop this notion of ideological war to impose the four freedoms on other nations by military force and against their will.

5. Devote ourselves to improving the four freedoms within our borders that the light of their success may stir the people of the world to their adoption.

6. We can hope a peace table will assemble some day, whether it be the result of stalemate or victory. The world will be glad to have America sit in at the peace table.

   When that day comes the other nations will be sufficiently exhausted to listen to the military, economic, and moral powers of the United States. And with these reserves unexhausted, at that moment, and that moment only, can the United States promote a just and permanent peace.

7. We should go to that peace conference without the hates which come with war. We should go with a plan thought out and matured. We should prepare a new concept of human relations that will give the world some hope of permanent peace.

Dr. Robert Maynard Hutchins, President of the University of Chicago, January 23, 1941

I wish to dissociate myself from those who want us to stay out of war to save our own skins or our own property. I believe that the people of this country are and should be prepared to make sacrifices for humanity. National selfishness should not determine national policy. . . .

What, then, should our policy be? Instead of doing everything we can to get into the war, we should do everything we can to stay at peace. Our policy should be peace. Aid to Britain, China, and Greece should be extended on the basis most likely to keep us at peace, and least likely to involve us in war.

At the same time we should prepare to defend ourselves. We should prepare to defend ourselves against military or political penetration. We should bend every energy to the construction of an adequate navy and air force and the training of an adequate army. By adequate I mean adequate for defense against any power or combination of powers.

In the meantime, we should begin to make this country a refuge for those who will not live without liberty. For less than the cost of two battleships we could accommodate half a million refugees from totalitarian countries for a year. The net cost would not approach the cost of two battleships, for these victims, unlike battleships, would contribute to our industry and our cultural life, and help us make democracy work.

But most important of all, we should take up with new vigor the long struggle for moral, intellectual, and spiritual preparedness. If we would change the face of the earth, we must first change our own hearts. The principal end that we have hitherto set before ourselves is the unlimited acquisition of material goods. The business of America, said Calvin Coolidge, is business. We must now learn that material goods are a means and not an end. We want them to sustain life, but they are not the aim of life. The aim of life is the fullest development of the highest powers of men. This means art, religion, education, moral and intellectual growth. These things we have regarded as mere decorations or relaxations in the serious business of life, which was making money. The American people, in their own interest, require a moral regeneration. If they are to be missionaries to the world, this regeneration must be profound and complete.

We must try to build a new moral order for America. We need moral conviction, intellectual clarity, and moral action: moral conviction about the dignity of man, intellectual clarity about ends and means, moral action to construct institutions to bring to pass the ends we have chosen.

A new moral order for America means a new conception of security. Today we do not permit men to die of starvation, but neither do we give them an incentive to live. Every citizen must have a respected place in the achievement of the national purpose.

A new moral order for America means a new conception of sacrifice, sacrifice for the moral purpose of the community. In the interest of human dignity we need a rising standard of health, character, and intelligence. These positive goals demand the devotion and sacrifice of every American. We should rebuild one-third of the nation's homes. We must provide adequate medical care in every corner of the land. We must develop an education aimed at moral and intellectual growth instead of at making money.

A new moral order for America means a new conception of mastery. We must learn how to reconcile the machine with human dignity. We have allowed it to run wild in prosperity and war and to rust idly in periodic collapse. We have hitherto evaded the issue by seeking new markets. In an unstable world this has meant bigger and bigger collapses, more and more catastrophic war. In Europe and Russia the efforts to master the machine are carried out by methods we despise. America can master the machine within the framework of a balanced democracy, outdistance the totalitarian despotisms, and bring light and hope to the world. It is our highest function and greatest opportunity to learn to make democracy work. We must bring justice and the moral order to life, here and now.

March 30, 1941

The President cannot literally mean that we are to fight on till the four freedoms ring everywhere. If we are to be responsible for the four freedoms everywhere, we must have authority everywhere. We must force the four freedoms upon people who might prefer to do without them rather than accept them from the armed missionaries of the United States. This new imperialism, this revised conception of the White Man's Burden, this modern version of America's Manifest Destiny is a repudiation of the presidential teaching that there never has been, isn't now, and never will be any race of people fit to serve as masters over their fellow men.

Of course, we must extend the four freedoms to our "allies" as well as to our "enemies." We must see to it that British possessions throughout the world have them. The hopes held out to India during the last war, disappointed after it, and now held out again must be fulfilled. China, Greece, and Turkey must reform, too. In the Latin-American countries we shall have no easy task. Few of them have the four freedoms now. From Mexico to Patagonia we must send our legions to convert our good neighbors by force of arms.

The President cannot mean this, for it is a program of perpetual war, war in Latin-America, war in the Far East, war in the South Seas, and even war with Britain. Mr. Roosevelt must mean that by defeating the Axis we shall rid the world of those governments at present most aggressive in their attack on the four freedoms. During or after the war we shall have to figure out the next steps: how to establish and maintain governments that believe in the four freedoms. The first step is war. Here, then, is the real issue. Is the path to war the path to freedom?

This war, if we enter it, will be long, hard, and bloody. We do not have the choice between a short war abroad and a prolonged period of militarization at home. The "enemy" now controls all of Europe and part of Asia, and is not yet driven from Africa. We have no evidence that the totalitarian regimes will fly to pieces when their opponents get superiority in the air, or even that superiority can be achieved.

Total war for total victory against totalitarian states can best be conducted by totalitarian states. The reason is simple. A totalitarian state is nothing but a military machine. A totalitarian state will be more effective in war than any other kind of state. A democratic state is organized for the happiness of its citizens. But their happiness cannot be considered in total war. Every one of them must become a cog in the military machine. If the United States is to proceed through total war to total victory over totalitarian states, it will have to become totalitarian, too.

Is total war, then, the path to freedom? We seek freedom from want, and we impoverish ourselves. We seek freedom from fear, and we terrorize ourselves. We seek freedom of worship and freedom of speech, and we suppress them.

And when total victory has been won, will the totalitarian administration end? We may find a clue in England. A responsible member of the British Cabinet, Sir Archibald Sinclair, publicly supports a proposal that there shall be no elections in England for three years after the war. The reason is clear. Poverty and disillusionment will make democracy dangerous. . . .

The path to war is a false path to freedom. It is a false path to freedom for America. It is a false path to the four freedoms everywhere. War is for the sake of peace. The spirit of the peace will be determined by the spirit of the countries which make it. An Englishman, J. Middleton Murry, said of England, "This country, as it is, is incapable of winning a Christian victory, because it simply is not Christian." This general principle is sound. No country can win a democratic victory unless it is democratic. Only those who understand, value, and practice democracy know what a democratic peace would be. Only those who understand, value, and practice justice can make a just peace. Only those who understand, value, and practice four freedoms can make a peace to establish them everywhere.

Senator Hiram Johnson, R-California, May 31, 1941

But, what will become of our United States of America while we are pursuing these Herculean tasks? We have seen, little by little, power concentrated in one man's hands. We have soothed our perturbed spirits by pretending that those powers were needed to be thus concentrated in order to meet the crisis, but when you are meeting crises on practically all lands of every continent, what will become, the ordinary citizen will ask, of the good old United States. It is no reply to talk in generalities. . . . What is to become of your Government, Mr. American? Is it not plain that all this fighting on every shore, and in practically every country will mean but one thing, perhaps the destruction of a dictatorship in other lands, but the certainty of the creation of a dictatorship in our own. You may live under a beneficent despot the rest of your days if you desire. I prefer the good old American way, and I will protest and fight to the bitter end. You cannot with this plan that apparently is mapped out for you, escape a dictatorship and perhaps worse. If ever there was a time in the history of this country when it is the duty of Americans to stand forth and be men it is now. It will soon be too late, and then the outstretched hands of liberty may no longer join yours.

General Hugh S. Johnson, head of Selective Service Administration during World War I, head of NRA [National Recovery Administration], September 5, 1940*

There are very few Americans who do not hate Hitler and hope that Britain wins. Our sympathies are all with England. But modern war is not risked by any wise nation, as George Washington was careful to tell us, for any reason other than its own defense or some other absolutely compelling cause. That is the reason why our friends who want us to take part in this war call their committee "Defend America," and add, "by helping Britain." They have gone a long distance with that slogan; their argument is that our peace depends upon the British navy.

They go a lot further than that. They say that our peace, our Monroe Doctrine and the tranquillity of the Americas always have depended on the British navy. Therefore they say Britain is fighting our war, that Britain is fighting to defend us. They say: we owe it, both to gratitude and to our own defense, to help Britain. So they want to strip our army, navy, and air power of ships and guns and ammunition, and by various blind-pig loopholes in our own statutes, our treaties and international law, bootleg these hundreds of thousands of tons of lethal weapons to England.

First of all, let me say that if that argument is true, we would cut a fine figure in history and with our own conscience and common sense and for our own defense, if we can be satisfied to pay so great a debt and fulfill so great a duty with a lot of undercover gun-running and international hypocrisy. If our peace and defense depended, and now depends, on England, and England is at bay, we ought to go to war with everything we have. . . .

This country should have seen enough of what is going on in the world today to know that any nation which must rely for its own peace and for its own defense on the strength of any other nation is lost. We cannot rely on any other power but our own—Great Britain or any other. We can rely on

* This is from the first radio broadcast sponsored by America First.

nothing on this earth but the strength of our own right arm, our own resources, and the patriotism, valor and fidelity of our own people and Thanks Be To God!—it's enough.

In the past three years, Europe has been strewn with the wreckage of nations that relied on other nations for their defense. Some of them relied on Britain. France had full power when Hitler started in 1933, full power to stop him there in his tracks. But she preferred to rely on her alliance with the little nations of Central Europe called the Cordon Sanitaire. They relied on her as she relied on them, and all relied on British sea power in the background.

Austria so relied. They stepped aside and saw her swallowed. Czechoslovakia so relied. They went to Munich and tossed her to the wolves. Earlier, Britain had relied on France to help keep Mussolini out of Ethiopia, and France wanted Britain to help keep Hitler out of the Rhineland which would have kept the peace of Europe in this good day. But each reliance failed. Each nation was tying its shoe and looking in the other direction when the call for help came.

Finally, on a pledge of assistance if she would resist, Britain and France pushed Poland into the line of fire. Poland fell. No help came, and all of Northern Europe crumbled. Holland relied on Belgium, Belgium on France, France and Norway on Britain. Where are those nations now? All, except Britain, "Gone With the Wind." And the epitaph of each could read—"She Relied for Her Peace and Safety on Some Strength Other Than Her Own." . . .

We are out there (in the Far East) to help preserve the British empire in Asia. Is that necessary in order to keep the British fleet between us and Hitler? It may help, but it's a pretty far cry to such a conclusion. The real effect of it is not to keep the British navy between us and Hitler. Its purpose is to rest the peace and defense of America on some force other than our own. Present indications are that we are in more danger of waking up some morning to find ourselves at war in the Far East, 7,000 miles away, than of anything that could conceivably happen to us on our Atlantic coast.

Philip La Follette, former governor of Wisconsin, November 1, 1941

There is no dispute among thoughtful and patriotic Americans over the fact that our way of life is in danger. The difference—and it is a profound difference—that divides us is *where* and *how* the United States can best meet that challenge and wisely serve the cause of freedom for mankind. This difference has shattered our old political lines. It is no longer a question of the Republican Party and the Democratic Party. Today the alignment is between the War Party and the American Party. The War Party maintains that American freedom is to be won or lost on the battlefields of Europe, Asia, and Africa. The American Party maintains that the future welfare and happiness of our people will not be determined by the defeat or victory of any other nation anywhere on earth, but by what we—we in America—do to protect and extend freedom and security of our people here. . . .

. . . Every step in the program, that has now led to *shooting* hostilities, was thrust on a reluctant and suspicious people as the one *sure* way to keep *out* of war. Whatever the intentions may have been, this program has produced exactly the opposite result from that upon which it was sold to the people. In spite of the barrage of pledges of peace, we are today in shooting warfare—armed hostilities concerning which neither the people nor the Congress has been consulted. . . .

A vast field awaits the constructive action of clear thinking and stout-hearted Americans. A greater, richer frontier lies ahead than any we have left behind. It belongs to the strong and not to the weak. It will be opened by red-blooded fighters fighting—not to destroy—but to restore again opportunity for those who build. When this new frontier is open—there will be unlimited opportunity for every man, woman and child in this land. The tragedy of the War Party is they cannot look ahead—they only look backward. They only see—and fight for yesterday. We see and fight for tomorrow. And as ghastly as the days ahead may be, not even Fascist-minded war-mongers here in Washington can wreck the future of America. The policies of this Administration may take a frightful toll in life and liberty and treasure, but this America of ours is strong enough and great enough and rich enough to build anew—to make the dream of economic security and the pursuit of happiness again come true.

Senator Robert La Follette, P-Wisconsin, February 24, 1941*

We have a job to do at home—a job that challenges the very best that we have and are—the job of putting our own house in order and proving by our example to oppressed peoples everywhere in the world that democracy can function, that democracy can meet head-on the problems, which, when left unsolved in Europe, spawned dictatorship and war.

We have the men, the machines, the brains, the brawn, the resources and the ingenuity. Here in America we move 40 percent of the world's freight, produce nearly 40 percent of the world's raw materials for industry, generate 50 percent of the world's horsepower, and 35 percent of its electric power.

Here in America we produce 34 percent of the world's coal, 62 percent of its petroleum. We are rich in iron ore, copper, lead, and zinc. We make more than a third of the world's pig iron and steel.

Here in America we grow half the world's corn. We have half the world's telephones. We have three-fourths of the world's automobiles, two-thirds of the trucks and buses, more than half of the world's radio sets.

We have the most gigantic productive capacity the world has ever seen.

We have 130,000,000 American men, women, and children who are ready—yes, they are anxious, if need be—to shed the last drop of their blood to defend America against any aggressor or any combination of aggressors.

* From *Congressional Record*, 77th Cong., 1st session, pp. 1307–8.

Mr. President, I appeal to my fellow countrymen to throw off this fear, this hysteria; to reject it for the false and hideous propaganda that it is.

Here in America we are richer in resources than Russia, Germany, France, Great Britain, Italy, and Japan combined.

If to our own breath-taking resources we add the resources of a friendly Latin America, we emerge with rubber as our major deficiency—rubber which was first developed in the Western Hemisphere and may now be brought back to satisfy our needs. Tin may be a problem also, but we have not explored it fully on a hemisphere basis. The administration has been fiddling around for months trying to decide to whom it will give the concession for establishing an American smelter for the reduction of low-grade South American tin ore.

With these fabulous resources, with the man power and machine power to convert them into goods to satisfy men's hunger for sustenance and significance we can end the paradox of poverty in the midst of plenty. We can hold aloft a beacon to light the free way of life for all mankind.

Mr. President, I offer this as an American alternative to the mad foreign adventure which the bill* envisions.

I urge that we make the "four freedoms" prevail in America before we try to ram them down the throats of people everywhere in the world.

I urge that we stop trying to solve other peoples' problems until we have lifted dispossessed and pauperized farmers in America out of the poverty which has been theirs for so long.

I urge that we shorten our gaze at least until we have done something constructive and permanent for the 10,000,000 unemployed Americans in urban and rural areas.

I urge that we stop trying to run the whole world until we have built decent homes here, until we have reconstructed our money and credit system, so that we can meet the challenge which is behind the hideous brutalitarian aspects of the Nazi-German revolution.

I urge that we stop trying to run the world until we have provided a program of sound and adequate medical and hospital care for the masses of our people, until we have provided a generous security for the old and full opportunity for our youth. Mr. President, in all sincerity I urge that we stop wearing a halo of righteousness until we do something about factors which have caused approximately 20 percent of our men—supposedly the flower of the Nation—to be rejected as physically or mentally unfit for military training.

I urge, likewise, that we end the campaign of fear. I urge, instead, that we buckle down to the job of national defense. I urge at the same time that we prepare to meet the inevitable dislocations which will follow the end of this armament boom.

* The Lend-Lease bill.

I urge that we stop misleading the valiant defenders of Britain, Greece, and China into thinking we are going to war; or stop misleading the American people into thinking that we are not going to war.

In short, Mr. President, I urge that we reject this bill and resume the job—the uncompleted job—we dropped a year ago, that we throw everything we have into the awe-inspiring challenge of our time.

I urge this, Mr. President, because in the long pull, such a course will not only preserve the American way of life, but it will liberate us from fear and doubt and impoverishment. In this way, and in this way only, will we be able to blaze a trail which the war-weary, blood-sick peoples of the world can follow on their long, weary, and painful trek back from war toward peace and prosperity.

Dr. Henry Noble MacCracken, president of Vassar College, August 20, 1941

If we can win such a war, is it well that we should win it? We had a president once who prayed for a peace without victory. I confess myself to be of Wilson's mind. For I do not see how such a victory could leave us with any idealism to carry out the points of the sea treaty. Instead we should be an empire, either a part of the British Empire, as some would have us be, or an American world-empire, the old independent United States forever gone.

We should have garrisons in Germany, Japan, and Italy; commissars of raw materials all over the world imposing an Anglo-American peace on the world, with an indispensable condition as its basis—the integrity of the British Empire.

The imperialistic temptation, to be lord of all the kingdoms of the earth, is the greatest of all temptations to a rich and powerful democracy. We know what happened to Athens when she maintained such a peace, what happened to Rome when she went the imperial way, and what a dilemma now confronts Britain, as she tries to develop democracy at home, and empire abroad.

You cannot evade that issue. Democracy and empire are incompatible terms. What our country needs is not empire abroad, but [a] new birth of freedom at home, if government by the people is not to perish from the earth.

Colonel Hanford MacNider, former assistant secretary of war, former U.S. minister to Canada, former head of American Legion, January 22, 1941 (radio address, WOL, Washington, D.C.)

Ever since the First World War the Americans who served in it have cried for an impregnable defense of our country, so that just such situations as this could not arise. We have demanded a small but powerful army fast on its feet and able to meet all comers, a navy and an air force second to none. We have usually won from the very people who now clamor loudest for intervention in Europe's everlasting quarrels, the name of militarists, war-mongers or worse. We were then and we are now for an impregnable defense for these United States. One does not have to be a military expert to know that no foreign power nor even group of powers will ever dare attack a prepared America. Meantime, while we are at last aroused to prepare, we can be of no real help to anyone else unless and until we are strong and unafraid ourselves.

I have no quarrel with aid to Britain, or to Greece and China. They are fighting a gallant fight against great odds, and I pray that they win, not for our sakes but for their own. I begrudge them no help which we may give them within the framework of our present laws, and which is not at the expense of our own proper defense.

I am, however, unwilling to commit my sons or any American's sons to the policing of the rest of the world, or the maintenance of the British Empire, much as I hope that it may survive. Our fathers came to this land to leave all that behind them. Europe and Asia have been in constant battle over the balance of power for thousands of years. They will be at it long after all of us here are gone. If we put ourselves back into it now, we shall lose this republic.

We are committed to the enforcement of the Monroe Doctrine. That is, we are to keep out of Europe's affairs and they are to keep out of those of this hemisphere. Are we to enforce one part of it and forget the rest?

I do not believe any nation has ever fought our battles or is fighting them now. Nor should they be allowed to fight them. That would be cowardly and un-American. Either the wars overseas are our wars, or they are not. If they are not, we should obey the laws upon our statute books, maintain our Constitution under which we have became the greatest nation in history, and preserve America as a great citadel of enlightened democracy to which men and nations can repair for guidance and a re[birth] of civilization. That is the greatest contribution we can give this troubled world.

The first responsibility of every American is to his fellow Americans. The first responsibility of our government is to the American people; not to the rest of the world, no matter how sorely beleaguered it may be.

Dr. Charles Clayton Morrison, editor of *The Christian Century*, October 23, 1941

The transcendently important fact for Americans to consider is that the present war is being waged in an international framework which is on the point of being shattered everywhere on the planet. There is nothing substantial and calculable to tie to. The whole political structure is being shaken by forces which have long been gathering. The world order as we have known it is in the grip of forces which the nations themselves cannot control. For the United States to consent to the doctrine that our future depends upon the continued existence of any other nation, and to tie itself to that nation, is to hang our destiny upon nails driven into rotting timbers.

The tight, snug, dependable world of nations in which all previous wars were fought has passed away. The other World War was the last to be waged in such a world. In that world, a war could be fought and a victory won. And a victory, then, was a victory. But now a victory may turn to ashes by the very disintegration and disappearance of the vanquished nation, leaving only a chaos behind. Up to and including the last World War the nations were, as entities, sure of themselves. Today they are in terror of themselves. Their very existence is precarious, and that not merely because of external enemies but because of the upsurge of powerful forces at home. The political structures of the world are no longer the trim, firm, calculable entities they once were. Today they are trembling on the brink of collapse.

Something is happening that is undermining the stability of every national state, including, though perhaps less threateningly, our own. What is it that is happening? This: The economic consciousness of mankind has become so massive, so insistent, and so potent, that it can no longer be controlled by the traditional political system. This is true not merely in the sense that economic interest dictates political policy (that has always been the case), but in the sense that it now is actually at the point of undermining the existing national state as a political entity.

This is the kind of world in which it is proposed that the United States shall tie its destiny to one of the existing empires. To do this goes against the grain of the whole proud tradition of American independence. But that is not the point I am now making. For this country to act upon the assumption that participation in this war in order to preserve American liberty or the democratic ideals which this country cherishes, is to make a momentous decision on the basis of assumptions which no longer have validity. We are being driven to take over a bankrupt war, in order to save a bankrupt imperial system as a means of escape from a bankrupt domestic economy. . . .

America's moral responsibility to humanity, as well as her own national interest, demands that this country be kept out of this war. In the face of an incalculable future, the United States should make herself strong enough within her own boundaries to defend the treasures of her civilization against whatever shapeless uncertainties lie hidden from her present view. We should therefore have as strong a Navy as we can build, as great an air force as we can develop, and as competent an Army as we need to defend the independence of this Nation should the hour come when we must do so.

But this is not enough. The democracy which is our sacred heritage must be preserved, vastly improved, evolved, and crowned with a kind of justice which it has not yet been able to achieve. . . .

But this is not enough—not enough for that America which we who love her cherish in our heart of hearts.

This Nation has a role of vast responsibility to play in the world order which will follow that which is now going down. The plea which I make for our nonintervention in the war is no plea of isolationism. I am not an isolationist. I am a cooperationist—perhaps I should say a critical cooperationist. Instead of throwing oil on the flames that are now devouring Europe, and cruelly prolonging the insensate slaughter of human life and the devastation of civilization, it is America's high duty to stretch forth a hand of sanity and humanity, to ease the terrors of the revolution now in process and inform it with some glimmer of reason and hope. America's true role is peace, not war. Her voice should be lifted up, not for slaughter, but for justice.

*William H. Murray,** former governor of Oklahoma, August 29, 1941

The only system is to follow the "Traditional American Policy" proclaimed by Washington in his farewell address, supplemented by Monroe in his "declaration," and so accurately stated by Jefferson in his "First Inaugural": "Peace, friendship, trade and commerce with all nations, entangling alliances with none."

So long as we followed that rule we had no quarrel with Europe; indeed, under the Monroe Doctrine we promised to stay out of European controversies and based the "Declaration" on the fact that we had never been a party to the quarrels of the Old World. If we now depart from that doctrine we shall be unable to maintain the Monroe Doctrine.

I, for one, would like to hold to the Doctrine that America's covenants with other nations, and confirmed by legislative authority of Congress, should be kept. We took the lead in the '90's to establish a World Court to adjudicate differences, that all could agree should be submitted to that court; for certainly we could not submit to any international authority the Monroe Doctrine, the form of our government, our independence, or constitutional or religious principles; but there are many things that we could with propriety agree to submit, and we did submit, and signed a covenant with other nations in 1907 that established the World Court, and the same was approved by the United States Congress, and is a law today. Among other things, in Article 6 of that covenant may be found the following language:

"Article 6. The supplying, in any manner, directly or indirectly, by a neutral power to a belligerent, of warships, ammunition, or war material of any kind whatever, is forbidden."

Under general principles of international law, we are not called upon to refuse to sell anything to any nation, even when at war, but we must needs treat them all alike. That is if we sell to England, we should sell also to her antagonist nations. That is neutrality. However, we went further in this covenant before quoted, and declared that we would not furnish war materials of any kind "directly or indirectly" to any nation at war, and we have been violating that provision ever since Hitler's first move in Europe—at all times with the cry of the authorities of our government that we are neutral; but is that true?

---

* "Alfalfa Bill" Murray, Oklahoma governor and an agronomist who developed a hybrid corn, was one of the last great shaggy embodiments of the old populist tradition.

Senator Gerald P. Nye, R-North Dakota, March 4, 1941*

Until the outbreak of the war these Americans could look at the British Empire coolly, calmly, and see it for what it is. It represented then the very acme of reaction, imperialism, and exploitation of subject peoples. Yet somehow today these same Americans talk of this empire as though it has become overnight, by virtue of the mere fact that it has become involved in the war, miraculously transfigured into a guardian of liberty and democratic rights. This rear guard of world reaction has by some inexplicable magic become the vanguard of liberal democracy.

But there is the other Britain about which nothing is being said; and this is the Britain that we are expected to forget while we debate such a bill as this [Lend-Lease]. There is the Britain that covers 27 percent of the habitable surface of the globe and embraces within its power a quarter of all the population of the earth. Do we realize, as we consider this bill, that in this vast empire fewer than one-seventh of all its inhabitants live under democratic forms of self-government? Perhaps nothing is so ominous in the present situation as the romantic view of this empire which so many Americans are now permitting themselves to take under the emotional stress of the war.

What has happened? Has the leopard really changed its spots? Has the British imperial policy undergone a transformation or fallen into the control of men with new ideas? Of course nothing of the sort has happened. Broadly speaking, the class which shaped British imperial policy during the last fatal decade and which proved unable to avoid the present catastrophe is still at the helm of the British Empire. All that has happened is that we have lost our mental balance. Hysteria has enslaved our judgment and warped our perspective.

Dr. John A. O'Brien, professor, University of Notre Dame, June 24, 1941

Propaganda that the United States must enter the war to save democracy and Christianity received its deathblow when developments brought Russia into the war on the side of Great Britain.

In duplicity and cruelty Stalin equals Hitler, and he surpasses him in his hatred of Christianity, or our system of private ownership and in our democratic way of life.

In asking the American people to turn our weapons against brave little Finland, the one country which has honored its obligations to America, to maintain on his bloody throne the worst butcher of Christians in the world, Prime Minister Churchill does violence to the feelings of our people.

---

* From *Congressional Record*, 77th Cong., 1st session, pp. 1724–25.

R. Douglas Stuart, Jr., national director of the America First Committee*

Here is the one fact which still stands out among the changing facts of the last two years—the united determination of the American people that we shall not enter war abroad is as strong today as it was when the war began.

Try as they may, the war party cannot question or refute it. Month after month, by every authentic test, by every reliable poll, the evidence has piled up against them. Not the bare majority—not two-thirds—but four-fifths of the American people stand agreed on this one ground. By every rule the people's will should be decisive. Yet how foreign to the democratic way is the spectacle which confronts us. The more the people's opposition to the war has grown, the closer the minority has brought us to the brink.

Here, then, is the threat that strikes at the very heart of the American way. For if there is one cardinal principle upon which this government is based, it is the principle of majority rule. The day Americans surrender this historic precept will be the day when our democracy, and all it stands for, can be pronounced dead. . . .

The Gallup poll, week after week, reveals its consistent anti-war majority of 80 percent. Every survey bears this out. Newspapers; members of Congress; a committee of college presidents, headed by Robert M. Hutchins of Chicago, all have conducted exhaustive tests in widespread areas. And always the result has been 70, 80 and, in some cases, 90 percent solidly opposed to our entry into Europe's war.

It avails the interventionist nothing to assert that of course no one wants war. In none of these polls was the question whether we want war or like war or favor war. Knowing all the facts, the voters were asked in the clearest language whether they thought the United States should enter this war.

That is the precise question which Congress may be called upon to decide.

America is united today—united for defense—a defense so strong that we need never fear the outcome of Europe's war. This is their verdict and the minority should accept it in the traditional American way.

The war party's new strategy, however, has left behind the traditions of America. Their approach now lies on more desperate and dangerous ground. In one final effort, they now invoke the totalitarian weapon of undeclared war. Here is the alien doctrine which is the last resort of the dictator—the measure by which a Hitler or a Stalin forces the hand of his unwilling people. It is one which the authors of our Constitution took strict pains to guard against. Bitter experience with the tyrants of the old world had taught them the danger of placing the most awful of all powers—the power of life or death—in the hands of one man, be he dictator or king. Carefully they made the Congress sole trustee of the nation's peace.

---

*From radio address on the National Broadcasting Company's Blue Network, August 1, 1941.

Yet today—in the hysteria of the moment—the proposal of executive war finds acceptance in the President's own cabinet.

As usual, the war party couches its proposal in soft, disarming terms. "Clear the Atlantic now," they urge—a suggestion which sounds attractive to the unwary. What they mean to say is that our navy and our air force should enter the war immediately as a full belligerent . . .

Who can be sure that a disillusioned America will ever return to the system which let war come in rank defiance of the people's will?

You and I have a faith to keep with those who gave us America. We are trustees of liberties which we alone can keep alive. Not in China, Russia, Africa, or other foreign lands—which neither know nor want our way of life—but here, here in a free and independent United States.

Unconfused by our sympathy for England or Finland, or any nation but our own, let us turn our eyes from the old world to the job at hand. Mindful of the lessons of the past, let us build a strong America, united for peace and free from foreign war.

Senator Robert A. Taft, R-Ohio, March 7, 1941*

I favor the defense on the oceans, because I think we can make our force sufficiently strong so that while we are defending that line no one, not Hitler himself, will dare attack us across those oceans, and we shall insure our peace. I say if we adopt the other policy, if we say that the British Channel is our frontier, if we say we cannot permit anyone, Hitler or anyone else, to have complete control of all Europe, then we will be in war the rest of our lives. We will be assuming the position the English had to take for many years. We will have to maintain the balance of power in Europe. We will have forever to defend the British Isles, across a very narrow vulnerable channel some 13 miles wide. We will have forever a vulnerable position, inviting attack from the continent, just as the Philippines make us vulnerable in the Far East.

I say that the course of going to war, the course of intervening in the European war, is a course which in the end is vain. We cannot war against philosophies, we cannot war against religions and "isms." War will kill democracy not save it. This policy really is a policy of manifest destiny about which we heard in the Spanish War time, the policy that we should go out and run the world. Either we are not going to send troops, in which case the war is certainly a deadlock, in which case Hitler is certainly going to remain the dominating factor in Europe, in which case we will have all the dangerous results of such a complete domination of Europe; or we are going to Europe, and when we get there, we are going to have to send our men and police Europe.

Are we going to leave an army of occupation in Germany, or are we to get out and let them do again what they have done in the past 20 years? Are we

---

* From *Congressional Record*, 77th Cong., 1st session, pp. 1973–74.

going to involve ourselves perpetually in European policy? Our policy should be to defend the Atlantic and Pacific Oceans.

Norman Thomas, head of the Socialist Party, former Socialist presidential nominee, in *Keep America Out of War: A Program* with Bertram D. Wolfe (Stokes, 1939).

We believe that the war raging in Europe is not our war. It is not our war because it is not our making. It is not our war because it is rooted in the age-old power politics of Europe in which we do not and should not participate. It is not our war because it is an outgrowth of the same conflicts as the war of 1914–1918; conflicts between "sated" imperialist powers and "hungry" ones, between those who acquired their colonies and spheres of influence a little earlier (were the Boer war, the Opium war, the Sepoy War, less brutal, aggressive and ruthless than the Russo-German invasion of Poland?) and those powers which arrived late upon the scene and demand a re-division of the spoils. . . .

In our opinion, there will be no lasting peace in Europe except as the peoples of Europe become conscious that they have no quarrel with each other (a consciousness that is already far more widespread than it was in 1914), and except as they take their own destinies fully into their own hands. The one hope of bringing permanent peace to Europe's blood-soaked soil lies in the peoples' joining hands across all frontiers, and together making peace and reorganizing their continent into a democratic and socialist United States of Europe, where only the war against ignorance and poverty and disease and degradation, and against death itself, can still find scope. We believe that there are no "military victory" methods of putting a permanent end to war or the evils that follow in its train.

Senator Charles Tobey, R-New Hampshire, September 27, 1941

I measure my words when I say that in my opinion the greatest menace to this country and to our form of government does not come from any enemy abroad, but rather exists right here in our country, and more particularly and specifically, under the Capitol Dome in Washington, where the people's representatives in the Congress have apparently lost their sense of responsibility under the Constitution to act as a separate but coordinate branch of the federal government and have yielded to pressure and blandishments of another branch, the executive.

We of America need a new Declaration of Independence by the American Congress—independence of any other branch of the Government, consistent with the oath of the Congress to preserve, protect and defend the Constitution of the United States, and if that oath means anything, it means the Congress should exercise and be true to the obligations that it assumes in that oath, in accordance with the provisions of our Constitution. . . .

August 16, 1941

They are the defeatists in this country who take fear at the suggestion that Hitler might be able to conquer Europe, conquer Great Britain, overcome famine and disease and economic ruin, which will inevitably follow in the path of this war, and overcoming a tremendous Fifth Column against him in all Europe—that he will be able to hold these people down and at the same time, start out on a costly venture to cross the ocean in a doubtful attempt to conquer a well-defended and well-equipped, powerful nation of 130 million indomitable Americans.

They are the defeatists who say that, in the face of this questionable possibility, America has no alternative but to send her sons 3,000 miles to die on foreign soil, as they died in 1917–18.

Senator Burton K. Wheeler, D-Montana, July 28, 1941*

(Senator Wheeler used a commercial mailing list of 1,000,000 names in circulating under his frank copies of speeches of the president and others taken from the *Congressional Record.* Three reached members of the armed forces. In a press conference Secretary of War Stimson commented: "Without expressing legal opinions, I will simply say I think that comes near the line of subversive activities against the United States, if not treason." The following paragraphs are taken from Senator Wheeler's speech on the floor of the Senate reporting the facts.)

Whatever temporary success this smear campaign has enjoyed can be attributed to the artful planning and the falsity of its foundation.

The Secretary apparently cares not for truth or facts. He wanted the American people to believe that I had circularized army camps. That impression was created, with cold and calculated cunning. It is false—but it sired those shrieking headlines.

This attack was not made against a particular United States Senator. or a particular individual. It was not made because of what appeared on the card or to whom they were addressed. It was made to silence all those who oppose and fight our entry into war. It is a part of a program to terrify the American people into submission—to make them accept participation in a foreign war.

Which is treasonable—to plunge this country into a disastrous and ruinous war, or to maintain peace?

Which is subversive—to deny freedom of speech, press and petition, or to maintain our civil liberties guaranteed by the Constitution of the United States?

Mr. Stimson apparently believes the suppression of Constitutional Government and war constitute a mark of patriotism. I do not.

* From *Congressional Record,* 77th Cong., 1st session, p. 6335.

A year ago, the move for an enlarged army was launched. National Guards-men assembled at Camps. The Army had begun its expansion program. Many people favored war. Willkie charged that President Roosevelt was leading the nation into war. As Willkie's strength seemed to be mounting, the Democrats insisted that the President go on the stump. Not once, not twice but many times in those last few days before election day of 1940, President Roosevelt stood before microphones and promised peace, peace.

Undoubtedly soldiers heard, read and believed those pledges. Secretary Stimson did not charge the President with "subversive activity"—he did not charge his Commander-in-Chief with "near treason." But when I reproduced and distributed President Roosevelt's peace pledges nine months later, then cries arose of "traitor," "Treason."

If one, two, certainly if three members of our armed forces are listening, then one can plead the cause of peace only under the penalty of being labeled a traitor. If a newspaper reaching an army camp publishes an antiwar speech then it engages in subversive activities.

Under this new formula announced by Stimson and approved by the President, freedom of speech, freedom of press, and freedom of petition are suppressed in America, by calling the utterances of speakers or writers treasonable.

. . .

If an American Senator cannot ask the people of America to petition the President to keep us out of war; if free speech and free assemblage is to be denied in this country, democracy in the United States will have been sabotaged while we talked of establishing the four freedoms all over the world.

We must not, we cannot ask American boys to die upon the bloody battlefields of Europe and Asia to establish liberties denied the people of the United States.

So long as this country remains at peace, so long as this Congress has not declared the United States to be at war, so long as we retain a remnant of democratic government, I will not be silenced.

I will speak the truth as I see it.

"Truth wears no mask, bows at no human shrine, neither seeks place or applause. It only asks a hearing. . . . "

Time and history will prove who was blinded by clouds of glory, who sought to sell America's birthright for a mess of pottage—and it will prove, too, who honestly and rightly fought to preserve this land as a free, democratic republic.

8

Closing the Books

If the decision for war were to be given affirmatively, General Wood had said in the early days of America First,

You will find Americans like myself, who sincerely believe such a course spells disaster to the nation, will be at their posts of duty in the service of this country. I am old fashioned enough to believe in the toast offered by Stephen Decatur back in 1816, "Our country! In her intercourse with foreign nations, may she always be in the right: but Our Country, right or wrong."

In harmony with that position, a few hours after the airways brought the news of the attack on Pearl Harbor, the National Committee of America First issued a statement pledging complete support to the government in the defense of our country:

The military forces of Japan have, without warning, attacked this nation, and the Japanese government has formally declared war upon us. This must be followed by a similar declaration on the part of the United States and by all-out hostilities. The America First Committee urges all those who have subscribed to its principles to give their support to the war effort of this country until the conflict with Japan is brought to a successful conclusion. In this war the America First Committee pledges its aid to the President as Commander in Chief of the Armed Forces of the United States.

The day after Pearl Harbor the chapter chairmen were invited by air mail[1] to submit their views immediately to the National Committee (which was to meet three days later) regarding the course the Committee should adopt:

1. Dissolution of the Committee and cessation of all activity.

2. Adjournment of all activity but preserving the organization structure.

3. Continued opposition to entry into the European war while supporting the war effort against Japan.

4. Support of national defense by working to fill the needs of the armed forces.

Within twenty-four hours telegrams came pouring into national headquarters from chapter chairmen urging that the committee not disband, that it continue in war as in peace to fight for the interests of America first. All but a half dozen of the chapters wanted to continue.

On December 11, the National Committee met and passed a resolution directing that the committee and all its affiliated subdivisions be dissolved.

Several days later, the chapters were ordered to liquidate their affairs as rapidly as possible (the Chicago, Pittsburgh, and St. Louis chapters and a few others had already taken independent action to dissolve), and to send their membership lists and records to Chicago, where they were to be impounded in the care of General Wood.

In behalf of the National Committee General Wood sent a letter of appreciation to all chapter chairmen.

Many of the chapter chairmen sent similar letters to their members, from which the following typical paragraphs are taken:

A battle has been lost in spite of your contributions of time, money and ability. The shooting war may be long but the war to preserve and develop our democracy will be longer. We must not suffer defeat in either struggle. The name "America First" remains, the organization does not. Our ideals remain, their realization does not.

The two principal aims of the AFC were: first, to avoid entanglement in foreign wars by opposing policies and methods of entanglement; and second, to promote the building of a strong national defense in armed forces, equipment, supplies, and organization, against any attack. The attack and the declarations of war that were made throw no shadow upon the correctness of the Committee's position, either before or since war was made upon us. Now that war has come, we are still for America First and that means now, before all things, victory for America.

Not one of us should have any apologies or regrets for the course of action we have taken. Our fundamental objectives as citizens of our country at war are the same as those of our Committee in peace—to adequately defend America, to achieve our independent destiny, and to preserve our democratic institutions. Toward the achievement of ultimate victory in the war and these fundamental objectives, each one of us will willingly continue to make the sacrifices required in the same spirit in which we have carried on the work of the Committee.

The National Committee signed a statement of gratitude to General Wood for his leadership:

In the summer of 1940 the America First Committee was organized, with one primary objective, to keep this country out of war in Europe and Asia. You were its leading spirit and throughout its existence acted as Chairman. Sustained by practical idealism, you were a patriotic and inspiring guide to all your co-workers in the interest of adequate defense and of peace.

When propagandists for intervention and war made bitter attacks on all who opposed them, your courage sustained us. When those attacks turned to slander and vilification, your integrity and character stood like a rock unshaken in the flood. As long as the way was open for democratic debate, your technical knowledge, ability and logic gave to millions of people a sound view of a correct national policy. Throughout the entire existence of the Committee you were a rallying point for all those who believe in defense of their country and in peace. Your patriotism was never questioned. When the forces of intervention brought about a situation which was bound to, and which did eventually, lead to war, you again volunteered your services to the United States army, as you had in 1917.

The courage and rightness of your course throughout will be acknowledged by all thoughtful Americans, and those who write the history of these times will record your statesmanlike leadership of a great national cause.

We, who served under that leadership in the battle against deliberate intervention and involvement in European and Asiatic wars, give you a final salute as we close all debate, and join with you in support of the war effort of our beloved country.

The day after Pearl Harbor, General Wood volunteered his services to General Marshall and was immediately placed on the staff of the Chicago Army Ordinance District as a full-time adviser. General Thomas S. Hammond, member of the National Committee, was appointed in a similar capacity. Colonel Hanford MacNider, of the infantry reserve, former National Committee member, immediately volunteered and later was sent to Australia to serve on General MacArthur's staff. Bobby Stuart, first lieutenant in the reserve, who had founded America First and had left Yale Law School to become its executive director, enlisted and in January went to serve at Fort Sill, Oklahoma. Colonel Lindbergh offered his services to the secretary of war and was accepted as a technical consultant.

General Wood's final letter to chapter chairmen, dated December 12, explained the sentiments of committee leaders at the critical hour of our country's plunge into the Second World War:

The National Committee of the America First Committee, at a meeting in Chicago yesterday, passed a resolution directing that the America First Committee and all its affiliated subdivisions be dissolved.

In view of the Japanese attack upon the United States and in view of our own Government's declaration of war against Japan, Germany and Italy, no alternative course is open to the Committee.

Since its formation in September 1940, the America First Committee has contended that the United States should build an impregnable national defense and avoid participation in foreign wars. We have held further that a policy of aid to other countries would weaken our own defense and tend to draw us into the conflict. We believe that our principles were right then and are right today. We believe that if the Government had followed the policy which we advocated, war could have been avoided and America and the world would have benefited. We make no apologies for the position which we have taken, and we firmly believe that history will prove that we were right.

However, whether or not the Government's policy in the past has been wise, we are today at war by constitutional declaration of Congress. The evening of December 7th the National Committee urged publicly that the declaration of war be made and pledged the full support of this Committee to its successful prosecution. We repeat that pledge now.

Thus, the principal purpose to which the America First Committee was dedicated and which bound together its members throughout the country no longer exists. As patriotic Americans, loyal to their Government, the members of the America First Committee now have no alternative but to disband, cease their activities and dedicate themselves to the job at hand—winning the war.

As Chairman of the National Committee of the America First Committee I deeply regret that this action has become necessary. It has been a privilege and an inspiration during the past fourteen months to participate in a program which has been distinguished by the unselfishness and patriotism of so many loyal Americans.

Together we have been privileged to conduct an American crusade, the only object of which was to promote the peace and happiness of the American people and to insure the carrying out of the popular will. It cannot be said that the members of the America First Committee have been moved by any consideration of personal gain. Your own sacrifice of time and effort, your own financial contributions, your own willingness to undergo criticism, is typical of the willingness of the America First members everywhere to take their stand in accordance with their conviction of right.

You can be sure that your work has not been in vain. You have acted in accordance with the rights and duties of American citizenship, and you have contributed in full measure to the furtherance of democracy in America. The only persons who have anything to regret are those who, having a conviction as to the best course for their country, have failed to speak out through cowardice or temporary selfish advantage.

We hope that as individuals you will exert your efforts in support of those members of the Senate and House of Representatives who have so bravely carried on this fight.

With all my heart I thank you for your unstinting patriotism and devotion to principle, which alone made possible the work of this Committee. Though we jointly cease our common activity today, we know our message will live on.

NOTE

1. The letter in full follows:

The National Committee will meet in Chicago, Thursday, December 11, to consider what course of action the Committee should take in view of the declaration of war against Japan. In order that the Committee may be fully informed of the attitude of its chapters and members, it is of the utmost importance that you communicate to us by telegram the recommendation of your chapter as to our policy for the future.

You have seen the statement issued by the National Committee the evening of December 7. Quite properly, this statement commits us to full support of the war effort against Japan. It makes no reference to our attitude in connection with the war in Europe.

Several courses of action are to be considered at this time. The principal alternatives are as follows:

Dissolution of Committee and cessation of all activity.

"Adjournment" of all activity. By this course we would cease activity but keep the organization intact until such time when it is deemed advisable to renew a loyal opposition in the interests of American democracy. Thus, issues may arise wherein the country will need a patriotic group to act as spokesman for a large proportion of the people. Possible issues are:

Conduct of the war. As in England, it may be necessary to carry on constructive criticism of the war, especially on such questions as an AEF [Allied Expeditionary Force], inefficiency, etc.

Preservation of two-party government. One of the great dangers to democracy would be destruction of the two-party system. There is a strong possibility that Mr. Roosevelt and Mr. Willkie may seek to remove all issues from the 1942 elections and to unite Republicans and Democrats on a platform of internationalism. In such event, it may be essential to renew our program of nonpartisan activity in the 1942 elections. Even in England the opposition party remains active during wartime and serves the important democratic function of preserving minority rights.

Peace terms. The America First Committee may be able to perform an important service in connection with war aims and peace terms. As the war progresses, there may well develop a serious issue of internationalism against Americanism; there may be a distinct trend toward imperialism. On both issues AFC can be the principal spokesman of the American people.

Union Now. There may well be a strong movement toward union with Great Britain. The Union Now organization will doubtless continue and become increasingly active. In the interest of the preservation of American independence it may be vitally necessary to continue activity in opposition to Union Now pressure.

Bill of Rights. In wartime, especially under the extreme conditions of modern war, the statement that "Eternal vigilance is the price of liberty" is doubly true. War especially threatens civil liberties as guaranteed by our Constitution and Bill of Rights. It is possible that the Committee can well continue as the chief guardian of these constitutional guarantees. December 15 is the 150th anniversary of the adoption of our historic Bill of Rights. This may be a fitting time for an announcement that the Committee will dedicate itself to the preservation of our traditional liberties.

N.B. It should be noted that on all these points the Committee will undertake no active program now. Instead it will "adjourn," holding itself in readiness to renew activity when the need arises as set forth above.

Continued opposition to the entry into the European war. While supporting the war effort against Japan, it is possible that we can continue our opposition to entering the European war. The facts and arguments against intervention in Europe remain the same as they were before the Japanese issue arose. If we enter the European war, it will still be necessary to defeat the Germans on the Continent, to send a huge AEF,* and to spend countless billions. All this involves the same threat to our democracy as it has from the outset. Our argument would be that we must not allow the Japanese situation to serve as a pretext upon which to circumvent the determination of the American people to stay out of Europe's war.

Support of national defense and the war effort against Japan. Special attention should be given to the needs of the American forces, making certain that they are properly equipped. Various possible courses of action come to mind, among them support of such organizations as the Red Cross, USO, or perhaps some new approach such as "Bundles for America."

These possible courses of action come to mind, at once; you may think of others. Some of them, or all of them, may be impractical. We are especially anxious to obtain your studied reaction as to the possible reception which would be given to the above suggestions in your area. Consider, especially, whether you can expect financial support and whether war sentiment will make the Committee ineffective. We do not want to undertake any of the above proposals if the possible reaction to the Committee will be so harsh as to endanger its effectiveness and good name.

* Allied Expeditionary Force.

The forthcoming decision is, of course, the most serious we have ever faced. The Committee is extremely anxious to give full consideration not only to your own views, but to the views of your chapter as represented by your Executive Committee. It is of the utmost importance, therefore, that you call a meeting of your Executive Committee or Advisory Board immediately and discuss fully the questions with which we are faced. We would like to have the different views of your Committee by telegraph so that they may be placed before the National Committee on Thursday. I hope we may have your cooperation on this important matter.

Meantime, please refrain from making any statements on activity relating to the Japanese situation or the future of the Committee. It is vital that in this critical period we all act together. Whatever decision the Committee reaches, I know we will have your full support and cooperation which has contributed so much to the success of the Committee.

Who Were the America Firsters?

Bill Kauffman

LIBBY AND RANKIN

In his memoir, *To End War: The Story of the National Council for Prevention of War* (1969), Frederick J. Libby recalls the populist vision that animated the NCPW's founding. He "had been deeply impressed that the grass roots of the nation—the farmers, the churches, the women, the laborers, the educators—are all natural foes of war."[1] The interest groups representing this quintet became "the 'big five'" of the NCPW. The council was founded on September 8, 1921, at the Shoreham Hotel on 15th Street in Washington, D.C. Among those present at the creation was Mrs. Robert M. (Belle Case) La Follette, "filled with determination to prevent America's involvement in another world war. America's recent participation in one of Europe's wars had been a costly experience. It must not be repeated."[2]

The NCPW, which historian Lawrence S. Wittner has called "[p]erhaps the most vigorous and effective of the groups in the peace movement's militant wing,"[3] acted as a pacifist clearinghouse for such decidedly nonradical groups as the National Education Association, Parent-Teacher Association, National League of Women Voters, Veterans of Foreign Wars, YMCA, Women's Christian Temperance Union, and more radical groups such as the American Union Against Militarism and the Fellowship of Reconciliation. Though Libby was a pacifist, most of his associates were not, and he eschewed sectarian infighting. "We must never forget that our great purpose is the prevention of a second World War," he emphasized. "We must not divide our forces between pacifists and non-pacifists."[4] He successfully defeated a move by Dorothy Detzer of the Women's International League for Peace and Freedom and John Nevin Sayre of the Fellowship of Reconciliation that would have had the NCPW formally adopt pacifism as its creed; as with General Wood and the America First Committee, Libby understood the necessity of broad coalitions in any antiwar movement.

For a decade and a half, the NCPW flourished. It raised $180,000 in 1926, its high point, and distributed 2 million pieces of literature in 1931, during the irenic, if cash-poor, presidency of the Quaker engineer Herbert Hoover. The

Quakers supplied the bulk of the NCPW's budget. The organization's single-biggest contributor was executive board member Mrs. J. Malcolm (Rose Dabney) Forbes of Milton, Massachusetts, whose donations totaled $105,000.

Frederick Libby gave Ruth Sarles her first major job in Washington. "As associate editor of *Peace Action*, and ably assisted by Carolyn Heine, Ruth Sarles made many constructive contributions to NCPW policies,"[5] Libby recalled years later. *Peace Action*, the NCPW monthly newsletter, reached a circulation of more than 20,000. Flush with the optimism characteristic of Middle American progressives, Libby placed female activists in critical roles; he had said in 1930 that women "constitute the backbone of the peace movement in America,"[6] which was true then and largely true in 1940–41: Ruth Sarles and Congresswoman Jeannette Rankin passed through both the NCPW and America First, and many other women—often derided for "primitive mother-love" by the utterly rational warhawks—made the same journey.

Libby's alliance with America First came naturally. His own inclinations were Quaker Republican and old-culture American, and, unlike his successors in the peace movement, he looked to Middle America rather than to the sons and daughters of privilege (and the marginalized groups they romanticized) for his peace constituency. "The grass roots are naturally against war," he understood. "[I]f all of the grass-roots organizations that are against war got together they would be irresistible."[7]

The fight against U.S. involvement in the Second World War was at once the NCPW's greatest moment and its downfall. Refusing to cut his pacifist principles to fit the prevailing winds of liberal belligerency, Libby was everywhere, speaking, lobbying, shaking the money tree, and shoring up morale. On May 4, 1938, he debated Earl Browder, general secretary of the Communist Party USA, on the question, "Should America Join in Concerted Action Against the Fascist States?" in front of 15,000 people at Madison Square Garden. (Browder's position changed with the signing of the Hitler-Stalin Pact, and then reversed on a ruble when Hitler reneged on the deal.)

Libby struggled manfully to keep his coalition together, though it suffered defections. "Our eleven Jewish organizations resigned one after another, reluctantly," he recalled. "Hitler's persecution of the Jews made these changes in our membership inevitable. Mrs. Louis D. Brandeis resigned from our executive board. We understood."[8] Note the last sentence, suggesting Libby's basic decency.

But he never renounced peace. "Were we indifferent to the sufferings of the victims of Nazi persecution? No, far from it. Our response was in positive action like that of the surgeon who keeps a clear head and a steady hand in the presence of tragedy. Our Council must not increase the scope of the disaster, nor the number of its victims. We were convinced that our greatest service to humanity required us to make every effort to keep the United States out of war."[9]

By spring 1939, NCPW staffers, Sarles among them, were going without pay. The defections were draining its treasury. Nevertheless, Libby kept at it, sending out 500,000 copies of speeches by Lindergh and Senators Walsh, Borah, La Follette, Nye, and McCarran in October 1939 alone. Sarles attended the 1940 GOP convention for the NCPW, distributing an antiwar newspaper she had written; at the 1940 Democratic convention, NCPW youth marched in prison clothing, ropes around necks, with placards reading, "I am twenty, [hawkish editor] William Allen White is 72."[10]

But war came, the young men went, and the complacent White settled into his utterly tame and much-laureled Emporia, Kansas, curmudgeonhood.

The NCPW did not disband after Pearl Harbor; instead, it committed itself to

1. Curb the growth of hate and intolerance.
2. Work for the earliest possible peace by negotiation.
3. Without obstructing the war effort, educate on the elements of a just and lasting peace.[11]

Noble goals, but thoroughly impractical in wartime. Though the council would unsoldier on, it never achieved even a fraction of its former influence, and after Libby resigned, no successor was ever named.

The NCPW's Washington lobbyist, Jeannette Rankin (1880–1973), was the once and future Montana congresswoman who by extraordinary coincidence cast votes against U.S. entry into both world wars, in 1917 and 1941, in her two widely spaced congressional terms.

The Missoula-born Rankin, the first woman to serve in Congress, had been a field secretary for the National American Woman Suffrage Association before her election to Congress in 1916 as a progressive Republican. Four days after taking her oath of office, she joined fifty-six stalwart American members of Congress in voting no to war. (The jingo press mendaciously reported that she cried upon casting her vote; this lie would annoy the tough and hardly lachrymose Montanan for the rest of her life.)

Rankin served as lobbyist for the National Council for Prevention of War from 1929 to 1939. As the war drums beat ever louder, she testified before Congress against Lend-Lease, against convoys, against the draft, against any and all of the administration's steps toward war. She was returned to the U.S. House of Representatives after winning the 1940 election with the help of Senator Burton K. Wheeler (D-Mont.). She spoke frequently from America First platforms, though like other members of Congress, she never officially joined the AFC. On December 8, 1941, she found herself even more alone than she had been twenty-four springs earlier. Throwing up her hands, she voted no, understanding full well that she was also throwing away her career. "I have nothing left now except my integrity,"[12] she declared. (Rankin toyed with the idea of running for the House in 1968, at the age of eighty eight, for she "wanted to go back to Congress to vote against a third war."[13] By that time, of course, the act of declaring war was a hopeless anachronism, and the dead in Vietnam were victims not of a war but of a bureaucratic "conflict.")

Rankin's voting pattern in presidential elections is a classic illustration of the coherence of the Peace Party—though to the guardians of orthodoxy, it seems helter-skelter. Rankin supported Douglas MacArthur in 1944; other isolationists (Hanford MacNider, Hamilton Fish, Philip La Follette) would do so in 1948, and there was a method to their madness, at least when one remembers MacArthur's prescient and tragically ignored proscriptions against U.S. military involvement in Southeast Asia. She mustered some enthusiasm for Eisenhower in 1956, crediting him with extricating the United States from Truman's Korean War (which Rankin, as an anti–cold warrior, dismissed as the latest in our "adventures in imperialism"[14]). She supported Goldwater in 1964, Eugene McCarthy in 1968, and McGovern in 1972, believing them to be substantially less warlike than their opponents. She confessed, however, that her favorite presidential candidate had been Socialist Norman Thomas—who was revered by many America Firsters, and who spoke from America First platforms during the great debate.

On January 15, 1968, 5,000 women calling themselves the Jeannette Rankin Brigade marched in Washington, D.C., against the Vietnam War. Their banners honored this America First orator; the peppery pacifist-isolationist Rankin had become a student favorite. Today, a celebration of Jeannette Rankin is almost unthinkable. After all—like four in five Americans before Pearl Harbor—she opposed the Good War fought by The Greatest Generation.

WARRIORS FOR PEACE

If Sarles, Libby, Rankin, and the Quakerish anti–foreign war legions are a usually untold part of the America First story, the men in uniform who honored the military but feared militarism are somewhat better known, if not appreciated.

The permanent "temporary chairman" of the America First Committee from September 21, 1940, until its dissolution was General Robert E. Wood, a West Pointer who was in the midst of a twenty-six-year career as chairman of the board of Sears, Roebuck. Wood was an excellent businessman; Sears, Roebuck grew from 27 retail stores and a $270 million volume when he took over to 700 retail stores with a $3 billion volume by his retirement in 1954. An admiring profile in *Harper's* placed Wood's profit-sharing plan for Sears, Roebuck on "the verge of radicalism"; it also expressed bafflement that this veteran of the Panama Canal construction and former quartermaster of the Army "distrusts the growing influence of the military."[15] (Sears, Roebuck director Lessing J. Rosenwald, Wood's mentor, joined the committee's national board in September 1940 but resigned soon thereafter; nonetheless professing continued sympathy for the antiwar cause.)

Wood sought constantly to cease acting as chairman and turn the job over to someone else, preferably Charles Lindbergh. For although "he has many enemies," said Wood of Lindbergh, "he is courageous and patriotic."[16] But Lindbergh, too much the lone wolf to take on the direction of a pack, did not want the post, and Wood remained chairman: unassailable (Lindbergh offered a far more tempting target for arrows), respected even by the most fervent interventionists.

After the war, Wood had no regrets. "They answered me then," he said in 1954, "by warning that if we let Hitler win, we would have to become an armed camp and spend as much as $50 billion on armaments. Well, what are we doing today?"[17] A supporter of Senator Joseph McCarthy, Wood told his *Harper's* profiler that he favored drastic cuts in military spending, with the savings applied to schools and roads. It was classic Midwestern progressivism—but by the 1950s, such a political profile was often seen as a mark of lunacy.

Wood and William Regnery—both, incidentally, early supporters of FDR and the New Deal—were based in Chicago, and so was the committee. Chicago would remain the financial and spiritual base of America First; for all of New York City's riches, even those men of business who were not eager to send other men's boys to die in Europe were reluctant to publicly identify themselves with the cause of peace. "I have been greatly annoyed by the shocking timidity of business leaders here,"[18] wrote old-style liberal John T. Flynn of the New York AFC chapter to Stuart.

The America Firsters found grim amusement in the sight of Midwestern isolationists fighting the war while their Eastern interventionist counterparts waxed bellicose from their editorial cubicles. For when war came, the young and not so young males of America First went. Many served with distinction, and rather enjoyed the sight of the 4-F warhawks wading through the malarial swamps of grad school or the newsroom while the boys of the peace movement were slinging grenades. In wartime, General Wood wrote Sarles that he enjoyed seeing photos of Hanford MacNider taking charge in the Southwest Pacific, adding, "I haven't seen anything about either of the Cowles brothers [interventionist publishers] of Des Moines and Minneapolis being at the front."[19]

A word on MacNider (1889–1968), the first national commander of the American Legion: He was the son of a Mason City, Iowa, banker, who, in worst bourgeois fashion, sent the boy to Milton Academy in Massachusetts and then to Harvard, where he played football, as did so many of the leading America Firsters. (Mason City was also the hometown of Meredith Willson of *Music Man* fame.)

If exile is the nursery of nationalism, as Lord Acton said, young Hanford was a star pupil, for his New England exile inspired in him a vision of "Iowa as the Promised Land."[20] After graduation he came home to Mason City and the bank. He enlisted in the Thirty-sixth U.S. Infantry in the First World War, serving with distinction. Upon his return he organized the American Legion of Iowa and was chosen national commander at the Kansas City convention for 1921–22. (Hamilton Fish was a coauthor of the Legion's preamble and constitution.)

We think of the American Legion today as a place to grab a beer with a friend who is a veteran, or as a hobbling and dwindling band of old men who sponsor Little League teams and Legion baseball clubs. (This is a MacNider legacy: his "Iowa idea" required each Legion post to "make some unselfish contribution to its community's welfare each year or lose its charter."[21]) But in the early 1920s the American Legion was a potent lobbyist for loot, in particular medical care for those maimed or mutilated during Mr. Wilson's War to End All Wars. Its commander was a national figure of some prominence, and Hanford MacNider, the martial banker from Mason City, served as assistant secretary of war and then acting secretary of war under President Coolidge. (There was a refreshing frankness about the old terminology: as Senator Eugene McCarthy has pointed out, the 1947 Defense Reorganization Act that retitled the Department of War the "Department of Defense" was a triumph of bureaucratic Orwellianism.)

MacNider's business interests soon included a cement company; his political stock went so high that in 1932 his name was placed in nomination to serve as President Hoover's running mate on a technically unconstitutional all-Iowa ticket. In 1940, he was nominated for president at the Republican national convention as a favorite son by the mercurial Verne Marshall, isolationist publisher of the Cedar Rapids *Gazette*. (Marshall, who headed the short-lived No Foreign War Committee, comes off badly in virtually every account by a contemporary. Lindbergh, usually generous in his personal assessments, expressed concern about "Marshall's nervous condition" after a meeting of December 12, 1940. Still, he recorded in his diary, "I like Marshall personally, but there is something about his attitude on life that disturbs me." Three days and several meetings later, Lindbergh concluded that he was "temperamental and irritable," and "quick to form impressions and has a violent temper." One month later, Lindbergh declared to the press that he would have nothing to do with the No Foreign War Committee: Marshall was simply intolerable.[22])

But back to a more equable Iowan. Hanford MacNider was a popular choice to head America First—"Most people concerned would prefer MacNider,"[23] wrote Lindbergh—but he declined, though he remained a director until just shy of closing time. On December 4, 1941, party man MacNider resigned from the AFC in protest against its stated intent to defeat pro-war candidates at the next congressional election. "[M]uch as a I sympathize with the good cause to which [the AFC] is dedicated . . . I am a Republican, a rabid Republican," he explained. "I believe that the only hope for the nation's future lies in the Republican Party."[24]

Three days later, the point was moot. Hanford MacNider volunteered for service, and after an initial refusal he was assigned to the Southwest Pacific, where his "Bushmasters" whacked their way through the Philippine Islands. He served with honor in the war he had labored so hard to prevent.

NOVELISTS ON BOARD

Among the best-kept secrets in American letters is the large number of American writers and poets who detested Franklin Roosevelt and/or opposed U.S. intervention in the Second World War. They range from Edmund Wilson to Sinclair Lewis to e.e. cummings to Robert Frost to Robinson Jeffers to William Saroyan. Lesser-known but more active than these men was novelist Janet Ayer Fairbank (1878–1951), who served as one of two vice chairmen of the America First Committee. (Hanford MacNider was the other.)

The sister of writer Margaret Ayer Barnes, Janet Ayer Fairbank had spent her adulthood working for liberal causes: she was a woman suffragist, the chairwoman of the Western Division of the Woman's Finance Committee of Theodore Roosevelt's Progressive Party, a member of the executive committee of the Democratic National Committee, and Democratic National Committeewoman from Illinois from 1924 to 1928. A Chicagoan by birth, education (University of Chicago), and social position, Fairbank was a liberal Democrat in an age when the adjective was not yet redundant. She smiled benignantly on various progressive causes, peace among them, and as the war clouds gathered she descried in their louring nimbi the end of her America. And so she acted.

The interventionist British front group Friends of Democracy compiled a "Confidential Report" on Fairbank, which read,

An outstanding social figure in Chicago. (Democrat). She has long been identified with social and political activities. She maintains one of the influential salons in Chicago. . . . Up to the threat of possible U.S. entry into the war, she took an active part in the liberally internationally-minded pro-British group around the Daily News. But with the threat of possible war, she reacted like a primitive mother—refusing to contemplate possible war danger for her sons.[25]

Note the sneering coda: mother-love is an atavism that must be extirpated in the Brave New World.

Looking back, the ever-courteous Robert D. Stuart, Jr. concedes that Fairbank was, shall we say, a tigress. She pestered young Stuart and his staff from the get-go. In a letter to General Wood of September 14, 1940, Fairbank complained, "I am somewhat distressed about the 'America First' Committee. It seems to me very unfortunate for so young a lad as Stuart to have complete authority to issue statements, to add people to the committee, and to shape policies."

Of course young Stuart did *not* have such authority, but Fairbank went on to suggest that she might serve on a committee that would make the AFC's public utterances. "I hope that you do not think I am trying to push myself into a position of importance," she expostulated. "It is merely that my profession is writing." Exhibiting a political shrewdness somewhat less than preternatural, Fairbank then proposed that Henry Ford be made president of America First, wondering only if this publisher of the anti-Semitic hoax *The Protocols of the Elders of Zion* is "too pacifist."²⁶ (General Wood assured her that "While young Stuart is doing practically all the work, none of the material has gone out without my approval."²⁷ An exasperated Stuart wrote Wood that "Mrs. Fairbank has caused a certain amount of ill-feeling amongst the people in this office because she is in the habit of calling up and ordering [us] to do something for her."²⁸)

Okay, so La Fairbank had termagant qualities. She was a hard worker who organized more than forty AF chapters in Illinois. She was also a fine novelist whose major work, *The Smiths*, is one of the best of a rich field of Chicago novels (her description of the Chicago fire is memorable), and whose major political novel, *The Lion's Den* (1930), is a worthy volume in the Progressive canon. These novels merit brief exegeses.

The Smiths (1925) concerns Peter Smith, "a real lover of his town,"²⁹ who returns to Chicago from being wounded at Antietam to become a driven steel titan. Peter and his like-minded friends are railroad and tariff Republicans whose "triumphant individualism"³⁰ contains the seeds of their own, and their nation's, destruction: they agree, for instance, that "the only good Indian was a dead Indian. . . . The West was theirs. Anything which interfered with their enjoyment of it must go."³¹ (Interestingly, all the main characters marry badly.)

Peter is an anachronism. He refuses to sell to National Steel, insisting that "I can run my plant a damn sight better than any group of men can run it as a part of a trust," to which his attorney replies, "[Y]ou are going against the tendency of the times, Pete. . . . The day of the individual is almost over."³² Its end, we learn, was hastened by such barons of industry as Peter, who once knew each of his men by name—as William H. Regnery did—and knew their families, too, but by the end of the Gilded Age Peter regarded them only as sullen, swarthy, babel-jabbering hordes ever ready to strike. Peter stubbornly refuses to throw in with J.P. Morgan. His weak sons counsel surrender, as do his directors. "He was thought old-fashioned, for he resented combinations, whether of labor or of capital. He felt that men who were unable to stand alone must be essentially soft-fibered, and he could not help showing it."³³ Only Peter's wife, Ann, urges him to hold out, but finally he bows to the inevitable, and Smith and Jefferson becomes part of the United States Steel Corporation.

All around him Peter sees weakness, flab, creeping iniquity. His ex-partner is expatriated in Paris, where he and his wife have become dissipated, listless, and wasted by unmooring themselves from their native soil. Peter and Ann stubbornly stay on the south side of Chicago, while their prosperous family deserts them for the newly fashionable north side. When Peter dies, Ann insists on a funeral cortege with horses and carriages rather than motor cars: a last futile protest against a new world of machines and exhaust. Yet hope is not extinguished: the only Smith descendant with spunk, a grandson, becomes a Bull Moose organizer, marries a Kansas suffragette, and sets out to reclaim an older America, when "democracy had not yet been ironed entirely flat."³⁴

Fairbank picks up this political thread in *The Lion's Den* (1930), which follows the fall and resurrection of Daniel Carson, a self-educated Wisconsin farmer who is elected to the U.S. House of Representatives as a Progressive-Republican only to find his fellow Progressives, excepting the monomaniacal radical Wolf Zimmer, to be go-along-to-get-along mediocrities.

Before you can say "La Follette," the rube Carson is ensorcelled by the feline wife of a corrupt senator who never can recall which state he hails from: Kansas, Iowa, one of those out there. Carson is seduced and laid waste, and the horny-handed son of toil becomes a horny stock-market gambler who loses it all in the Crash. The naive Badger has "forgot all about his moral sense."[35]

The firebrand Wolf Zimmer, dying in penury, passes the progresssive torch to a disheartened Daniel Carson. As Zimmer lies dying, Fairbank eulogizes him in terms that might have been applied to the America Firsters a decade later:

Here lay this old man dying. He was poor. He was called a crank. He had been a thousand times defeated. He had no money, and he had no power. And yet, he had something. Daniel leaned closer to see the pugnacious thrust of the jaw, the integrity in the line of the mouth. He looked for some time at the worn idealistic face on the pillow. . . . [H]is face as he lay dying showed no trace of the world, no weakness or defeat. Why, Daniel wondered. Was it because he had never allowed expediency to interfere with his sponsoring a cause, no matter how forlorn, which he believed to be right? Was it because in all the lost causes he had supported, he had never lost his own soul?

Money and power? Could a man who paid the necessary price for those two worldly weapons ever hope to wear that triumphant look upon his face when he lay dying?[36]

Rededicating himself to the People, the Cause, and the girl next door, Carson achieves renomination and a promise of love. A decade later, Janet Ayer Fairbank bruised feelings and earned anything but love from the America First staff, but her soul, at least, remained her own.

The most indefatigable of the literary people who campaigned for America First was Kathleen Norris (1880–1966), daughter of a prominent Bay Area banker father and devoutly Roman Catholic mother. Young Kathleen Thompson was, for all intents and purposes, home-schooled. Her parents "feared schooling for their children";[37] Kathleen and her five siblings had been "overschooled" and paid for it with blinding headaches and indigestion. So at age eight her family decamped from San Francisco to the "mountain forests below Tamalpais Mountain, where there was not a school for miles. Here, for exquisite years, we ran wild."[38]

This idyll lasted until Kathleen was nineteen, when her parents died within one month of each other, leaving an estate smaller than any banker's bequest this side of George Bailey's father. The spirited girl and her older brother took whatever work was available (in Kathleen's case, bookkeeping, caring for children and invalids, and librarian) and raised their younger siblings. In her mid-twenties, Kathleen hooked on with a series of San Francisco newspapers, and within this milieu she met Charles Norris, brother of novelist Frank Norris, and the man with whom she would have an "enduring and affectionate"[39] marriage of forty-five years.

Once Kathleen Norris started writing novels, she could not stop. She cranked out eighty-one novels for the "woman's market"; they received scant critical respect but sold more than 10 million copies. Think of her as an Irish Catholic Danielle Steel, without the hanky-panky. She became "America's favorite author"[40] and quite possibly its richest as well.

As Norris recalled in her autobiographical sketch *Noon* (1925), her father "read us the Declaration of Independence and the Gettysburg Address, and talked to us of the glories of our own nation."[41] Properly instructed, his daughter grew to be a patriot and reformer (and, to her husband's good-natured consternation, a prohibitionist). Alexander Woollcott, the man who came to dinner, called her "the ideal lady president of all the women's clubs in the world."[42] She was a cultural America Firster as well, and whether you find her stirring or saccharine, Norris's ingenuousness was genuine—and she understood that it could not survive the transmogrification of America from republic to empire:

Europe has given the world great stories, great music, Europe is filled with great pictures, thousands of sweet sleepy babies in their aureoled mothers' arms. But we have pictures in America finer than any that the Old Masters painted, or that de Balzac and Goethe made immortal in words.

We have the living scene: tree-shaded villages where every baby is started straight and strong, where his eyes and his schooling and his morals and his rights are important; we have women with serene eyes and hearts at peace; we have glimpses—from a passing motor car—of dinner tables set in grassy backyards, and little cars in open garages, and little libraries at crossroads.[43]

Kathleen Norris was yet another pacifist in the front ranks of America First. An America First national committeewoman, Norris was also a member of the Women's International League for Peace and Freedom and a crusader against capital punishment.

Norris became one of America First's most popular speakers. Her "motherliness," sneered the pro-war social democrat polemicists of New York City's *PM*, was manifested by her "exploitation of the emotion of grief for the dead."[44] Note how to the War Party, a mother's tears are mere "sentiment" that cannot get in the way once the tanks roll and bombs drop.

Kathleen Norris frequently shared a stage and a dinner table with Charles Lindbergh. Charles and his wife, Anne, spent several days in June 1941 visiting the Norris family at their ranch in the mountains near Saratoga, California. "Wonderful woman—real character," wrote Lindbergh in his diary. A passel of Norris nieces and nephews were present. "The family represented all shades of politican opinion," marveled Lindbergh, who noted that four members of the Communist Party USA were at supper. "How they all manage to get on together I don't know. As Anne says, it must be due to the character of Mrs. Norris."[45]

So you see, Kathleen Norris had experience in cementing transideological alliances, whether for purposes of dinner or keeping out of war.

The literary men of America First—Lewis, cummings, Frost, Vidal—tended to combine a crusty individualism with old-fashioned populist political inclinations. A classic specimen was Lincoln Colcord (1883–1947), storyteller of the Maine seacoast, a "man of outstanding vitality and gusto," as his friend Walter Muir Whitehill recalled, who "met life eagerly, equally alert for the savor of a situation, a bowl of chowder, a bottle of rum, an idea, an anecdote, or a stretch of landscape."[46]

Colcord was born at sea, off Cape Horn, in the ship commanded by his father. He grew up in Maine and on the oceans, navigating the China Sea with his parents, and it seems from his earliest political incarnation as a Progressive that his childhood peregrinations lent an oceanic capaciousness to his visions. A writer of short stories, Colcord became Washington correspondent of the *Philadelphia Public Ledger*, an associate editor with *The Nation*, and a close friend of Colonel Edward House, the Texas Progressive and American Rasputin who advised President Wilson. (House had written the anonymously published novel *Philip Dru: Administrator* (1912), in which a dictatorial administrator from West Point sets things right in the United States and conquers Mexico to boot.[47])

Despite an initial burst of enthusiasm for Mr. Wilson's war, Colcord soon bolted from Wilson's House. His subsequent rejection of the impulse to play world missionary is presaged in a June 23, 1916, letter to Colonel House. Colcord wrote of his hometown of Searsport, Maine, "It's not a bad place, much like many others, but the secret of our love for it lies in what I have just said—we know it intimately. This is the lesson I get from Thoreau. Love your own pond. All are beautiful. Be contented where you are. Content!—a lost word in our America. This restless ambition—I cannot feel the truth of it. I cannot follow there. I am quite willing to be out of touch with my times. I would live as if the times were out of touch with me."[48]

In his admiration of Thoreau he was in the company of his fellow America Firster Sinclair Lewis; his willingness to live "out of touch with my times" bespeaks the pull of ancestral voices: Colcord came from five generations of Maine seafarers, and historian Christopher Lasch notes that "his origins evoke a much earlier period of American history" than his birth in 1883. "His tastes and habits of mind mark him as a survivor, even in his own time, of an earlier New England tradition with which, in fact, he liked to identify himself."[49]

Colcord remained a Democrat and a friend to populist causes both political and literary. His greatest service to American letters was his co-translation of O.E. Rolvaag's *Giants in the Earth* (1927), which has as good a claim as any to being *the* American epic novel.

By 1929, Colcord had repatriated himself for good to the seacoast of Maine. From his home, which overlooked Penobscot Bay, he proselytized for maritime history and hurled anathemas at the New Deal. "The nearer the country moved to war, the more vociferously isolationist he became," recalled Whitehill. "Yet he would happily lend his friend Samuel Eliot Morison nineteenth-century blue-backed charts of the Pacific to take with him on his cruises as historian of United States naval operations."[50] To the good man, friendship always trumps ideology.

In Colcord's view, the America First Committee was too conciliatory. The United States ought to be "strictly neutral,"[51] he asserted; he criticized the pro-British tilt he detected in General Wood, for example, who proposed the sale of U.S. ships and the extension of long-term credits for food and materiel to Britain.

"[T]he war in Europe should have been no business of ours, since we did nothing to bring it about and since our self-interest was nowhere involved," Colcord wrote Wood on January 6, 1941. "I come of British stock, with ten generations in New England behind me," testified Colcord. "I personally should be heartsick to see totalitarianism triumph in Europe; every fibre of my being is democratic, everything I feel and know is opposed to autocracy in any form. But . . . I do not believe that it is the office of my nation to save the British Empire."[52]

Colcord saw the future, and it was grim. Perhaps there was no longer a place for Americans of his sort. Whitehill pronounced an epitaph that might be applied, with appropriate variation, to any number of the older America Firsters: "This all-engrossing concern for the independence of the individual led him to decry our contemporary processes of regimentation, and to exalt the past, particularly the seafaring past of New England, which, to his imagination, had fostered the hardihood of man."[53]

Let us take a closer look at yet another aged America First liberal: Samuel Hopkins Adams (1871–1959), chronic novelist, pioneering muckraker, curmudgeonly regionalist, and AFC National Committeeman. The sage of Owasco Lake's Stakhanovite output—more than fifty novels and numberless magazine articles—makes his sister Upstate New Yorker Joyce Carol Oates look as though she suffers from a protracted case of writer's block.

Samuel Hopkins Adams was born in Dunkirk, New York, in 1871 to a liberal Congregationalist minister and his evocatively named wife, Hester, descendant of the Declaration of Independence signer Stephen Hopkins. Grandfathers Adams and Hopkins fired the boy's imagination. The former, a Rochesterian, told tales of the Erie Canal, on which he once worked and in which Sam (nickname: Huck) and his cousins swam. Grandfather Adams had what today we would call a healthy measure of self-esteem: asked by a "visiting New England lady" if he claimed kinship with the Adamses of her section, he replied, "There is a Boston branch, I believe." To young Sam, he vouchsafed the opinion that "the Boston Adamses [were] rather an effete and unenterprising lot."[54]

Grandfather Hopkins, though lacking the cachet of the canaller, introduced Sam and the cousinage to his friend Harriet Tubman, who sang "Go Down Moses" to the children and attended a matinee of *Uncle Tom's Cabin* with Sam's grandmother. (Tubman liked it well enough but "was critical of Eliza's escape across the ice, declaring the affair ill-managed."[55])

As a young journalist, Adams raked muck for *McClure's* and *Collier's*, spattering the trusts and President Theodore Roosevelt (whom, as a good liberal Democrat, Adams disdained). In 1905, Adams made his mark on American journalism with a six-part series in *Collier's*, "The Great American Fraud," one of those titles that might apply to many subjects. Adams's exposure of the patent medicine industry, with its absurd claims for magical syrups and alcoholic elixirs, spurred the passage of the Pure Food and Drug Act. He was rather less successful, if no less prolific, as a novelist: his torrential output earned middling reviews, though under the pen name Warner Fabian he wrote *Flaming Youth* (1923) a *success de scandale*. Frank Capra turned Adams's short story "Night Bus" into the smash film *It Happened One Night*.

The duality that runs through Upstate New York political history (and through Adams's own family)—earnest reformism on the one hand, and demotic plainspokenness on the other—was embodied by Samuel Hopkins Adams. He supported prohibition—but once demon rum had been banished from freedom's land by constitutional amendment, he became a latitudinarian who told the *Cleveland Press* that his favorite hobby was "[w]atching my friends violate the Volstead Act."[56] A Wilsonian Democrat, Adams participated in the most ridiculous excesses of World War One propaganda, signing up as a Four Minute Man for George Creel's Committee on Public Information and slandering any pacifist, German-American, or Socialist who had the temerity to question Mr. Wilson's war—and then in 1941 he joined the America First Committee in an effort to "keep the war spirit out of America."[57]

Adams was a cantankerous New Dealer who served on the Cayuga County Re-Employment Committee of the National Recovery Administration. He supported FDR in 1940 and remained a fighting liberal until the end of his days. Never before or never after 1941 did he make common cause with people or organizations even remotely belonging to the Right.

So why did Samuel Hopkins Adams become an America Firster? Because he understood that his America, the America of Huck swimming in a canal and free-thinking Congregationalists going their own way and grown men crying at the strains of the Hamilton College anthem, was about to go under. "I had an awfully good time when I was a boy," he recalled in 1955. "We got a lot out of life: simple things. . . . We played croquet, shot at birds that we never hit, collected butterflies, indulged in whist or cribbage, sang the newest college songs, read aloud or went in a group to the church entertainment. In those days most of our entertainments were in the home."[58] This is the voice of a well-born son of the Old Republic, secure in his Americanism, looking back on a world vanished. As with the America Firsters of the Right, he knew that something was going. Hereafter, boys were conscripted when they ought to have been out chasing butterflies, or footballs, or coeds. Even his father's Plymouth Church in Rochester had been razed—to make way for a highway. This landmark of his youth was gone, "thanks to the juggernaut of a misguided progress."[59]

Adams would end his days writing regional novels set in the nineteenth century and compiling the stories of his forebears, particularly Grandfather Adams, into his most enduring book, the charming *Grandfather Stories* (1955). His country was now located in the past.

Irvin Shrewsbury Cobb (1876–1944) was the Paducah, Kentucky, born and bred humorist and novelist best known for his Old Judge Priest character, the wise rural judge given to translating scripture into Kentucky vulgate. Judge Priest was immortalized by Cobb's friend Will Rogers in John Ford's 1934 film *Judge Priest*. (Obscure as Cobb has become, he was, for a time, twinned with Rogers as the two funniest men in America. Rogers died five years before he almost certainly would have joined the left flank of the America First Committee; his attitude toward intervention in foreign wars was summed up by his remark "America has a great habit of always talking about protecting American Interests in some foreign Country. PROTECT 'EM HERE AT HOME! There is more American Interests right here than anywhere."[60])

Irvin S. Cobb was something of an America First anomaly: he was, first and foremost, a Southerner, and most confidently so—in Judge Priest's chambers hangs a "steel engraving of President Davis and his Cabinet";[61] an annual highlight of the judge's year is the festively bibulous gathering of the survivors of "Company B, of the Old Regiment of mounted infantry serving under General Nathan Bedford Forrest."[62]

Yet as Wayne S. Cole has written, "in no section of the nation did the America First Committee encounter such uninterrupted, vehement, and effective opposition as it met in the South."[63] How desperate was the AFC to find Southern sympathizers? Ruth Sarles reported to the committee's leadership on a November 1941 meeting she had with Representative James P. Richards (D-S.C.), who had "voted with the Administration on every measure in this session" before breaking with FDR over revisions to the Neutrality Law. Richards was friendly but absolutely refused to speak under AFC auspices. He told Sarles that "if it is necessary for us to send forces halfway around the world he will support it." Sarles ended her report on this unwilling Southern paladin of isolationism with the observation that Richards "is much relieved when he is free to find a crooked pole and some worms and go and sit on the bank of some creek."[64] So much for the Southern flank.

Cobb was a Southerner long exiled in perhaps the only piece of the country that was even less fertile for isolationists: New York City. But just as Sinclair Lewis never shed what he called his "Saukcentricities," Cobb remained Paducah at his core. "There never was but one Paducah; there never will be but one Paducah,"[65] he said as an old man, and he understood that Paducah would not thrive—and in fact might disappear as a distinct entity—in an America that scattered its young men to the corners of the globe.

Cobb was unable to apply much of his folksy charm in the cause of America First. "The plain people have always respected you tremendously,"[66] wrote Bob Stuart on August 4, 1941, but "doctor's orders" kept Cobb from a requested radio address and other speaking engagements for America First.[67] "I wish I might take an active part in this campaign to make America sane," he told Richard A. Moore of the AFC's National Speakers' Bureau. "It irks me that in this great emergency I can do so little of what I conceive to be my duty as a citizen of this imperiled Republic."[68]

Irvin S. Cobb would die in 1944, his ashes interred in Paducah.

WHAT WAS LEFT?

Like Samuel Hopkins Adams and Lincoln Colcord, another America First "liberal of the old school" who saw the coming war as an illiberal menace was John T. Flynn, raker of plutocratic muck and columnist for the *New Republic* until his antiwar heresies got him booted. Like such America First senators as Rush Holt (D-W.V.), Burton K. Wheeler (D-Mont.), Robert La Follette, Jr. (P-Wis.), and Gerald Nye (R-N.Dak.), Flynn indicted the New Deal not for its putative egalitarianism but because of its fascistic potential for "forming society into regiments, subjecting it to orders, drills, commanders."[69]

Flynn was chairman of the New York City chapter of America First—an "urbane and sophisticated"[70] group in the "interventionist capital city"[71]—and as a result of his labors, as he wrote General Wood, he "sacrificed all of my own personal income and even the connection out of which I made that income."[72] Hearken the echo, borne on the night-wind of the past; something about lives, fortunes, and sacred honor.

The men and women of America First laid down their reputations in a cause they believed to be just. Even an impeccable member of the establishment, once tainted by the antiwar brush, was marked for life. As Milton Mayer wrote of his boss, the one-time boy wonder president of the University of Chicago who took his stand against intervention, "Five years earlier Robert Maynard Hutchins had nowhere to go but up to the presidency or the chief justiceship; by 1941 he had nowhere to go."[73] The cost of principle is sometimes measured in broken careers.

John T. Flynn also served as a national chairman of the Keep America Out of War Congress, which was founded in March 1938 to organize the Left in opposition to U.S. engagement in the European war. The Socialist Party sponsored the KAOW's first rally; Norman Thomas was its leading light, Oswald Garrison Villard its first chairman. Frederick J. Libby led its governing committee. Chester Bowles provided light eleemosynary.

The overlap with the America First Committee is significant. Though the KAOW consisted of the Socialist Party and such peace groups as the National

Council for Prevention of War, the War Resisters League, the Fellowship of Reconciliation, the World Peace Commission of the Methodist Church, the Peace Section of the American Friends Service Committee, and the American Section of the Women's International League for Peace and Freedom, it co-sponsored rallies with the "right-wing" America First Committee. The AFC contributed up to $1,000 to the KAOW and sponsored radio broadcasts by perennial Socialist Party presidential candidate Norman Thomas and KAOW executive secretary and Socialist organizer Mary Hillyer. (The America First Committee later sponsored an extensive speaking tour by Norman Thomas, who preached the antiwar gospel at Cornell, Vassar, Madison Square Garden, and the universities of Illinois, Wisconsin, Kansas, Minnesota, Michigan, and elsewhere.)

The KAOW's student contingent added a welcome dash of irreverence to the antiwar cause. "Jobs, not graves,"[74] demanded the young Socialists, who gave away doughnuts to bemused passersby under the slogan "Doughnuts not Doughboys."[75] Again, note the minatory reflection of the First World War.

The KAOW, presaging America First, warned in 1938 that "a war against fascism abroad will bring fascist dictatorship at home."[76] Although the United States should open its shores to refugees from fascist persecution—a position championed as well by H.L. Mencken—Hitler's war against Stalin was not worth "one American penny, one American man, or one American hour."[77]

Oswald Garrison Villard (1872–1949) also provided a link between left and right; between the Keep America Out of War Congress and America First; between the classical liberalism of *The Nation* of the Gilded Age and the bellicose fellow travelers who had hijacked *The Nation* by 1940; between the anarchism of conscience of his grandfather William Lloyd Garrison and the rooted anarchism that one finds in many of the alleged "conservatives" of America First.

Villard, the "liberals' liberal," was a patrician pacifist who edited *The Nation* from 1918 to 1932, boosting its circulation from 7,200 to 35,409. He served thereafter as a columnist until he was forced from the magazine—whose fine reputation he more than anyone else had made—by the Stalinist Freda Kirchwey.

By reason of genetics and temperament, Villard considered himself heir to the abolitionists, "the finest and most successful group of Americans who ever lived."[78] He was a devout free-trader, a cofounder of the NAACP, a defender of civil liberties and the early New Deal who, like many of the best old liberals, was driven to the other camp in horror when FDR tried to pack the Supreme Court in 1937. By 1939, his break with what he viewed as a furtively belligerent administration was almost complete; he wrote in his August 5, 1939, column,

America must keep out of the whole revolting European mess and free ourselves from the delusion that we have got to back England and France in order to save democracy. . . . Not all my tremendous sympathy for the British people and the French estops my saying today, 'America first.' I do not speak in any selfish or holier-than-thou spirit: everyone who has followed my life's work knows that I have never been an isolationist except in the matter of war and peace.[79]

For choosing peace over war, Villard had his pay per column cut by Kirchwey from $50 to $30—shabby treatment for the editor who had made *The Nation* the essential magazine of the early twentieth-century American Left, but then Kirchwey was determined to sever the magazine's last link to an older liberalism of peace and civil liberties. Villard charged that Kirchwey, who by now had enlisted *The Nation* in what the old liberal regarded as the fascistic campaign for universal military service, had "prostituted"[80] the magazine. He quit, but not before a magnificent two-part valedictory published in *The Nation* of June 22 and June 29, 1941.

Villard predicted that like Hitler's Germany, Roosevelt's America would become "a nation in arms, in which every single phase of industrial and economic life is subordinated to the military machine." Say good-bye to "democracy, freedom of the press, the right to criticize the government, personal liberty," and other quaint vestiges of the Old Republic.

"I still believe in the defense afforded us by the Atlantic Ocean," ventured Villard, but "the masters of America no longer do."

"[M]y retirement," wrote Villard, "has been precipitated at this time by the editors' abandonment of *The Nation*'s steadfast opposition to all preparations for war, to universal military service, to a great navy, and to *all* war, for this in my judgment has been the chief glory of its great and honorable past."[81]

Villard had joined the national committee of America First on August 21, 1940, reserving, as he told R. Douglas Stuart, Jr., "the right to differ with the committee as to what constitutes an impregnable defense for America."[82] To Kirchwey's taunts that he was trafficking with reactionaries, he replied, "With me the supreme objective is to keep the United States out of war. You know it has always been my main purpose in life so far as I could bring it about. I am willing to be associated with any non-Communist group that is working sincerely for the same end."[83]

General Wood's emphasis on military defense discomfited Villard enough that he resigned soon after he joined, on the grounds that a potent army "carries within it the seeds of death for our democracy."[84] As he explained his pacifism, "There are many things above the State and superior to it, and one of these is Christianity. Where the teachings of Jesus and allegiance to the State conflict, you will invariably find me putting Jesus above the State. Reverence for the State? . . . Why *should* we reverence it? It is meant to be the servant of peoples, and it has become their master and beyond their control, slaughtering millions as well."[85]

Despite his resignation, he remained close to many America Firsters, and was one of the foremost defenders of Charles Lindbergh's Des Moines speech. Like Lindbergh, Villard had been denounced by Harold Ickes, hatchetman of the Roosevelt administration, as a "Nazi fellow traveler,"[86] a libel that was doubly unfair given Villard's reputation as something of a Semitophile. Villard had long been regarded as the great journalistic defender of American Jews; he had once castigated Adolph Ochs for shying from his coreligionists lest his *New York Times* be "criticized as a Jew paper."[87]

In October 1944, Villard suffered a heart attack in the office of his old friend Norman Thomas—two old antiwar lefties adrift in the age of total war, relics from an era in which the Left had regarded war as the health of the state. In 1946, Villard prophetically wrote his isolationist friend Robert L. O'Brien, "I will bet the few normal remaining teeth I have that when you and I have passed off the scene the country will be called upon by some cheap poor white like Harry Truman to save the world from bolshevism and preserve the Christian religion."[88]

Villard died in 1949, as the long dark night of the cold war was descending. He had become a man out of time.

At least Oswald Garrison Villard could take some satisfaction in a long and distinguished career. Moreover, his reputation afforded him a certain impregnability against the arrows of slander. The less well known were rather easier to defame.

Among the more unjustly calumnied America First politicians was ex-Senator Rush Holt, the West Virginia Democrat and "Boy Senator" whose image faded from that of fiery Populist to Nazi symp almost overnight.

In 1934, Rush Holt, son of a small-town doctor who had campaigned for Socialist Eugene V. Debs, became the youngest man ever elected to the U.S. Senate. He had to wait until June 1935, when he turned thirty, to take his seat. He was very much his father's boy, a defender of the United Mine Workers of America and a consistent opponent of U.S. involvement in foreign conflicts, whether in Europe, Asia, or Latin America. "Holt viewed war as destructive of constitutional liberties, unnecessarily sacrificial of human life and material goods, and in most cases immoral," writes historian William E. Coffey, a fellow West Virginian. "Isolation, rigid neutrality and antimilitarism remained his prescription for avoiding war."[89]

Holt's anti-imperialism acted upon his domestic politics; he came to view the New Deal as a form of American imperialism, in which Washington, D.C., played the imperium and West Virginia the subjugated outland. Thus he opposed the WPA as well as military spending, earning himself the opposition of the Roosevelt administration and a defeat in the 1940 senatorial primary.

Shortly after his defeat—he was a political has-been at age thirty five—the lame-duck Holt lit into the pending conscription bill with an incendiary fervor seldom experienced in the medium-cool world of the Senate. The military draft, he charged, was conceived in the plutocratic mire of the "Hahva'd Club" by men with "very decided, large, strong foreign investments," for instance in the wire industry. "[W]e need wire in war," Holt remarked mischievously. "It is very usual to see a boy, one of these conscripted boys, hanging over a barbed wire, with his stomach torn open by a bomb." He went on in this vein, and one could imagine the veins bulging in senatorial foreheads as he indicted the merchants of death, "the same individuals who were anxious to push America into the World War before 1917." He named names: Henry Stimson, Lewis Douglas, Grenville Clark, Jullius O. Adler—a serious breach of etiquette, for populist bluster is tolerated as long as the villains are never identified—and closed with the ringing declaration that "as long as Americanism is present in Congress, there will be opposition to this alien doctrine of conscription, and the conscription program, which did not come from America, but came from foreign shores, and was incubated in the banks and law firms of New York City on Wall Street."

Applause rocked the galleries; the lame-duck Boy Senator had told 'em.

That did it. It is one thing to ramble on about rights and liberties and such guff on the stump, but Holt had vituperated Wall Street; he had asked, in the tradition of Senator Gerald Nye and the First World War revisionists, if the Eastern financial interests had a stake in war. The Boy Senator had to be taken to the woodshed.

Senator Sherman Minton (D-Ind.)—the "smear artist of the New Deal," in Holt's tangy phrase—took aim at the West Virginian's Socialist father. "I get a little impatient at being lectured from a slacker family," Minton sneered in a precocious bit of Red-baiting. Holt ejaculated that "as soon as the Senator concludes I will answer his malicious lie!" and it took Majority Leader Alben Barkley (D-Ky.) to restore order. (Barkley, who would be Truman's vice president, intervened only when Holt attacked Minton; the Indiana senator's animadversions upon Holt's family he let pass.)

"Mr. President," Holt responded after Minton's Socialist-baiting, "I do not know what caused the Senator from Indiana to get in the spirit that he has gotten into. I notice he has been going back and forth out of that door." After implying that Minton was stewed, Holt called him a stooge, noting that "there never has been a time in recent history when the administration wanted some dirty, filthy, low job done, that they could not get the Senator from Indiana to do it."

An emotional Holt enumerated a lengthy list of ancestors who had fought in the French and Indian War, the Revolutionary War, the War of 1812, the Civil War, and the First World War. "My father was against the world war, and I am against this war, because I know that the same path which we took in 1916 and 1917 is being taken in 1939 and 1940."[90]

The next day, August 7, 1940, Senator Holt rose once more to elucidate the Holt family philosophy. The Holts, he explained,

do not teach that professional patriots should stay at home and reap millions out of war . . . my father protested against that. No; the Holts do not teach that free speech should be destroyed and that mob rule should be substituted. My father was attacked by such a group, most of whom apologized as time proved my father right. No; the Holts do not teach that men should be allowed to raid the Treasury under the name of patriotism. No; the Holts do not believe in boys being killed on the battlefield while favorites sit in swivel chairs in Washington, far removed from the scene of action. No; the Holts are not professional pay-roll patriots.[91]

"I don't like Hitlerized methods in America to conquer Hitler overseas,"[92] he said, trying to frame the debate over the draft as a conflict between the old individualistic America and the regimented new world run by the people in gray. And then he was gone, absent from a Senate of Mintons.

Ex-Senator Holt was among the America First Committee's most tireless speakers: accepting only expenses, no fees, he and his wife barnstormed the country in the summer and fall of 1941, covering 25,000 miles.

William E. Coffey, who wrote his dissertation on Holt, found that the much-maligned Boy Senator was in nowise a fascist sympathizer or even an anti-Semite. He had many Jewish friends and supporters, spoke before Jewish groups, and "eschewed racial or religious jokes and slurs in his personal language."[93] If he was guilty of anything it was an indiscriminate willingness to make common cause with any and all who opposed the war; he was friendly with Father Charles Coughlin and the anti-Semitic orator Gerald L.K. Smith. (In fairness, it should be pointed out that Smith did not descend into the lower gutters of Jew-baiting until a few years later. As an organizer for Huey Long, he had been almost respectable in the 1930s, writing for *The New Republic,* among others. H.L. Mencken adjudged Smith "the greatest rabblerouser seen on earth since Apostolic times. . . . Gerald never stoops to talk sense. He confines himself to pure hooey, and it is of the highest voltage."[94]) Holt also stood side by side with Socialists (including the ubiquitous Norman Thomas) and activists of the antiwar Left.

We have grown so used to ascribing sinister or corrupt motives to dissenters in our quondam land of liberty that we risk losing sight of the very simple reason that Senator Rush Holt threw himself into this war against war: in Coffey's conclusion, "it was chiefly abhorrence of war, anti-imperialism, and belief in individual liberty and constitutional government that motivated his foreign policy views."[95] And although America First was ideologically versicolored, that is not a bad description of many of the men and women mentioned in the editor's introduction and this appendix.

A more unorthodox figure of the Left who vocally supported America First was the architect Frank Lloyd Wright. Bob Stuart was dissuaded from asking Wright to join the National Committee by publicity director Sidney Hertzberg, who wrote, "On second thought Frank Lloyd Wright may not be a good man to have on the committee. He is a great architect but he has quite a reputation for immorality."[96]

Wright is not easily boxed and put on the ideological shelf. He was a Jeffersonian agrarian and follower of the social credit theories of C.H. Douglas; he called himself a "liberal individualist and moderate democratic nationalist."[97] The editor of his collected writings deems as "zany"[98] Wright's proposal in

1932 that every American have reserved for him or her one acre at birth. Zany? Impractical, perhaps, but evidence of Wright's healthy Middle American reverence for land ownership.

Wright's zaniness extended to his—perhaps prophetic—vision of a United States broken into three self-governing regions: New England, Texas and the South, and the "great intermediate body of the union"; or "Usonia, Usonia South, and New England."[99] Given another fifty years, philoprogenitive Mexican Americans and their immigrant kin may yet redeem at least a portion of Wright's prophesy.

In his self-published Taliesin Square Papers, Wright designed an agrarian and autarkist defense of isolationism. "The democratic people must know, at heart, that going to war is the natural basis of Empire," he wrote. "[N]ational defense and salvation lie ahead of these United States of America in ordered decentralization, in social reintegration with the ground, in a natural capitalist economy: in effective solidarity of the will and the purpose to grow independent and strong here at home."[100]

Three of his young apprentices at Taliesin were sent to prison as conscientious objectors, provoking Wright to tell the judge who sentenced one of them, "Were I born forty years later than 1869 I too should be a conscientious objector."[101]

All over his beloved country he saw the lights of liberty and independence going out: "Here in our national home, the U.S.A., the atmosphere is becoming so loaded with false implication and impurities, now so heated and close that any voice telling truth is like an open window letting in fresh air. Already the open window is regarded as a danger. . . . An Independent is named an Isolationist and patriotism is degraded to a level where no true Patriot would stand."[102]

"I love England but I hate Empire,"[103] protested the architect, and within a generation such diction was tantamount to thought-crime. "Empire" was virtually banished from the national lexicon until Senator J. William Fulbright's courageous disinterment of the term in the early 1960s; even today, one uses the "e"-word at the risk of being dismissed as a Red, an America-hater, an irrelevancy.

Typically, in 1994 a reviewer for *Publishers Weekly* huffed of Wright's collected works, "The architect's outspoken pacifism and isolationism, voiced in repetitious, often strident essays, led him to stubbornly misperceive Hitler's Germany as a distant economic threat rather than as a totalitarian power bent on world domination."[104] Although the evidence of Hitler's invasion plans for the United States have yet to surface, Wright's political views—which seem a natural extension of his belief in an architecture suited to local conditions—are seldom if ever given a hearing.

Wright, Norman Thomas, Rush Holt, Oswald Garrison Villard: the America First Left was, well, American. Its adherents generally came from older families, almost never first-generation immigrants, and like Edmund Wilson and Gore

Vidal (both America Firsters themselves) they evinced a "proprietary patriot-ism": that is, they acted as though the country were theirs, as though it really belonged to them, and thus dissent became an act of love, of fealty.

This is not to say that recent immigrants were altogether absent from the antiwar movement. (I except, of course, the few German-American Bundists and recent Italian immigrants whose loyalties lie on the other side of the ocean.) Nevertheless, the antiwar Left was nowhere near as polyglot as the more gen-eral Left, and for a shard or two of evidence we call the man Ruth Sarles was to marry during the war, Bertram Benedict.

Bertram Benedict's book *The Larger Socialism*, published by Macmillan in 1921, reveals its author to be somewhat less vatic than, say, Nostradamus. Read in the light of the disastrous seventy-five-year experiment in state socialism, claims of "capitalism's inefficiency in the kinds of commodities produced"[105] and paeans to the superiority of the planned economy are best left to molder in Benedict's long-forgotten tome. Capitalism may be indicted on many counts, but its inefficiency in comparison with the Soviet model is not among them.

Yet before relegating Ruth's husband's magnum opus to a footnote, we can shake two or three pertinencies from its clotted branches.

Benedict is most interesting in his discussion of the failure of the Socialist Party to displace the Republicans or Democrats. (Benedict performed his au-topsy near the peak of Socialist Party health: the noble Eugene V. Debs, cam-paigning from the prison cell to which the vindictive Wilson had assigned him, won 915,490 votes in the 1920 presidential campaign, or more than 3 percent of the total.)

"The membership of the Socialist Party of America has been recruited to an abnormally large extent from the foreign-born,"[106] observed Benedict, accu-rately. Its polylingual babble had a rebarbative effect on inland Americans; the farmers who had flocked to the Populists distrusted the Socialists as adherents of an alien ideology. Withal, the Socialists displayed a "rudely overbearing intolerance"[107] right out of Marx.

Benedict concluded that

the Socialist Party of America seems to labor under appalling ignorance as to the nature of most Americans. The reasons are obvious. The Party membership is recruited largely from the foreign-born. It has been almost entirely industrial, and it does not understand the problems and the concepts of the great mass of Americans, even in the cities, who are not industrial workers. It also is predominantly urban, and does not appreciate the nature of the life and the people in the agricultural districts and in the small towns.[108]

This is an acutely America Firstish diagnosis; among Benedict's prescriptions for the party is that it promote an advisory referendum on declarations of war—a cause that his future wife took up, with some success, in the councils of the America First Committee.

THE DEANS OF ISOLATION

There were noninterventionist college presidents, such as Henry Noble Mc-Cracken of Vassar, a neighbor and friend of Roosevelt's—the candidate had spoken from McCracken's front porch in the 1932 campaign—who braved the laird's displeasure by speaking three times under AFC auspices. But none blazed so brightly as Robert Maynard Hutchins, the Yale Law School graduate and professor who in 1929 was made president of the University of Chicago at the tender age of thirty. Hutchins "boils with vision, likes idiosyncrasy, and is absolutely fearless, honest, and independent,"[109] wrote the awestruck John Gunther.

Under Hutchins, the University of Chicago was something of an isolationist brain trust: William Benton, Chester Bowles's partner who had earned his millions and was looking for a way to serve, was Hutchins's vice president of public relations, and a fine young Jewish pacifist writer named Milton Mayer worked for the university's Radio Office.

Academic wunderkind Hutchins resisted the "begging" of America First leaders to join the committee. ("You could almost make us respectable," joked Chester Bowles.[110]) He never did join, nor did he speak under its auspices. "I am not an isolationist," insisted the liberal internationalist Hutchins. "I have not joined the America First Committee. I do not like its name. I should like to join a Committee for Humanity First."[111]

But by spring 1941, he wondered if his apolitical fastidiousness hadn't been a mistake. He wrote his friend Professor Philip Jessup of Columbia, "I now wonder if I was right in not joining America First. Although I do not like some of them, like Henry Ford, I know absolutely nothing against General Wood or Douglas Stuart, the director. On the contrary, I admire them both. . . . The reason why I am drifting toward America First is that it is the only group that is working with real effect on the problem."

Hutchins drifted closer and closer to America First, pulled in large part by its most magnetic body, Lindbergh. "I recently spent an evening with Lindbergh," he reported to Jessup. "I regard him as the most misrepresented and maligned individual I have ever known. Perhaps I'm blind, but I can't see anything wrong with him whatsoever."[112] (Hutchins would ever defend Lindbergh against the fallout from the Des Moines speech. In a February 17, 1976, interview, Hutchins said of Lindbergh's speech, "There were probably rich Jews in favor of intervention but it was not a timely remark.")[113]

Although Hutchins is the college president most closely identified with America First, in some ways Alan Valentine, president of the University of Rochester, is a more representative figure.

Though George Eastman, University of Rochester patron extraordinaire, had been as belligerent as the next Four-Minute Man in 1917, the school his riches built stood as an academic beacon of the peace movement. University President

Alan Valentine (like his medical school dean George Hoyt Whipple, about whom more anon) was an athletic intellectual who felt no need to prove his virility by whooping it up for war.

Valentine was a member of that once-flourishing tribe that is now rarer than the Mohicans: a Quaker conservative. An honorable-mention Walter Camp All-America lineman on that gridiron oxymoron known as the Swarthmore football team, Valentine won a gold medal in Paris as player-coach on the 1924 U.S. Olympic rugby team.

A Rhodes scholar and professor of English whose academic reputation rested on his biographies of British diplomats—hardly the profile of a cheap Anglo-phobic demagogue baiting John Bull—Valentine was made president of the University of Rochester in 1935.

He was a nominal Democrat, having voted for Smith in 1928, FDR in 1932, and Landon in 1936; in 1940 he took temporary leave of his position, if not his senses, to serve as executive director of Democrats for Willkie.

Valentine worked closely with the America First Committee but seems never to have formally joined the organization. He testified against Lend-Lease on February 5, 1941, telling the Senate Foreign Relations Committee that it was "ironical that anyone who advocates peace in Europe, or a hands-off-the-war policy, risks immediate name calling as disloyal, anti-British, or pro-Nazi"[114]— ironical because few if any of the Bundles for Britain crowd had as deep a knowledge or love of that land as Valentine. But you see, he loved his own country more. (As a senior at Swarthmore, Valentine ignored the bigoted pro-testations of his fraternity—Phi Kappa Psi—and selected a Jewish independent as a roommate. But we live in curious times, when the only honest defense against a charge of bigotry or racism—"Some of my best friends. . . ."—is ridiculed, and the effortless exhalations of empty slogans about brotherhood or multiculturalism are accepted as proof of a pure heart.)

Valentine's exceedingly strange autobiography, *Trial Balance: The Education of an American* (1956), makes no mention of his antiwar activities. With an eye toward Henry Adams, Valentine writes in the third person, rechristening himself "Angus"—and no one under forty can read this without thinking of Angus Young, knickered lead guitarist of hard-rock bad boys AC/DC. We get a good deal of "Angus" as chief of the Marshall Plan in the Netherlands, and "Angus" as a fairly minor economic adviser to President Truman, but somehow old Angus never gets around to voicing an opinion in the great debate of 1940–41. As AC/DC never sang, What's too painful to remember, we simply choose to forget. . . .

The medical schools of Hutchins's and Valentine's universities were repre-sented on the America First National Committee by University of Chicago physiologist Anton Julius Carlson and George Hoyt Whipple, the Nobel Prize–winning pathologist at the University of Rochester.

Whipple was an archetypal America Firster. A tenth-generation New En-glander, he grew up at the foothills of the White Mountains playing baseball, hunting squirrels and rabbits, and catching sunfish, bullheads, and shiners, in an idyllic boyhood not unlike Whittier's "barefoot boy, with cheek of tan . . . kissed by strawberries on the hill."[115]

Whipple's father and grandfather were doctors, and after an education at Phillips Academy, Yale, and Johns Hopkins School of Medicine (where he starred on undergraduate baseball and football teams), he earned the family honorific. In 1921, George Eastman lured him from his position as dean of the University of California Medical College to take over the new University of Rochester Medical School, which the extraordinarily philanthropic Eastman had heavily endowed.

It was yet another of Eastman's wise investments. Whipple, George Minot, and William P. Murphy shared the 1934 Nobel Prize in physiology and medicine for their roles in discovering a liver-based cure for pernicious anemia. The Nobel Laureate built one of the country's outstanding medical schools, though not without controversy: he held fast to an old-fashioned parti pris in favor of American medical students. As his biographer noted, "Applicants from foreign countries, Whipple thought, were in general unacceptable, however well prepared, because this was an American enterprise, planned to train physicians for work in our country, not abroad under very different conditions; every foreigner admitted would keep out an American."[116] Today, Whipple's simple loyalty to his countrymen would earn him at the very least a visit from the Thought Police; more likely, he would spend his fifteen minutes on the national cross.

Whipple's politics were made of Yankee adamant. He had "a wisdom born in New Hampshire's hills/And a high disdain for useless frills,"[117] as a colleague apostrophized him at a 1955 retirement party; he despised Franklin D. Roosevelt and the New Deal. (When, at a medical school lunch, a colleague observed that FDR was his own worst enemy, Whipple grunted, "Not while I'm alive."[118])

His "idealistic, self-reliant, home-centered individualism"[119] under assault, Whipple broke with his practice of not associating with political groups by joining the America First National Committee. Though he was not overly active in committee doings, his presence made Rochester—home of Whipple, Valentine, novelist and America First supporter Henry W. Clune, and ancestral home of Samuel Hopkins Adams—an America First redoubt. But as is the case in New York State politics, Rochester was no match for Manhattan.

RURAL AMERICA FIRST

America First was so closely tied to Chicago and the domestic manufacturers of the Midwest that we often ignore its agrarian base. The agrarian and economic nationalist strains of America First come together in the person of George N. Peek, a stubbornly confident eighth-generation American whose

New England grandfather went west, to Illinois, following his brother-in-law
. . . John Deere.

George N. Peek's career path was thus furrowed before his birth: he became
vice president of John Deere and president of Moline Plow Company. "You
can't sell a plow to a busted customer,"[120] he said, by way of explaining why a
farm implements executive soon took up the cause of farmers. Peek became
the nation's foremost advocate of farm parity, which he viewed as essential to
his vision of a self-sufficiently rural nation. Like most other Republicans of his
era, he was a committed high-tariff man who loathed free trade.

Whereas Oswald Garrison Villard considered the free trade of goods as a
condition of peace—"If goods can't cross borders, troops will," as the old libertarian adage goes—George N. Peek, like Rush Holt, viewed the tariff wall as
a protective rampart. Something of the same split is present among the early
twenty-first-century America Firsters, who meet on the common ground of
opposing "managed trade" deals, à la NAFTA and GATT, in which statutory
power is vested in unelected supranational bodies, but who cleave over the
matter of unilateral tariff reductions and the eliminaton of import quotas.

The cities, Peek believed, were fetid spawning grounds of un-American socialism. "Red doctrine thrives in industrialism," he declared. "It fails in a community of land owners."[121] Despite his business pedigree, "Peek was an agrarian
at heart," writes his biographer, Gilbert C. Fite. "Like Jefferson, his ideal America was one where independent and self-reliant farmers were a dominant
group."[122]

Peek left the GOP when it would not endorse his pet scheme of farm parity.
He became administrator of the Agricultural Adjustment Act, but he bolted
the Roosevelt administration in 1935 when he became convinced that its tinge
was urban, industrial, and socialist, rather than rural, agrarian, and Jeffersonian. In a memo titled "America's Choice," Peek contrasted "A Policy for Internationalists" with "A Policy for America": one of its eight points pitted
"[a]utomatic intervention in European or Asiatic political disputes" versus "In
case of wars in Europe or Asia, strict neutrality and avoidance of 'moral' judge-
ments on belligerents." Roosevelt called the memo "silly," and the proud Peek
resigned to write economic nationalist manifestoes and needle the administration.[123]

This son of a Quaker mother contributed several hundred dollars to the
America First Committee, made speeches on its behalf, and served as honorary
chairman of the Moline, Illinois, chapter. He died December 17, 1943, during
a war whose primary issue, he would insist until the end, was "Americanism
versus Internationalism."[124] If that rings xenophobic, well, perhaps it is, although the impeccably progressive Jeannette Rankin, like other America Firsters, understood that by renouncing whatever remained of the Monroe Doctrine's pledge to forswear involvement in European affairs, the United States
would emerge from the war with "responsibility for the rest of the world."[125]
We would be ensnared in perpetual war for perpetual peace: in Europe, yes,

and who knows where else? Korea, the Dominican Republic, Vietnam, Grenada, Iraq, Serbia . . . no land would be too remote for the armed legions of the American Century. If those who preferred not to cover the globe with American troops were "xenophobes," then perhaps there was something to be said for that pejorative word.

NOTES

1. Frederick J. Libby, *To End War: The Story of the National Council for Prevention of War* (Nyack, NY: Fellowship Publications, 1969), p. xiii.

2. Ibid., p. 1. To an enormous extent, the American experience in the abattoir of the First World War shaped the isolationist view in the late 1930s. The connection was often made explicit, as with this 1919 poem (by W.A. Flynn) reprinted in the Pittsburgh *America First Herald:*

My Old Pal Steve

My old pal Steve is back again
From out the land of missing men
He said, "No more in France I'll roam,
I'm glad I'm home, back home, back home."

"I'm glad to see the old home folk,
The village smith, the old town soak,
And even my worst enemy,
His mug looks good to me—to me."

"And my old dog, a mongrel cur
With stubby tail and shaggy fur,
He wags his tail with unfeigned joy.
A welcome home, old boy—old boy."

"War is all right for writer-men,
They conquer worlds with ink and pen.
But cannon's roar and shrieking shell
Makes soldiers' life a hell—a hell."

Take *that*, Archibald MacLeish. (Or MacArchibald MacLapdog MacLeish, as e.e. cummings dubbed the rhymester of the New Deal.) "My Old Pal Steve," W.A. Flynn, *America First Herald* (Pittsburgh), December 5, 1941, p. 2.

3. Lawrence S. Wittner, *Rebels Against War: The American Peace Movement, 1933–1983*, rev. ed. (Philadelphia: Temple University Press, 1984), pp. 9–10.

4. Libby, *To End War*, p. 67.

5. Ibid., p. 116.

6. Wittner, *Rebels Against War*, p. 5.

7. Libby, *To End War*, p. 2.

8. Ibid., p. 147.

9. Ibid., pp. 147–8.

10. Ibid., p. 159.

11. Ibid., p. 171.

12. Joan Hoff Wilson, "'Peace is a woman's job . . .' Jeannette Rankin and American Foreign Policy: Her Lifework as a Pacifist," *Montana: The Magazine of Western History* (spring 1980), p. 47.

13. Ibid., p. 50.

14. Wilson, "The Origins of Her Pacifism," p. 33.

15. Irving Pflaum, "The Baffling Career of Robert E. Wood," *Harper's* (April 1954), p. 68.

16. R.E. Wood, "To the Members of the America First Executive Committee," April 9, 1941, America First Collection, Box 291, Hoover Institution.

17. Pflaum, "The Baffling Career of Robert E. Wood," pp. 72–3.

18. Stenehjem, *An American First*, p. 44.

19. R.E. Wood to Ruth Sarles, November 27, 1942, Mobilization Folder, Box 1, Hoover Presidential Library.

20. Dorothy H. Rankin, "Hanford MacNider," *Annals of Iowa*, 33, no. 4 (April 1956), p. 235.

21. Ibid., p. 249.

22. Lindbergh, *The Wartime Journals of Charles A. Lindbergh*, pp. 426–40.

23. Ibid., p. 426.

24. Hanford MacNider to Robert E. Wood, December 4, 1941, *In Danger Undaunted*, p. 444.

25. FOD Confidential Report, undated, Wayne S. Cole research notes, Janet Ayer Fairbank Folder, Box 1, Hoover Presidential Library.

26. Janet Ayer Fairbank to R.E. Wood, September 14, 1940, Wayne S. Cole research notes, Janet Ayer Fairbank Folder, Box 1, Hoover Presidential Library.

27. R.E. Wood to Janet Ayer Fairbank, September 18, 1940, Wayne S. Cole research notes, Janet Ayer Fairbank Folder, Box 1, Hoover Presidential Library.

28. R. Douglas Stuart, Jr., to R.E. Wood, December 26, 1940, Wayne S. Cole research notes, Janet Ayer Fairbank Folder, Box 1, Hoover Presidential Library.

29. Janet Ayer Fairbank, *The Smiths* (Indianapolis: Bobbs-Merrill, 1925), p. 2.

30. Ibid., p. 171.

31. Ibid., p. 133.

32. Ibid., p. 381.

33. Ibid., p. 384.

34. Ibid., p. 413.

35. Janet Ayer Fairbank, *The Lion's Den* (Indianapolis: Bobbs-Merrill, 1930), p. 134.

36. Ibid., p. 353.

37. Kathleen Norris, *Noon: An Autobiographical Sketch* (Garden City, NY: Doubleday, Page & Co., 1925), p. 6.

38. Ibid.

39. Elinor Richey, "Kathleen Thompson Norris," *Notable American Women: The Middle Period* (Cambridge: Belknap Press, 1980), p. 510.

40. Alexander Woollcott, "A Portrait of Kathleen Norris," *The Portable Woollcott*, (New York: Viking, 1946), p. 149.

41. Norris, *Noon*, pp. 13–14.

42. Woollcott, "A Portrait of Kathleen Norris," p. 148.

43. Norris, *Noon*, p. 85.

44. Wayne S. Cole, *America First: The Battle Against Intervention, 1940–1941* (Madison: University of Wisconsin Press, 1953), p. 108.

45. Lindbergh, *The Wartime Journals of Charles A. Lindbergh,* pp. 511–2.

46. Walter Muir Whitehill, "Lincoln Ross Colcord," *Dictionary of American Biography,* Supplement Four: 1946–1950 (New York: Scribner's, 1974), p. 172.

47. Edward M. House, *Philip Dru, Administrator* (New York: B.W. Huebsch, 1912).

48. Quoted in Christopher Lasch, "Lincoln Colcord and Colonel House: *Dreams of Terror and Utopia,*" in *The New Radicalism in America, 1889–1963* (New York: Knopf, 1965), p. 226.

49. Ibid., pp. 225, 228.

50. Whitehill, "Lincoln Ross Colcord," p. 172.

51. Lincoln Colcord to Robert E. Wood, January 6, 1941, in Doenecke, *In Danger Undaunted,* p. 221.

52. Ibid.

53. Whitehill, "Lincoln Ross Colcord," p. 173.

54. Samuel Hopkins Adams, *Grandfather Stories* (New York: Random House, 1955), p. 22.

55. Ibid., p. 275.

56. Samuel V. Kennedy III, *Samuel Hopkins Adams and the Business of Writing* (Syracuse: Syracuse University Press, 1999), p. 129.

57. Ibid., p. 190.

58. Ibid., p. 10.

59. Ibid., p. 298.

60. Will Rogers, *The Autobiography of Will Rogers,* ed. Donald Day (Boston: Houghton Mifflin, 1949), p. 116.

61. Irvin S. Cobb, *Old Judge Priest* (New York: George H. Doran, 1916), p. 12.

62. Ibid., p. 83.

63. Wayne S. Cole, "America First and the South, 1940–1941," *Journal of Southern History* (February 1956), p. 43.

64. Ruth Sarles Memo, November 25, 1941, Mobilization Folder, Box 1, Hoover Presidential Library.

65. Wayne Chatterton, *Irvin S. Cobb* (Boston: Twayne, 1986), p. 2.

66. R. Douglas Stuart, Jr., to Irvin S. Cobb, August 4, 1941, America First Collection, Box 44, Hoover Institution.

67. Irvin S. Cobb to General Wood, August 26, 1941, America First Collection, Box 44, Hoover Institution. "[M]any have come to believe the 'America First' position is expressed only by Senator Wheeler and Colonel Lindbergh," Stuart wrote Cobb. "This is certainly not true and I think we strengthen our case with spokesmen from various walks of life." R. Douglas Stuart, Jr. to Irvin S. Cobb, August 4, 1941, America First Collection, Box 44, Hoover Institution.

68. Irvin S. Cobb to Richard Moore, July 16, 1941, America First Collection, Box 44, Hoover Institution.

69. John T. Flynn, "Whose Child Is the NRA?" *Harper's* (September 1934), reprinted in *Forgotten Lessons: Selected Essays of John T. Flynn,* ed. Gregory P. Pavlik (Irvington-on-Hudson, NY: Foundation for Economic Education, 1996), p. 10.

70. Stenehjem, *An American First,* p. 9.

71. Ibid., p. 39.

72. John F. McManus, "Principles First," *New American* (January 31, 2000), www.thenewamerican.com.

73. Mayer, *Robert Maynard Hutchins,* p. 223.

74. Libby, *To End War*, p. 148.

75. Justus D. Doenecke, "Non-interventionism of the Left: The Keep America Out of War Congress, 1938–41," *Journal of Contemporary History* 12 (April 1977), p. 230.

76. Ibid., p. 226.

77. Ibid., p. 229.

78. Michael Wreszin, *Oswald Garrison Villard: Pacifist at War* (Bloomington: Indiana University Press, 1965), p. 270.

79. Ibid., p. 259.

80. Ibid., p. 262.

81. Villard, "Valedictory," p. 782.

82. Wreszin, *Oswald Garrison Villard*, p. 266.

83. Ibid.

84. Doenecke, *In Danger Undaunted*, p. 14.

85. D. Joy Humes, *Oswald Garrison Villard: Liberal of the 1920's* (Syracuse: Syracuse University Press, 1960), p. 196.

86. "Ickes Offers a List of Nazi 'Tools' Here," *New York Times*, April 14, 1941.

87. Humes, *Oswald Garrison Villard*, p. 96.

88. Wreszin, *Oswald Garrison Villard*, p. 271.

89. William E. Coffey, "Isolationism and Pacifism: Senator Rush D. Holt and American Foreign Policy," *West Virginia History* 51 (1992), p. 5. Rush Holt's son and namesake was elected to Congress from New Jersey in 1998. A liberal Democrat, he became the only plasma physicist in the House. He disgraced his father in 1999 with his vote in favor of U.S. military action against Serbia.

90. *Congressional Record*, 76th Cong., 3rd Sess., Vol. 86, Part 9, August 6, 1940, pp. 9921–5.

91. Ibid., August 7, 1940, p. 9979.

92. Coffey, "Isolationism and Pacifism," p. 7.

93. Ibid., p. 9.

94. *The New Mencken Letters*, ed. Carl Bode (New York: Dial, 1977), p. 393. For more on the strange arc of Gerald L.K. Smith's career, see Leo P. Ribuffo, *The Old Christian Right: The Protestant Far Right from the Great Depression to the Cold War* (Philadelphia: Temple University Press, 1983), pp. 128–77.

95. Coffey, "Isolationism and Pacifism," p. 11.

96. Doenecke, *In Danger Undaunted*, p. 14.

97. Frank Lloyd Wright, "Of What Use Is a Great Navy With No Place to Hide?" *Frank Lloyd Wright: Collected Writings*, vol. 4 (1939–1949), ed. Bruce Brooks Pfeiffer (New York: Rizzoli, 1994), p. 74.

98. Ibid., p. 8.

99. Ibid., p. 91.

100. Ibid., p. 77.

101. Wright, "An Open Letter to Patrick Stone Et Al.," in Pfeiffer, p. 105.

102. Wright, "Usonia, Usonia South, and New England," in Pfeiffer, p. 89.

103. Wright, "Of What Use Is a Great Navy With No Place to Hide?" p. 77.

104. "Forecasts," *Publishers Weekly* (November 28, 1994), p. 49.

105. Bertram Benedict, *The Larger Socialism* (New York: Macmillan, 1921), p. 15.

106. Ibid., p. 96.

107. Ibid., p. 102.

108. Ibid., pp. 188–9.

109. Quoted in Joseph L. Jaffe, Jr., "Isolationism and Neutrality in Academe, 1938–1941," (Ph.D. diss., Case Western Reserve University, 1979), p. 24.

110. Quoted in Mayer, *Robert Maynard Hutchins*, p. 221.

111. Doenecke, *In Danger Undaunted*, p. 54; Mayer, *Robert Maynard Hutchins*, p. 218.

112. Mayer, *Robert Maynard Hutchins*, p. 220.

113. Ibid., p. 72.

114. Ibid., p. 175.

115. John Greenleaf Whittier, *The Complete Poetical Works of Whittier* (Boston: Houghton Mifflin, 1894), p. 396.

116. George W. Corner, *George Hoyt Whipple and His Friends: The Life-Story of the Nobel Prize Pathologist* (Philadelphia: J.B. Lippincott Co., 1963), p. 162. Rochester's preeminent writer of the age, novelist and newspaper columnist Henry W. Clune, was also an America First sympathizer. Clune's magnum opus, *By His Own Hand* (1952), features a fictionalized George Eastman making isolationist arguments against U.S. entry into the First World War. The real Eastman had been hawkish on Mr. Wilson's war, disparaging the pacific efforts of industrialist Henry Ford: "[H]e makes me both sick and tired," complained Eastman when Ford's "Peace Ship" set sail. Elizabeth Brayer, *George Eastman: A Biography* (Baltimore: Johns Hopkins University Press, 1996), p. 409.

117. Ibid., p. 155.

118. Ibid., p. 219.

119. Ibid., p. 217.

120. Gilbert C. Fite, *George N. Peek and the Fight for Farm Parity* (Norman, OK: University of Oklahoma Press, 1954), p. 38.

121. Ibid., p. 43.

122. Ibid.

123. Ibid., pp. 282–4.

124. Ibid., p. 297.

125. Wilson, "Peace is a woman's job . . . " p. 33.

Appendix B

An Interview with
Robert Douglas Stuart, Jr.

In February 2000, I spoke with Robert Douglas Stuart, Jr., who had been national director of the America First Committee. We met in the offices of Conway Farms, a real-estate development company in Stuart's hometown of Lake Forest, Illinois. The precocious Yale Law student described in Ruth Sarles's book went on to a distinguished career in business and diplomacy. After his wartime service, Stuart graduated Yale Law but opted for the family concern: beginning as a West Coast salesman, he eventually became president, CEO, and chairman of the board of Quaker Oats. Stuart kept a hand in Republican Party politics: the capstone of his political career was his service as U.S. ambassador to Norway from 1984 to 1989. In recent years, Stuart's chief political interests have been campaign finance reform, specifically the elimination of "soft money" from campaigns, and finding ways to combat the coarsening of American popular entertainment, especially television. Mr. Stuart was eighty-three at the time of the interview.

Kauffman: It seems remarkable that a small group of Yale Law students launched what became the largest antiwar organization in American history. How did you come to be involved in the battle against U.S. involvement in the Second World War?

Stuart: Most of us of our generation who were in any way thoughtful about history and international affairs learned that the U.S. didn't accomplish very much in committing troops to the First World War, which was a terrible slaughter of the talent of the Western world—an internecine conflagration. The best genes on both sides of the lines were heroically exhausted in combat.

The bottom line was that it had not been a rewarding experience for the United States. Therefore, we'd be smart if we stayed the hell out of the conflagration that seemed to be emerging by the time we were all talking up at law school.

The law school is not a very large place. A group of us that knew each other talked, in addition to legal subjects, about the political scene. The extraordinary thing is that so many of those people became major figures. Potter Stewart was a good friend of mine. S-t-e-w versus S-t-u: we sat next to each other. Sargent Shriver was a very close friend. We weren't partisan.

Now there is concern versus doing something about it. We would have these huddles, and we put together a letter: we thought we could reach others feeling just the way we did. So with my late wife and wonderful companion, we'd type up these letters and circulate them to other universities and other undergraduate groups.

Our objective was to get some action from the people, and we got a lot of responses to these letters. But it became pretty clear to all of us that we needed some heavies to make an impact. Kingman Brewster, who later became president of Yale, and I decided to go to the Republican National Convention in Philadelphia to see if we could get this point of view across. We were not ever pacifists nor were we anti-Semitic, but we just felt we could make ourselves strong and focus U.S. efforts on the Western Hemisphere. So Kingman Brewster and I went down to the Philadelphia convention.

Kauffman: This is the convention at which Wendell Willkie, the barefoot boy from Wall Street, snatched the nomination away from various antiwar Republicans. Any particularly vivid memories of that convention?

Stuart: We testified before these committees, but Senator Taft and others said the person to see was General Robert E. Wood. I had known General Wood. One of the things we'd done as young people at the law school, we got a poll done as to how people in the student body felt about the European war. It was done in response to President Seymour of Yale, who had recommended that America has the responsibility to prepare to save Britain.

And so this poll was in a sense responsive to that, and the student opinion was against getting involved in the war.

I had previous to this gotten a one-line note, saying, "Dear Bobby: Your friends at the law school show a great deal more sense than the president of your university. Signed, Robert E. Wood." (Laughter)

When I got a response from Senator Taft and others down there, we began to realize that we needed bigger oars to be very effective. But going back to Willkie: it all reminds me of what a huge influence Henry Luce had. Luce was convinced Willkie was the right man.

And Luce had a huge impact exposing Willkie to the brokerage community, the investment and banking community, who packed the galleries. In those days, the primaries weren't very significant as opposed to the actual convention.

And it was just frustrating to hear—I can still hear all these brokers from Philadelphia and New York who packed the galleries: "We want Willkie! We want Willkie!"

Kauffman: Voice of the people, huh?

Stuart: Voice of the people, boy. "We want Willkie" won. We didn't have as good a chant for the Taft forces.

Kauffman: Nothing alliterative with Taft?

Stuart: So that was our first effort, and then we decided, well, equal time, we're going to have to talk to Democrats, too.

So we're coming out to the Chicago convention of Democrats, who are rallying to nominate FDR again. I went to the convention and testified again. Senator Wheeler was there, and . . .

Kauffman: He was your strongest ally within the Democratic Party.

Stuart: . . . and Champ Clark. That's right. And they both got us together with some senior people. So from that experience at the two conventions, people began to mention General Wood as the ideal leader for this organization. He was a huge success for this cause.

He'd been for Roosevelt, initially. He was a businessman, highly respected, very decisive, perfect guy.

Kauffman: You were mostly Republicans, would it be fair to say?

Stuart: No, Sargent Shriver sure wasn't.

Kauffman: Did the swiftness with which America First caught on surprise you? I mean, one minute you and your wife were working out of your home in New Haven, and the next minute it was this enormous national organization.

Stuart: Well, as you know, Bill, we were just tapping into a whole reservoir of feeling across the country, but there had been no organizing mechanism to put it into some kind of a movement, to give it political cohesiveness.

And so we started sending out letters, first to college types, and then we shifted to the more senior leadership: General Wood, Hanford MacNider, Bob Hutchins, Bill Benton, Chester Bowles. They knew people, and then we started to work with them, and our objective was to get chapters, units across the country, to develop a strong mass organization.

But it wasn't because we were so clever, because we weren't. It's there was a reservoir of opinion that was sympathetic to Britain but feeling we shouldn't be in the war. And that's how it all sort of came together, because the thinking, the point of view was out there with the people.

Kauffman: America First included on its national committee a variety of manufacturers like W.H. Regnery and Sterling Morton; writers like John T. Flynn and Oswald Garrison Villard; and colorful figures including Alice Roosevelt Longworth, Eddie Rickenbacker. . . . It must have been a chore to keep a set of strong-willed individualists like this rowing together, wasn't it? Were there factions, was there a lot of infighting?

Stuart: Well, that was probably one of the advantages of being a young man. They would be sort of tolerant. And they admired General Wood. I saw them all and made a point of kind of bringing them up to date on things and getting their ideas.

I think one of the members, a woman named Janet Ayer Fairbank . . .

Kauffman: Chicago novelist?

Stuart: Novelist, yes. And well known, and high opinion of herself, she always felt that young Bobby, at twenty-four or twenty-five, shouldn't be the honcho, and someone like herself should probably be the director of the thing. And that was a bit of a struggle but General Wood was patting her a little bit. (Laughter)

The others had different points of view. If you know anything about Benton and Bowles, it was really quite a remarkable story. Bill Benton and Chester Bowles put this agency together, and had been classmates at Yale. Bill had always said when he made his first ten million he was going to leave business and try to be a public servant and be useful.

Bill went on to the University of Chicago as business manager, but the two of them were great friends. Chester Bowles, as you know, was a Democrat, and ran for the Senate in Connecticut at one point. He went to India as the ambassador. He was head of price controls after the war. Those two were very helpful. Bill Benton obviously didn't sleep very well at night; he had this fiendish habit. He would have a dictaphone right by his bed so he could wake up with these ideas. And so every day I'd have some new thoughts from Bill. (Laughter) They were dictated about three in the morning.

Kauffman: Half-coherent?

Stuart: Half. No, there were disadvantages in being as inexperienced as I was, but I think there were *some* pluses because people wanted to be helpful.

Kauffman: What were your duties as national director? What would a typical day be like?

Stuart: Putting out fires. (Laughter) We needed to insulate ourselves as best we could against the contention of the Eastern interventionists that we were just a tool of the Germans, and we were just a front for German propaganda. So we made a conscious effort to—I had a wonderful secretary named Bertha Tallman, who I constantly employed because she had a Jewish background, and I had a very good guy named Sidney Hertzberg who did public relations and things like that.

We were trying to avoid Father Coughlin, and keep ourselves separate from those people. Some of their people were more extremist.

Our issue was not in any way connected with taking sides on the German issue or anything like that. You know, most of us were of British ancestry and so many of us were sympathetic to Britain, but we just felt we shouldn't be entrapped in the war.

Chapter chairmen had a series of principles that they had to agree to. But it was sometimes pretty hard to keep them on track, or make them sensitive to these bigger issues, because as the storm gathered in intensity in Britain the willingness of the media to beat up on us just increased all the time. So we had to make our chapters conscious of the need to be careful whom they brought into their sanctum and worked with.

Because there were elements that may have had more Germany's interest at heart. And of course the whole role of the Communist Party: at first, they were very much on the side of nonintervention. And then when the Nazi Germans rolled into Russia, they attacked the hell out of us (laughter) for opposing support to Russia, and they were all for getting the United States in the war as a way of helping to stop Germany.

Kauffman: According to Ruth Sarles, you were something of a New Dealer. She says you wanted to work for the National Labor Relations Board after graduation.

Stuart: You know, when you come out of college, you're idealistic as hell, want to save the world. I don't know if I was consciously a New Dealer or not; I certainly was not as conservative a Republican as I am today. (Laughter)

Kauffman: The perception today of the America First Committee is that it was composed primarily of anti-FDR Republican conservatives. Is that accurate?

Stuart: Inaccurate. Of course, your opposition hopes to paint you that way. God knows Chester Bowles, Bill Benton, Senator Wheeler, and Champ Clark were Democrats.

We tried always to achieve a balance. Kathryn Lewis was John L. Lewis' daughter. He thought she'd be better on the committee; the United Mine Workers were not a leading Republican organization.

We tried like hell to keep a nonpartisan flavor. We had nothing against FDR, but he was a major force in leading us gradually, step by step, toward involvement.

Kauffman: Cole writes that you "actively sought the support of liberals" in America First. Was it difficult? Did you find a lot of prominent liberals or Democrats saying, "I agree with you, but I don't want to be associated with the committee"?

Stuart: No, nothing like that. You know, Bob and Phil La Follette were so liberal they had a different party up in Wisconsin.

Kauffman: The National Progressives.

Stuart: I remember telling Phil we were going to rent a room in Wisconsin or Minnesota, and I said, "Phil, I'm not sure if we'll have a very successful meeting. I sure haven't got enough acceptances." Phil said, "A lesson to learn in politics: get a room that is too small for the group and then everybody thinks it's a huge success when they crowd them into a small quarter." (Laughter)

Kauffman: Lillian Gish was on the national committee until it became apparent that pro-war Hollywood would not give an antiwar actress work. Were you aware at the time of the career pressures on Miss Gish?

Stuart: I think I've spent my life worrying about what the media are doing to us. There were a lot of very bright Jewish people in the media who were very much for getting involved in the war, and so it became very difficult for Miss Gish to get contracts and things like that.

Kauffman: A number of Kennedys and Kennedy associates supported the America First Committee and the like-minded College Men for Defense First.

Stuart: Jack Kennedy ended up being a chapter chairman up there at Harvard.

Kauffman: How helpful or supportive or involved were the Kennedys?

Stuart: The future president was active up there at Harvard. I went to call on Ambassador [Joseph] Kennedy in Palm Beach, and he gave us some money. I persuaded him to make a couple of talks for us on the radio. At that time he was very out with Roosevelt and Roosevelt was out with him.

Kauffman: Talk about a guy who's gotten a terrible press posthumously . . . Was the ambassador as dreadful as we read today?

Stuart: I, to be honest with you, was not evaluating his personal behavior. I was evaluating the fact that he was a big name that could be helpful to us on the radio and could be helpful financially. So I was making no judgments. (Laughter)

Kauffman: In Charles Lindbergh's *Wartime Journals,* he writes that your father "is by no means in agreement with his son's outlook, and is apparently not too happy about Bob's position in America First."
Was Lindbergh's perception accurate?

Stuart: Dad was the most wonderful father, and he believed in my doing what I thought was right, and in fact helped us to some extent. He had some extra space in the Board of Trade Building, Quaker offices; they gave us that extra space to get us started.
I think that, push come to shove, Dad would have preferred that I not do it, but he was one of those wonderful guys that never put any pressure on me to change.

Kauffman: What was Gerald Ford's role in the genesis of the America First Committee? He was central to it at first, wasn't he?

Stuart: He signed that first letter. We got him to sign it because everyone knew he was a hell of a football player. Ford was a wonderful man. I don't think he was terribly active in all these discussions, but he signed on, was helpful. Jerry Ford was just a friend, and he believed the same thing and signed this letter, but I don't think after that he . . .

Kauffman: He became, as a congressman, a pretty thoroughgoing internationalist. Do you think he was embarrassed by the America First connection at all?

Stuart: He and I never talked about that. You know, all of us that were involved ended up in a very kind of sensitive role.

Kauffman: Did anyone ever bring it up to you during your wartime service?

Stuart: An old friend told me he'd been in some sort of OSS [Office of Strategic Service] counterintelligence role, vetting all the appointments to different positions, and my name had gone across: at the time I was being assigned to take a sensitive role.

I never knew until later that the file had come in with a big question mark to flag Ike about this, and my friend was in a position to say, "Oh, this is ridiculous; he's signed on and is as good an American as any of us," so that's the only time I ever heard of it.

Kauffman: What was Ruth Sarles like?

Stuart: I thought of her as a very conscientious, thorough, dependable, trustworthy person who worked very hard and was very loyal.

Kauffman: Was she an attractive woman?

Stuart: She was attractive. And I always felt we connected. We never had any romantic affiliation or anything like that, but I had a sense that when we coordinated or cooperated the chemistry was good.

Kauffman: She was loaned to the committee by Frederick Libby and the National Council for Prevention of War. Libby was a Quaker pacifist with a real fondness for right-wing Republicans. He must have been an interesting character. Did you have much contact with him?

Stuart: Not much. More letter writing. We felt that Libby, although we weren't pacifists, his objective and ours was to keep the country out of Europe, so we can cooperate, and we did. But our constant emphasis with General Wood as our leader was to emphasize that we were very much for a strong defense and were not pacifists.

Kauffman: The coalition ranged from conservative Republicans to Socialists, and it included a fair number of pacifists and Quakers. Was there ever tension or significant disagreement between America First people with pacifist backgrounds like Ruth Sarles and those in the General Wood tradition, who were in favor of a strong defense? Were these disagreements muted in interest in the higher cause?

Stuart: They were muted. Because you're really focusing on the one issue. So they didn't surface.

Kauffman: Who were your most impressive allies in Congress? Intellectually, morally . . . who were the most impressive statesmen you worked with?

Stuart: Well, Senator Wheeler gets a bad rap, but he was terrific. And Senator Taft was awfully good. And Bob La Follette was very good. Those were the three, I think, that I spent more time with.

Kauffman: As you mentioned earlier, interventionists then and now have sometimes implied or more than implied that the America First Committee was anti-Semitic. What's your response to that?

Stuart: That it is a wonderful bit of demagoguery, like the race card, that people pull out of the hat to discredit. But we were not. Witness personnel and other things like that.

But, you know, it's damn tough. We were trying very hard to avoid any label attack, but we always found it frustrating that we sensed a great deal of pressure from the active Jewish organizations against us.

We were trying to keep our shirts completely clear of that kind of stuff, because it isn't American. We believed in those principles, as did Sidney Hertzberg, Bertha Tallman, and others.

Kauffman: Was it a mistake putting Henry Ford on the National Committee for a short while?

Stuart: Probably. I mean, from the point of public relations. On the other hand, Henry Ford was a great guy. And working with Charles Lindbergh was . . . Charles was famous. We went to see Mr. Ford with Charles, and I was very impressed; we went to him for funding. One time, with Charles, we went up to camp with Mr. Ford in Michigan, and through Mr. Ford, Charles was assigned a little single-engine monoplane, which obviously he knew how to fly. (Laughter)

For me as a kid, my great dream in life was to cross the Atlantic. He was my hero. We had a garden, about three and a half acres, and somehow the *Spirit of St. Louis* would have to come down there—(laughing)—I would get to meet him. And then fast forward to, I was flying with Charles up through Michigan, and he would say, "Now, Bob, try this."

So he turned it over and God, we'd zig and we'd zag, and he said, "Steady as we go." I mean, the fact that my hero was letting me fly his plane, and he was teaching me, was just, you know, a wonderful experience.

Then on the way back we got into rain squalls and storms. And as we were flying back through the storm, lightning and stuff, we couldn't see the ground, and Charles said, "Well, Bob, you just have to do what we used to do when flying the mail. We'll get down on the deck and get the road map out."

He'd have a road map here, and we were not very far, a couple hundred feet in the air, and we tracked the road using a road map, right into Detroit with that big field where Ford had his manufacturing plant. We came out right on the nose. Willow Run.

Kauffman: Navigating for Charles Lindbergh: That's impressive.

Stuart: He said, "The young fellows that are flying today can't do that, but we just learned. We had to. We had nothing else." And so it was always a great thrill for me to think that that was my hero.

Kauffman: Here you are, side by side, working with your boyhood hero. Were you awestruck at first? Were you tongue-tied in his presence?

Stuart: Not really. [He was] very easy once you had his confidence. My wife, Barbara, who was really much more intellectual than I am, and Anne [Morrow Lindbergh] became great friends.

Charles even stayed with us at Lake Forest. We would visit and Barbara and Anne used to fly back and forth together. They loved to talk philosophy and all those things. We were very fond of the Lindberghs.

Kauffman: It's often said, "Never meet your heroes—you'll be disappointed." But Lindbergh, I take it, lived up to advance billing.

Stuart: Oh, he lived up to every bit of it. He was remarkable. You've read Scott Berg's book [*Lindbergh,* Putnam's, 1998]. In terms of flying ability, just think of the trips that he and Anne took before there were all these sophisticated guidance systems.

He jumped out a couple times on air runs when he was a mail pilot. But think of the places they went. All over the world. He had to be the greatest flyer of all time.

Kauffman: Lindbergh was also Gore Vidal's boyhood hero. Vidal, in an essay on Berg's book, said that Lindbergh was the closest thing we're ever going to have to a real American hero.

Stuart: Good for him. He said that?

Kauffman: Yes. Vidal was a member of the America First Committee at Exeter, and through the years he's always defended it. Vidal's essay was supposed to be in the *New York Review of Books,* with which he's had this long relationship, and they refused to publish it because, you know, Lindbergh is one of the impermissibles.

He had to publish it in London in the *Times Literary Supplement.* Here you have probably the greatest living American man of letters writing about the great American hero, and he can't be published in his own country. It's sad.

Stuart: Bias is terrible. I mean, it's anti-intellectual, everything else.

Kauffman: Did you have any misgivings about tying Lindbergh so closely with the committee, making him its public face? Because of the German medal and all?

Stuart: I always felt a little guilty about that. I tried to moderate his being too much out front. He was my personal hero and a hero to all of us, because he was such a great guy. But . . . you know, I'm married to a Scandinavian lady now; I understand him perfectly. (Laughter)

Having received that medal in the interests of the United States in an American ambassador's home and to have everybody insist he give it back—he just wasn't, goddamn it, he wasn't going to do it.

He'd received hundreds of other medals, he hadn't given any of them back. And from other people that weren't particularly heroes to everybody. The strength of his stubbornness. . .

Kauffman: Perhaps the most controversial incident in the history of America First was Lindbergh's Des Moines speech of September 1941 in which he said, "The three most important groups who have been pressing this country toward war are the British, the Jewish, and the Roosevelt administration."

Lindbergh was widely reprimanded, or some would say smeared, for anti-Semitism, as a result. Were you dismayed by the speech or did you think that Lindbergh's critics were overreacting and using this unfairly against him?

Stuart: I had to be the public-relations man for the committee, and I knew what a handle it would give the critics. I was concerned about it and uncomfortable and so it was a difficult problem. Because it just gave the Walter Lippmanns of the world a chance to make him seem pro-German and anti-Semitic.

Kauffman: Lindbergh didn't consult with anyone before the speech, I assume?

Stuart: No, he didn't show it to Anne, either. He never vetted his speeches with us. It may have had something to do with the fact we were about twenty-five years old and he was a little older than that. We never saw them. Usually he showed Anne. This time he did not.

Kauffman: But the next day when you woke up, did you think "Oh, no"? Did you realize that this firestorm was going to sweep over you?

Stuart: Oh, sure. You can't be in a politically sensitive role without recognizing what does trigger storms. And so I was very conscious of it and troubled by it.

Kauffman: If New York City was the interventionist capital, Chicago was the stronghold of the America Firsters. Why Chicago?

Stuart: Well, it's kind of a Midwestern tradition. I think there were a whole number of reasons for that.

　　We had a vocal supporter in Colonel Bertie McCormick of the *Chicago Tribune*, so there was an articulate medium out here through the newspaper. This part of the world was more solidly opposed to getting involved in the war than the eastern seaboard. The eastern seaboard had lots of refugees who migrated through the horrors.

Kauffman: Was there a point before December 7, 1941, when you thought, "The game is up, U.S. intervention is inevitable"?

Stuart: No, Congress was pretty evenly divided on some of those important things, like just by one vote.

　　The country got in the polling business long before Bill Clinton used them to govern. We ran a poll in November [1941]—Bob Hutchins of the University of Chicago and Bill Benton [oversaw it]—and it showed that seventy-five to eighty percent of the people were opposed to our involvement in a European war. So the people were still very much against involvement.

Kauffman: Where were you on December seventh when you heard what happened?

Stuart: I'd just come back from church. It was Sunday. Barbara turned on the radio, and we were headed over to have a drink with some friends. And I just couldn't believe it.

　　And then I began to realize the implications thereof. I was a reserve officer, and it looked like we were obviously going to be at war, and so we got on the phone with others. We called an emergency meeting of the committee.

　　There was a marvelous guy named Dick Moore, who was in the Nixon White House, and we put our heads together and quickly recognized that the continued efforts to keep us out of the war weren't going to work.

　　That was cinched when the Germans declared war on us, which was a dumb thing for them to have done. But anyway, I just remember feeling sick. Not only over the loss of Pearl Harbor, but what it meant. The game was over.

Kauffman: Did your America First involvement come up in the confirmation hearings on your appointment as ambassador to Norway?

Stuart: You know, it's funny. No, it didn't. I was very prepared to not apologize for it. I believed in it. At the time there were no intercontinental missiles or long-range bombers or things like that.

Kauffman: It never did during Chester Bowles's various confirmations, either. In his autobiography, there's this hole from 1940 to 1941, as though Bowles had a long nap during these years.

Stuart: He was writing a lot of memos to me.

Kauffman: Did the founders of the committee keep in touch over the years?

Stuart: Not in any sort of conscious alumni sense, but I worked for Ford, and I'd see Whizzer White from time to time. Sargent Shriver is a good friend of mine still, even though he's on the other side of the aisle.

Kauffman: Never had an America First reunion?

Stuart: No, we did not. We may be a little sensitive to the fact that the world still thinks we're the bad guys.

Appendix C

Speakers and National Committee Members of America First

Senators and Congressmen Who Spoke for America First.
This list and the two following include radio as well as platform speakers.

Senators

Wayland C. Brooks	(R-Illinois)
Arthur Capper	(R-Kansas)
Bennett C. Clark	(D-Missouri)
D. Worth Clark	(D-Idaho)
John A. Danaher	(R-Connecticut)
Rufus D. Holman	(R-Oregon)
Edwin C. Johnson	(D-Colorado)
Hiram W. Johnson	(R-California)
Robert M. La Follette	(P-Wisconsin)
Henry Cabot Lodge	(R-Massachusetts)
Pat McCarran	(D-Nevada)
Gerald P. Nye	(R-North Dakota)
Robert R. Reynolds	(D-North Carolina)
Henrik Shipstead	(R-Minnesota)
Robert A. Taft	(R-Ohio)
Charles W. Tobey	(R-New Hampshire)
Arthur H. Vandenberg	(R-Michigan)
David I. Walsh	(D-Massachusetts)
Burton K. Wheeler	(D-Montana)
Raymond E. Willis	(R-Indiana)

Congressmen

William B. Barry	(D-N.Y.)	Louis Ludlow	(D-Ind.)
C.W. Bishop	(R-Ill.)	Karl E. Mundt	(R-S.Dak.)
Fred Bradley	(R-Mich.)	George D. O'Brien	(D-Mich.)
J. Edgar Chenoweth	(R-Colo.)	James F. O'Connor	(D-Mont.)
John M. Coffee	(D-Wash.)	Jeannette Rankin	(R-Mont.)
Carl T. Curtis	(R-Neb.)	Harry Sauthoff	(R-Wis.)
Stephen A. Day	(R- Ill.)	Paul W. Shafer	(R-Mich.)
Hamilton Fish	(R-N.Y.)	Dewey Short	(R-Mo.)
Fred A. Hartley, Jr.	(R-N.J.)	Raymond S. Springer	(R-Ind.)
Knute Hill	(D-Wash.)	William G. Stratton	(R-Ill.)
Clare E. Hoffman	(R-Mich.)	Jessie Sumner	(R-Ill.)
Joshua L. Johns	(R-Wis.)	Martin L. Sweeney	(D-Ohio)
Robert F. Jones	(R-Ohio)	Lewis D. Thill	(R-Wis.)
Frank B. Keefe	(R-Wis.)	James E. Van Zandt	(R-Pa.)
Harold Knutson	(R-Ill.)	John M. Vorys	(R-Ohio)
William P. Lambertson	(R-Kans.)	Albert L. Vreeland	(R-N.J.)
Gerald W. Landis	(R-Ind.)	Roy O. Woodruff	(R-Mich.)
		Henry C. Luckey (former)	(D-Neb.)

Other Speakers Scheduled by America First

Father John L. Bazinet	-	St. Mary's Seminary, Baltimore, Md.
Mrs. [Miriam] Bennett Champ Clark	-	Wife of Senator Clark, (D-Mo.)
Gertude Coogan	-	Economist and lecturer (Chicago)
John Cudahy	-	Former U.S. ambassador to Belgium
John T. Flynn	-	Economist and writer
Rev. James M. Gillis	-	Editor, *Catholic World*
Lillian Gish	-	Stage and screen actress
Major Horace Greeley, Jr., M.D.	-	Grandson of renowned newspaper publisher
Rev. Arman Guerrero	-	Methodist minister
Gen. Thomas S. Hammond	-	Industrialist, World War I veteran
Rush Holt	-	Former U.S. senator from West Virginia
Rev. Charles M. Houser	-	Fort Wayne, Indiana (Congregationalist)
Professor Cary Jacob	-	Smith College
Gen. Hugh S. Johnson	-	Columnist, former head of NRA, head of Selective Service in World War I

Laura Ingalls	-	Flyer; early in 1942, was convicted and sentenced as an agent of the German government.
Philip La Follette	-	Former governor of Wisconsin
Charles A. Lindbergh	-	Flyer
Dr. Hyman Lischner	-	Former president of San Diego B'nai B'rith
Hanford MacNider	-	Former national commander of American Legion, former U.S. minister to Canada, former assistant secretary of war
Dr. Clarence Manion	-	Dean of Notre Dame Law School
Dr. Henry Noble McCracken	-	President of Vassar College
Irene Castle McLaughlin	-	Former dancer
Charles Clayton Morrison	-	Editor of *Christian Century*
William H. ("Alfalfa Bill") Murray	-	Former governor of Oklahoma
Kathleen Norris	-	Novelist
Father John A. O'Brien	-	University of Notre Dame
Honorable Hjalmar Peterson	-	Former governor of Minnesota
Samuel B. Pettengill	-	Attorney, former member of Congress from Indiana
Henry Rademacher	-	Lecturer
David A. Reed	-	Former U.S. Senator from Pennsylvania
Michael Strange	-	Author
R. Douglas Stuart, Jr.	-	National director, America First Committee
Mrs. [Martha] Robert A. Taft	-	Wife of senator Taft (R-Ohio)
Norman Thomas	-	Chairman of Socialist Party, Socialist nominee for president
Charles W. Vail	-	Attorney
Bishop Raymond T. Wade	-	Methodist bishop
Gen. Robert E. Wood	-	Acting chairman, America First Committee

Speakers Whose Addresses Were Announced by America First but Not Under America First Auspices

Most Reverend Francis J.L. Beckman	-	Catholic archbishop of Dubuque, Iowa
Thomas E. Dewey	-	former district attorney of New York, Republican candidate for governor of New York
John H. Finerty	-	New York attorney and chairman of the Keep America Out of War Congress
Herbert Hoover	-	former president of the United States
Robert Maynard Hutchins	-	President of the University of Chicago
Joseph P. Kennedy	-	former ambassador to England
Alfred M. Landon	-	Republican candidate for president (1936)
Frederick J. Libby	-	Executive secretary of National Council for Prevention of War
Joseph Scott	-	California attorney, Knight of St. Gregory (nominated Hoover in 1928)
Most Reverend Gerald Shaughnessy	-	Catholic bishop, Seattle, Washington
Freda Utley	-	English writer, author of *The Dream We Lost*
Oswald Garrison Villard	-	author and journalist, former owner and editor of *The Nation*

Members of the National Committee

	Elected to membership	Resigned	Reason given for resignation
General Robert E. Wood, chairman of the board of Sears, Roebuck and Co.			
R. Douglas Stuart, Jr., Yale law student and son of the vice president of Quaker Oats Co.			
Janet Ayer Fairbank, author, former Democratic National Committeewoman from Illinois			
J. Sanford Otis, vice president of the Central Republic Bank of Chicago			
Charles Francis Adams, chairman of the board, State Street Trust Co., Boston	November 1, 1940	December 3, 1940	American First affiliation was embarrassing to the former secretary of the navy and president of the bank of which Mr. Adams was chairman of the board, since he was active in the Committee to Defend America.
Samuel Hopkins Adams, author, member of Executive Committee, National Consumers' League	October 20, 1940		
Chester Bowles, president of Benton and Bowles, New York advertising agency	September 21, 1940		

(continued)

	Elected to membership	Resigned	Reason given for resignation
Dr. Anton J. Carlson, head of Department of Physiology, University of Chicago, lieutenant colonel in the Sanitary Corps, B.S.A., 1917	November 1, 1940		
Otto Case, treasurer of the state of Washington	October 20, 1941		
William R. Castle, former undersecretary of state, former U.S. ambassador to Japan	November 1, 1940		
Mrs. [Miriam] Bennett Champ Clark, wife of Senator Clark (D-Mo.)	November 1, 1940		
Irvin S. Cobb, author, Chevalier of the French Legion of Honor	December 27, 1940		
Ellen French Vanderbilt FitzSimons, Republican National Committeewoman from Rhode Island; awarded Victory Medal of Society of Social Sciences for distinguished service in the Red Cross, 1919	October 20, 1941	November 26, 1941	In view of her close affiliation with the Republican Party, thought it unwise to continue with an organization that would support Democrats as well as Republicans in the coming election.
John T. Flynn, author, economist	September 21, 1940		
Henry Ford, manufacturer	September 21, 1940		
Lillian Gish, screen and stage actress	March 28, 1941		

Bishop Wilbur E. Hammaker, Methodist bishop of the Rocky Mountain states and Methodist bishop of China from 1936 to 1939	September 21, 1940	
Gen. Thomas S. Hammond, president of the Whiting Corporation	September 21, 1940	
Jay C. Hormel, president of the Hormel Meat Packing Co.	September 21, 1940	Believed America First program too "anti-" not constructive enough; thought that with our economy dedicated to war it was too late to urge avoidance of participation in war.
	December 9, 1941	
William L. Hutcheson, first vice president of the AFL; general president of the United Brotherhood of Carpenters and Joiners of America; member of War Labor Board, 1917–1919	October 20, 1941	
General Hugh S. Johnson, columnist, former head of NRA	September 21, 1940	
Clay Judson, Chicago attorney; former president of the Chicago Council on Foreign Relations	September 21, 1940	
Florence Kahn	January 21, 1941	From "circumstances beyond my control," to "strictly personal and confidential consideration."
	May 12, 1941	

(continued)

	Elected to membership	Resigned	Reason given for resignation
Kathryn Lewis, secretary-treasurer of Local 50, United Mine Workers of America	September 29, 1940	October 20, 1941	Not in accord with the position stated in Colonel Lindbergh's speech; greater responsibilities in her job with the United Mine Workers.
Charles A. Lindbergh, flyer	October 20, 1941		
Alice Roosevelt Longworth, daughter of Theodore Roosevelt, wife of late Speaker of the House Nicholas Longworth	September 21, 1940		
Frank O. Lowden, former governor of Illinois	December 27, 1940		
Hanford MacNider, president of the Northwestern States Portland Cement Co.; former national commander of the American Legion; former assistant secretary of war; former U.S. minister to Canada	September 21, 1940	December 4, 1941	Believed that hope for the nation's future lay with the Republican Party; could not go along with a nonpartisan organization.
Thomas N. McCarter, president of the New Jersey Public Service Co.	September 21, 1940	September 29, 1941	Thought that "What was originally an honest difference of opinion has developed into a controversy that is being conducted by both sides along lines that are not helpful in the crisis with which we are confronted."
Ray McKaig, master of the Idaho National Grange	September 21, 1940		
Dr. Clarence Manion, dean of the College of Law, Notre Dame University	October 20, 1941		

Mrs. John P. Marquand, wife of author of *J.P. Pulham, Esquire*	October 20, 1941	
Gregory Mason, anthropologist, author, head of Department of Journalism, College of the City of New York.	October 20, 1941	
Sterling Morton, president of the Morton Salt Co.	September 21, 1940	
Kathleen Norris, novelist	January 21, 1941	
Rev. John A. O'Brien, Notre Dame University	October 20, 1941	
Dr. Albert Palmer, president of Chicago Theological Seminary	September 21, 1940	
Isaac Pennypacker, Philadelphia attorney	October 20, 1941	
Amos R.E. Pinchot, lawyer, philanthropist	December 27, 1940	
George N. Peek, former AAA administrator; special adviser to President Roosevelt on foreign trade, 1934–1935; former president of the Export-Import Bank.	February 7, 1941	December 3, 1940 — Because of early restriction against pacifists.
William H. Regnery, president of Western Shade Cloth Co., Chicago	September 21, 1940	
Edward Rickenbacker, flyer, president of Eastern Air Lines	September 21, 1940	January 16, 1941 — "Due to the many complications within the America First Committee."

(continued)

	Elected to membership	Resigned	Reason given for resignation
Lessing J. Rosenwald, former chairman of the board, Sears, Roebuck and Co.	September 21, 1940	December 3, 1940	"Some of the members have taken such action and hold to such ideologies that I cannot afford to be associated with them, although still in accord with Committee's basic principles."
Edward L. Ryerson, Jr., president of the Inland Steel Corporation	September 21, 1940	September 17, 1941	Although "abhorring" the "hysteria about our defense requirements," believed the time had come for national unity.
Ruth Hanna McCormick Simms, former member of Congress from Illinois; former Republican National Committeewoman	October 20, 1941		
Carl G. Snavely, football coach, Cornell University; coach of 1941 College All Stars	October 20, 1941	November 28, 1941	
Harry L. Stuart, president of Halsey, Stuart and Co., Chicago	October 20, 1941		
Louis J. Taber, master of the national Grange	September 21, 1940		
M.W. Thatcher, general manager of the Farmers' Union Grain Terminal Assn., St. Paul, Minnesota	September 21, 1940	December 3, 1940	
Oswald Garrison Villard, author and journalist, former owner and editor of *The Nation*	September 21, 1940	December 3, 1940	Because of early restriction against pacifists.
Mrs. [Lulu White] Burton K. Wheeler, wife of senator (D-Montana)	December 21, 1940		

Dr. George H. Whipple, Nobel Prize winner in medicine, 1934	September 21, 1940
Edwin S. Webster, Jr., senior partner of Kidder, Peabody and Co.	October 20, 1941
Major Alford J. Williams, flyer, columnist	December 21, 1940
Robert Young, financier	November 28, 1941

Index

About the Author and Editor

RUTH SARLES was chief researcher and Senate lobbyist for the America First Committee. A former editor with the pacifist National Council for Prevention of War, Sarles represents the often-unacknowledged liberal face of the anti-intervention movement of 1940–41. After marrying Bertram Benedict in 1943, Sarles worked as a Washington Daily News reporter and a State Department analyst. She died in 1996.

BILL KAUFFMAN is the author of four books: *With Good Intentions? Reflections on the Myth of Progress in America* (Praeger, 1998), *America First! Its History, Culture, and Politics* (1995), *Country Towns of New York* (1994), and the novel *Every Man a King* (1989).